Change and Continuity in the 1980 Elections

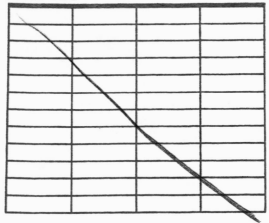

Politics and Public Policy Series

Advisory Editor

Robert L. Peabody

Johns Hopkins University

Change and Continuity in the 1980 Elections

Revised Edition

Paul R. Abramson
Michigan State University

John H. Aldrich
University of Minnesota

David W. Rohde
Michigan State University

CQ Press
a division of
CONGRESSIONAL QUARTERLY INC.
1414 22nd Street N.W., Washington, D.C. 20037

Library of Congress Cataloging in Publication Data

Abramson, Paul R.
    Change and continuity in the 1980 elections.

    Bibliography: p.
    Includes index.
    1. Presidents — United States — Election —
1980. 2. United States. Congress — Elections, 1980.
I. Aldrich, John Herbert, 1947-   . II. Rohde, Da-
vid W. III. Title.
JK526 1980e   324.973'0926   83-1961
ISBN 0-87187-270-6   AACR2

To

David

Heather and Lee

Jennifer and Margaret

Foreword

Every four years millions of Americans are confronted with two fundamental questions: first, should they vote at all; and second, if they decide to go to the polls, who should they choose for president? Of the more than 150 million Americans who were eligible to vote in 1980, some 86 million cast a ballot for president, which represents the lowest voter turnout (53 percent) since 1948. When all the ballots were tabulated, Ronald Reagan, the Republican challenger, won the electoral votes of 44 states with a total of 50.7 percent of the popular vote. Incumbent president Jimmy Carter, the Democratic nominee, won 41.0 percent of the vote, carrying only seven electoral units—the District of Columbia, Georgia, Hawaii, Maryland, Minnesota, Rhode Island, and West Virginia. Unable to obtain a plurality in any state, Independent candidate John Anderson ended up with 6.6 percent of the vote. The remaining 1.7 percent was scattered among more than a half-dozen candidates representing such ideological extremes as Ed Clark of the Libertarian party and Barry Commoner of the Citizens party.

The election of 1980 continued a pattern of relative Republican dominance in presidential elections since World War II. Of the nine postwar elections, Republican candidates have won five, including three of the last four. In addition, the 1980 election continued a pattern of electoral volatility. Since 1952, neither major party has been able to win more than two presidential elections in a row.

In addition to regaining the presidency in 1980, the Republican party made major strides toward becoming the dominant party in Congress. With a net gain of 12 seats in the Senate, the GOP won control of that body for the first time since 1952. When the 97th Congress convened in 1981, the Senate had 53 Republicans, 46 Democrats, and one Independent (Harry F. Byrd, Jr., of Virginia). With a net gain of 33 seats in the House of Representatives, the Republicans were in striking range of gaining control of that chamber. Democrats maintained nominal party, if not always ideological, control of the House with 243 seats compared with the Republicans' 192.

The election results were quickly known by voters clustered about their television sets that night of November 4, 1980. But the implications of voters' choices were less clear. With the publication of *Change and Continuity in the 1980 Elections*, we now have what is likely to become the definitive analysis of the election results. Professors David W. Rohde and Paul R. Abramson of Michigan State University and John H. Aldrich of the University of Minnesota interpret voters' decisions in 1980, analyze recent voting patterns in the context of earlier elections, and explain the implications of these trends for the American political system. Relying extensively on data collected by the Survey Research Center-Center for Political Studies at the University of Michigan, the authors present an excellent account of the 1980 contests and a penetrating analysis of the elections' historical significance. Twenty figures and 52 tables help the reader to understand the important trends in voting behavior in the postwar period.

The book's analysis and data provide a framework to study certain fundamental questions that cannot yet be answered. One of the most important is whether the 1980 elections signal a basic realignment in political allegiance in the United States. As the authors observe, "realignments involve 'durable' or 'lasting' shifts in the balance of partisan forces." To satisfy the minimum conditions for the beginnings of a major party alignment as of 1980, Republicans will have to maintain or increase their hold on the Senate and win control of the House. If unsuccessful in 1982, then GOP House candidates perhaps could ride the coattails of a successful Republican presidential candidate in 1984. Above all, significantly larger numbers of voters will have to shift to identification with the Republican party. While it is too soon to assess the full impact of the 1980 elections, the authors identify the important political landmarks that signal electoral realignment.

The authors also examine the extent to which the 1980 elections constituted an endorsement of Republican party policies. They make a strong case that the election results are most reasonably interpreted as a rejection of Carter's performance as president rather than as a mandate for Republican policies. The authors argue that "most voters felt Carter was unsuccessful in handling the two basic economic issues—inflation and unemployment. And most of those who judged Carter a failure voted for Reagan. Similarly, the electorate will hold the Reagan administration responsible for its success or failure in solving these same two problems."

Numerous books and articles on the 1980 contests have been published already. Using the University of Michigan's SRC-CPS rich survey data and grounded in solid historical analysis, *Change and Continuity in the 1980 Elections* promises to be the definitive study.

Robert L. Peabody

Preface to the Revised Edition

A remarkable series of political events took place between November 4, 1980, and November 2, 1982. The Republican triumphs in the 1980 election quickly led to major cutbacks in domestic programs and a fresh attempt to handle the nation's economic ills. But by the fall of 1982, with unemployment at 10 percent, many Americans already were questioning whether President Ronald Reagan's policies could work. The midterm elections of 1982 gave the electorate an opportunity to judge those policies. What then was its verdict?

When viewed as a referendum on the president, the 1982 elections provided an ambiguous message. The Democrats gained 26 seats in the House but made little headway in the Senate where the party balance— 54 Republicans, 46 Democrats—remained the same. Still, by early 1983, it was apparent that the changes in the House would severely restrict Reagan's ability to introduce new programs in the 98th Congress.

Should the 1982 elections be viewed as a Democratic victory? How do the results affect the 1984 presidential contest and the chances for a pro-Republican realignment in the electorate? In Part V, 1982 Election Update, we analyze the reasons for and the political implications of these congressional outcomes. In light of the events of 1982, including the November elections, we look forward to the 1984 contest and assess the long-term prospects for the American party system.

Like the first edition, the revised edition is a collective enterprise, but, once again, we divided the labor. David Rohde had the primary responsibility for Chapter 12, John Aldrich for the first two sections of Chapter 13, and Paul Abramson for the last section. None of us is willing to take any responsibility for the 98th Congress.

We wish to thank Ada Finifter, Jack Knott, and Joseph Schlesinger for their suggestions. Iris Richardson provided valuable secretarial assistance. We also thank Joanne Daniels of Congressional Quarterly for her encouragement and editorial help and Barbara R. de Boinville for the speedy production of this updated edition.

Paul R. Abramson
John H. Aldrich
David W. Rohde

Preface to the First Edition

The Republican victories of 1980 brought to power political leaders committed to changing the direction of public policy. Within a year of the election of Ronald Reagan as president and the Republican sweep of the Senate, Congress had enacted major reductions in domestic social programs and substantial cuts in federal taxes. In campaigning for public office, Republican leaders advanced explicit programs. But were the 1980 elections a mandate for these conservative policies or a vote against Jimmy Carter? Did they signal a realignment of political power in America or reflect a postwar pattern of continued electoral volatility? To answer these questions we will view the 1980 presidential and congressional elections from a social-scientific perspective. While we cannot judge yet the full impact of the Reagan administration's policies on the economy, it is clear that the 1980 elections may prove to be among the most important in American history.

Our goal in writing this book was to provide a solid social-scientific analysis of the elections using the best data available for studying voting behavior. The major study we used is the 1980 survey of the American electorate conducted by the Survey Research Center-Center for Political Studies of the University of Michigan as part of an ongoing project funded by the National Science Foundation. The Inter-University Consortium for Political and Social Research released the preliminary version of these data in late April 1981; a final version was released in mid-July 1981. Most of the other surveys analyzed for this book also were made available through the Consortium. Unless otherwise indicated, all the tables and figures in Chapters 2, 4 through 8, and 10 are based upon data it provided. The standard disclaimer holds: the Consortium is responsible for neither our analyses nor our interpretations.

We are grateful to Harriet Dhanak of the Politometrics Laboratory at Michigan State University for helping us analyze these surveys. The assistance of Joan Campbell and Rebecca Martin also is appreciated. Our thanks go to Jean Woy and Barbara de Boinville of Congressional Quarterly Press who provided invaluable support throughout the editing and production of the book. Several of our colleagues gave us useful suggestions about the presentation of materials, and we are particularly grateful to Joseph A. Schlesinger for his insights on American party politics. Richard G. Niemi of the University of Rochester and William Claggett of the University of Mississippi provided extensive and helpful comments.

This book was a collective enterprise, but we did divide the labor. Paul Abramson had the primary responsibility for Chapters 3, 4, 5, and 11, John Aldrich for Chapters 1, 6, 7, and 8, and David Rohde for Chapters 2, 9, and 10. Only one of us, a Reagan voter, can claim any responsibility for the presidential election result. Two of us split our votes between Carter and Anderson. While none of us voted with enthusiasm, we were enthusiastic when we turned to our role as political scientists, for the policy consequences of the elections already have proved to be far-reaching. Explaining why voters elected Reagan and why they gave the Republicans a majority in the Senate and more seats in the House is of crucial importance for understanding American politics.

Paul R. Abramson
John H. Aldrich
David W. Rohde

Contents

Figures and Tables

(Unless otherwise noted in the text, these figures and tables are based upon our analyses of survey data provided by the Inter-University Consortium for Political and Social Research, Ann Arbor, Michigan.)

Figures

Tables

PART I

The 1980 Presidential Election Contest

The race for the American presidency is a long, tortuous process that culminates in selecting the most powerful freely elected leader in the world. Yet the effort necessary to gain this uncommon office forces the aspirants to earn the votes of millions of common citizens. To win those votes, candidates must first earn the time and money of thousands of more active citizens. Individuals who would seek to be commander in chief of a major nuclear arsenal must press the flesh of thousands of average Americans and show themselves to be common as well as extraordinary.

The ultimate prize of the presidency commands prestige as well as power. The American president is considered not only the leader of the United States, but of the entire free world. And yet the prestige and tremendous resources of the presidency do not ensure that citizens will return an incumbent president to office, as both the 1976 and 1980 presidential elections show.

The fascination with the presidency grows largely from the power of the office. Of course, the president is limited by Congress, the courts, and by the very nature of the federal system that shares power with 50 states. Often presidents have been unable to implement changes in domestic policies. It is generally argued that they have greater power to influence foreign policy, although Congress's passage of the 1973 War Powers Act attempted to limit the president's authority to send American forces into combat. Despite these limits, the president has the capacity to influence greatly, if not totally to dictate, the nation's major policy decisions.

It is precisely because presidents have immense powers that presidential elections, from time to time, have played a major role in determining the course of American history. The election of 1832, in which incumbent Democratic president Andrew Jackson defeated Henry Clay (National Republican) was fought over the issue of rechartering the Bank of the United States. Jackson's landslide victory,

54 percent of the popular vote to 37 percent for Clay, led to the downfall of the Bank and increased the importance of local banks. The election of 1860, which brought Abraham Lincoln and the Republicans to power and ousted a divided Democratic party, focused on the issue of whether slavery should be extended into the western territories. Following Lincoln's victory, 11 southern states attempted to secede from the Union, the Civil War erupted, and, ultimately, slavery itself was abolished. An antislavery plurality that did not necessarily favor the abolition of slavery (Lincoln received only 40 percent of the popular vote) set in motion a chain of events that freed some four million black Americans. And the election of 1896, in which the Republican William McKinley defeated the Populist and Democrat William Jennings Bryan, beat back the challenge of western and southern agrarian interests against the prevailing financial and industrial power of the East. Although Bryan mounted a strong campaign, winning 47 percent of the popular vote to 51 percent for McKinley, the election set a clear course for a policy of high tariffs and the continuation of the gold standard for American money.

The twentieth century also has witnessed presidential elections that determined the future fate of public policy. The 1936 contest, in which incumbent Franklin D. Roosevelt won 61 percent of the vote and his Republican opponent, Alfred E. Landon, only 37 percent, allowed the Democrats to continue and consolidate the economic policies of the New Deal. And Lyndon B. Johnson's 1964 landslide victory over Republican Barry M. Goldwater probably provided the clearest set of policy alternatives of any election in this century. Johnson, who received 61 percent of the popular vote to 38 percent for Goldwater, saw his triumph as a mandate for his Great Society reforms, the most far-reaching social legislation enacted since World War II. Goldwater provided "a choice, not an echo," advocating far more conservative social and economic policies than Johnson, and the electorate rejected the choice he offered. Ironically, the election also appeared to offer a choice between escalating American involvement in Vietnam and restraint. Given Johnson's subsequent moves to escalate the war, most of Goldwater's policies ultimately were implemented by Johnson himself.

Only the future can reveal the ultimate importance of the 1980 election. The Carter-Reagan contest, however, did provide clear policy alternatives. Jimmy Carter proved to be a fairly conservative president, especially in his vacillating economic policies. Although Carter never pushed for major civil rights, national health, or full employment legislation, he was not, as Ted Kennedy charged in the heat of the nomination contest, a "clone of Ronald Reagan." Clearly, he was more committed to strong federal involvement in the economy, to improving conditions for minorities, and to such symbolic policies as the enactment of the Equal Rights Amendment. Reagan proposed massive cuts in federal income taxes, urging a 10 percent reduction for three years, while Carter strongly opposed such cuts, and even opposed a tactical pre-election tax cut. Reagan favored scrapping the SALT II arms limitation treaty, while Carter supported its ratification, and Reagan favored substantial increases in military spending. The initial success Reagan has enjoyed in cutting spending for social services reveals that the 1980 election may have profound policy consequences.

Although many voters were apparently dissatisfied with the choices they were offered, the positions of the two major candidates were clearly different. And voters who rejected the policies of the two major candidates could opt for John B. Anderson (Independent party) or for the dramatically different policies offered by Ed Clark (Libertarian party) or Barry Commoner (Citizens party).

In fact, a majority of voters chose Reagan. In addition, the Republicans won control of the United States Senate for the first time since 1952 and gained 33 seats in the House of Representatives. These Republican victories raise two fundamental questions. Did the 1980 elections constitute an endorsement for Republican policies? And did they provide the basis for a shift in partisan fortunes that will establish the Republicans as the dominant political party?

While Reagan and the leaders of his party view the election as a mandate for their programs, the Republican victories do not necessarily demonstrate that voters support their policies. On November 4, 1980, presidential voters were not only choosing among policies but among men; they selected a specific individual to be entrusted with vast political as well as military power. To a large extent, voters make choices based upon their evaluations of the candidates, their perceived leadership abilities, and their personal qualities. When one of the candidates is an incumbent president, the incumbent's performance in office may be the deciding factor.

We believe the Republican victory in 1980 was more a rejection of Carter's performance as president than a mandate for Republican policies.[1] Did it signal the beginning of a partisan realignment? This is a far more difficult question to answer. Political scientists define realignment differently. V. O. Key, Jr., developed a theory of "critical elections" that specified conditions under which "new and durable electoral groupings are formed."[2] He later argued that a realignment takes place over a series of elections in which "shifts in the partisan balance of power" occur.[3] James L. Sundquist defines realignment as "a durable change in patterns of political behavior."[4] And Lawrence G. McMichael and Richard J. Trilling define it as "a significant and durable change in the distribution of party support over relevant groups within the electorate."[5]

Realignments usually do not involve across-the-board shifts toward the same party by all segments of the electorate. Shifts occur instead in the regional bases of party support and in the partisanship of social groups. They may result from the mobilization of new social groups into the electorate. Sundquist and others stress the importance of new issues in leading to realignments. Realignments occur not just from shifts in voting behavior, but from shifts in the party loyalties of the electorate.

Political leadership also contributes to partisan realignments. Jerome M. Clubb, William F. Flanigan, and Nancy H. Zingale argue that several potential realignments failed to materialize because political leaders did not take advantage of conditions that were favorable to their party. For example, they claim that Lyndon B. Johnson's 1964 landslide could have led to a pro-Democratic realignment were it not for his escalation of American involvement in Vietnam. Usually realignments occur when leaders capitalize on conditions by introducing policies that secure the long-term loyalties of new and potential supporters. "The role of political leadership, governmental action, and the course of historical events," according to Clubb, Flanigan, and Zingale, are "central to the formation of new distributions of partisan attitudes and to consequent lasting shifts in dominance over government from one party to the other." [6]

Since realignments involve "durable" or "lasting" shifts in the balance of partisan forces, and since they are more likely to occur if political leaders introduce successful policies, it is too soon to evaluate the ultimate impact of the 1980 elections. Nonetheless, by placing the 1980 elections in a broad historical context, we may be able to assess the conditions that could lead to a pro-Republican realignment. [7] We should recognize, however, that a partisan realignment merely implies a shift in the balance of partisan forces. This has occurred already. The move from Democratic dominance to a more competitive balance between the parties could be called a realignment although political scientists have used the term "dealignment" to describe the process through which old voting patterns break down without being replaced by new ones. [8]

SURVEY RESEARCH SAMPLING

Our book relies heavily upon surveys of the American electorate, especially upon the 1980 survey conducted by the Survey Research Center and the Center for Political Studies of the University of Michigan. Readers may question our reliance upon this survey of 1,614 Americans, when more than 160,000,000 Americans are of voting age. [9] Would we have obtained similar results if all adults were surveyed?

The Michigan SRC-CPS uses a procedure called multistage probability sampling to select the specific individuals to be interviewed.

These procedures ensure that the final sample is very likely to represent the entire United States adult citizen population (except for Americans living in institutions, military reservations, or abroad).[10] Because the SRC has been studying American electoral behavior since 1948, we are able to examine American voting behavior for the entire postwar period. Since 1952, party identification and feelings of political effectiveness have been measured. The Michigan data provides the best and most comprehensive source of information on the issue preferences, political attitudes, and partisan loyalties of the American electorate.

Given the probability procedures the SRC-CPS uses to sample the electorate, we are able to assess the likelihood that the results of these surveys represent the total United States resident citizen population. Although the 1980 survey sampled only about one adult American in 100,000, the representativeness of the sample depends far more upon the size of the sample than upon the size of the population being studied. For most purposes, samples of about 1,500 respondents are adequate to study the American electorate. With a sample of this size we can be fairly confident (confident to a level of .95) that the result we obtain falls within plus or minus three percentage points of the result we would get if the entire adult population were surveyed.[11] For example, when we find in Chapter 6 that 56 percent of the electorate named an economic issue as the most important problem facing the nation, we can be fairly confident that between 53 percent and 59 percent of the entire electorate considered an economic problem as most important. The actual result for the entire electorate *could* be less than 53 percent or more than 59 percent. But a confidence level of .95 means that the odds are 19 to one that the entire electorate falls within this range.

The range of confidence becomes wider when we look at subgroups of the electorate. When we examine groups of 500 respondents, the range of confidence grows to plus or minus six percentage points. For only 100 respondents, the range of confidence expands to plus or minus 14 percent. Since the likelihood of error grows as our subsamples become smaller, we will often supplement our analyses with the reports of other surveys.

Somewhat more complicated procedures are necessary to determine whether the difference between two groups is likely to reflect relationships that would obtain if the entire population were surveyed. The probability that such differences reflect real differences in the total population is largely a function of the size of the samples of the groups being compared.[12] Generally speaking, when we compare the results of the total 1980 survey with the result of a previous survey, a difference of about four percentage points is sufficient to be reasonably confident that the differences are real. When we are comparing subgroups of the electorate sampled in 1980 (or subgroups sampled in 1980 with the same subgroup sampled in earlier surveys), a larger percentage difference is necessary to be confident that differences did not result from chance. For example, if we compare men with women, a difference of about six percentage points would be necessary. When we compare blacks with whites, a difference of about nine percentage points would be necessary since one of the two subgroups is relatively small (generally only about 200 blacks are sampled in any given survey). These procedures provide only a quick "ballpark" estimate of the chance that the reported results are likely to represent the entire population. However, more precise estimates are possible using formulas presented in many statistics texts. To conduct such calculations, or even to conduct a "ballpark" estimate of the chance of error, the reader must know the size of the groups being compared. For this reason we usually report in our tables and figures the numbers upon which the percentages are based.

THE 1980 CONTEST

Part I of our book follows the chronology of the campaign itself. We begin with the struggle to gain the two major-party nominations. Chapter 1 examines the long process of earning delegates through party caucuses and presidential primaries and shows how the dynamics of momentum help candidates gain the delegates needed to win. As we shall see, the major political reforms after 1968 have greatly increased the number of primary contests and have altered the chances for different types of candidates to win their party's nomination. Chapter 1 concludes with the spectacle of the 1980 party nominating conventions themselves.

Once the party nominations have been won, the race usually narrows to a struggle between the two major political parties. Candidates who fail to win their party's nomination have virtually no chance to be elected. In 1980, Anderson rejected this logic and after failing to gain the Republican nomination launched an independent candidacy which, although ultimately unsuccessful, enlivened the campaign. Chapter 2 describes the major-party campaigns in light of the Anderson challenge. The major presidential candidates' election strategies and the electoral consequences of the presidential debates are analyzed. We also examine the media's role in shaping the public's perception of the campaign.

Chapter 3 presents and interprets the election results themselves in the context of postwar presidential elections and then in the larger context of all presidential elections since 1832. Because states are the building blocks upon which electoral vote majorities are won, the results are discussed on a state by state basis. As we will see, the Republicans have built an electoral vote base that may aid them in future presidential elections. We do not think that a new party realignment is necessarily in the making, nor do we think that the Republicans have become a majority party. But we do see signs of change that point to electoral volatility in the remaining presidential elections in this century.

NOTES

1. Numerous political scientists who have begun to study the 1980 election have come to a similar conclusion. See Everett Carll Ladd, "The Brittle Mandate: Electoral Dealignment and the 1980 Presidential Election," *Political Science Quarterly* 96 (Spring 1981): 1-25; Kathleen A. Frankovic, "Public Opinion Trends," in *The Election of 1980: Reports and Interpretations,* Gerald M. Pomper with colleagues (Chatham, N.J.: Chatham House, 1981), pp. 97-118; and Warren E. Miller, "Policy Directions and Presidential Leadership: Alternative Interpretations of the 1980 Presidential Election" and Arthur H. Miller and Martin P. Wattenberg, "Policy and Performance Voting in the 1980 Election" (Papers delivered at the annual meeting of the American Political Science Association, New York, New York, September 3-6, 1981).
2. V. O. Key, Jr., "A Theory of Critical Elections," *Journal of Politics* 17 (February 1955): 4.
3. V. O. Key, Jr., "Secular Realignment and the Party System," *Journal of Politics* 21 (May 1959): 198.
4. James L. Sundquist, *Dynamics of the Party System: Alignment and Realignment of Political Parties in the United States* (Washington, D.C.: The Brookings Institution, 1973), p. 5.
5. Lawrence G. McMichael and Richard J. Trilling, "The Structure and Meaning of Critical Realignment: The Case of Pennsylvania, 1928-1932," in *Realignment in American Politics: Toward a Theory,* ed. Bruce A. Campbell and Richard J. Trilling (Austin: University of Texas Press, 1980), p. 25.
6. Jerome M. Clubb, William H. Flanigan, and Nancy H. Zingale, *Partisan Realignment: Voters, Parties and Government in American History* (Beverly Hills, Calif.: Sage Publications, 1980), p. 268.
7. William Schneider argues that a pro-Republican realignment has occurred already. See Schneider, "The November 4 Vote for President: What Did it Mean?" in *The American Elections of 1980,* ed. Austin Ranney (Washington, D.C.: American Enterprise Institute for Public Policy Research, 1981), pp. 249-262.
8. See Ronald Inglehart and Avram Hochstein, "Alignment and Dealignment of the Electorate in France and the United States," *Comparative Political Studies* 5 (October 1972): 343-372; Paul Allen Beck, "Partisan Dealignment in the Postwar South," *American Political Science Review* 71 (June 1977): 477-496; and Ivor Crewe, "Prospects for Party Realignment: An Anglo-American Comparison," *Comparative Politics* 12 (July 1980): 379-400.
9. For most of our tabulations we confine our analyses to the 1,408 respondents included in the 1980 SRC-CPS postelection survey.
10. For an excellent introduction to the sampling procedures used by the University of Michigan Survey Research Center, see Herbert F. Weisberg and Bruce D. Bowen, *An Introduction to Survey Research and Data*

Analysis (San Francisco: W. H. Freeman & Co., 1977), pp. 27-35. For a more detailed description of SRC survey methods, see Survey Research Center, *Interviewer's Manual*, rev. ed. (Ann Arbor, Mich.: Institute for Social Research, 1976).

11. The probability of sampling error is partly a function of the result for any given question. The probability of error is greater for proportions near 50 percent, and diminishes somewhat for proportions above 70 percent or below 30 percent. The probability of error diminishes markedly for proportions above 90 percent or below 10 percent. For the sake of simplicity, we will report the confidence levels for percentages near 50 percent.

12. For an excellent table that allows us to evaluate differences between groups, see Leslie Kish, *Survey Sampling* (New York: John Wiley & Sons, 1965), p. 580. Kish defines the difference between two groups to be significant if the results are two standard deviations apart.

1

The Nomination Struggle

Presidential campaigns can be divided into four phases. The first phase begins sometime after the last presidential election and continues until the media start to cover the next presidential campaign extensively. In this phase before the public campaign begins in earnest, presidential prospects must decide whether or not to become candidates. If they choose to run, they must build a campaign organization and plan a strategy to win.

The second phase of presidential campaigns covers the 50 state primaries and caucuses at which delegates are chosen to attend the national convention. For all intents and purposes, the winner of this phase is the nominee. In 1980, Jimmy Carter and Ronald Reagan amassed their winning coalitions at or before the last primaries in June, as we will see in Figure 1-3.

During the third phase, the nominee is officially selected at the party's national nominating convention. Even though the candidates already have won or lost the nomination by this time, the convention remains important. At the convention the party as a whole adopts rules to govern it and chooses its policy platform. Barring renomination of an incumbent, the winner must pick a vice-presidential running mate. He also must begin the transition from competing within his own party to competing against the other party and its nominee. This transition is to the last phase, the general election campaign itself.

In this chapter we will review the first three phases: the decision to run, the primary and caucus campaigns, and the national conventions. We will also examine the rules, laws and institutions that govern the preconvention campaign period. The last phase, the general election campaign, will be discussed in Chapter 2.

In many important ways, the 1976 and 1980 nomination campaigns were remarkably similar. This is due to both the particular institutional arrangements of our nominating system and the goals and incentives of the major actors involved. Therefore, if the 1980 election proves to be a realigning election, the realignment occurred in spite of the nature of the nomination campaign.

All four nominations were contested vigorously from the opening shot to the last few primaries. In 1980, perhaps even more than in 1976, the nominations were won and lost well before the conventions began. The crowded field in the challenging party quickly diminished to a handful of plausible candidates. Carter was challenged by just two candidates in 1980, and his only serious challenger was Edward M. (Ted) Kennedy, just as Reagan was Gerald R. Ford's only opponent in 1976. In both years the nomination was in serious doubt. Kennedy in 1980 and Reagan in 1976 actively pursued the incumbent president through the initial stages of the convention itself, even though their opponents had the votes necessary to win before the convention. Their losses were not certain until each had launched a "test vote" of their strength on a procedural issue and lost it on the convention floor.

Are the similarities between the 1976 and 1980 campaigns purely coincidental? At least one similarity is. It is coincidental for there to be an incumbent seeking nomination in two consecutive election years. In other respects, however, the parallels are not surprising. To see why, let us look first at the history of presidential primaries in America and the institutions governing the nomination process.

THE NOMINATION PROCESS

The Republican and Democratic parties select their presidential nominees by a simple majority vote of delegates attending their respective national conventions.[1] The obvious goal of any nomination hopeful is to win the support of half of the delegates or more. At one time, this goal could be attained during the convention itself. In 1896, William Jennings Bryan's "Cross of Gold" speech supposedly convinced large numbers of delegates that he was able to win nomination. More commonly, nomination contenders have attempted to win delegate support either by obtaining the backing of party leaders (who would then deliver the votes of "their" delegates) or by ensuring that delegates favorable to their candidacy were selected to attend the convention in the first place. Historically, candidates relying on the latter source of support turned to the presidential primary, and they did so because they were challenging the established party leadership.

The primary was initiated early in the twentieth century to involve more citizens in nominations and to reduce the control of party machines. Florida passed the first presidential primary law in 1901, and the popularity of primaries grew rapidly. By 1916, 20 states held primaries. For the next 30 years few additional states adopted primaries, some even dropped them. In 1948, 14 states used the primary to select national convention delegates. Of these, two were Democratic primaries only, while in six more there was only one choice on the ballot in both party "competitions." Because many states did not adopt the primary or did not bind the delegates selected to vote in any particular way at the convention, no candidate who "went the primary route" won nomination.

For example, Theodore Roosevelt won 9 of the 12 primaries held in 1912, but incumbent president William Howard Taft, the winner of but a single primary, was able to gain the support of most of the delegates through the traditional party network. In subsequent contended nomination campaigns, the candidate who won the most primary votes usually lost the nomination. In 1960, John F. Kennedy won two major Democratic primaries in Wisconsin and West Virginia. He used those victories to convince party leaders that he was popular enough to be elected. Thus, while these primary victories were important ingredients in his successful nomination campaign, they were used as evidence to convince key party figures to support him.

Primary Reforms

After the 1968 campaign, the role of the primary changed radically. Democratic senators Eugene McCarthy and Robert Kennedy focused their 1968 campaigns on the primaries. McCarthy's surprisingly large vote in New Hampshire and projected win in Wisconsin may have encouraged President Lyndon B. Johnson to retire, but the nomination was won by then Vice President Hubert Humphrey, who did not enter a single primary. The tumultuous convention in Chicago that year led the Democratic party to initiate a series of reforms to involve the Democrats in the electorate in the nomination process.

One outgrowth of this reform effort in the late sixties was a resurgence in the use of the primary: 15 states in 1968, 21 in 1972, 30 in 1976, and 37 in 1980. About three-quarters of all Democratic delegates were chosen in primaries in the last two presidential elections. Because primaries are established by state law, the spread of primaries affected the Republican party as well. Related party provisions tied more closely the delegates selected in primaries to the voters' presidential preferences.

About one-quarter of the states do not use the presidential primary. Instead they hold caucuses or conventions to select their representatives to the national conventions. These caucuses ordinarily attract many fewer participants than primaries attract voters. As a result, they are more easily dominated by strong party organizations or committed ideological or presidential candidate organizations. The Democratic party reform efforts focused on making the caucus system more open to public participation and less responsive to organizational control. In many cases the reforms had the effect of making caucuses quasi-primaries. The attention the media gave to the Iowa caucus and others reinforced their primary-like role. While the reforms affected only Democratic party organizations, there has been an inevitable spillover to the Republican party.

In short, the delegate selection procedures enacted during the last decade give the electorate a greater and more direct role in influencing presidential nominations. As a result, candidates for the nomination spend far more time, effort, and resources appealing to the public than ever before. In 1980, as in 1972 and 1976, the nomination campaign was won or lost in public and by appeal to the public.

Campaign Financing Reforms

The federal government enacted a series of sweeping reforms of presidential campaign financing at the same time the primary reforms were going into effect. One set of reforms concerned the contribution of money by citizens. Individuals who wish to donate money to a presidential campaign were limited to giving $1,000 to any one candidate and a total of $25,000 in any one election period. The intent of this reform was to limit the role of "fat cats" who provide large sums of money to individual candidates. Because of the success of this reform, candidates have been forced to raise money from a large number of donators of small sums. In effect, candidates appeal to the public for money as well as votes.

Broad-based financial appeals are reinforced by federal matching funds, which became available for the first time during the 1976 campaign. If a presidential candidate meets certain qualifications, the federal government will match, dollar for dollar, any individual's contribution of $250 or less, up to a total of $7.36 million in 1980. Candidates are not required to accept matching funds although most do.

John Connally chose not to accept matching funds in his campaign for the 1980 Republican nomination, however. He did so because acceptance of federal support would have limited the amount he could spend. Candidates accepting matching funds in 1980 were limited to spending in their nomination campaigns no more than $14,720,000. (Some other expenditures, such as for fund-raising efforts themselves, are permitted.) In addition, the amount a candidate could spend in any one state primary or caucus campaign was limited. Ford and Carter could each spend no more than $10.9 million in their 1976 nomination campaigns and $21.8 million in their general election campaigns, or a total of $32.7 million. In 1972, Richard Nixon spent $51.4 million for his renomination and re-election campaigns. In 1980, Reagan and Carter, even George Bush and Kennedy, rapidly approached their total nomination expenditure limits and had to economize near the end.

In important state contests, state expenditures limits can be crucial. Not bound by the $477,196 spending ceiling in South Carolina, Connally planned to outspend his opponents by about twice as much on the assumption that higher spending would provide the margin for victory. Ironically, having spent $8.2 million in 1979, he began to run out of money as the South Carolina primary neared and was unable to spend more than the limit anyway.[2]

Two important aspects of the campaign finance reforms, the "Political Action Committee" (PAC) and the independent campaign committee, played a strategic role in the 1980 elections. As part of the 1974 financial reform package, Congress permitted businesses and corporations to contribute money to candidates via PACs. The PAC contribution was first used in 1976, but 1980 saw a phenomenal growth in their number and influence. For the first time, PAC contributions by the business community exceeded those by labor unions. According to the *New York Times,* by the end of June 1980 corporations had donated $23 million, while union PACs had contributed $17.5 million.[3] The *Times* also reported differences in PAC contributions to political parties in 1980. The Republican National Committee received $37.2 million, the Democratic National Committee $8.0 million; the National Republican Senatorial Committee received $9.0 million, the Democratic Senatorial Campaign Committee $0.9 million. The two congressional totals were $16.4 and $1.3 million, respectively. Clearly, PACs benefited the Republicans.

Federal law permits committees that are independent of candidates and their organizations to spend unlimited amounts on behalf of any candidates they choose. These independent committees benefited Ronald Reagan and other Republican candidates. The National Conservative Political Action Committee (NCPAC), for example, raised many millions of dollars for such expenditures. No comparable Democratic-supporting independent committees were active during the 1980 presidential campaign, although several were created after the election. George McGovern, the former Democratic senator from South Dakota who was targeted by NCPAC and was defeated for re-election, founded Americans for Common Sense in December 1980.

Technological Advances and the Media

Technological advances provide a third set of major changes in the electoral process of the 1970s and 1980s. Computerized mailing lists, polling techniques, marketing and advertising technology, and the capabilities of the print and broadcast media have transformed campaigning. Most candidates employ professional specialists in campaign techniques. New technological possibilities have enabled candidates to circumvent the much more labor-intensive local and state party organizations, contributing to the so-called "decline" of political parties in American elections. Many party-oriented campaign organizations have been replaced by the more personalized, candidate-dominated organizations common to both presidential nomination and election campaigns.

The changed role of the media is the most important of these technological advances. Not only have the media benefited from the technological improvements of the last few decades, but their role in presidential nomination campaigns has altered as the nature of campaigns has changed. Because candidates now wage public nomination campaigns nationwide in the search for primary votes, money, and campaign workers, the media cover campaigns more closely on a day-to-day basis. They cover who is ahead at every stage of the race ("horse race coverage") and conduct state- and national-level polls of the electorate.

These changes in the media's campaign coverage have influenced the strategy of the candidates. For example, it is far more efficient for a candidate to appear on television than to try to contact a similar number of citizens directly. If the media establish qualifications for federal funding as a crucial "benchmark" of early success, it behooves the candidate to qualify as soon as possible. If dramatic confrontations make the evening news, it makes sense for John Anderson to address a hostile audience on gun control. The support he might lose in that audience may be made up many times in the televised coverage of his "courageous" stance. If the media criticize Reagan's failure to attend the Republican debate in Iowa, apparently contributing to his loss there, he had better attend the next debates in New Hampshire. At the same time, candidates exercise some control over which issues the media cover, which primaries are important and to whom. Thus, the candidates and the media personnel are almost symbiotically related. Each benefits from the relationship with the other, at least as long as the candidate's campaign remains viable.

THE FIRST PHASE: WHO RUNS FOR PRESIDENT

The presidency is by far the most attractive public office to politicians. Yet in any election year only a very few make a serious bid for a major-party nomination. The reasons why so few seek what so many desire are evident. A presidential candidacy is an arduous, costly, and even physically dangerous endeavor requiring great personal and sometimes professional sacrifices. Only a handful of presidential hopefuls can have anything approaching a realistic expectation of surviving the primary season, winning the nomination, and then defeating the opponent(s) in the fall.

Many, but not all, serious candidates for a presidential nomination have the nearly exclusive goal of winning. They can be understood best as office seekers, per se. Yet few if any candidates want only the nomination and the election. Nearly all want to shape public policy in the United States. Indeed, the intensity of the campaign is such that many candidates see vast differences for the future of the country if they, instead of their opponents, are elected. While candidates are often charged with ambiguous views and waffling on the issues, most identify themselves, and become identified by others, as espousing particular kinds of policies.

The general labeling of candidates—Kennedy as a liberal and Carter as less liberal, Reagan and Phil Crane as conservatives, Bush and Howard H. Baker, Jr., as more moderate conservatives, and Anderson as a relatively liberal Republican—is grounded in their career histories as well as in their campaign rhetoric. In short, virtually all candidates want to win the nomination and election, but they also have goals for public policy. Some attempt to lay the groundwork for attaining these goals in the future.

Kennedy, Edmund G. (Jerry) Brown, Jr., and several of the Republican candidates in 1980 may be contemplating a presidential bid in 1984. Phil Crane was hoping to assume the Reagan mantle of conservative spokesman. Still others, Bush, for example, may have seen the potential for a vice-presidential nomination in 1980 if the presidential nomination could not be won. Anderson developed, if he did not already have, a desire to restructure the party system in the United States, either by redefining the coalitions of the two major parties or by establishing a third party. One thing is clear, however. Whether a candidate hopes to win office, affect public policy, or realize goals in the future, the candidate will be more likely to achieve those goals by doing better in the campaign than by doing worse. Thus, most candidates seek to win delegate support through campaigning for public votes in state primaries or caucuses; the more they get, the better.

Given the very high costs of campaigning, the strength of opposition, and the relatively low chance of success, only a few will find it worthwhile to enter the fray. In 1980, as in prior elections, serious candidates were drawn from the small set of visible, current or recent public officeholders. Indeed, the need to win votes from a broad segment of the public who know little or nothing of most politicians has exaggerated the importance of prior visibility—as well as the necessity for those less well known to start campaigning as early as possible. All serious candidates in 1980 held or had held the office of president, U.S.

senator, U.S. representative, or governor. The strong electoral base these offices provide is a crucial ingredient of success and separates those who run from many who might like to be president but do not try.

In 1980, a number of candidates were out of public office. Reagan, Bush, and Connally had not held elective or major appointive office for four years and more, just as Carter and Reagan, among others, held no office in 1976. The extreme demands of running for president mean that officeholders are disadvantaged in comparison to those freer to run every day for six months or a year before the conventions. Baker, as Senate minority leader, was torn between performing the duties of his office and needing to get out on the hustings. His poor showing at the outset has been attributed in part to his inability to wage a daily campaign, and it led to his early withdrawal. Kennedy and Anderson essentially gave up their duties as incumbent members of Congress, sacrifices that were necessary ingredients of their strong, if losing, candidacies. (Anderson had announced already that he was retiring from Congress and felt freer to slight his congressional tasks.) Thus, the new nomination system of the seventies and eighties places a premium on visibility and prominence and gives a relative advantage to those free (or willing to free themselves) of current commitments.

The sacrifices necessary to run for president compared to the difficulty of winning nomination also explain why relatively few challenge a sitting president. Here the key is the probability of success. The president, regardless of how popular or unpopular, commands tremendous resources. Ford and Carter may have been perceived as weak incumbents compared to Dwight D. Eisenhower in 1956, Johnson in 1964, or Richard M. Nixon in 1972, but they were able to do many things their challengers could not simply because they were president. The prestige of the office, the ability to shape policy, the vast media coverage of the daily conduct of the office of president, and the resources of party leaders and organizations are assets no challenger can match.

Only a few unusually attractive and powerful figures in the incumbent's party can imagine any reasonable chance of defeating an incumbent president. Ted Kennedy, for example, had assets of the Kennedy legacy, high poll standings, and the apparent support of many influential Democrats. Jerry Brown, a late-starting candidate in 1976, created considerable attention (dubbed the "Brown phenomenon" by reporters) after he defeated Carter in several primaries. In 1976, only Reagan could attract the kinds of ideological, party, and mass support necessary to challenge even an unelected president. Kennedy, Brown, and Reagan were all unsuccessful. Rarely can anyone match the sort of nomination resources an incumbent can employ. As a result, incumbents, although beatable, have been and will be challenged seriously only by one or two opponents. In nominations involving no incumbent, the field of contenders is much larger precisely because no one is likely to be as strong at the outset as an incumbent.

THE SECOND PHASE: THE PRIMARY CAMPAIGNS

The Democratic Primary Campaign

Having considered who runs for president, why they run, and what sort of nomination system they face, let us examine how the nomination campaigns of Carter and Reagan unfolded and why they won, turning first to the Democratic campaign.

In 1980, much of the "action" in the incumbent's nomination bid occurred before the actual delegate selection phase began. In part, the action started in the summer and fall of 1979 because of the 1976 experience when Carter caught the media and the country by surprise in Iowa. R. W. "Johnny" Apple of the *New York Times* reported on an unofficial, "straw" ballot in Iowa and was credited with first recognizing Carter's rise there. The importance of the Iowa victory to Carter's successful bid in 1976, as well as the professional gain from first spying the eventual winner, led the media to search very early in 1980 for signs of the "next Carter." As a result, Florida Democrats saw that they could receive a lot of media attention and perhaps play a great role in the nomination by holding an unofficial vote of their partisans as early as possible. The Florida straw vote was late in 1979. Supporters of both Kennedy and Carter (who won), seeing the opportunity of attention and an early victory, campaigned hard in Florida. The media, the Florida party structure, and both candidates and their supporters turned this "non-event" into an important juncture in the quest for the nomination.

While the "system" forced the opening of the campaign back into 1979, even more important events happened before then. One of the first questions on reporters' lips about the 1980 Democratic campaign was "Will Teddy run?" This question was asked in 1968 after Robert Kennedy's assassination, in 1972, and once again in 1976. In these prior campaigns, Kennedy's only problem was how to say no convincingly without precluding a presidential bid. He said yes in 1979.

Several factors, motives, and rationales informed Kennedy's decision to run. First, he stood very high in the polls; Carter did not. Figure 1-1 depicts their relative Gallup Poll standings among Democrats in the electorate. Many key groups and Kennedy backers were encouraging him to run. Kennedy's vision of the policies this country needed differed substantially from Carter's. It is fair to guess that Kennedy did not want Carter to be president for four more years. An equally fair guess is that Kennedy would have disliked a Brown nomination at least as much as a

Figure 1-1 Democrats' Choices for the Nomination, Gallup Polls, February 1979-February 1980

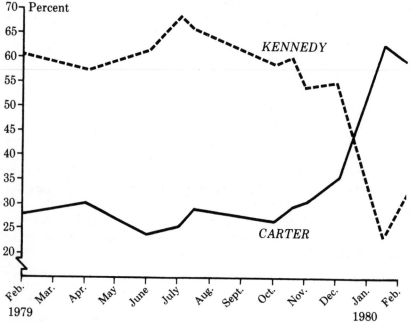

NOTE: About 675 Democrats were asked this question in the typical Gallup Poll.
SOURCE: *Gallup Opinion Index*, Report No. 183, December 1980, p. 51.

Carter renomination. If Carter won in 1980, new candidates such as Vice President Walter F. Mondale might emerge by 1984. And it appeared in the summer of 1979 that Carter was vulnerable. Figure 1-2 reports the Gallup Poll standings of Carter versus Reagan during the course of the nomination campaign.

Many pundits all but declared Kennedy the victor with his entrance into the race. After all, he led Carter among Democrats in the July Gallup Poll by 36 percentage points. Virtually with Kennedy's entrance, however, his lead fell. By the time the 1980 campaign got under way in Iowa in late January, he was behind by 29 points. Kennedy was never able to recover. What happened and, more importantly, why did it happen? There were two separate sets of factors: those that hurt Kennedy and those that boosted Carter.

First, the height of Kennedy's pre-announcement popularity was chimeric. He was, after all, not a real candidate. Undoubtedly, many thought fondly—but only vaguely—of a Kennedy candidacy. By entering the race, Kennedy changed from one of the Kennedy brothers to Ted Kennedy, a serious candidate for the presidency. Secondly, he opened himself up to careful scrutiny. Commentators and politicians

Figure 1-2 Carter-Reagan Support, Gallup Polls, March 1979 through Conventions in August 1980

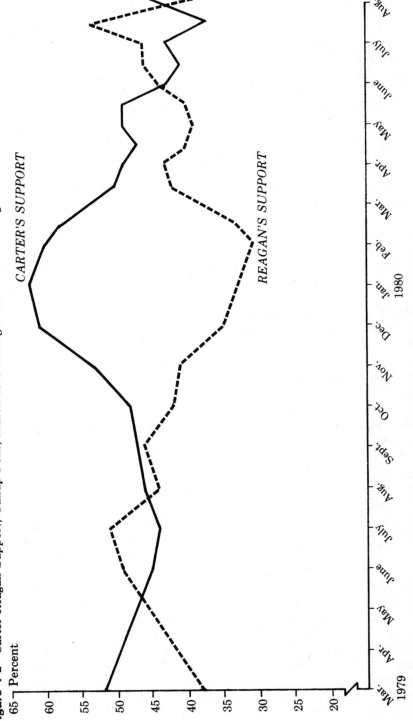

Percent

CARTER'S SUPPORT

REAGAN'S SUPPORT

65
60
55
50
45
40
35
30
25
20

Mar. Apr. May June July Aug. Sept. Oct. Nov. Dec. Jan. Feb. Mar. Apr. May June July Aug.

1979

1980

NOTE: Virtually all of the 1,500 respondents in a typical Gallup Poll were asked this question.
SOURCE: *Gallup Opinion Index*, Report No. 183, December 1980, pp. 13-15.

began to examine both his personal qualifications and his policy concerns. Doubts about his personal behavior centered on the now-famous incident on Chappaquiddick Island off the coast of Martha's Vineyard. In July 1969, Kennedy was driving with a former Robert Kennedy campaign worker, Mary Jo Kopechne. It was late at night, and he missed a narrow bridge and plunged into the river. He survived, but she did not. Questions were raised not only about the circumstances of her death, but of his handling of the incident, particularly his failure to report the death to the police until the following morning. Such questions were raised in public by reporters and politicians in numerous direct or not so subtle, indirect ways.

Kennedy's political views attracted attention as well. Long an active liberal, he was seen by many as out of step in an era in which inflation and relatively slow economic growth seemed to call for fiscal conservatism. Some feared expensive liberal programs not only would exacerbate federal deficits, but also fall victim to a sort of Lyndon Johnson-Great Society programs backlash epitomized by the phrase "throwing money at problems."

Presumably, an adept politician could anticipate these problems, but in 1979 and early 1980 Kennedy proved to be remarkably inept. He appeared hesitant, even inarticulate, in public appearances (leading to comical satirization in *Doonesbury* and elsewhere). He seemed unable to organize his campaign and displayed occasional outbursts of ill-judged rhetoric (e.g., criticizing the Shah of Iran shortly after the seizure of hostages there). In a nationally televised interview broadcast in early November by then CBS correspondent Roger Mudd, Kennedy not only appeared confused, but stumbled over questions that seemed to be easy enough for a veteran politician. Why? Our belief is that he launched his campaign too soon. It began well before he thought deeply about why he wanted to be president and why he should ask Democrats to support him instead of a sitting president, before he developed a sense of his campaign or a theme to present to the electorate, and before he had developed a campaign organization and a strategic plan for winning the nomination. In short, he responded to pressure, decided to run, and then started campaigning without planning it out.

As Kennedy's popularity started to plummet in the polls, Carter's began to rise, as Figure 1-1 illustrates. Carter's improved public standing late in 1979 can be attributed in large part to the electoral advantages of incumbency. Historically, the public supports the president in times of crisis. On November 4, 1979, Iranian students seized American hostages in the U.S. embassy in Teheran. The next month the Soviets invaded Afghanistan. These two crises led to the so-called "rally 'round the flag" phenomenon, boosting Carter's standing.[4] The Gallup polling organization regularly asks the public whether they approve of the president's handling of his duties. In October, Carter's "popularity" was 30 percent. In the next two months, he scored a 26 point increase, the largest short-term increase in presidential popularity since Gallup began asking the question in 1938.

President Carter placed inflation at the top of his economic priorities. In January 1980, the annual inflation rate peaked at 20 percent, a record high. In March, the Federal Reserve Board began to take actions intended to quell inflation. The result was an unprecedented increase in the prime interest rate, or the rate banks charge their preferred customers. Rightly or wrongly, Carter, as president, was held responsible by many for high inflation and interest rates. One would expect these problems to hurt rather than to help the incumbent, but Carter was particularly open to attack from conservative economic positions. Liberal fiscal and economic policies were not the medicine seen to be effective in curing 20 percent inflation and 20 percent interest rates. Thus, Kennedy's liberal instincts and political history were especially inappropriate at just the wrong moments as the Iowa caucuses and the New Hampshire primary loomed near.

The fall in Kennedy's popularity and the rise in Carter's reflect both the strategic aspects of pre-primary campaigning and the intrusion of particular events. Kennedy and Carter shifted places by the opening of the public campaign. Carter had become the front-running candidate that incumbents ordinarily are. Kennedy fell victim to his own poor planning, Carter's incumbency advantages, and just plain bad luck.

This reversal in fortunes posed an opportunity for Carter and a problem for Kennedy. As president and front-runner, Carter could—and did—rely on the "Rose Garden" campaign strategy. Throughout most of the primary season, he remained near the White House, letting the day-to-day campaigning fall to his family, the vice president, the cabinet, and other "surrogates." Carter abandoned this strategy only after the aborted attempted rescue of the hostages in late April, but by then he was well on the way to the nomination.

As president, Carter was able not only to draw on a very impressive list of officials to "work" individual states for him, but also to generate as much media coverage as he desired. Moreover, the coverage was of Carter as president, thus keeping him above the fray and not letting him get on the defensive in any campaign exchanges. He justified his actions by citing Iran, thereby keeping the electorate rallied around the flag.[5] Kennedy, although able to generate considerable attention himself, was forced to do so in the usual travel-motorcade-speech-interview campaign fashion. He thus appeared "political" and could not entice the leading candidate to engage in debate.

Carter's tactics would have changed had he been unsuccessful. He was not. He led in the electoral polls as well as in the public opinion polls. He won easily in Iowa and New Hampshire, came remarkably close to Kennedy in Massachusetts, won three southern primaries, and then pulled out a major victory in Illinois. While Kennedy was able to win primaries or caucuses in several key industrial states—Michigan, New York, and Pennsylvania—as well as in California, New Jersey, New Mexico, Rhode Island, and South Dakota (all on the last primary election date), he was unable to affect either the substantial initial delegate lead Carter held or Carter's accumulation of delegates outside of the urban states. Carter's "competitive standing" based on delegates won during the nomination campaign is presented in Figure 1-3. This standing is based on how many more delegates Carter had won than Kennedy and Brown (with 1 delegate), divided by the remaining "pool" of delegates, chosen as uncommitted or yet to be selected.

In short, Kennedy, faced three problems: how to define his candidacy, how to reverse Carter's early momentum, and how to keep Carter from accumulating a majority of delegates. Kennedy was unable to develop a theme, program, or purpose quickly. Beginning with a major address at Georgetown University in late January his candidacy began to evolve a core that fully matured only at the convention itself. As interest rates fell, as inflation slowed, as unemployment increased, and as he, perhaps, began to look toward 1984, Kennedy returned to his liberal "home." The culmination was his spectacular address to the Democratic National Convention.

Unable to generate a major victory early on, Kennedy lost momentum to Carter. As Figure 1-3 illustrates, the early losses to Carter were relatively unimportant in terms of delegates. They were important because such failures made fund raising difficult (the lack of money plagued Kennedy for the rest of the campaign), dispirited campaign workers, and generated media analyses of Kennedy's failures and of how hard it would be for him to win. Kennedy was never able to break this cycle. The sheer accumulation of delegates by Carter, combined with the Democratic party rule that delegates are awarded to candidates in proportion to the votes candidates win, meant that Kennedy simply could not overtake Carter. Carter had a majority of delegates committed to him (either by law or by personal preference) well before the convention opened.[6]

Carter's strategy and Kennedy's refusal to quit the campaign had several major consequences. First, Kennedy was successful at winning support among key traditional Democratic groups in pivotal states. His success in the spring made Carter's job in the fall that much harder. Second, Kennedy's continued campaign through the convention meant that Carter could not begin his campaign against Reagan. Moreover, Kennedy's campaign continued to improve, culminating in a more adept handling of his role in the convention. By then, Carter was on the

Figure 1-3 Carter's and Reagan's Competitive Standing Based on Delegates Won, 1980

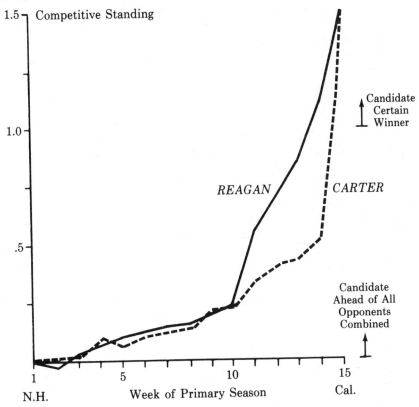

Formula: $$\frac{\text{Delegates for Carter [Reagan] - Delegates for Other Dems. [Reps.]}}{\text{Total Dem. Delegates (3,331) [Rep. Delegates (1,994)] - Delegates Committed}}$$

SOURCE: *Congressional Quarterly Weekly Reports.*

defensive, trying to hang on to his majority and granting policy concessions to Kennedy. Finally, by staying out of the ordinary campaign routine, Carter won the nomination but missed the opportunity to build enthusiasm among Democratic campaign workers.

Jerry Brown's campaign never got off the ground. The media image of the "Brown phenomenon" of 1976 had turned by 1980 to an image of "flake" and "Governor Moonbeam." He was unable to make contact with either Iowans or New Hampshirites. As a result he was not able to generate any momentum. His campaign ended in Wisconsin, a state he had set as the make-or-break showing. It broke him. By failing to obtain at least 10 percent of the vote in two consecutive primaries, he became disqualified for federal matching funds. Without popular or financial support, his campaign ended in virtual anonymity.

The Republican Primary Campaign

The Republican campaign was more one of jockeying for position. Commentators saw Reagan as front-runner, but they also saw potential vulnerabilities such as his age. Furthermore, they refused to ignore any candidate completely, not wanting to be surprised by another Carter-like "rise from obscurity." Indeed, George Bush received attention precisely because he followed the tactics of the Carter 1976 campaign. If anyone was seen as the most serious threat to Reagan it was John Connally, in part because of his visibility and in part because of the substantial sums of money he collected. His decision to refuse federal matching funds was intentionally eye-catching to reporters. In general, however, there was no solid consensus about likely winners or likely losers. Figure 1-4 reports the preferences of Republicans for their party's nomination. Obviously, many favored Reagan and Ford, but the other candidates were relatively unknown.

Thus, the Republican campaign "really" began in 1980 during the delegate selection phase itself. The Iowa precinct caucuses on January 21 and the New Hampshire primary February 26 were extremely

Figure 1-4 Republicans' Choices for the Nomination, Gallup Polls, January 1979-February 1980

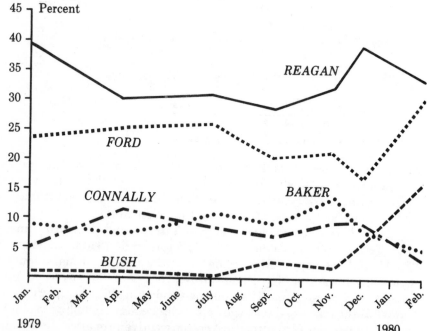

NOTE: About 350 Republicans were asked this question in the typical Gallup Poll.
SOURCE: *Gallup Opinion Index,* Report No. 183, December 1980, p. 32.

important. Each had a unique feature for Republican nomination politics—formalized debates.

All the major candidates but Reagan attended the Iowa debate. At the time, his strategy was to conserve energy and resources, to husband his lead in the polls, and to avoid getting involved in the normal give-and-take of campaigning. Bush's narrow defeat of Reagan in Iowa was attributed to Reagan's absence from the debate, although Reagan's more important failing—his refusal to campaign hard—was cited by some analysts. That Bush won at all, no matter how narrowly, was seen as a major breakthrough. His Iowa victory generated momentum for him, leading to a massive increase in contributions and a jump in the Gallup Polls. At the Iowa debate, Anderson was the only candidate to support Carter's embargo of grain shipments to the USSR because of the invasion of Afghanistan. Coverage of this stance led to the first signs of Anderson support from disaffected liberals.

In New Hampshire, Bush and Reagan switched tactics. Assuming the mantle of front-runner, whether true or not, Bush decided to stay "above the fray," while Reagan plunged into heavy, day-to-day campaigning. Poll reports indicated that Bush's popularity began to wane as Reagan's increased. In a debate in Nashua, New Hampshire, Reagan won a major symbolic victory.

The debate's sponsor, the *Nashua Telegraph,* scheduled a two-man confrontation between Reagan and Bush. The other candidates, however, filed a complaint with the Federal Election Commission demanding equal time and showed up at the hall. When the debate's moderator decided to stick to the original format, Anderson, Baker, Crane, and Robert Dole protested. Bush just sat there, but Reagan grabbed the initiative—and the headlines—by inviting the others to stay. When the moderator tried to prevent Reagan from speaking on their behalf, Reagan replied, "I paid for this microphone," since he had paid for the air time himself and transformed the debate to "paid political advertising" instead of "hard news." Even though in the end the others did not participate, Reagan's appeal won over the crowd. The four uninvited candidates retired to another room where they roundly denounced Bush to reporters. The debate itself was not televised, but newscasts across the country featured the rejected speakers' comments. Three days later on February 26 Reagan beat Bush in the New Hampshire primary by more than a 2-1 margin.

Since Bush's poll standings in New Hampshire were already in decline, his loss to Reagan in the primary may or may not have been directly attributable to the debate performance. Whatever the cause, Reagan reasserted himself as the clear front-runner. Late in the afternoon of the primary, the Reagan campaign announced the "resignation" of his campaign manager, John P. Sears, and several other top aides, culminating the reversal of his campaign strategy.

Connally set South Carolina as his make-or-break primary. He poured money, time, and effort into it, but to no avail. Reagan beat Connally solidly perhaps because of his recent win in New Hampshire and/or his natural popularity among Southern Republicans, and Connally withdrew.

Anderson's strong second-place finishes in the March 4 Vermont and Massachusetts primaries (to Reagan and Bush, respectively), established him as a serious, moderate-to-liberal alternative. For all intents and purposes, the campaign became a three-man race, but with one man ahead—Reagan.

Reagan's strong conservative credentials served him well. He amassed primary victories and delegates in the South and other conservative Republican bastions. Anderson never won a primary, but he did "put the squeeze" on Bush, who was caught in the middle between Reagan on his right and Anderson on his left. Bush maintained that if Anderson would let him face Reagan one-on-one, he could beat Reagan.[7] It was a reasonable argument, apparently confirmed in subsequent head-to-head confrontations with Reagan. Bush not only won several major primaries in less conservative Republican states such as New York, Connecticut, and Michigan, but he even came remarkably close to surprising Reagan in Texas.

Bush finally fell victim to the same unbeatable combination that stopped Kennedy: key early primary victories and consistent delegate acquisition by his opponent. On the very night of Bush's most spectacular victory in Michigan, Reagan assured his own nomination by winning just enough delegates in Michigan and Oregon to reach an outright majority. Bush withdrew shortly thereafter, but his strong and consistent support in the key industrial states helped win him the vice-presidential slot at the convention. Reagan's inexorable drive towards the nomination can be seen via his competitive standing measure, which is reported in Figure 1-3.

And what about Baker, Crane, Dole, and the other candidates? They fell victim to the same momentum phenomenon as Connally. Only Anderson, Bush, and Reagan were able to win substantial support in the early Iowa caucuses and the first few primaries. These three front-runners enjoyed the benefits of momentum, media attention, money, and therefore voter support down the road. The others failed to gain a minimal amount of support early on. They, like Connally, were winnowed out of contention before getting even a handful of delegates. This narrowing of a crowded field of candidates is the rule. It happened in the 1976 and 1972 Democratic campaigns, and it happened in the 1980 Republican campaign.

In many ways the Democratic and Republican campaigns of 1980 were very similar. On both sides attention focused on the few candidates who received substantial support in at least a few early primaries. Brown on the Democratic side and Baker, Crane, Connally, and Dole on the Republican side were eliminated early in the campaign. The front-runners did not win all or even nearly all of the remaining primaries, but both Carter and Reagan did run campaigns virtually everywhere while Anderson, Bush, and Kennedy did not. By receiving their proportionate share of delegates, the front-runners were able to win nomination before their conventions. As front-runners, they had built up too much momentum and too much of a lead to be stopped.

Reagan was, in part, fortunate. On the one hand, Bush did do well when Anderson was not competing. Perhaps a two-man race from beginning to end would have been different. On the other hand, Reagan seriously tried to get delegates in nearly all the states, while Bush did not. Reagan's efforts cost money, however. Since he accepted federal matching funds, he also accepted spending limits. As the campaign neared the end, Reagan began to approach these overall spending limits. A little closer contest might have meant that Reagan would not have been able to spend enough to campaign as effectively and, hence, would not have been as likely to win.

Anderson, the lone Republican tagged a "liberal," discovered the lesson learned by other liberal Republicans in recent years: conservative Republicans far outnumber liberal Republicans. Anderson was never able to win a primary, although he came close in several states where normally Democratic voters or Independents crossed party lines and voted for him. His strongest showings came in Massachusetts, Vermont, Illinois, Wisconsin, and Connecticut; only the last was a Republicans-only primary. Certainly, it seemed that his support in the nomination campaign was drawn from Democrats and Independents as much as from Republicans. Seeing his chances of winning a Republican nomination dwindling toward zero, Anderson withdrew and launched a third-candidate (conspicuously *not* called a third-*party*) campaign.

By July, then, Carter and Reagan had their nominations secured. As the conventions neared, it appeared they would be "coronations" as much as conventions.

THE THIRD PHASE: THE PARTY CONVENTIONS

National party conventions were invented in the early nineteenth century for the selection of the presidential and vice-presidential nominees. Yet since 1952 no convention has needed more than one ballot to choose a presidential nominee, and most nominees were assured of victory before the convention ever opened. The selection of the vice-presidential nominee has been even less competitive. No presidential nominee of recent times has faced serious opposition to his choice of running mate. We have argued that reforms after 1968 have reduced the importance of the convention in the selection of nominees, yet conventions serve a number of other purposes.

Three major decisions besides selection of nominees are made at conventions: the approval of the credentials of delegates for seating at the convention, the adoption of the rules to govern the party, and the selection of the party platform. All of these decisions have been controversial in some recent conventions.

Conventions not only make these formal decisions, but they also affect public opinion. The nominees address their acceptance speeches to the public at least as much as to the delegates. In fact, the convention can be considered a week-long advertisement for the party, even with its warts showing. The intense coverage of the convention naturally leads party leaders toward the goal of party unity. Whatever the divisions in the party, it is hoped, at least by the end of the convention, that the viewer will receive the impression of a party united by principle, united behind its candidates, and united in opposition to its competitors.

If unity is a major aspiration of the party, the 1980 conventions presented striking contrasts. The Republican convention displayed an almost overwhelming sense of unity; the Democratic convention revealed a party divided over rules, policy, and candidates. Again, the parallels with the 1976 conventions are strong. Then the Democrats appeared to be as united behind Carter as the Republican party was behind Reagan four years later. The 1976 Republican convention was contentious; ideological, procedural, policy, and candidate divisions surfaced. As divided as the Republicans were in 1976, however, they portrayed at least a semblance of unity by the closing gavel. In 1980, attempts at unity in the Democratic party were transparent failures.

The Republican Convention

On the Republican side, unity was no problem. The main source of disunity, the presidential nomination, was resolved before the convention. Bush, Reagan's last opponent, had withdrawn gracefully six weeks before the Republican convention convened in Detroit on July 14. Reagan's selection of Bush as his running mate, however, was somewhat less graceful.

Rumors circulated that Reagan was considering Gerald Ford as his running mate, a move that was seen to lead toward a Republican "dream ticket." The negotiations centered on whether or not Reagan could ensure a sufficiently important role for Ford as vice president to entice him to join the Reagan ticket. Ford, after all, had been president, and John Nance Garner equated the value of being vice president with "a bucket of warm spit." But no suitable arrangements could be worked out. The rumors, however, had gotten out of hand. In fact, they dominated TV coverage of the convention on the very night Reagan was to be nominated. CBS even announced that the Reagan-Ford ticket was certain. Reagan had to make the unprecedented move of appearing before the convention late that evening to announce that, while he had considered Ford as his running mate, he wanted Bush. Although entertaining for television viewers and embarrassing to the principals, this sequence of events did little to disrupt the united party front.

The Republican platform presented a stark contrast with the Democratic one.[8] The Democrats adopted a platform that was largely a continuation and reaffirmation of the policies of the incumbent. The exceptions, notably the planks enacted with Kennedy's aid, were in accord with traditional Democratic liberalism. Taken as a whole, therefore, the platform was moderate to liberal and provided continuity with traditional Democratic positions.

The Republican platform, however, departed from tradition in a few significant respects. It did not endorse the Equal Rights Amendment for the first time in 40 years, and it took a much stronger pro-life position than in prior platforms. Moreover, supply-side economic policies were put into the platform for the first time. The Republican party as a whole had endorsed these positions in the 1978 midterm elections. The Kemp-Roth bill and the rest of the supply-side provisions were key elements in Reagan's nomination and election campaigns. They were to become his first priority in office. Finally, the platform's foreign policy provisions marked a departure from the policies of the last two Republican presidents. For example, Nixon and Ford and their secretary of state, Henry A. Kissinger, pursued a policy of negotiation with the Soviet Union called "détente." Reagan had campaigned against Ford in 1976 in part by attacking Kissinger and détente, and the 1980 Republican platform emphasized a much harder line in our relations with the USSR.

Thus, with relatively little dissension, and at times relatively little discussion, the Republican party put forward an economic policy at odds with their last platform, proposed different directions in foreign policy than recent Republican incumbents had followed, and moved to a more conservative stance on social issues. The conservatives were in power in the party, even more clearly than in 1964, for then there was significant opposition from more moderate wings. Moreover, the meaning of "conservative" had come to include new elements, such as supply-side economics.

The Democratic Convention

When the Democratic convention convened on August 14 in New York City, Carter's main problem was Kennedy. He had the votes, but Kennedy refused to accept defeat, thus disrupting party unity. In 1976, Reagan also had refused to accept defeat by the opening of the convention. The 1976 Republican race, however, was even closer than the 1980 Democratic one, and there were fewer Republican delegates bound by law to support a candidate. The closer and more uncertain race made Reagan's continued campaign understandable. Kennedy, on the other hand, knew he had too few votes. Trailing Carter by nearly 650 delegates and with the president already possessing the majority needed to win, Kennedy realized he had little hope of getting the nomination without a rules fight. He challenged the proposed party rule that would require all delegates to vote on the first ballot for the candidate under whose banner they were elected.

Kennedy justified his call for an "open convention" on the grounds that circumstances had changed substantially in the months since the primaries had been held. Kennedy was right, of course. Although the Iranian and Afghanistan crises in November and December 1979 buoyed Carter in the polls, his popularity was waning. In January and February, Carter held a substantial lead over Reagan. This lead shrank during the course of the primary season as we saw in Figure 1-2. By early August, Reagan led Carter by more than 15 percentage points. The proposal for an open convention received the support of other prominent Democrats who, however, wanted neither Carter nor Kennedy selected. These Democrats were afraid that neither candidate could defeat Reagan. They also weren't delegates. The vote on the proposed rules change was defeated; the delegates voted for the position backed by their preferred presidential candidates. While reasonable and principled arguments were advanced on both sides, the vote was cast as a test vote of the strength of the two contenders.

In 1976, Reagan had launched a test vote at the Republican convention. The question was whether presidential candidates must announce their vice-presidential choice in advance of the presidential nomination balloting. Reagan, seeing that he was coming close but apparently losing, had announced already that Senator Richard S. Schweiker, a liberal senator from Pennsylvania, was his choice for vice-presidential nominee. This move did not dislodge Ford backers, and Reagan hoped that Ford, if forced to pick a running mate in advance, also would make a mistake. As with the open convention movement in 1980, reasonable ethical arguments were advanced on both sides, but the vote was divided by candidate preference. Procedural moves become test votes of candidate strength because of the dominance of concern about the presidential nomination. Candidates cannot afford to let their supporters "vote their consciences" in a test vote, lest the attendant uncertainty weakens their delegate strength.

When Kennedy lost the test vote, he lost his last chance for nomination, and he withdrew formally. The Democratic platform was selected the next night. Kennedy appeared before the convention in support of several minority planks that were opposed by Carter. His speech eloquently articulated his ideals. It was received enthusiastically by the delegates, regardless of their presidential choice, and was acclaimed widely by media analysts. In losing, Kennedy had found and expressed the purpose and theme of his candidacy. At this point Carter was simply trying to hold on to his majority. He capitulated immediately, and several of the Kennedy-backed proposals were accepted by voice vote. Carter won the nomination, but Kennedy won the hearts of many delegates.

The platform proceedings echoed the 1976 Republican convention where committed conservative Republicans were able to impose "minority" platform planks that were opposed by Ford. In some cases these options were outright embarrassments to the Ford administration, notably those in direct opposition to the foreign policy of Ford and Secretary of State Kissinger. An observer could see that the forces supporting Reagan in policy terms held the hearts of the Republican party.

Similarities between the 1980 Democratic convention and the 1976 Republican convention end here. Carter's acceptance speech was much less successful than Ford's. More importantly, Ford and Reagan made a clear gesture of mutual respect and admiration, and the convention closed on an apparently reunited party. While Kennedy, after long, agonizing moments, did appear on stage with Carter after Carter's acceptance speech, Kennedy's appearance made it clear that he barely forgave Carter and certainly did not forget. Any semblance of Democratic unity was a sham.

The stage was now set for the general election campaign. The two parties had nominated very different candidates. The incumbent president was perceived as unsuccessful and trailed the challenger in the polls. He ran on a platform that was a combination of his past policies and traditional Democratic positions. Reagan headed a united party and ran on a platform that was distinctly conservative and differed from past Republican positions. Each candidate would try to make the opponent the issue. Reagan would try to make Carter's record and its perceived failures central. Carter would try to make Reagan the issue, a candidate whom he believed to be out of step with the beliefs of the public and whom he tried to portray as unsuited for the office. Neither would emphasize themselves except as foils to the other.

These basic strategies are at odds with the ideas of mandate and realignment. If a candidate believes that the public is willing to give him a mandate, that is, vote for him because they agree with his policies, he will make his platform the centerpiece of the campaign. Similarly, he will make the supposed realigning issues the core of the campaign if he believes the electorate is ripe for realignment. In either case, he will not, as both Reagan and Carter did, make his opponent the focus of his campaign.

NOTES

1. Other rules are possible. For example, until the 1936 convention, the Democratic party required that the presidential nominee be selected by a vote of two-thirds of the delegates. See John H. Aldrich, *Before the Convention: Strategies and Choices in Presidential Nomination Campaigns* (Chicago: University of Chicago Press, 1980). Results of prior campaigns can be found in *Guide to U.S. Elections* (Washington, D.C.: Congressional Quarterly, 1975) and *Guide to 1976 Elections: A Supplement to CQ's Guide to U.S. Elections* (Washington, D.C.: Congressional Quarterly, 1977). For details on 1980 primary votes and key convention votes, see *The Election of 1980: Reports and Interpretations*, Gerald M. Pomper with colleagues (Chatham, N.J.: Chatham House Publications, 1981).
2. *Congressional Quarterly Weekly Report*, March 1, 1980, p. 601.
3. E. J. Dionne, Jr., *New York Times*, September 25, 1980, p. B10.
4. The "rally 'round the flag" phenomenon was studied and named in the context of public opinion about presidents and their conduct in office by John E. Mueller in *War, Presidents and Public Opinion* (New York: John Wiley & Sons, 1973).
5. A more blatant than usual example of these advantages was Carter's announcement at a hastily called press conference on the morning of the Wisconsin primary that the Iranian government might take charge of the hostages. This move was seen as a crucial first step toward the release of the hostages. There are strong similarities with then Secretary of State Henry Kissinger's announcement in October 1972 that "peace was at hand" in Vietnam. Both Carter and Kissinger had reason for real optimism. In both cases the optimism was false, but in both cases the timing was almost too good to be true for the incumbent. For more on this and other campaign incidents, see Jack W. Germond and Jules Witcover, *Blue Smoke and Mirrors: How Reagan Won and Why Carter Lost the Election of 1980* (New York: The Viking Press, 1981).
6. The estimates used to form Figure 1-3 are from various issues of *CQ Weekly Reports*. By that count, Carter and Reagan were assured of victory on the basis of the results of the last primaries.
7. For a theoretical account of the "middleman squeeze" in three-candidate races, see Steven J. Brams, *The Presidential Election Game* (New Haven, Conn.: Yale University Press, 1978).
8. For a more detailed discussion of the platform, see Michael J. Malbin, "Conventions, Platforms, and Issue Activists," in *The American Elections of 1980*, ed. Austin Ranney (Washington, D.C.: The American Enterprise Institute for Public Policy Research, 1981), pp. 99-141.

2

The Campaign

When candidates enter a general election campaign, their choice of strategies will be dictated by what they estimate their chances of winning to be, by what they think the electorate wants, and by what they perceive to be their own strengths and weaknesses and those of their opponents. A candidate who is far ahead in the polls will run a different campaign than he would if he were far behind. A candidate who perceives political vulnerabilities in his opponent is more likely to wage an aggressive, attacking campaign than is a candidate who doesn't perceive such vulnerabilities.

Both major-party candidates in 1980 perceived their opponents as vulnerable, and each chose to make these vulnerabilities the focus of his campaign. Ronald Reagan approached the electorate in the following spirit: "Carter has failed as president. He, therefore, ought not to be returned to office." Reagan offered his economic and defense programs in a manner reflecting that point of view, saying in effect: "Carter was a failure, but I will do better. Here is my program. It is different from his, so you know that I will not repeat the same mistakes." Thus Reagan's strategy was to attack Carter's *performance,* but not to attack the president personally. He knew that one of Jimmy Carter's major assets was the positive reaction the electorate still had to him as a person. On this score Reagan merely wanted to behave in a fashion that would lead the voters to react similarly to him.

Carter's campaign can be seen as presenting this view: "Reagan is awful. Don't vote for him." Since Reagan was not the incumbent, he did not have a specific record of performance for Carter to attack (although Carter could and did attack Reagan's record as governor of California). Therefore, Carter's "Reagan is awful" theme required a more personal kind of campaign against Reagan than Reagan's plan entailed against Carter. Alternatively, Carter could hope for mistakes by Reagan on policy statements that would convey an impression of incompetence. This, however, was out of candidate Carter's hands and could not be depended on. To go on the offensive, Carter would need to attack Reagan and "expend" some of the personal good will the electorate had for him. And an offensive apparently would be necessary, due to the relative standings of the candidates in the polls.

The president had rallied from a 45 percent to 29 percent deficit in the Gallup Poll just before the Democratic convention to a virtual dead heat (38 percent for Reagan, 39 percent for Carter, 13 percent for Anderson, 10 percent undecided) at the end of August.[1] A one percent lead, however, was not an enviable cushion for an incumbent president at the beginning of a general election campaign, and it certainly was not the basis for passive, "ignore your opponent" tactics. Carter would have to strike at Reagan as well as defend himself against Reagan's attacks by convincing the electorate that while he (the president) had made mistakes, he had learned from them and the experience made him even better qualified to hold office.

For John B. Anderson, the future did not look bright as the campaign opened. His poll support had been in the low twenties since early spring; now it stood in the low teens. Due to his decline in the polls, Anderson was not sure of an invitation to the presidential debates sponsored by the League of Women Voters; only candidates with at least 15 percent in the polls would be invited. He was having trouble raising money and did not know whether he would qualify for partial reimbursement from public campaign funds after the election (although he did receive approval early in September for reimbursement—if he received at least 5 percent of the popular vote).

It was clear to most observers at the beginning of September that Anderson had no chance to be elected or to run second to one of the major candidates. However, he could carry a few states and perhaps even deny a majority of the electoral vote to Carter or Reagan. To increase the probability of this result occurring, Anderson had to convince the voters that he was different from and preferable to both Reagan and Carter. First he named Patrick J. Lucey, a former Democratic governor of Wisconsin and a 1980 supporter of Ted Kennedy for president, as his running mate. Then he announced his campaign platform, a series of proposals that emphasized what was called his "wallet on the right, heart on the left" political philosophy. The platform stressed revitalization of the economy, self-sacrifice, no massive new federal spending but maintenance of a range of liberal social programs. To succeed in selling his program to the electorate, Anderson would need to raise a significant campaign fund and get widespread exposure for his views.

The individual chapters in Part II of this book will analyze in detail the effects of different aspects of the campaign: the role of issues, evaluations of Carter's performance as president, the impact of partisan loyalties, and the success of Anderson's appeals. This chapter provides an overview—an account of the course of the campaign and a context in which to set what occurred.

THE OPENING GUNS

The traditional starting date for presidential general election campaigns is Labor Day. Working-class whites make up more than one-third of the electorate, and they are concentrated in the big industrial states whose large "chunks" of electoral votes swing presidential election outcomes. The working-class vote, as we shall see in Chapter 5, is crucial for the Democrats, who have never won the presidency without majority support from the white working class. To make a first symbolic grab for this significant group of voters, most presidential candidates in the postwar years have opened their campaigns on Labor Day in a major industrial city of the Northeast or Midwest.

Carter's campaign was different, however, in this respect as in many others. He opened his campaign in the South, as he had in 1976. Then his problem had been convincing the mainstream northern elements of the party that he deserved their support, so he spoke on Labor Day at Warm Springs, Georgia, Franklin D. Roosevelt's frequent vacation spot and the place where he died. This served to symbolize the link between the moderate southern Democratic tradition that Carter represented and the New Deal tradition of the national Democratic party.

In 1980, Carter's problems were different. Since he was now the incumbent, his position with the mainstream of his party was stronger than in 1976. Unlike 1976, however, he faced an opponent who had a strong southern base. In 1976, Carter could take southern support almost for granted; in 1980, he would have to fight for it. Thus on Labor Day 1980, he opened his re-election campaign in Tuscumbia, Alabama, a town in an industrial and agricultural area in the Tennessee Valley. He surrounded himself with southern labor and political leaders, including George C. Wallace. Carter asked his listeners to "stick with me," and said:

> It was you who put me on the road to the greatest honor that any American can possibly have, to serve as your president, and today I've come home.[2]

The president then went on to denounce the Ku Klux Klan, some of whose members were demonstrating at the rally, and to identify with the gains of the workers' movement in Poland.

Reagan, on the other hand, reflecting the happy fact that he stood even with an incumbent president in the polls, chose a more traditional opening for his campaign. He spoke on the Hudson River waterfront in Jersey City, New Jersey, with the Statue of Liberty in the background. The event was billed as an "ethnic picnic" and attracted people from a variety of eastern European backgrounds. In a media coup, Reagan was joined on the podium by Stanislaw Walesa, the father of the leader of the Polish workers' movement. Reagan's speech mixed attacks on the Carter administration's economic record with patriotic appeals. He also attacked Carter for refusing to agree to a three-way debate that would include Anderson. Reagan said: "I look forward to meeting Mr. Carter in debate, confronting him with the whole sorry record of his administration—the record he prefers not to mention." [3]

Thus the nine-week general election campaign was under way. Before we recount the details, we should ask a basic question: Did the campaign as a whole matter, or would the outcome have been just the same if the electorate voted on Labor Day? A postelection poll by the University of Michigan's Survey Research Center-Center for Political Studies asked respondents when they made up their minds on their presidential choice. Table 2-1 shows the reported presidential choice of respondents according to when they decided and controlling for their party identification.

It appears that the campaign may well have affected voting choices. For example, for both Democrats and Republicans, the later a voter decided, the more likely was that voter to support someone other than the candidate of the voter's party. That is, if a voter decided before the campaign began, that voter was likely to stick with his or her party. If, however, the voter waited to make a presidential choice until the campaign had begun, the chance of deviation from party identification grew substantially. Apparently, the advertising and news coverage of the candidates that voters encountered during the campaign could make a difference. The results in Table 2-1 suggest that the campaign had an effect upon voters, and that these effects may have been greatest among Democrats who decided how to vote during or after the Carter-Reagan debate.

Democrats were more likely to deviate from their party than Republicans. This reflects both the historically greater defection rates among Democrats and the fact that Democrats were more dissatisfied with Carter than Republicans were with Reagan. Indeed, among Democrats who made up their minds at or after the time of the Reagan-Carter debate, Carter received less than majority support, compared to the 85 percent support that Reagan received from Republicans who made up their minds at this time.

Table 2-1 Presidential Vote by Time of Vote Decision, Controlling for Party Identification, 1980

Time of Vote Decision Vote	Democrats			Independents			Republicans		
	Through Conventions	Before Debate	Debate and After	Through Conventions	Before Debate	Debate and After	Through Conventions	Before Debate	Debate and After
Reagan	14%	16%	39%	67%	52%	53%	91%	87%	85%
Carter	84	69	49	24	21	32	5	6	6
Anderson	2	15	12	9	27	16	4	6	8
Total percent	100%	100%	100%	100%	100%	101%	100%	99%	99%
(Number)	(243)	(62)	(94)	(139)	(48)	(95)	(189)	(31)	(48)

Finally, among Democrats and Independents, those who made up their minds after the campaign began were more likely to vote for Anderson than were people who made up their minds earlier. It would appear, therefore, that the campaign did matter in voters' decisions, and we will proceed to look at a few of the details.

REAGAN'S STUMBLING START

Even though Reagan had been a presidential candidate in two previous elections (1968 and 1976), this was his first general election campaign for the office and he ran into difficulties at the beginning. Reagan likes to talk to reporters, so frequently topics would come up on which he did not have adequately prepared responses. These "off-the-cuff" answers often provoked negative reactions that the Reagan campaign didn't need or want. For example, Reagan talked of establishing official ties to Taiwan (when the agreement establishing relations with Peking severed such ties), referred to the Vietnam war as a "noble cause," and supported the teaching of "creationism" as well as evolution in the public schools.

Perhaps Reagan's most politically damaging remark was his criticism of Carter's opening of his campaign in Tuscumbia, Alabama. Speaking at the Michigan State Fair, he said:

> I am happy to be here where you are dealing at first hand with economic policies that have been committed, [*sic*] and he's opening his campaign down in the city that gave birth to and is the parent body of the Ku Klux Klan.[4]

Reagan was incorrect; Tuscumbia was not the birthplace of the Klan, thus the remark added to the impression that he was less than capable. Correct or not, however, the remark risked the Republicans' progress in eating away at Carter's southern base. Seven angry southern Democratic governors condemned Reagan's comments. Governor William Winter of Mississippi said, "I thought it was a particularly unfair slap at our area of the country."[5]

The response of the Reagan campaign team to these problems was to minimize their impact when questioned about them by the press and to attempt to ensure that such events would not continue to occur. A top level political adviser was included in the campaign entourage each trip to check Reagan's speeches and advise the candidate on tactics. Furthermore, the staff tried to guard against impromptu Reagan comments by literally running interference for him when he moved from place to place. These tactics worked well and gaffes were rare in the remainder of the campaign. The Democrats, of course, tried to gain points by arguing that Reagan's handlers were afraid to permit their candidate to speak for himself, demonstrating that Reagan was unfit to be president. These Democratic arguments were not very effective since their candidate was getting himself in a lot of trouble at the time.

CARTER "GETS MEAN"

It was no secret that Jimmy Carter disliked Ronald Reagan. It was also obvious that a sense of desperation was developing in the Carter campaign because of the president's continued low level of popularity, the intractability of the problems the administration was facing (particularly the economy and the hostage situation in Iran), and the fact that Carter was trailing in the large northern states, a majority of which he needed to win. These factors induced the Democratic candidate to make a series of comments about Reagan that were extreme to say the least and which combined to become the "meanness" issue.

Actually, this personal tone was present from the beginning of the campaign, but the earlier comments were masked by Reagan's own difficulties. For example, in the first week of the campaign Carter declared:

> I believe in peace, I believe in arms control, I believe in the rights of working people of this country, I believe in looking forward and not backward, I don't believe the nation ought to be divided one region from another. In all these respects, Governor Reagan is different from me.[6]

In mid-September, several statements of this kind began to draw press attention. "You've seen in this campaign the stirrings of hate and the rebirth of code words like 'state's rights'...," Carter said in an Atlanta speech. "This is a message that creates a cloud on the political horizon. Hatred has no place in this country."[7] The Democratic candidate denied that he was calling Reagan a racist, but a few days later his campaign published in 100 newspapers this ad aimed at blacks: "Jimmy Carter named 37 black judges. Cracked down on job bias. And created 1 million jobs. That's why the Republicans are out to beat him."[8] Republicans charged that this ad was a "smear" by the Democrats. A few days later, Carter told a labor convention in Los Angeles that the electorate would have a choice in November between "whether we have peace or war."[9]

This rhetorical trend culminated in a speech by Carter at a Democratic fund-raising event in Chicago on October 6:

> You'll determine whether this America will be unified or, if I lose the election, whether Americans might be separated, blacks from whites, Jews from Christians, North from South, rural from urban.[10]

Reagan reacted mildly, stating that he was "saddened" but "not angry." Carter was "prejudiced about me," he said, and "owes the country an apology." [11] (This was a frequent practice of Reagan's during the campaign. When attacked by Carter, he would react mildly and charitably showing that he was too nice a guy to be a "racist warmonger.") The reaction of the press and media, however, was much harsher and uniformly negative.

Nor was Carter's rhetoric his only problem; it was, rather, a reflection of his difficulties. On September 21 in Baltimore, the first presidential debate occurred—without the president. When the League of Women Voters decided to invite Anderson, Carter declined. Clearly, the Carter campaign believed that Anderson would take more votes from Carter than from Reagan and was unwilling to do anything to enhance Anderson's chances. Most observers of the debate agreed that both Reagan and Anderson came across as competent, and that the only loser was the absent Carter.

At the beginning of October, the national polls showed the two major candidates to be in about the same position they were at the beginning of September: virtually even. Anderson had been unable to break through with the electorate. He was getting little exposure on his own because of lack of funds, and while he made an adequate showing in the debate with Reagan, he apparently didn't give anti-Carter voters sufficient reason to prefer him to the Republican nominee. Whatever negative reaction there was to Carter's refusal to participate in the debate, it was not reflected in the polls at this time. Most analyses based on state polls, however, showed Reagan with a significant lead, and there was little doubt that the sense of momentum was with the Reagan campaign. But the presidential campaign roller coaster had not finished its run.

THE PENDULUM SWINGS AGAIN

October 7, the day after Carter made his "separated, blacks from whites" statement, probably marked the beginning of another shift in campaign fortunes, this time in Carter's favor.[12] The Carter White House team had been pressuring the media to end Reagan's "free ride." They argued that the press coverage of the Republican candidate had been too uncritical and that contradictions in his record were being ignored. Whether for this reason or because of the natural ebb and flow of coverage in a campaign, on October 7 the CBS Evening News followed a critical report on Carter's speech with a report by Bill Plante on Reagan's "shifting from the right to the center of the spectrum."

To show that Reagan was abandoning or ignoring his previous policy positions, Plante used film clips of Reagan calling for the abolition of the departments of Education and Energy, proposing to abolish the inheritance tax, recommending antitrust laws to weaken unions, and opposing aid for the Chrysler Corporation and New York City. For each example, Plante used a graphic with Reagan's face which was covered with an electronically drawn "X" to illustrate that Reagan had shifted his position. Plante then asked:

> Which is the real Ronald Reagan? Does he plan to deliver on his conservative promise? Or is he really a closet moderate? His aides say that it's simply that he understands the politics of getting elected. In any case it presents President Carter with the problem of convincing voters that he's talking about the same Ronald Reagan who looks and sounds so much more moderate today.[13]

Numerous viewers called CBS to complain about Plante's report. The next night CBS anchorman Walter Cronkite apologized for the graphic x-ing out of Reagan's face, but not for the substance of Plante's commentary.

A new round of negative Reagan coverage had begun. The Republican candidate added fuel to the fire himself when, on October 9, he said that air pollution was under control and that Mount St. Helens' volcanic eruptions and the country's forests were responsible for a significant amount of air pollution. Regarding Mount St. Helens he said:

> I'm not a scientist and I don't know the figures, but I have a suspicion that that one little mountain out there, in these last several months, has probably released more sulphur dioxide into the atmosphere of the world than has been released in the last 10 years of automobile driving or things of that kind that people are so concerned about.[14]

The press naturally sought a comment from the Environmental Protection Agency. Unfortunately for Reagan, the EPA estimated that man-made sulphur dioxide emissions amounted to 81,000 tons a day, while the emissions from Mount St. Helens were in the 500 to 2,000 ton range. These facts were duly reported on television. Furthermore, the networks showed clips of videotape with Reagan denying that he had claimed pollution was under control, and another clip from a few days before showing him claiming exactly that. In succeeding days, the networks gave more coverage to Carter's attacks on specific Reagan statements and policies.

Shortly after this rise in negative media coverage of Reagan, Carter appeared on national television (in an interview with Barbara Walters of ABC) to admit that he had permitted the tone of the campaign to fall to a low level and to promise not to be nasty anymore. He indicated that he would cease personal attacks on Reagan and concentrate his criticism on his opponent's policies.

A few days later, the Reagan campaign announced what may have been the most important decision of the presidential campaign: Reagan would debate Carter one-on-one. After Carter's earlier refusal to join in a three-way debate and Anderson's decline in the polls, the League of Women Voters decided to invite only Reagan and Carter to a final debate. Carter agreed, but because his campaign was going so well Reagan stood on principle, said Anderson should have been included in any debate, and refused to participate. Now he changed his mind.

Various elements appear to have played a part in this decision. The momentum in the campaign had clearly shifted again. And this shift apparently was having concrete political consequences. Reagan's own surveys in key states showed his lead over Carter narrowing.[15] His campaign aides were also worried about an "October surprise"—a dramatic move by an incumbent president that would shift political support to his side. This concern centered on a possible resolution of the Iranian hostage crisis, and speculation about just such a possibility was receiving increasing media coverage. Whatever the reasons, Reagan's acceptance set the stage for a final dramatic confrontation in Cleveland, Ohio, on Tuesday evening, October 28—one week before election day. Campaign strategists on both sides of this apparently close election saw the debate as promising to be the single event that could swing the vote either way. As we shall see, some evidence supports this "single roll of the dice" view.

THE "GREAT" DEBATE

Compared to the debates of 1976, the Reagan-Carter debate was uneventful. There were no major rhetorical errors, such as Gerald R. Ford's statement that the Russians did not dominate Poland or Robert J. Dole's intimations that the Democrats were the party of war. Nor was there any of the "meanness" that characterized the early part of the Carter campaign. Each candidate was respectful of his opponent, while attacking his policy positions.

A panel of four journalists from the print and electronic media each asked two questions of the participants. Three of the questions concerned foreign and defense policies, specifically: the use of military power, terrorism, and SALT II. Four dealt with domestic and economic questions: inflation, urban decay and racial inequality, energy and alternative fuels, and social security. The eighth and final question asked each candidate to outline the greatest weakness of his opponent.

Both candidates were unresponsive to specific questions when it suited their purposes, Carter more so than Reagan. Instead, each used the questions as opportunities to make the points they wanted to make. Even though he was the incumbent, Carter was more aggressive and on the attack. He criticized what he claimed were actions taken by Reagan, some dating from the Republican's days as governor of California.

Reagan argued that Carter was distorting his positions. Late in the debate, after Carter claimed that Reagan had opposed Medicare, Reagan responded in smiling exasperation: "There you go again," and said that he had merely favored an alternative piece of legislation at the time Medicare was adopted.

In their closing statements, both candidates indicated that they thought the electorate was presented with a clear choice. As he had throughout the debate, Carter portrayed himself in the "mainstream" of his party and of the "bipartisan list of presidents who served before me." [16] Reagan was on the fringe of his party, Carter implied. He cited again his experience as president, alluding to the continual judgments he had had to make on questions of war and peace. Carter then closed with the following statement:

> There is a partnership involved in our nation. To stay strong, to stay at peace, to raise high the banner of human rights, to set an example for the rest of the world, to let our deep beliefs and commitments be felt by others in other nations, is my plan for the future. I ask the American people to join me in this partnership.

Reagan had the last word with his summation. He began by saying that he was sorry that the "third candidate" couldn't be brought into the debate. He then offered his own characterization of the choice facing the voters and a call for their support:

> Next Tuesday is Election Day. Next Tuesday all of you will go to the polls, will stand there in the polling place and make a decision. I think when you make that decision, it might be well if you would ask yourself, are you better off than you were four years ago? Is it easier for you to go and buy things in the stores than it was four years ago? Is there more or less unemployment in the country than there was four years ago? Is America as respected throughout the world as it was? Do you feel that our security is as safe, that we're as strong as we were four years ago? And if you answer all of those questions yes, why then, I think your choice is very obvious as to whom you will vote for. If you don't agree, if you don't think that this course that we've been on for the last four years is what you would like to see us follow for the next four, then I could suggest another choice that you have. . . .
>
> I would like to have a crusade today, and I would like to lead that crusade with your help. And it would be one to take government off the backs of the great people of this country, and turn you loose again to do those things that I know you can do so well, because you did them and made this country great. Thank you.[17]

Most press observers scored the debate as fairly even. The important thing, however, was how the voting public scored it. A CBS News poll the day after the debate indicated that 44 percent of the viewers thought Reagan had won, while 36 percent chose Carter. Six percent said they had changed their vote choice because of the debate; these viewers went for Reagan two to one.[18]

A poll by the Survey Research Center-Center for Political Studies permits us to take a more detailed look at the impact of the debate. In that survey respondents were asked: "Which of the two candidates impressed you as being the more qualified to be President?" [19] Table 2-2 relates responses to this question to reported presidential vote, controlling for party identification. The data clearly indicate that Reagan was judged to be more impressive. Among voters who watched the debate, a substantial minority of the Democrats, a majority of Independents, and the overwhelming majority of Republicans chose Reagan on this question.

The data also strongly suggest that the respondents' reactions to the debate often influenced their vote choice. [20] Among Democrats who said they were more impressed by Carter, only one percent chose Reagan; if they were more impressed by Reagan, 71 percent chose the Republican nominee! A similar pattern, albeit less extreme in degree, is present among Independents and Republicans. Among Independents who were impressed by either Carter or Reagan, only 11 percent voted for Anderson. Among Independents who said that neither Reagan nor Carter impressed them, 30 percent chose Anderson. Few Republicans said they were more impressed by Carter, but Carter gained far more votes from this group than he did among other Republicans.

Apparently, Reagan's gamble paid off. He was judged by the voters who watched the debate to have been the better man, and this judgment appears to have been translated into votes.

APPROACHING JUDGMENT DAY

In the last week of the campaign, Carter lost the momentum he had regained in October. The debate showed Reagan to be a competent and confident person. This may have assuaged some of the doubts that the Democrats had created about him. Furthermore, the final inflation figures released before the election showed a substantial jump from the previous two months. The July figure had showed no gain and August was .7 percent; September, however, had a 1 percent inflation rate, for a 12.7 percent annual rate. These figures were cited frequently by Reagan in the last week. Finally, the hopes that had been raised in the previous few weeks about a possible break in the impasse over the hostages in Iran were dashed. There would be no release of the hostages before the election. [21]

The strategies with which the three candidates began the campaign were pursued with varying degrees of success. Reagan attacked Carter's performance throughout, but suffered at times when he tried to present his own case. The last part of the campaign and particularly the Carter-Reagan debate, however, seemed to have given Reagan an advantage on this score. Carter waged an offensive against Reagan from beginning to

Table 2-2 Presidential Vote by Evaluation of Carter-Reagan Debate, Controlling for Party Identification

Who was more impressive in debate Vote	Democrats				Independents				Republicans			
	Reagan	Carter	Neither	Didn't Watch	Reagan	Carter	Neither	Didn't Watch	Reagan	Carter	Neither	Didn't Watch
Reagan	71%	1%	16%	18%	85%	23%	46%	50%	93%	58%	91%	88%
Carter	24	95	73	72	4	66	24	35	2	37	0	6
Anderson	5	4	11	10	11	11	30	15	5	5	9	6
Total percent	100%	100%	100%	100%	100%	100%	100%	100%	100%	100%	100%	100%
(Number)	(66)	(140)	(37)	(115)	(124)	(53)	(37)	(60)	(175)	(19)	(11)	(48)

end, but he pushed too far at certain points and had to spend time
defending his campaign rather than attacking his opponent. Here, too,
the debate was important. In the end, Carter was not able to make the
extremist/incompetent image stick to Reagan for a sufficiently large
share of the electorate. Carter tried to hold together the coalition of
blacks, working-class whites, Democratic liberals, southern conservatives, and those persons who had been dissatisfied with aspects of eight
years of Republican rule that had elected him in 1976. Reagan built on
the Republican conservative base that had nominated him and reached
out to centrist and conservative voters of all party, ethnic, and religious
identifications who were not satisfied with Carter's performance. Anderson reached the same types of voters as Reagan, but those whose policy
views placed them from the center to the left of the spectrum, plus the
dwindling group of liberal Republicans. Election day would determine
whose strategies were more successful.

Most of the final poll results published before the election showed
pretty much the same thing: Reagan was ahead, but the race would be
close. Of all the major public opinion pollsters, only Louis Harris was
willing to "call" the election for Reagan. Even he predicted that Reagan
would win by only five percentage points.[22] The campaign had yielded
many surprises, but Carter had not accomplished an "October surprise."
The electorate, however, provided a "November surprise" of its own.

NOTES

1. For polling data comparable to the data in Figure 1-2, but for all three
   candidates, see the *Gallup Opinion Index,* Report No. 183, December 1980,
   pp. 13-15.
2. Steven B. Weisman, "President Denounces the Klan," *New York Times,*
   September 2, 1980, pp. A1, B8.
3. Howell Raines, "Republican Stresses Economy," *New York Times,* September 2, 1980, pp. A1, B8.
4. Adam Clymer, "First Week of the Presidential Campaign," *New York
   Times,* September 9, 1980, p. A1.
5. Ibid.
6. Ibid.
7. Francis C. Clines, "Carter Suggests Turn to Racism in Reagan Views," *New
   York Times,* September 17, 1980, p. B10.
8. Adam Clymer, "Carter Campaign Ad Attacked as a 'Smear,' " *New York
   Times,* September 21, 1980, p. 10.
9. Terence Smith, "Carter Reiterates Doubt About Reagan," *New York Times,*
   September 24, 1980, p. A26.
10. Douglas E. Kneeland, "Reagan Declares Carter Is at 'a Point of Hysteria,' "
    New York Times, October 8, 1980, p. B6.
11. Ibid.
12. This section relies on Richard Harwood, "October," in *The Pursuit of the
    Presidency 1980,* ed. Richard Harwood (New York: Berkley Books, 1980),
    pp. 294-305.

13. Ibid., p. 297.
14. Douglas E. Kneeland, "Reagan Defends His Record on the Environment Issues," *New York Times,* October 10, 1980, p. D14.
15. See Hedrick Smith, "Reagan, in Shift, Agrees to Debate With Carter Alone," *New York Times,* October 19, 1980, p. 8.
16. *Congressional Quarterly Weekly Report,* November 1, 1980, p. 3289. All the quotations from the debate are from the same page.
17. Note how the logic of Reagan's argument almost explicitly followed the logic of "retrospective" voting that we will discuss in Chapter 7. To a very large extent, voters' decisions were based upon their evaluation of Carter's performance as president.
18. Hedrick Smith, "Carter and Reagan Express Confidence on Debate Showing," *New York Times,* October 30, 1980, p. A1.
19. The SRC-CPS did not ask a comparable question after the 1960 and 1976 presidential elections.
20. We cannot tell from these data whether the respondents are simply "projecting" their vote choice onto the debate question. That is, the respondents may have decided how to vote and then simply picked their candidate as the winner of the debate. Thus causality would work in the opposite direction from what we have surmised in the text. It would be difficult to sort out the direction of causality from the SRC-CPS data since the question about the debate was asked several weeks after the election. More may be learned, however, from other more limited surveys specifically designed to measure the impact of the debate.
21. Some commentators attribute the magnitude of Reagan's final victory to the feelings engendered by the flurry of activity in Iran and the U.S. about the hostages in the last weekend of the campaign. See Jack W. Germond and Jules Witcover, *Blue Smoke and Mirrors: How Reagan Won and Why Carter Lost the Election of 1980* (New York: Viking Press, 1981).
22. *ABC News-Harris Survey,* November 4, 1980. (News release for Tuesday a.m.).

3

The Election Results

The 1980 presidential contest contained many surprises, but the biggest came on election day itself, November 4. Most political commentators expected Ronald Reagan to win, and he was the odds-on favorite among bookies in both London and Las Vegas. Yet the results were expected to be close. Reagan's victory came swiftly and decisively. By 8:15 p.m. (Eastern Standard Time), fifteen minutes after the polls closed in many eastern states, NBC News projected Reagan to be the winner. While ABC and CBS were more cautious— projecting Reagan's win at 9:52 p.m. and 10:32 p.m., respectively—it was clear that Reagan's election was certain. By 9:45 p.m., before the final network projection, and an hour before the polls had closed in Alaska, California, Hawaii, Idaho, Oregon, and Washington State, Jimmy Carter conceded.

Reagan's victory was impressive. He tallied nearly 44 million votes, while Carter won only 35 and a half million. John B. Anderson won 5.7 million votes, Ed Clark (Libertarian party) won more than 900,000 votes, and Barry Commoner (Citizens party) more than 200,000 votes. Reagan won more than half the popular vote cast (50.7 percent), while Carter won just two out of five (41.0 percent). Table 3-1 presents the official presidential election results by states.

The electoral college margin was even more impressive. As Figure 3-1 illustrates, Carter carried only the District of Columbia, Georgia, Hawaii, Maryland, Minnesota, Rhode Island, and West Virginia, while Reagan swept the remaining 44 states. No region of the country could be called a Carter stronghold; he won only the adjoining units of D.C., Maryland, and West Virginia. Moreover, Carter carried only three electoral units—D.C., Georgia, and Rhode Island—by more than 10 percentage points. His other four wins were all by less than five points.

Table 3-1 Official Presidential Election Results by States, 1980

State	Total Vote	Republican	Democratic	Independent	Other*	Percentage of Total Votes		
						Rep.	Dem.	Ind.
Alabama	1,341,929	654,192	636,730	16,481	34,526	48.8%	47.4%	1.2%
Alaska	158,445	86,112	41,842	11,155	19,336	54.3	26.4	7.0
Arizona	873,945	529,688	246,843	76,952	20,462	60.6	28.2	8.8
Arkansas	837,582	403,164	398,041	22,468	13,909	48.1	47.5	2.7
California	8,587,063	4,524,858	3,083,661	739,833	238,711	52.7	35.9	8.6
Colorado	1,184,415	652,264	367,973	130,633	33,545	55.1	31.1	11.0
Connecticut	1,406,285	677,210	541,732	171,807	15,536	48.2	38.5	12.2
Delaware	235,900	111,252	105,754	16,288	2,606	47.2	44.8	6.9
Florida	3,686,930	2,046,951	1,419,475	189,692	30,812	55.5	38.5	5.1
Georgia	1,596,695	654,168	890,733	36,055	15,739	41.0	55.8	2.3
Hawaii	303,287	130,112	135,879	32,021	5,275	42.9	44.8	10.6
Idaho	437,431	290,699	110,192	27,058	9,482	66.5	25.2	6.2
Illinois	4,749,721	2,358,049	1,981,413	346,754	63,505	49.6	41.7	7.3
Indiana	2,242,033	1,255,656	844,197	111,639	30,541	56.0	37.7	5.0
Iowa	1,317,661	676,026	508,672	115,633	17,330	51.3	38.6	8.8
Kansas	979,795	566,812	326,150	68,231	18,602	57.9	33.3	7.0
Kentucky	1,294,627	635,274	616,417	31,127	11,809	49.1	47.6	2.4
Louisiana	1,548,591	792,853	708,453	26,345	20,940	51.2	45.7	1.7
Maine	523,011	238,522	220,974	53,327	10,188	45.6	42.3	10.2
Maryland	1,540,496	680,606	726,161	119,537	14,192	44.2	47.1	7.8
Massachusetts	2,524,298	1,057,631	1,053,802	382,539	30,326	41.9	41.7	15.2
Michigan	3,909,725	1,915,225	1,661,532	275,223	57,745	49.0	42.5	7.0
Minnesota	2,051,980	873,268	954,174	174,990	49,548	42.6	46.5	8.5
Mississippi	892,620	441,089	429,281	12,036	10,214	49.4	48.1	1.3
Missouri	2,099,824	1,074,181	931,182	77,920	16,541	51.2	44.3	3.7

Montana	363,952	206,814	118,032	29,281	9,825	56.8	32.4	8.0
Nebraska	640,854	419,937	166,851	44,993	9,073	65.5	26.0	7.0
Nevada	247,885	155,017	66,666	17,651	8,551	62.5	26.9	7.1
New Hampshire	383,990	221,705	108,864	49,693	3,728	57.7	28.4	12.9
New Jersey	2,975,684	1,546,557	1,147,364	234,632	47,131	52.0	38.6	7.9
New Mexico	456,971	250,779	167,826	29,459	8,907	54.9	36.7	6.4
New York	6,201,959	2,893,831	2,728,372	467,801	111,955	46.7	44.0	7.5
North Carolina	1,855,833	915,018	875,635	52,800	12,380	49.3	47.2	2.8
North Dakota	301,545	193,695	79,189	23,640	5,021	64.2	26.3	7.8
Ohio	4,283,603	2,206,545	1,752,414	254,472	70,172	51.5	40.9	5.9
Oklahoma	1,149,708	695,570	402,026	38,284	13,828	60.5	35.0	3.3
Oregon	1,181,516	571,044	456,890	112,389	41,193	48.3	38.7	9.5
Pennsylvania	4,561,501	2,261,872	1,937,540	292,921	69,168	49.6	42.5	6.4
Rhode Island	416,072	154,793	198,342	59,819	3,118	37.2	47.7	14.4
South Carolina	894,071	441,841	430,385	14,153	7,692	49.4	48.1	1.6
South Dakota	327,703	198,343	103,855	21,431	4,074	60.5	31.7	6.5
Tennessee	1,617,616	787,761	783,051	35,991	10,813	48.7	48.4	2.2
Texas	4,541,636	2,510,705	1,881,147	111,613	38,171	55.3	41.4	2.5
Utah	604,222	439,687	124,266	30,284	9,985	72.8	20.6	5.0
Vermont	213,299	94,628	81,952	31,761	4,958	44.4	38.4	14.9
Virginia	1,866,032	989,609	752,174	95,418	28,831	53.0	40.3	5.1
Washington	1,742,394	865,244	650,193	185,073	41,884	49.7	37.3	10.6
West Virginia	737,715	334,206	367,462	31,691	4,356	45.3	49.8	4.3
Wisconsin	2,273,221	1,088,845	981,584	160,657	42,135	47.9	43.2	7.1
Wyoming	176,713	110,700	49,427	12,072	4,514	62.6	28.0	6.8
Dist. of Col.	175,237	23,545	131,113	16,337	4,242	13.4	74.8	9.3
United States	86,515,221	43,904,153	35,483,883	5,720,060	1,407,125	50.7%	41.0%	6.6%

* Other includes Ed Clark (Libertarian party), who received 921,299 votes, Barry Commoner (Citizens party), who received 234,294, and a variety of other candidates.

SOURCE: *America Votes 14: A Handbook of Contemporary American Elections Statistics*, compiled and edited by Richard M. Scammon and Alice V. McGillivray (Washington, D.C.: published for the Elections Research Center by Congressional Quarterly, 1981), pp. 19-20.

Reagan, on the other hand, won by a margin of 10 or more points in 24 states and by a margin of 20 points or more in 14 states. Figure 3-1 presents the official 1980 presidential election results by states.

Was Reagan's triumph a landslide as some have argued? When compared with the landslide elections of 1956, 1964, and 1972, it was not. Dwight D. Eisenhower defeated Adlai E. Stevenson, Lyndon B. Johnson defeated Barry M. Goldwater, and Richard M. Nixon defeated George S. McGovern by more than a 15 percentage point margin. Moreover, in these three elections the winning total was substantially more than a majority of the vote cast (57 percent for Eisenhower, 61 percent for Johnson, and 61 percent for Nixon), while Reagan scored just 51 percent. On the other hand, Eisenhower, Johnson, and Nixon were all incumbents running against unpopular opponents. Reagan was the first challenger to defeat an *elected* incumbent president since Franklin D. Roosevelt defeated Herbert Hoover in 1932.

WERE THE POLLS WRONG?

Since we rely heavily on public opinion data in this book we must answer a potentially embarrassing question: Why did the pollsters

Figure 3-1   Electoral Votes by States, 1980

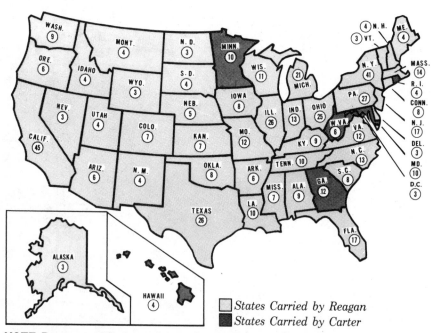

States Carried by Reagan

States Carried by Carter

NOTE: Reagan won 489 electoral votes; Carter won 49 electoral votes.

SOURCE: *Congressional Quarterly Weekly Report*, November 8, 1980, p. 3297.

predict a close election when Reagan won by a very comfortable margin? First, let us look at the pollsters' predictions.

The final pre-election Gallup Poll showed that among likely voters 46 percent supported Reagan, 43 percent supported Carter, and 7 percent supported Anderson. The CBS News/*New York Times* polls showed Reagan ahead with 44 percent, Carter with 43 percent, and Anderson with 8 percent. Louis Harris, the only major national pollster who clearly predicted a Reagan victory, predicted Carter would win 40 percent of the vote and Reagan 45 percent—six points less than Reagan's actual margin. In polls conducted six weeks prior to the election, the Survey Research Center-Center for Political Studies at the University of Michigan showed Carter slightly ahead of Reagan, 41 percent to 37 percent. Of course, all polls have a "margin of error" of three or four percent, but even the Harris Poll was off by six percentage points.[1]

Although these polls were off target they serve a very useful purpose by revealing the dynamics of the 1980 election contest.[2] They portray a highly volatile electorate. Many voters apparently had weak preferences and many changed their candidate preferences during the campaign. Moreover, the polls show a last minute shift to Reagan, who apparently benefited both from his head-to-head debate with Carter and from disillusionment over the president's handling of the Iranian hostage situation. In fact, the polls that were conducted until the day before the election captured this last minute shift. Apparently, one main reason the ABC News/Harris Poll came closer to predicting the result than the other published polls was that it continued surveying until election day itself. Moreover, the private polls conducted by Richard B. Wirthlin for Reagan and by Patrick H. Caddell for Carter both projected a solid Reagan victory. Caddell's last poll showed Carter 10 percentage points behind Reagan, the actual margin of Carter's defeat.

The pre-election polls thus document a volatile electorate that shifted at the last minute. A CBS News/*New York Times* poll of 2,200 respondents a few days before and a few days after the election revealed that there were individual shifts in all possible directions. For example, most persons who favored Reagan before the election actually voted for him, but some voted for Carter, some for Anderson, some did not vote, and some would not say how they voted. Carter and Anderson supporters shifted as well. On balance, however, Reagan gained about one percentage point from these last minute shifts, while Carter lost six points, and Anderson lost two.[3] The Michigan SRC-CPS data also show a net shift to Reagan. Respondents who preferred Reagan were more likely to vote for him than those who preferred Carter, and Reagan gained a majority of the voters who defected from Anderson, as well as of those who were undecided.

In short, the pre-election polls were probably basically correct, although they appear to have underrepresented Reagan's strength slightly, even when last minute switching is taken into account. While the failure to predict Reagan's victory may have embarrassed the pollsters, it should not lead us to question seriously the value of public opinion polls. Without these pre-election polls we would not be able to understand the dynamics of electoral change.

THE RESULTS IN
HISTORICAL PERSPECTIVE

Although Reagan's victory may have been cemented in the last few days before the election, he ultimately scored a narrow popular vote majority, a decisive popular vote margin over Carter, and a massive electoral vote majority. It is useful to examine the election in broader historical perspective, first by placing it in the context of all postwar presidential elections, and then in the context of competitive party elections since 1832.

No president since Eisenhower has served two full terms. Several commentators have stressed this result of the 1980 election. While it is true, and while Reagan's age (69 at the time of his election) makes him an unlikely man to break this trend, its importance has been overemphasized. John F. Kennedy was not a successful president (although he is remembered as one), but he might very well have been re-elected. And Nixon was re-elected and failed to serve his second term because he had the bad judgment to tape-record his Oval Office conversations.

A second basic result is that the 1980 election continues a pattern of Republican dominance in postwar presidential elections. Most political scientists consider the Democrats to be the majority party because more people say they are Democrats than Republicans and because Congress has been dominated by the Democratic party since 1930. But elections are not conducted through public opinion polls that register party loyalties, and the United States government is not a parliamentary system where the legislature chooses the key political executives.

Of the nine postwar presidential elections, the Republicans have now won five. And as of 1968, they have won three of the last four. The Republicans won a majority of the popular vote cast four times (1952, 1956, 1972, and 1980), while the Democrats gained a majority only twice (1964 and 1976). The average (mean) level of Republican support in the nine postwar elections is 49.8 percent, while the average level of Democratic support is only 46.4 percent. Moreover, during these elections Republican presidential candidates have won 23 million votes more than Democratic candidates have. (A total of 314,781,000 cast for Republican candidates, 291,558,000 for the Democrats.)

Although the Republicans hold an edge over the Democrats, no party has been able to win more than two successive presidential elections since World War II. The failure of either party to develop a string of victories sets the postwar era in sharp contrast with most of pre-war electoral history. Table 3-2 shows the presidential election results since 1832, the first year the candidate of the modern Democratic party, Andrew Jackson, stood for re-election. Since 1832 we find four periods in which a single political party won a series of three or more elections. The Republicans won six consecutive elections between 1860 and 1880 (although the 1876 victory of Rutherford B. Hayes over Samuel J. Tilden was by a single electoral vote, and although Tilden had a majority of the popular vote cast). They also won four elections between 1896 and 1908, as well as three between 1920 and 1928. The Democrats won five straight elections between 1932 and 1948.

While no party has managed three straight wins during the postwar era, until 1980 the winning party was able to pull off a second presidential victory. The Republicans won in 1952 and 1956, the Democrats in 1960 and 1964, and the Republicans again in 1968 and 1972. Regardless of the margin of victory in the first win, the second win was always of landslide proportions. The Democrats under Carter won in 1976, but they failed to hold on to the advantage of incumbency and stay in power. The 1980 election is unique because it marks the first time in the twentieth century that the party in the White House lost two successive elections.

The incumbent party lost four successive elections between 1840 and 1852, a period of alternation between the Democrats and the Whigs, and between 1884 and 1896, a period of alternation between the Republicans and the Democrats. Both of these intervals preceded major partisan realignments among the electorate. After Whig losses in 1852 and 1856, the newly formed Republicans replaced them as the second major party. Although many Whigs, including Abraham Lincoln, became Republicans, the Republican party was not just the Whig party renamed. The Republicans had a strong anti-slavery position and a different regional base, drawing upon many midwestern states, as well as California.

In 1896 the Republicans emerged as a dominant party, gaining a solid hold in New York, Connecticut, New Jersey, and Indiana, states which they had frequently lost between 1876 and 1892. After William McKinley's 1896 defeat of William Jennings Bryan, the Republicans had a far more substantial regional base in the midwest, mid-Atlantic, and New England states, and they lost the presidency only in 1912, when the GOP itself was split, and in 1916 when Woodrow Wilson stood for re-election.

The Great Depression ended the Republican dominance, and the emergence of the Democrats as the majority party between 1932 and 1936 was not preceded by a series of incumbent losses. The Democratic

Table 3-2   Presidential Election Results, 1832-1980

Election	Winning Candidate	Party of Winning Candidate	Success of Incumbent Political Party
1832	Andrew Jackson	Democrat	Won
1836	Martin Van Buren	Democrat	Won
1840	William H. Harrison	Whig	Lost
1844	James K. Polk	Democrat	Lost
1848	Zachary Taylor	Whig	Lost
1852	Franklin Pierce	Democrat	Lost
1856	James Buchanan	Democrat	Won
1860	Abraham Lincoln	Republican	Lost
1864	Abraham Lincoln	Republican	Won
1868	Ulysses S. Grant	Republican	Won
1872	Ulysses S. Grant	Republican	Won
1876	Rutherford B. Hayes	Republican	Won
1880	James A. Garfield	Republican	Won
1884	Grover Cleveland	Democrat	Lost
1888	Benjamin Harrison	Republican	Lost
1892	Grover Cleveland	Democrat	Lost
1896	William McKinley	Republican	Lost
1900	William McKinley	Republican	Won
1904	Theodore Roosevelt	Republican	Won
1908	William H. Taft	Republican	Won
1912	Woodrow Wilson	Democrat	Lost
1916	Woodrow Wilson	Democrat	Won
1920	Warren G. Harding	Republican	Lost
1924	Calvin Coolidge	Republican	Won
1928	Herbert C. Hoover	Republican	Won
1932	Franklin D. Roosevelt	Democrat	Lost
1936	Franklin D. Roosevelt	Democrat	Won
1940	Franklin D. Roosevelt	Democrat	Won
1944	Franklin D. Roosevelt	Democrat	Won
1948	Harry S Truman	Democrat	Won
1952	Dwight D. Eisenhower	Republican	Lost
1956	Dwight D. Eisenhower	Republican	Won
1960	John F. Kennedy	Democrat	Lost
1964	Lyndon B. Johnson	Democrat	Won
1968	Richard M. Nixon	Republican	Lost
1972	Richard M. Nixon	Republican	Won
1976	Jimmy Carter	Democrat	Lost
1980	Ronald Reagan	Republican	Lost

SOURCE: *Presidential Elections Since 1789*, 2d ed. (Washington, D.C.: Congressional Quarterly, 1979).

coalition, forged between 1932 and 1936, relied heavily upon an emerging industrial working class, and the mobilization of new social groups into the electorate. A series of incumbent losses is not a prerequisite for a major party realignment. Nor is it necessarily a sufficient condition.

The two incumbent party losses of 1976 and 1980 do not necessarily provide an early warning signal that a realignment is imminent. In the first place, the realignments following the 1840-1852 and the 1884-1896 periods came after four incumbent losses, not two. Moreover, although the failure of incumbent parties to hold the White House may indicate instability in the party system, such instability will not necessarily be followed by a new alignment of political forces. Many political scientists today predict partisan *dealignment* rather than *realignment*. They project that the political parties will continue to weaken and argue that the remnants of past alignments are likely to disappear without being replaced by any new alignment. The pattern of incumbent losses during the postwar years, now marked by two incumbent losses, may merely be a forerunner of continued electoral instability.

STATE BY STATE RESULTS

Politicians, journalists, and political scientists are fascinated by the success of presidential candidates in winning states. The contest for president can be viewed as 51 separate elections, one for each state and one for the District of Columbia. To win a state a candidate need only carry a simple plurality of the popular vote cast, that is to say, more votes than any opponent.

Although there are some minor exceptions, the candidate with the plurality of the vote within each state wins all of its electoral votes. The number of electoral votes for each state is the sum of the number of its senators (two) plus the number of its representatives in the House. In 1980, the number of electoral votes per state ranged from a low of three in Alaska, Delaware, Nevada, North Dakota, Vermont, Wyoming, and the District of Columbia to a high of 45 in California. To be elected president a candidate must win an absolute majority of the electoral votes or 270 out of 538. Naturally, in the quest for electoral votes attention is focused on the more populous states, especially those that have switched their allegiance from election to election.

States are the building blocks of winning electoral coalitions, but state by state results can be overemphasized and may even be misleading. First, in every presidential election since 1892, the candidate with the largest number of popular votes also gained the majority of electoral votes. In this sense, winning coalitions are national coalitions based upon demographic and social groups in the nation as a whole. Given the logic of the American electoral system, which usually translates popular vote pluralities into electoral vote majorities, presidential candidates must run national electoral campaigns.

Second, a comparison of state by state results can be misleading because such an emphasis may conceal change. To illustrate this point we will compare the state by state results of two of the closest postwar presidential elections, John F. Kennedy's 1960 win over Nixon and Carter's 1976 win over Gerald R. Ford.

Many striking parallels exist between these two elections. In 1960 and 1976 the Republicans succeeded in the West, and both Kennedy and Carter needed southern support to win.[4] Kennedy carried six of the eleven states of the old Confederacy (Arkansas, Georgia, Louisiana, North Carolina, South Carolina, and Texas), as well as some support in Alabama, for a total of 81 electoral votes. Carter carried 10 of these states (all but Virginia), for a total of 118 electoral votes.

The demographic basis of Carter's support in the South was completely different, however. In 1960, only 29 percent of black adults in the South were registered to vote, compared with 61 percent of the whites. According to our analysis of survey data from the University of Michigan's Survey Research Center, only one out of fifteen of Kennedy's southern votes came from blacks. (See Chapter 5, p. 106.) After the Voting Rights Act of 1965, however, black registration and voting increased dramatically. In 1976, 63 percent of black adults were registered to vote, compared with 68 percent of white southerners.[5] According to our estimates, about one out of three southern voters for Carter was black. A comparison of state by state victories conceals this massive change in the social composition of the Democratic presidential coalition.

Third, state by state comparisons do not tell us why a presidential candidate received support. Of course, such analyses can lead to interesting speculation, especially when the dominant political issues are clearly related to regional differences. But we must turn to survey research that questions individual voters to understand the dynamics of electoral choices.

With these three qualifications in mind we turn now to the state results. The relatively dull, two-tone map showing the states carried by Reagan and Carter (Figure 3-1) becomes more interesting once we depict Reagan's margin of victory (Figure 3-2).

As this map reveals, Reagan's largest margin of victory was in the prairie and mountain states. In the area officially designated as "mountain" by the U.S. Bureau of the Census, Reagan held a 20 point or greater lead in seven of eight states and held an 18 point lead in the eighth. Carter did best in his native South. Although he gained only one of the eleven states of the old Confederacy, his margin of defeat was five points or less in six of the remaining states. That Carter did less poorly

Figure 3-2 Reagan's Margin of Victory Over Carter

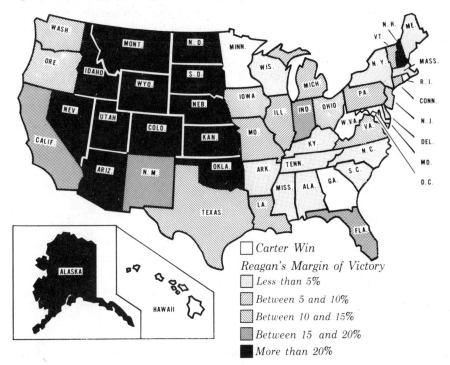

Carter Win

Reagan's Margin of Victory

Less than 5%

Between 5 and 10%

Between 10 and 15%

Between 15 and 20%

More than 20%

in these states is largely a result of their large black population; blacks were the only major demographic group to give him their solid support. Carter's margin of defeat was also relatively small in the six New England states, where he won one state, and lost by five points or less in two others. (On the other hand, he lost New Hampshire by 29 percentage points.)

What Figure 3-2 shows most dramatically is the massive margin of Reagan's victory west of the five states bordering the west bank of the Mississippi River. The western boundaries of Minnesota, Iowa, Missouri, Arkansas, and Louisiana roughly parallel the 96th meridian of longitude, a line that Walter Dean Burnham points out "bisects the United States remarkably cleanly." [6]

Of the 19 states west of this line, Carter carried only Hawaii in 1980, earning only four of the 155 electoral votes in this region. (In 1976, he also carried Texas, with its 26 electoral votes.) Moreover, Carter lost 13 of these western states by a margin of 20 or more percentage points, and he lost another two by between 15 and 19 points. He lost by 11 points in Washington, a state that Hubert H. Humphrey carried in 1968, and by nine points in Oregon, which is generally considered one of the most liberal states in the West.

Reagan's victory was so great that it diminished the importance of Anderson's candidacy, even though he received 10 percent of the vote or better in nine states, as Table 3-1 indicates. Throughout the campaign Carter argued that Anderson was a spoiler, who could serve only to help elect Reagan. In fact, even if every Anderson vote had gone to Carter, Reagan would still have carried 30 states with a total of 331 electoral votes.

To the extent that Anderson had a regional base, he did best in New England, the region where George C. Wallace, the American Independent party candidate in 1968, fared worst. And Anderson fared worst in the southern and border states, where Wallace was most successful. A more crucial difference is that Wallace actually attained a plurality in Alabama, Arkansas, Georgia, Louisiana, and Mississippi and thus earned 46 electoral votes (including one faithless elector from North Carolina).

The 1980 results appear to continue two basic trends in postwar American politics: Republican dominance in the West and a break-down of Democratic dominance in the South. These shifts began to occur well before the 1980 election and can best be illustrated by maps that capture the watershed elections in which they took place.

Figure 3-3 presents six maps that portray this shifting regional strength. Maps 3-3A and 3-3B show election results by state in the five elections between 1932 and 1948, that is, the four Roosevelt victories and Harry S Truman's defeat of Thomas E. Dewey. Maps 3-3C and 3-3D show the results for the three elections between 1952 and 1960, that is, Eisenhower's two wins and John F. Kennedy's win over Nixon. Maps 3-3E and 3-3F present the results of the five most recent elections, of which the Republicans have won three. Maps 3-3A, 3-3C, and 3-3E show the states that supported the Democratic candidate a majority of the time during each of these periods, while Maps 3-3B, 3-3D, and 3-3F show the states that supported the Republican candidate most of the time.

The Democrats generally prevailed throughout the country during the Roosevelt-Truman era. What is especially interesting is the Democratic victories in the West.[7] The Democrats failed to carry the prairie states from North Dakota south to Kansas, but they won six of the eight mountain states in all five elections and most of the elections in the remaining two. In addition, the Democrats carried Oklahoma, Texas, Washington, and California in all five elections. Map 3-3A also shows the beginnings of a chink in the "Solid South." Alabama, Louisiana, Mississippi, and South Carolina voted for J. Strom Thurmond, the States' Rights Democrat in 1948, although no southern state went Republican during this era.

The 1932-1948 period was a lean time for Republicans, as Map 3-3B illustrates. The GOP carried only Kansas, Nebraska, the Dakotas, and Indiana in three of the five elections, and Maine and Vermont in all five.

The years between 1952 and 1960 show a marked shift away from the Democrats among the western states. It is not surprising that these states voted Republican during Eisenhower's triumph. What is more important is that few western states returned to the Democratic fold in 1960. Kennedy, with Lyndon Johnson of Texas as his running mate, carried Texas, but he lost six of the eight mountain states, as well as all three Pacific Coast states. (As Eisenhower carried all the western states in 1952 and 1956, the western states with two out of three Republican wins in map 3-3D all voted for Kennedy in 1960.)

While all the western states but Arizona returned to the Democratic camp during Johnson's landslide over Goldwater, most western states have been consistently Republican since 1964, as Map 3-3F makes apparent. In fact, once we move west of the five states on the western bank of the Mississippi, we find that the Republicans have dominated 17 of 19 states. If we total the results in Maps 3-3D and 3-3F, we find they have won in 12 of these states in seven of the last eight elections, won Arizona in all eight, and carried Alaska in five of the six elections in which it could participate. The Republicans have also won seven out of eight times in four states east of the Mississippi, as well as in Iowa, but nowhere is their dominance greater than in the West. The Republicans have failed to dominate only two "western" states: Texas, which has been carried four times by each party, and Hawaii, which is predominantly Democratic.

As Map 3-3C shows, the Democrats won only nine states a majority of the time between 1952 and 1960, and seven of these were states of the old Confederacy. However, the Republicans made some inroads, carrying Virginia, Tennessee, and Florida in all three elections, and Texas in both Eisenhower contests. They also gained Louisiana once in 1956. The Republicans never succeeded in capturing Mississippi or Alabama. Adlai Stevenson carried these states in both 1952 and 1956, although in 1960 Harry F. Byrd won all of Mississippi's electoral votes and a majority of Alabama's.

As Maps 3-3E and 3-3F show, since 1960 neither party has dominated the South, although the Republicans have been more successful than the Democrats. The major breakthrough for the Republicans occurred in 1964, when Goldwater carried Alabama, Georgia, Louisiana, Mississippi, and South Carolina. In 1968, Humphrey carried only one former Confederate state (Texas), while Wallace carried five (listed above). In 1972, Nixon carried all 11 Confederate states, but in 1976 Carter captured every former Confederate state but Virginia. Four years later he held only his home state, Georgia.

Figure 3-3 How States Voted for President Between 1932 and 1948, 1952 and 1960, 1964 and 1980

Map 3-3A States that Voted Democratic at Least Three Out of Five Times Between 1932 and 1948

■ *Won 5 Times*
▨ *Won 4 Times*
☐ *Won 3 Times*

Map 3-3B States that Voted Republican at Least Three Out of Five Times Between 1932 and 1948

■ *Won 5 Times*
▨ *Won 3 Times*

Map 3-3C States that Voted Democratic at Least Two Out of Three Times Between 1952 and 1960

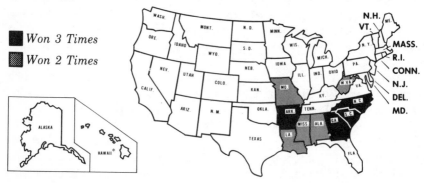

■ *Won 3 Times*
▨ *Won 2 Times*

Hawaii attained statehood in 1959 and voted Democratic in 1960.

Map 3-3D States that Voted Republican at Least Two Out of Three Times Between 1952 and 1960

*Alaska attained statehood in 1959 and voted Republican in 1960.

Map 3-3E States that Voted Democratic at Least Three Out of Five Times Between 1964 and 1980

Map 3-3F States that Voted Republican at Least Three Out of Five Times Between 1964 and 1980

NOTE: States that voted for third party candidates are as follows: Alabama, Louisiana, Mississippi, and South Carolina voted for J. Strom Thurmond in 1948; all of the electors from Mississippi and the majority of the electors from Alabama voted for Harry F. Byrd in 1960; and Alabama, Arkansas, Georgia, Louisiana, and Mississippi voted for George C. Wallace in 1968.

During the last five elections, Texas has been the only southern state carried by the Democrats in a majority of presidential elections. The Republicans have prevailed in eight, but they have carried only Virginia and South Carolina in four of the five contests, and none in all five. Arkansas and Georgia have split evenly, twice for the Republicans, twice for the Democrats, and once for Wallace. Clearly, the South can no longer be considered part of the Democratic presidential coalition.

What explains the Republican strength in the West? No simple answer accounts for this regional shift. Historically, the Democratic party enjoyed western support after William Jennings Bryan's Democratic and Populist candidacy of 1896. In the 1920, 1924, and 1928 Republican victories, however, the West voted solidly Republican. Franklin D. Roosevelt's agricultural policies may have earned him western support, and Harry S Truman's appeals to farmers may have helped him carry the region. Perhaps Kennedy failed to regain the West partly because he was a Roman Catholic, since most western states are less Catholic than the nation as a whole.

During the Bryan contests in 1896 and 1900, and perhaps during the Roosevelt years, many westerners looked to the federal government to protect them from powerful banking and railroad interests in the East. Since then the West has become more conservative. Today, when most social and economic policies emerge from Washington itself, westerners may resent the federal government and vote for the party that favors less federal regulation. And the Democratic reliance on black votes hurts them in this region, since many western states have a smaller proportion of blacks.

The reasons for the Democratic loss of the South are readily apparent. As V. O. Key, Jr., brilliantly demonstrated in *Southern Politics in State and Nation* (1949), the crucial factor in southern politics is race: "In its grand outlines the politics of the South revolves around the position of the Negro. . . . Whatever phase of the southern political process one seeks to understand, sooner or later the trail of inquiry leads to the Negro." [8] And it is the changed role of the national Democratic party toward black Americans that smashed the southern dominance of the Democratic party.

During the 12 presidential elections between 1880 (after Reconstruction ended) and 1924, the Democrats won all 11 former Confederate states, with the single exception of Tennessee in 1920. Even in 1928, when the Democrats ran Alfred E. Smith, a Roman Catholic, six of the most "solid" of these states voted Democratic (Alabama, Arkansas, Georgia, Louisiana, Mississippi, and South Carolina), even though all but Louisiana are overwhelmingly Protestant. During this period, and especially after the de facto disfranchisement of blacks during the late nineteenth and early twentieth centuries, the Republicans did not contest these states. While the Republicans, as the party of Lincoln, had black support in the North, they did not attempt to enforce the Fifteenth Amendment that bans restrictions on voting on grounds of "race, color, or previous condition of servitude."

In 1932 a majority of black voters remained loyal to Hoover, although by 1936 Roosevelt won the support of northern blacks. He made no effort to win the votes of southern blacks, and even as late as 1940 as much as 70 percent of the nation's blacks lived in the 11 states of the Confederacy. Few of these blacks voted, but Roosevelt did not need their support. He carried all 11 states of the old Confederacy in all four of his elections.

World War II led to substantial black migrations to the North, and by 1948 Truman, through his support of the Fair Employment Practices Commission, made explicit appeals to blacks. This support led to defections to Thurmond by Alabama, Louisiana, Mississippi, and South Carolina. Stevenson de-emphasized appeals to blacks and held most of the deep southern states, although Eisenhower made some inroads. Kennedy also played down appeals to blacks, and southern support was essential for his narrow victory over Nixon.

Lyndon Johnson's support for the Civil Rights Act of 1964 and his specific appeals to blacks helped end the Democratic domination of the South. Goldwater, who had voted against the Civil Rights Act, won five of the states of the deep South despite Johnson's nationwide landslide. By 1968, Humphrey, who had long been a champion of black demands, carried only a single southern state (Texas), which he won with 41 percent of the vote. He was doubtless aided by Wallace's candidacy, since Wallace gained 19 percent of the Texas vote, and, as survey data show, more Wallace supporters favored Nixon than Humphrey. Even in 1976, Carter carried a minority of the votes of white southerners.

Today the South clearly belongs to neither political party. In 1976, Carter won the South with the massive support of black voters perhaps because southern pride led a substantial minority of whites to support him. Carter failed to carry the South four years later, despite the continued support of southern blacks. The 1980 results are probably more indicative of the problems the Democrats face in this region. As long as the Democratic party is identified as the supporter of blacks, it will have substantial difficulties holding enough white southern support to carry this region. And yet without black support the Democrats are unlikely to carry the northern industrial states that they also need to gain the presidency.

CONCLUSION

The 1980 election results, especially when placed in the historical context of postwar American politics, present a pessimistic outlook for the Democratic party. As Figure 3-3 reveals, the Democratic party lacks a solid electoral vote base. In seven of the last eight elections, no state has voted consistently Democratic, and only one state, West Virginia, has voted Democratic in six of these contests. Only the District of Columbia has voted consistently Democratic in the five most recent elections, and only six states have voted Democratic in four of these five elections. Moreover, none of the states rich in electoral votes has voted solidly Democratic, although New York, Pennsylvania, and Texas have gone Democratic in three of the last five elections.

The Republican electoral vote base is impressive, especially in the West. Once we move west of the five states bordering the west bank of the Mississippi, the Republicans have consistently held 16 states, including California, winning these states in all four elections since 1968. In 1980, these states provided a core of 116 electoral votes, 45 of which were in California. More than two-fifths of the 270 electoral votes needed to win the presidency are provided by this Republican core. Moreover, after congressional redistricting following the 1980 census, these 16 states will have a total of 123 electoral votes.

Does the electoral college favor the Republicans by providing them with this solid base? Howard Busby, a political consultant, calls the electoral college "a Republican institution." *New York Times* columnist Tom Wicker argues that the solid strength of the Republicans in the West gives them a major advantage. This asset will increase after 1980, he predicts.[9] Many commentators believe the electoral college should be abolished and some form of direct election introduced in its place.

There are problems with the electoral college, and the present system for electing the president clearly affects electoral strategy. But we see no compelling evidence that the college provides any major advantage for either political party because, as we have already noted, in every presidential election since 1892, the popular vote winner has won the majority of the electoral votes.

In any event, we do not see the Republican advantage as firmly rooted in any regional base. The core of the West is California, which has voted Republican in seven of the last eight elections. But California is not a solidly Republican state. It has a Democratic governor, one Democratic senator, and its congressional delegation has 22 Democrats to 21 Republicans. Both houses of its state legislature are currently controlled by the Democratic party. In the 1980 presidential election it supported Reagan by a 17 point margin over Carter, but at the same time re-elected its liberal Democratic senator, Alan Cranston, by a 20 point margin over his Republican opponent. More importantly, California can be won by Democratic presidential candidates, even in close elections.

California has not voted very differently from the nation as a whole. During the nine postwar presidential elections, its mean level of Republican support has been 50.5 percent, less than a percentage point more Republican than the nation as a whole. In 1968, it voted four points more Republican than the nation as a whole, but in two elections, 1956 and 1972, it voted less Republican than the nation. Given that the Republicans have run a Californian for president or vice-president in seven of the nine postwar presidential elections,[10] and that the Democrats have never run a Californian for either office, it is hardly surprising that the Republicans have a minimal edge. In every close election since World War II, the margin of victory in California also has been close, and it is a state that the Democrats will always contest. Since California could be won by the Democrats, the Republican base is far less solid than it initially appears.

The 1980 election should lay to rest the myth that the Democrats are the majority party. In postwar presidential elections, the Republicans have a clear edge, whether one counts elections won, popular votes cast, or states that usually vote Republican. We should not judge Republican prospects, however, without a close examination of the attitudes and behavior of individual voters, the subject of Part II of our study.

NOTES

1. For a discussion, see Mervin Field, "Presidential Election Polling: Are the States Righter?" *Public Opinion* 4 (October/November 1981): 16-19, 56-58. Field argues that the state polls provided a more accurate basis for predicting the election results.
2. For a discussion of the pre-election polls, see Everett Carll Ladd and G. Donald Ferree, "Were the Pollsters Really Wrong?" *Public Opinion,* 3 (December/January 1981): 13-17, 20.
3. Adam Clymer, "Poll Shows Iran and Economy Hurt Carter Among Late-Shifting Voters," *New York Times,* November 16, 1980, pp. A1, A19.
4. Although the U.S. Bureau of the Census classifies several border states as well as the District of Columbia as southern, we use an explicitly political definition of the South—the 11 states of the old Confederacy: Alabama, Arkansas, Florida, Georgia, Louisiana, Mississippi, North Carolina, South Carolina, Tennessee, Texas, and Virginia.
5. U.S., Department of Commerce, Bureau of the Census, *Statistical Abstract of the United States,* 101st ed. (Washington, D.C.: U.S. Government Printing Office, 1980), Table 849, p. 514.
6. Walter Dean Burnham, "The 1980 Earthquake: Realignment, Reaction, or What?" in *The Hidden Election: Politics and Economics in the 1980 Presidential Campaign,* ed. Thomas Fergusen and Joel Rogers (New York: Pantheon Books, 1981), p. 111.
7. According to the U.S. Bureau of the Census, only Alaska, Arizona, California, Colorado, Hawaii, Idaho, Montana, Nevada, New Mexico, Oregon, Utah, Wyoming, and Washington are classified as the West. Kansas,

Nebraska, North Dakota, and South Dakota are the westernmost states of the West North Central region, while Oklahoma and Texas are the westernmost states of the West South Central region. According to the Census Bureau, Oklahoma and Texas are southern states. Although we will occasionally compare Texas with the western states, its presidential voting behavior is clearly more southern than western. In its presidential voting behavior, Oklahoma is a western state.

8. V. O. Key, Jr., *Southern Politics in State and Nation* (New York: Alfred A. Knopf, 1949), p. 5.
9. Tom Wicker, "A Good Republican College," *New York Times,* November 28, 1980, p. A27.
10. We count Nixon as a Californian in 1968, even though he officially ran as a resident of New York.

PART II

Voting Behavior in the 1980 Presidential Election

The collective decision reached by the electorate on November 4, 1980, was a product of more than 150 million individual decisions. Two choices faced American citizens 18 years of age or older: whether to vote and, if they decided to go to the polls, how to cast their ballots. The way voters make up their minds is one of the most thoroughly studied subjects in political science—and one of the most controversial.

Voting decisions can be studied from at least three theoretical perspectives. First, individuals can be viewed primarily as members of social groups. Voters belong to primary groups of family members and peers; secondary groups, such as private clubs, trade unions, or voluntary associations; and broader reference groups, such as social classes and ethnic groups. Understanding the political behavior of these groups is the key to understanding voting itself, according to the pioneers of this approach, Paul F. Lazarsfeld, Bernard R. Berelson, and their colleagues. Using a simple "index of political predisposition," they classified voters according to their religion (Catholic or Protestant), socioeconomic level, and residence (rural or urban) to predict how they would vote in the 1940 presidential election. Lazarsfeld and his colleagues maintain that a "person thinks, politically, as he is, socially. Social characteristics determine political preference." [1] This perspective is still very popular, although more so among sociologists than among political scientists. The writings of Robert R. Alford, Richard F. Hamilton, and Seymour Martin Lipset provide excellent examples of this sociological approach. [2]

A second approach emphasizes psychological variables. To explain voting choices in the 1952 and 1956 presidential elections, Angus Campbell and others at the University of Michigan's Survey Research Center (SRC) developed a model of political behavior based on social-psychological variables. [3] They focused on attitudes likely to have the greatest effect just before the moment of decision. Party identification emerged as the major social-psychological variable that influences voting decisions. The Michigan approach is the most prevalent among political scientists, although many de-emphasize its psychological underpinnings. The SRC has collected data on presidential elections since 1948, and scholars of voting behavior throughout the country often use the questions originally developed by the Michigan researchers. Indeed, in the following chapters we shall rely mainly upon the Michigan data because they clearly provide the best surveys of the American electorate. Perhaps the most outstanding example of this research tradition is the work of Philip E. Converse.[4]

A third and more recent approach to voting decisions draws heavily upon the study of economics. According to this perspective, voters weigh the costs of voting against the expected benefits of voting when deciding whether or not to go to the polls. And when deciding who to choose on election day, voters calculate which candidate favors policies closest to their own policy preferences. Voters are thus viewed as rational actors who attempt to maximize their expected utility. The major theoretical founders of this tradition are Anthony Downs and William H. Riker.[5] The writings of Riker, Peter C. Ordeshook, John A. Ferejohn, and Morris P. Fiorina provide excellent examples of this tradition.[6]

How, then, do voters decide? In our view none of these perspectives provides a complete answer. Although individuals are members of groups, they are not always influenced by these memberships. Moreover, classifying voters by social groups often does not explain why they are influenced by social forces. On the other hand, too great an emphasis on psychologically-based variables can lead us away from the important political forces that shape voter behavior. And while the assumption of economic rationality may result in clearly testable propositions, the data necessary to test them are often weak and the propositions themselves are sometimes trivial.

Although individually none of these perspectives adequately explains voting behavior, taken together they are largely complementary. Therefore, we have chosen an eclectic approach that draws upon the most useful insights from each research perspective. Where appropriate, we focus on sociological variables, but we also employ such social-psychological variables as party identification and sense of political efficacy. The rational choice approach guides our study of how issues influence voters' decisions.

Part II begins with an examination of the most important decision of all: whether or not to vote. One of the profound changes in postwar American politics has been the decline in electoral participation. Although turnout grew fairly consistently between 1920 and 1960, it decreased in 1964 and in each subsequent election. From a record high of 63 percent of the adult population voting for president in 1960, turnout fell to only 53 percent in 1980. Although turnout was low in 1980, it was not equally low for all social groups, and we will examine group differences in detail. From a social-psychological perspective, Chapter 4 studies the attitudes that contribute to electoral participation and attempts to account for the recent decline in turnout. Lastly, we try to determine whether the low turnout in 1980 affected the election results.

In Chapter 5 we examine how social forces influence the vote. Data from the Survey Research Center and Center for Political Studies (created in 1970) enable us to analyze the Carter, Reagan, and Anderson election results by race, sex, region, age, occupation, union membership, educational level, and religion. As we will see, the impact of these social divisions on the vote has changed considerably during the last three decades. Support for the Democratic party among the traditional "New Deal" coalition of southerners, union members, the working class, and Catholics has eroded, and it is unlikely that this coalition will ever be restored in its previous form.

Did Reagan's victory constitute a mandate for his policies? Chapter 6 attempts to answer this important question by looking at how issues influence the way Americans vote. We compare issue preferences among the electorate in the last three presidential elections and conclude that a major shift toward conservative policy preferences did not occur in 1980. Issue preferences did contribute to voting choices, but we show that Republican gains between 1976 and 1980 did not result from a pro-Republican shift in such preferences.

This leads to a consideration of the way presidential performance influences voting choices. Recent research suggests that many voters decide how to vote on the basis of "retrospective" evaluations of incumbents. In other words, what the incumbent has done while in office—not what he promises he will do if re-elected—affects how the voter decides. In Chapter 7 we assess the role of retrospective evaluations in 1972, 1976, and 1980—three presidential elections in which an incumbent ran. Voters' evaluations of Ford's and Carter's performance in the White House played a major role in electing Carter in 1976 and defeating him four years later. Reagan's election was in large part a rejection of Carter's presidency.

How closely do voters identify with a political party? And how does this identification shape issue preferences and retrospective evaluations of the incumbent? Chapter 8 explores the impact of party loyalties on voting choices in the postwar era, with special attention to the Anderson candidacy in 1980. We discuss how party loyalties affect voting in an election that offers a reasonably viable candidate who attempts to stand outside the party system. Even though party loyalties have declined, endorsement by one of the two major parties still provides important advantages that candidates outside the party system are denied.

NOTES

1. Paul F. Lazarsfeld, Bernard Berelson, and Hazel Gaudet, *The People's Choice: How the Voter Makes Up His Mind in a Presidential Campaign* (New York: Columbia University Press, 1944), p. 27. See also Bernard R. Berelson, Paul F. Lazarsfeld, and William N. McPhee, *Voting: A Study of Opinion Formation in a Presidential Campaign* (Chicago: University of Chicago Press, 1954).
2. See Robert R. Alford, *Party and Society: The Anglo-American Democracies* (Chicago: Rand McNally & Co., 1963); Richard F. Hamilton, *Class and Politics in the United States* (New York: John Wiley & Sons, 1972); and Seymour Martin Lipset, *Political Man: The Social Bases of Politics,* expanded edition (Baltimore, Md.: Johns Hopkins University Press, 1981).
3. Angus Campbell, Gerald Gurin, and Warren E. Miller, *The Voter Decides* (Evanston, Ill.: Row, Peterson, 1954); and Angus Campbell, Philip E. Converse, Warren E. Miller, and Donald E. Stokes, *The American Voter* (New York: John Wiley & Sons, 1960).
4. See Philip E. Converse, "Public Opinion and Voting Behavior," in *Handbook of Political Science, Volume 4: Nongovernmental Politics,* ed. Fred I. Greenstein and Nelson W. Polsby (Reading, Mass.: Addison-Wesley Publishing Co., 1975), pp. 75-169. This essay is the single best summary of Converse's views on voting behavior.
5. Anthony Downs, *An Economic Theory of Democracy* (New York: Harper & Row, 1957); and William H. Riker, *The Theory of Political Coalitions* (New Haven, Conn.: Yale University Press, 1962).
6. See, for example, William H. Riker and Peter C. Ordeshook, "A Theory of the Calculus of Voting," *American Political Science Review* 62 (March 1968): 25-42; John A. Ferejohn and Morris P. Fiorina, "The Paradox of Not Voting: A Decision Theoretic Analysis," *American Political Science Review* 68 (June 1974): 525-536; and Morris P. Fiorina, *Retrospective Voting in American National Elections* (New Haven, Conn.: Yale University Press, 1981).

4

Who Voted

Before attempting to discover how people voted in the 1980 presidential election, we should answer an even more basic question: who voted? In an election in which only 53 percent of the adults went to the polls, high levels of turnout by some social groups and low levels by others could potentially have affected the outcome. Even given Ronald Reagan's 10 percentage point margin of victory, the 47 percent who did not vote could have made Jimmy Carter the winner. In principle, nonvoters could have selected any alternative candidate, since many more Americans chose not to vote than chose to vote for Reagan. But this is not unusual. The winning presidential candidate has never received as many votes as the number of nonvoters. Before we study turnout in the 1980 elections, it is useful to place the low turnout for this contest in a broader historical perspective.

TURNOUT BETWEEN 1920 AND 1980

Although we can trace turnout into the nineteenth century, it is difficult to gather comparable statistics before 1920, the first year in which women were enfranchised throughout the United States. Table 4-1 shows the percentage of the voting age population that voted for the Democratic, Republican, and minor-party candidates in the 16 presidential elections between 1920 and 1980. It also shows the percentage that did not vote. As we can see, Reagan received the votes of only 27 percent of the voting age population.[1] Many previous winners exceeded this total: Hoover in 1928, Roosevelt in all four of his victories, Eisenhower in both his wins, Kennedy in 1960, Johnson in 1964, and Nixon in 1972. In fact, one *losing* candidate (Nixon in 1960) exceeded Reagan's total,

Table 4-1 Percentage of Adults Who Voted for Each Major Presidential Candidate, 1920-1980

Election Year	Democratic Candidate		Republican Candidate		Other Candidates	Did Not Vote	Total Percent	Voting Age Population
1920	14.8	James M. Cox	26.2	*Warren G. Harding*	2.4	56.6	100%	61,639,000
1924	12.7	John W. Davis	23.7	*Calvin Coolidge*	7.5	56.1	100%	66,229,000
1928	21.1	Alfred E. Smith	30.1	*Herbert C. Hoover*	.6	48.2	100%	71,100,000
1932	30.1	*Franklin D. Roosevelt*	20.8	Herbert C. Hoover	1.5	47.6	100%	75,768,000
1936	34.6	*Franklin D. Roosevelt*	20.8	Alfred M. Landon	1.5	43.1	100%	80,174,000
1940	32.2	*Franklin D. Roosevelt*	26.4	Wendell Willkie	.3	41.1	100%	84,728,000
1944	29.9	*Franklin D. Roosevelt*	25.7	Thomas E. Dewey	.4	44.0	100%	85,654,000
1948	25.3	*Harry S Truman*	23.0	Thomas E. Dewey	2.7	48.9	100%	95,573,000
1952	27.3	Adlai E. Stevenson	34.0	*Dwight D. Eisenhower*	.3	38.4	100%	99,929,000
1956	24.9	Adlai E. Stevenson	34.1	*Dwight D. Eisenhower*	.4	40.7	100%	104,515,000
1960	31.2	*John F. Kennedy*	31.1	Richard M. Nixon	.5	37.2	100%	109,672,000
1964	37.8	*Lyndon B. Johnson*	23.8	Barry M. Goldwater	.3	38.1	100%	114,090,000
1968	26.0	Hubert H. Humphrey	26.4	*Richard M. Nixon*	8.4	39.1	100%	120,285,000
1972	20.8	George S. McGovern	33.7	*Richard M. Nixon*	1.0	44.5	100%	140,068,000
1976	27.2	*Jimmy Carter*	26.1	Gerald R. Ford	1.1	45.7	100%	150,127,000
1980	21.8	Jimmy Carter	27.0	*Ronald Reagan*	4.4	46.8	100%	162,761,000

NOTE: The names of winning candidates are italicized.

SOURCE: U.S., Department of Commerce, Bureau of the Census, *Statistical Abstract of the United States: 1972* (Washington, D.C.: U.S. Government Printing Office, 1972), Table 597, p. 373; *Statistical Abstract of the United States: 1980*, Tables 825 and 851, p. 498, p. 515; and *America Votes 14: A Handbook of Contemporary American Elections Statistics*, compiled and edited by Richard M. Scammon and Alice V. McGillivray (Washington, D.C.; published for the Elections Research Center by Congressional Quarterly, 1981), p. 19. The 1980 voting age population is based upon the unpublished U.S. Bureau of the Census count of the U.S. population of 18-year olds and above as of April 1, 1980. Since the voting age population grew between April 1 and November 4, the percentage not voting is probably somewhat higher than reported in the table.

one equalled it (Stevenson in 1952), and several others came close (Willkie in 1940, Humphrey in 1968, and Ford in 1976).

Reagan's low overall total is the combination of two factors: he received just over half the total number of votes cast, and a low proportion of the adult population voted. That Reagan received the vote of just over one out of four adults reinforces our conclusion in Chapter 3 that his election was not a landslide. We should bear in mind, however, that just over one adult in five voted for Carter.

The low turnout in 1980 appears to be part of a trend that has been under way for the past two decades. Turnout increased, however, in 7 of the 10 elections between 1920 and 1960. Two of the three exceptions— 1944 and 1948—resulted largely from social dislocations caused by World War II. Specific political events explain why more people vote in certain elections. The jump in turnout between 1924 and 1928 resulted from the candidacy of Alfred E. Smith, the first Roman Catholic to receive a major party nomination, and the increase between 1932 and 1936 resulted from Franklin D. Roosevelt's efforts to mobilize voters from the lower social strata, particularly from the industrialized working class. The extremely close race between another Catholic candidate, John F. Kennedy, and Richard M. Nixon partially accounts for the high turnout in 1960. Nonvoting fell that year to 37.2 percent, a record low for the 1920-1980 period as Table 4-1 shows. Roughly 63 percent of the adult population voted in 1960.

Changing social characteristics of the electorate contributed to this long-term trend toward increased turnout. For example, older women who were enfranchised by the Nineteenth Amendment often failed to exercise their franchise before they died. Since it was necessary to be a citizen to vote (a requirement imposed by state legislation, not by the Constitution), many immigrants failed to enter the electorate. But after 1921, as the result of restrictive immigration laws, the percentage of the population that was foreign-born declined. Moreover, levels of formal education have been growing throughout the twentieth century—a change that should increase turnout since Americans with higher levels of education are much more likely to vote than those with lower levels.

By 1960, the decline in the foreign-born population was no longer pushing turnout upward. Although educational levels have continued to rise, turnout has not. Nonvoting increased in 1964, and it has risen consistently since then. By 1980, the percentage voting fell to only 53 percent, a 10 point decline in two decades.

TURNOUT AMONG SOCIAL GROUPS

Turnout was low in 1980, but it was not equally low among all social groups, as Table 4-2 shows. Because respondents sometimes claim to

Table 4-2   Percentage that Voted for President According to Voter Validation Study, by Social Group, 1980 (Percentages Read Across)

Social Group	Voted	Did Not Vote	Total Percent	(Number)
Electorate, by Race				
White	58	42	100%	(1179)
Black	45	55	100%	(163)
Whites, by Hispanic Identification				
Identify as Hispanic	38	62	100%	(40)
Do not identify	59	41	100%	(1136)
Whites, by Sex				
Male	61	39	100%	(519)
Female	56	44	100%	(660)
Whites, by Region				
New England and Mid Atlantic	60	40	100%	(257)
North Central	58	42	100%	(336)
South	49	51	100%	(291)
Border	60	40	100%	(84)
Mountain and Pacific	68	32	100%	(211)
Whites, by Birth Cohort				
Before 1924	64	36	100%	(338)
1924-1939	68	32	100%	(255)
1940-1954	57	43	100%	(394)
1955-1962	36	64	100%	(190)
Whites, by Social Class				
Working class	52	48	100%	(504)
Middle class	66	34	100%	(537)
Farmers	61	39	100%	(36)
Whites, by Occupation of Head of Household				
Unskilled Manual	49	51	100%	(114)
Skilled, Semi-skilled Manual	53	47	100%	(390)
Clerical, Sales, Other White-Collar	60	40	100%	(150)
Self-Employed, Managerial	68	32	100%	(191)
Professional and Semi-professional	69	31	100%	(196)

Table 4-2 (Continued)

Social Group	Voted	Did Not Vote	Total Percent	(Number)
Whites, by Annual Family Income				
Less than $5,000	39	61	100%	(95)
$5,000 to $9,999	44	56	100%	(154)
$10,000 to $14,999	57	43	100%	(184)
$15,000 to $19,999	56	44	100%	(149)
$20,000 to $24,999	64	46	100%	(194)
$25,000 to $29,999	71	29	100%	(116)
$30,000 to $34,999	65	35	100%	(84)
$35,000 to $49,999	70	30	100%	(100)
$50,000 and More	68	32	100%	(74)
Whites, by Whether Respondent or Family Member in Union				
Member	58	42	100%	(303)
Nonmember	58	42	100%	(870)
Whites, by Level of Education				
Eight Grades or Less	44	66	100%	(119)
Some High School	45	55	100%	(146)
High School Graduate	57	43	100%	(433)
Some College	59	41	100%	(257)
College Graduate	76	24	100%	(211)
Whites, by Religion				
Protestant	60	40	100%	(723)
Catholic	57	43	100%	(283)
Jewish	62	38	100%	(39)
No preference	50	50	100%	(104)
Whites, by Social Class and Religion				
Middle-class Protestants	68	32	100%	(310)
Working-class Protestants	54	46	100%	(314)
Middle-class Catholics	67	33	100%	(129)
Working-class Catholics	48	52	100%	(132)

NOTE: The 47 respondents for whom a validated vote check was not completed have been excluded from these calculations, as well as from calculations for Tables 4-3 and 4-4.

vote when they have not, reports of electoral participation derived from postelection surveys lead to overestimates of turnout. Fortunately, the 1980 survey by the Survey Research Center-Center for Political Studies (SRC-CPS) at the University of Michigan checked voting records to determine which respondents actually voted. In this chapter we shall use this actual check of the voting records to derive highly reliable estimates of voting participation.[2]

Race, Sex, Region, and Age

Race is the basic social division in American politics, so we will begin by comparing turnout among whites and blacks in 1980.[3] Whites were more likely to vote than blacks, although these differences are reduced when we consider that whites had higher levels of formal education. The low turnout of blacks is politically significant because blacks are the only major social group that voted heavily Democratic in the last five presidential elections.

Since relatively few blacks were sampled, we could not examine turnout differences in detail. However, some of the same basic factors that are related to turnout among whites (social class, income, and level of education) are related to turnout among blacks. Of all these factors, level of education is the most strongly related to turnout. On the other hand, black women were more likely to vote than black men.

Among whites, those who identified as Hispanic had much lower levels of turnout, mainly because few Chicanos voted.[4] Males have consistently outvoted women during the postwar years, but these differences have been diminishing.[5] In 1980, men once again voted more than women, but by a narrow margin, and these differences seem to result from women having less formal education. Regional differences among whites were also small, although whites from the mountain and Pacific Coast states were more likely to vote than those in other regions, again because of higher educational levels. Turnout in the Pacific Coast states might have been somewhat higher were it not for the early network projections of Reagan's victory and Carter's early concession.

Differences by age run counter to our general finding that groups with higher levels of education tend to vote more. Young Americans have substantially higher levels of formal education than their elders, but turnout was very low among whites born after 1954 (between the ages of 18 and 26), that is, the birth cohort that entered the electorate after the 1972 presidential election. Just over one-third of these youths voted.[6]

Social Class, Occupation, and Family Income

Social class differences were pronounced, a finding consistent with the relationship of formal education to turnout. Middle-class respondents (here defined as nonmanually employed workers and their dependents) were substantially more likely to vote than were members of the working class (manually employed workers and their dependents). Farmers registered average levels of turnout, but the number of farmers sampled was too small to lead to reliable conclusions. Although the distinction between the middle class and the working class is crude, it appears to capture a politically meaningful division, for when we further divide respondents according to the occupation of the head of the household, we find a substantial drop in turnout between the clerical, sales, and other white-collar groups and the skilled and semi-skilled manual workers.

Annual family income was also related to turnout, with substantially lower turnout among whites with family incomes below $10,000 a year.[7] Turnout was highest among persons with family incomes above $25,000. While persons with a high family income tend to have higher levels of formal education, and while both income and high education contribute to turnout, level of education is more consistently and strongly related to electoral participation.

Surveys over the years have found only a weak and inconsistent relationship between union membership and turnout. While being in a household with a union member leads to organizational ties that should stimulate turnout, members of union households tend to have somewhat lower levels of formal education. In 1980, among whites there were no differences at all in turnout between members of union households and persons in households with no union member.

Religion

In most elections white Catholics have voted more than white Protestants, but in 1980 there were no differences. Jews have much higher levels of formal education than gentiles and have always had high levels of turnout. They registered slightly higher levels of turnout in 1980, although the number of Jews sampled was too small to allow reliable comparisons.

Given the great interest in how religious factors influenced the vote, we examined turnout among white Protestants in considerable detail, although our results are not presented in Table 4-2. Among white Protestants, the highest levels of turnout were registered by Episcopalians and Presbyterians, denominations with high levels of formal education. We also explored turnout among white Protestants with differing religious values. For example, we measured whether white Protestants identified with an evangelical group, whether they said religion played an important role in their lives, whether religion provided guidance in their day-to-day lives, whether they had "deep religious experiences," such as being "born again," and whether they accepted the Bible as literally true. On balance, we found very little evidence that fundamentalist attitudes were related to turnout, despite the promise of the Moral Majority to deliver millions of votes. When religion (Catholic versus Protestant) is combined with social class, differences between Catholics and Protestants are negligible, while differences between the middle class and working class persist, as Table 4-2 indicates.

Education

Our most impressive finding is the strong relationship between formal education and turnout. As Raymond E. Wolfinger and Steven J. Rosenstone brilliantly document, education is the major variable explaining turnout in the United States.[8] Better educated Americans are more likely to develop attitudes that contribute to participation, especially feelings that citizens have a duty to vote and can be politically effective. Among whites who had not graduated from high school, less than one-half voted in 1980. Among college graduates, 76 percent voted—a higher level of turnout than for any other social or demographic group in Table 4-2.

The correlation between level of education and turnout underscores the paradox of declining levels of electoral participation. After all, levels of education have been rising since 1960. Why haven't these increases in education pushed participation upward, continuing the 1920 through 1960 trend of increased participation?

WHY HAS TURNOUT DECLINED?

Clearly, turnout within educational groups must have been declining so fast that it cancelled out the impact of rising educational levels. We therefore examined the relationship between education and *reported* turnout in all presidential elections since 1952, dividing the white electorate into five educational levels: college graduate, some college, high school graduate, some high school, and eight grades or less. Blacks have substantially lower levels of formal education than whites, and southern blacks have been effectively enfranchised only since 1965. Therefore, including blacks in any analysis of *trends* in participation would partly obscure the relationships we are studying.

College graduates have maintained high levels of turnout throughout the postwar period and were as likely to vote in 1980 as they were two decades earlier. But turnout declined among all four of the remaining educational categories. Therefore, consistent with patterns found in examining U.S. Bureau of the Census data, the greatest declines in turnout have occurred among Americans who are relatively disadvantaged.[9]

While increased education did not prevent turnout from declining, it at least slowed down the decline. Between 1960 and 1980 the educational level of the white electorate rose substantially. According to SRC-CPS data, the percentage of the white electorate that had not graduated from high school decreased from 47 percent in 1960 to 25 percent in 1980. During the same period the percentage that were college graduates rose from 11 percent to 17 percent. Nevertheless, reported turnout among the white electorate between 1960 and 1980 dropped 10 percentage points. If there had been no increases in educational levels, the decline would have been 16 percentage points.[10] In other words, if levels of formal education among the electorate had not increased during the last two decades, the decline in turnout would have been half again as great as the decline that actually occurred.[11]

Why was turnout low in 1980? Even more importantly, why has it continued to decline since 1960? Demographic changes and changing attitudes toward the political system appear to have contributed to the decline. As we saw in Table 4-2, young adults are less likely to vote than their elders. This is apparently because they are more socially mobile and have not yet established the community ties that contribute to voting. Because young adults are less likely to vote, the enfranchisement of 18-, 19-, and 20-year olds in 1971 served to reduce turnout. While the total number of voting age adults increased by definition, the total number of actual voters increased by a smaller rate. Wolfinger and Rosenstone estimate that about one percentage point of the decline in turnout between 1968 and 1972 results from enfranchising young Americans. Moreover, as the "baby boom" generation entered the electorate, young adults made up a growing share of the voting age population. Richard W. Boyd estimates that about one-fourth of the decline in turnout between 1960 and 1976 resulted from the changing age distribution of the electorate.[12]

Changing attitudes toward the political system also have eroded electoral participation. Our analyses focus on the erosion of party loyalties and the declining belief that the government is responsive, or what George I. Balch and others have called feelings of "external" political efficacy.[13] The measure of party identification is based upon questions designed to gauge psychological attachment to a partisan reference group.[14] It is widely recognized that partisan loyalties have declined, although closer examination reveals that this decline has been most marked among whites. The percentage of whites who strongly identified with either the Republican or Democratic party dropped from 36 percent in 1964 to 23 percent in 1980. In all the SRC-CPS surveys between 1952 and 1964, the percentage of Independents with no party leanings never rose above 9 percent. This figure rose to 14 percent by 1980. For a more detailed discussion of party loyalties and tables showing the distribution of party identification among whites and blacks between 1952 and 1980, see Chapter 8.

Strong feelings of partisan identification contribute to psychological involvement in politics, as Angus Campbell and his colleagues argue.[15] We also would expect partisanship to contribute to electoral participation, since partisan loyalties reduce information costs and thus reduce the costs of voting.[16] Many studies document the relationship between party loyalties and electoral participation. Indeed, in every presidential election since 1952, strong partisans have been more likely to report voting than any other partisan strength category. In every survey since 1960, Independents with no partisan leanings have been the least likely to say that they voted.

During the past two decades, feelings of political effectiveness also have declined markedly. Measures of "external" political efficacy make this clear. Scores on our measures were based upon responses to these two statements: "I don't think public officials care much what people like me think," and "People like me don't have any say about what the government does." [17] In 1956 and 1960, 64 percent of the white electorate were scored as highly efficacious. The decline in "external" political efficacy began after 1960. By 1976, 40 percent scored high, and by 1980, only 39 percent did. Likewise, the percentage scoring low on our measure was only 15 percent in 1956 and 1960, but it has risen fairly steadily since then. Thirty-four percent of the white electorate scored low in 1976, 30 percent in 1980. Persons who are politically efficacious may be more psychologically involved in politics and also may be more likely to see benefits from voting. In every presidential election since 1952, persons scoring "high" on our measure have been the most likely to report voting, those scoring "low" the least likely.

As we have seen, feelings of partisan loyalty and feelings of efficacy are both related to turnout. They are, however, only weakly related to each other. In other words, there is little tendency for persons who have strong party loyalties to have high levels of "external" political efficacy. Table 4-3 examines the combined effect of these attitudes for the entire electorate in 1980. We report actual turnout as measured by the voter validation study. Since there were virtually no differences in turnout between weak partisans and Independents who leaned toward a party, we have combined both groups into a single category.

By reading across the rows of Table 4-3 we can see that partisan strength is related to turnout regardless of scores on our political efficacy measure. By reading down each column we can see that feelings of political efficacy are strongly related to turnout regardless of partisan strength.

The partisanship-efficacy model succeeds remarkably well in accounting for the decline in turnout after 1960. As we have seen, both

Table 4-3 Percentage that Voted for President According to Voter Validation Study, by Strength of Party Identification and Sense of "External" Political Efficacy, 1980

	Strength of Party Identification		
Scores on "External" Political Efficacy Index	Strong Partisan	Weak Partisan Or Independent Who Leans Toward a Party	Independent, With No Partisan Leaning
High	74% (145)	65% (299)	50% (50)
Medium	69% (108)	56% (248)	48% (58)
Low	53% (99)	48% (254)	34% (59)

NOTE: Numbers in parentheses are the totals upon which percentages are based.

partisan loyalties and beliefs about government responsiveness have declined during the past two decades. We have tested the effects of these attitude changes, using both simple algebraic methods and more complicated probability techniques. Examining change among the white electorate, we found that the weakening of party loyalties accounts for about one-fourth of the decline in reported turnout between 1960 and 1980, while about half of the decline resulted from eroding feelings of "external" political efficacy. When we examined the combined effects of these attitude changes, we found that between two-thirds and seven-tenths of the decline in reported turnout resulted from the erosion of partisanship and declining feelings of political effectiveness.

Political parties—a major mechanism for mobilizing the electorate—appear to be losing their appeal. While older Americans often retain their strong party loyalties, young adults, who enter the electorate with weak partisan attachments, have not become stronger partisans as they age. Thus, as old cohorts, who learned their loyalties in a more partisan era, leave the electorate through death, and as newer cohorts with weak partisan ties enter the electorate, overall levels of partisanship erode.[18]

Low feelings of political effectiveness appear to spring from a generalized disaffection that may be seen as a response to political events. Disaffection with government policies over race-related issues, government policies in Vietnam, the Watergate scandals, and a more general sense that the government has failed to solve economic and social problems may have contributed to the feeling that the government does not respond to the people.[19]

We see the low level of turnout in 1980 as part of a long-term change, caused by long-term attitude trends. But we also recognize that low turnout may result from factors specific to the 1980 election. For example, only 54 percent of the whites interviewed in 1980 "cared a good deal" which party won the election. Concern was measured by responses to this question: "Generally speaking, would you say that *you personally* care a good deal which party wins the presidential election this fall, or that you don't care very much which party wins?"—a question that has been used in every SRC presidential election survey since 1952. The record low level of 54 percent results at least partly from short-term reactions to the alternatives that faced the electorate in 1980—for example, from the unpopularity of both major party candidates. As people who care which party wins are more likely to vote, the low turnout in 1980 partly results from short-term conditions.[20]

Even if we are correct in concluding that the decline in turnout results mainly from long-term forces, this does not mean that the decline will continue. New political conditions and new political leaders could attract nonvoters to the polls. Turnout would rise markedly if those conditions mobilized young Americans who have had very low levels of turnout, especially in the last two presidential elections. But we see little in our analyses that will encourage those who wish to increase political participation. The decline in party identification is largely the result of generational replacement. Given the very low levels of partisan loyalties among young adults, party loyalties are likely to remain weak for the remainder of this century.[21] On the other hand, feelings of "external" political efficacy are somewhat stronger among young adults than among their elders. Whether beliefs in government responsiveness will increase probably will depend upon the future actions of political leaders. We cannot predict those actions, but our analyses suggest that it will be difficult to restore higher levels of electoral participation unless the attitudes of the American electorate toward the political system are changed.

DOES LOW TURNOUT MATTER?

While in principle nonvoters in 1980 easily could have elected Carter, or even John B. Anderson, Ed Clark, or Barry Commoner, only massive differences between nonvoters and voters could have overcome Reagan's margin of victory. As we will see in Chapter 5, Carter outpolled Reagan among very few social groups: blacks, Hispanics, whites with family incomes below $5,000 a year, whites who had not graduated from high school, Jews, and working-class Catholics. And among these groups all but Jews had lower than average turnout.

Even if these five low participation groups had voted at the same rates as the electorate as a whole, and assuming that the extra voters thus brought to the polls would have voted Democratic at the same rate as members of these groups that did vote, this increased turnout would have added only about one and a half percentage points to Carter's total share of the vote. This increased turnout might have deprived Reagan of his absolute majority of the popular vote, but it would not have affected the outcome.

Indeed, some scholars have argued that low turnout matters little unless it can be shown that the partisan or policy preferences of voters and nonvoters differ markedly. Wolfinger and Rosenstone's analysis of the 1972 SRC-CPS survey suggests that there were negligible differences in the policy preferences of voters and nonvoters. Similarly, a recent analysis of SRC-CPS data by Stephen D. Shaffer suggests that the policy preferences of voters and nonvoters during the postwar years have differed only slightly.[22]

Our analysis of the 1980 SRC-CPS election survey confirms these findings. Differences in the partisanship or the policy preferences of voters and nonvoters were few. Table 4-4 summarizes our results, again using actual turnout as measured by the voter validation study. First, we examined turnout according to party identification. While strong Republicans outvote strong Democrats, while weak Republicans outvote weak Democrats, and while Independents who lean toward the Republican party outvote Independent Democrats, these differences are not great. Even if each Democratic group had voted at the same level as its Republican counterpart, and assuming that these extra voters had voted Democratic at the same rate as members of each Democratic group that did vote, this increased turnout would have added only about one and a half percentage points to Carter's share of the vote.

When we turned to the aggregate policy preferences of voters and nonvoters, we found no evidence that low turnout hurt Carter. The balance of issues measure in Table 4-4 summarizes each respondent's preferences across nine political issues.[23] Turnout was high among respondents who held issue preferences close to Carter's, but unfortunately for Carter, only two percent of the electorate held such preferences. Turnout was lowest among persons with slightly pro-Democratic preferences, but, on balance, persons with pro-Democratic preferences, that is, persons with liberal issue preferences, were as likely to vote as those with pro-Republican preferences.

Respondents who thought the Republican party was better able to handle the nation's economic problems were more likely to vote than those who thought the Democrats were better able to handle them. This is revealed by our summary measure of "retrospective" evaluations of the parties.[24] However, even if persons with favorable views toward the

Table 4-4   Percentage that Voted for President According to Voter Validation Study, by Party Identification, Issue Preferences, and Evaluation of Which Party Better Handles Inflation and Unemployment, 1980 (Percentages Read Across)

Attitude	Voted	Did Not Vote	Total Percent	(Number)
Electorate by Party Identification				
Strong Democrat	64	36	100%	(234)
Weak Democrat	49	51	100%	(305)
Independent, Leans Democratic	56	44	100%	(156)
Independent, No Partisan Leaning	43	57	100%	(171)
Independent, Leans Republican	62	38	100%	(147)
Weak Republican	65	35	100%	(198)
Strong Republican	70	30	100%	(122)
Electorate, by Balance of Issues Measure				
Clearly Democratic	72	28	100%	(29)
Moderately Democratic	64	36	100%	(70)
Slightly Democratic	49	51	100%	(146)
Neutral	55	45	100%	(443)
Slightly Republican	57	43	100%	(372)
Moderately Republican	59	41	100%	(224)
Clearly Republican	57	43	100%	(77)
Electorate, by Evaluation of Which Party Better Handles Inflation and Unemployment				
Clearly Democratic	56	44	100%	(129)
Slightly Democratic	61	39	100%	(125)
Neutral	50	50	100%	(583)
Slightly Republican	71	29	100%	(146)
Clearly Republican	66	34	100%	(252)

Democratic party had voted at the same rates as those with pro-Republican views, and assuming they voted as Democratic as those with favorable views who did vote, this increased turnout would have added only about one percentage point to Carter's total.

We also found that respondents who favored Carter before the election were less likely to vote than those who favored Reagan. This differential turnout is offset by the fact that a third of the respondents who favored Carter, and who failed to vote, no longer preferred him after the election. In fact, there were only negligible differences in the postelection presidential preferences of professed nonvoters. Thirty-three percent favored Carter, 32 percent Reagan, five percent Anderson, one percent Clark, and 29 percent had no preference.

Does the low turnout in 1980 really matter? Increased turnout probably would not have altered the results, and the policy preferences of nonvoters were similar to those who went to the polls. Turnout was low, one could argue, but the Americans who bothered to vote reflected the sentiments of the electorate as a whole.

While there is some truth in such an argument, we are reluctant to endorse it. Ever since the Johnson-Goldwater contest of 1964, turnout has been declining most among the relatively disadvantaged sectors of our society. While black turnout is up from the early 1960s, as a result of the enfranchisement of southern blacks, turnout among disadvantaged whites has declined markedly. So has turnout among blacks outside the South. Some believe this is because political leaders are structuring alternatives in a way that provides the disadvantaged little choice. The similarity of issue preferences among voters and nonvoters results from the way political choices are structured, they argue.[25]

We cannot endorse this argument either, mainly because the empirical evidence to support such conclusions is weak. The difficulty in supporting this perspective may result from the nature of survey research itself, since questions about policy preferences are usually framed along the lines of controversy as defined by mainstream political leaders. Occasionally, however, surveys pose radical policy alternatives, and they often ask open-ended questions that allow respondents to state their preferences. We find little concrete evidence current political leaders are ignoring the preferences of the electorate.

Nevertheless, the very low turnout in America today can scarcely be healthy for a democracy. Even if current low levels of turnout seldom alter electoral outcomes, they may undermine the legitimacy of elected political leaders. Moreover, the large bloc of nonparticipants in the electorate may be potentially dangerous since this means many potential voters have weak ties to established political leaders. The prospects for electoral instability, and perhaps political instability itself, are thus increased. Some scholars, such as Seymour Martin Lipset, have argued that while high participation may be desirable, sudden increases in participation can be dangerous for a democratic political system.[26] The prospects for rapid increases in participation are greater when current levels of participation are very low.

Regardless of the broader, long-term consequences of low turnout for American democracy, the low level of turnout in 1980 has led some scholars to question whether the election signals a pro-Republican realignment. As Gerald M. Pomper argues, "Elections that involve upheavals in the party coalitions have certain hallmarks, such as popular enthusiasm...." In 1980, however, "Turnout actually falls, instead of showing the increase that would be expected in the enthusiasm of a rising cause." [27] Of course, this evidence is not definitive, for even if all past realignments were preceded by increases in participation, surges in turnout would not be a necessary precursor of future realignments. Perhaps more important, as we shall document in the next chapter, the Republicans fare poorly among the social groups with relatively low turnout. Even though our analyses suggest that increased turnout by these groups would not have changed the outcome of the 1980 contest, a surge in turnout by disadvantaged Americans in future elections could weaken the Republican prospects for building a majority party.

NOTES

1. For somewhat different estimates, see Walter Dean Burnham, "The 1980 Earthquake: Realignment, Reaction, or What?" in *The Hidden Election: Politics and Economics in the 1980 Presidential Campaign*, ed. Thomas Ferguson and Joel Rogers (New York: Pantheon Books, 1981), pp. 100-101. Because Burnham's estimates of the voting age population exclude aliens, his estimates of turnout are slightly higher than ours. According to Burnham, turnout in 1980 was 55 percent, and Reagan received the support of 28 percent of the voting age citizen population.
2. Voting records can be checked to determine whether respondents are registered to vote, and whether they voted. Naturally, they cannot be used to determine how people voted. According to the 1980 voter validation study, 57 percent of the electorate voted, whereas reported turnout was 71 percent. There were 47 respondents for whom a voter validation check was not completed, and they have been excluded from our analyses. In measuring turnout with the voter validation study, we considered all persons as voters if records indicated that they voted, except for four validated voters who said they did not vote for president.
3. For the most part, the 1980 voter validation study demonstrates that there are few systematic biases introduced when reported turnout is used. However, the study shows that blacks are more likely to overreport voting than whites. Racial differences in turnout are thus more pronounced when the voter validation study is used than when reports of turnout are employed. In addition to the 1980 voter validation study, similar studies were carried out by the SRC in 1964, 1976, and 1978. In all these studies blacks were more likely to overreport voting than whites.
4. Respondents with Hispanic origins were divided into three categories—Chicanos, Puerto Ricans, and other Hispanics—but the total number of Hispanics surveyed was too small to permit careful analyses of their political behavior.
5. Warren E. Miller, Arthur H. Miller, and Edward J. Schneider, *American National Election Studies Data Sourcebook, 1952-1978* (Cambridge, Mass.: Harvard University Press, 1980), p. 317.
6. The Census Bureau survey of voter participation also shows low turnout among the young, with only a third of the 18- to 20-year-old whites *claiming* that they voted. See U.S., Department of Commerce, Bureau of the Census, *Voting and Registration in the Election of November 1980 (Advanced Report)* (Washington, D.C.: U.S. Government Printing Office, 1981), Table 1.

7. Our income measure is based upon the respondent's estimate of his or her family's 1979 income before taxes. For respondents who refused to answer this question, and for those for whom the interviewer thought the respondent answered dishonestly, we relied upon the interviewer's assessment of family income.

8. Raymond E. Wolfinger and Steven J. Rosenstone, *Who Votes?* (New Haven, Conn.: Yale University Press, 1980), pp. 13-36.

9. Walter Dean Burnham, "The 1976 Election: Has the Crisis Been Adjourned?" in *American Politics and Public Policy*, ed. Walter Dean Burnham and Martha Wagner Weinberg (Cambridge, Mass.: M.I.T. Press, 1978), p. 24; and Thomas E. Cavanagh, "Change in American Voter Turnout, 1964-1976," *Political Science Quarterly* 96 (Spring 1981): 53-65.

10. These estimates assume that the proportion of respondents at each educational level remained the same as in 1960, but that turnout for each educational group remained at the levels reported in each subsequent survey. For a discussion of these procedures, see Paul R. Abramson and John H. Aldrich, "The Decline of Electoral Participation in America" (Paper delivered at the annual meeting of the American Political Science Association, New York, New York, September 3-6, 1981).

11. For similar estimates, see Stephen D. Shaffer, "A Multivariate Explanation of Decreasing Turnout in Presidential Elections, 1960-1976," *American Journal of Political Science* 25 (February 1981): 68-95.

12. Richard W. Boyd, "Decline of U.S. Voter Turnout: Structural Explanations," *American Politics Quarterly* 9 (April 1981): 133-159.

13. George I. Balch, "Multiple Indicators in Survey Research: The Concept 'Sense of Political Efficacy'," *Political Methodology* 1 (Spring 1974): 1-43.

14. Respondents are asked, "Generally speaking, do you usually think of yourself as a Republican, a Democrat, an Independent, or what?" Persons who call themselves Republicans or Democrats are asked, "Would you call yourself a strong (Republican, Democrat) or a not very strong (Republican, Democrat)?" Respondents who call themselves Independents are asked, "Do you think of yourself as closer to the Republican Party or to the Democratic Party?"

15. Angus Campbell, Philip E. Converse, Warren E. Miller, and Donald E. Stokes, *The American Voter* (New York: John Wiley & Sons, 1960), pp. 120-167.

16. This expectation follows from a rational-choice perspective. For the most extensive discussion of party identification from this point of view, see Morris P. Fiorina, *Retrospective Voting in American National Elections* (New Haven, Conn.: Yale University Press, 1981), pp. 84-105.

17. Respondents who disagreed with both these statements were scored as highly efficacious; those who disagreed with one, but agreed with the other, were scored as medium; those who agreed with both were scored as low. Respondents with ambiguous responses to one question were scored as either high or low according to their response to the remaining question, and those with ambiguous responses to both questions were excluded from our analysis.

18. Paul R. Abramson, "Generational Change and the Decline of Party Identification in America: 1952-1974," *American Political Science Review* 70 (June 1976): 469-478; and Abramson, "Developing Party Identification: A Further Examination of Life-Cycle, Generational, and Period Effects," *American Journal of Political Science* 23 (February 1979): 78-96.

19. For a discussion of the decline of feelings of political efficacy among the American electorate, see Philip E. Converse, "Change in the American Electorate," in *The Human Meaning of Social Change,* ed. Angus Campbell and Philip E. Converse (New York: Sage Publications, 1972), pp. 311-337; James S. House and William M. Mason, "Political Alienation in America, 1952-1968," *American Sociological Review* 40 (April 1975): 123-147; and James D. Wright, *The Dissent of the Governed: Alienation and Democracy in America* (New York: Academic Press, 1976), pp. 168-200.
20. See John A. Ferejohn and Morris P. Fiorina, "The Decline of Turnout in Presidential Elections" (Paper delivered at the National Science Foundation Conference on Voter Turnout, San Diego, California, 1979). Ferejohn and Fiorina argue that the decline in turnout can be explained by short-term forces that are specific to given elections, and they focus on the decline in concern with electoral outcomes as the major variable in their analysis. For an extensive discussion of the reasons we reject their conclusions, see Abramson and Aldrich, "The Decline of Electoral Participation in America."
21. See the projections in Philip E. Converse, *The Dynamics of Party Support: Cohort-Analyzing Party Identification* (Beverly Hills, Calif.: Sage Publications, 1976), pp. 112-115.
22. Wolfinger and Rosenstone, *Who Votes?*, pp. 109-114; and Stephen D. Shaffer, "Issue Differences between Voters and Non-Voters in Federal Elections" (Paper delivered at the annual meeting of the Midwest Political Science Association, Cincinnati, Ohio, April 15-18, 1981).
23. The balance of issues measure, explained in more detail in Chapter 6, includes these nine issues: jobs and standard of living guarantees, aid to minorities, women's rights, defense spending, government spending and service cuts, inflation and unemployment, abortion, income tax cut, and relations with Russia.
24. Our measure of retrospective evaluations, explained in more detail in Chapter 7, is based on the respondent's evaluation of which party is better able to handle the problems of inflation and unemployment.
25. Walter Dean Burnham, "Shifting Patterns of Congressional Voting Participation in the United States" (Paper delivered at the annual meeting of the American Political Science Association, New York, New York, September 3-6, 1981).
26. Seymour Martin Lipset, *Political Man: The Social Bases of Politics,* expanded edition (Baltimore, Md.: John Hopkins University Press, 1981), pp. 226-229.
27. Gerald M. Pomper, "The Presidential Election," in *The Election of 1980: Reports and Interpretations*, Gerald M. Pomper with colleagues (Chatham, N.J.: Chatham House, 1981), p. 86.

5

Social Forces and the Vote

Despite the low percentage turnout in 1980, more than 86 million Americans voted for president, the largest number that ever voted in a presidential election. Viewed from one perspective, the electoral outcome was the product of 86 million individual voting choices. But most Americans also belong to primary groups comprised of families and friends and to secondary groups such as social classes, ethnic groups, and religions. Many formally belong to voluntary associations, such as trade unions, that provide concrete membership in a secondary group.

While voting is an individual act, social group memberships influence voting choices. Persons who share social characteristics may share political interests. Group similarities in voting behavior may reflect political conditions that existed generations earlier. The partisan loyalties of blacks, for example, were shaped by the Civil War and postwar Reconstruction, with black loyalties to the party of Lincoln lasting through the 1932 presidential election. And the Democratic voting of southern whites, a product of the same historical circumstances, lasted even longer, perhaps through 1960.

It is not difficult to see why group-based loyalties persist over time. Studies of pre-adult political learning suggest that partisan loyalties are often transmitted from generation to generation. And since religion, ethnicity, and, to a lesser extent, social class are often transmitted from generation to generation, social divisions among the electorate have considerable staying power. Moreover, the interaction of members of a social group with other members of that group reinforces similarities in political attitudes and voting behavior.

Politicians often think in group terms. They recognize that to win they must mobilize those social groups that have supported their party

95

in the past, and that it is helpful to cut into their opponents' established bases of support. The need to hold on to traditional sources of social support may be particularly great for the Democrats since they are a coalition of minorities. To win they must earn high levels of support from the social groups that have comprised their broad-based coalition. In fact, the failure of the Democratic party to capture the White House in 1980 may be attributed to its failure to hold the basic loyalties of the social groups that made up the winning coalition forged by Franklin D. Roosevelt back in the 1930s.

This chapter examines social groups' voting preferences in the 1980 presidential election. To put the 1980 results in perspective, the voting choices of key social groups for the entire postwar period are then considered. By studying the social bases of partisan support since 1944, we will show how the 1980 election results are part of a long-term trend that has severely weakened the New Deal coalition upon which Democratic victories traditionally have depended.

HOW SOCIAL GROUPS VOTED IN 1980

Our basic results are presented in Table 5-1, which shows how numerous social groups voted for president in 1980.[1] Excluding respondents for whom presidential voting choices were not ascertained, 50.8 percent said they voted for Reagan, 39.4 percent for Carter, 8.3 percent for Anderson, and 1.4 percent for other candidates—results that are very close to the official voting statistics. (See Table 3-1.) Because the total number of voters sampled by the SRC-CPS was relatively small (only 972), we will occasionally refer to larger surveys such as the CBS News/*New York Times* poll and the ABC News poll.[2]

Race, Sex, Region, and Age

Race is the fundamental social division in American politics; no other social cleavage approaches it in importance. According to the SRC-CPS survey, 92 percent of the black voters supported Carter compared to only 33 percent of the white voters. Other polls also report very large differences in support for Carter between blacks and whites. The CBS News/*New York Times* survey showed that 82 percent of the blacks voted for Carter, while only 36 percent of the whites did, and the ABC News poll showed that 82 percent of the blacks voted for Carter, while only 34 percent of the white voters did. A Gallup survey conducted shortly before the 1980 election suggests that 86 percent of the "nonwhites" voted for Carter, while only 36 percent of the white voters supported him.[3] Even though blacks make up only one-ninth of the electorate and have relatively low turnout, a very large proportion of Carter's total vote came from black voters—25 percent.[4]

Because race is such a profound social division, our analyses will examine divisions among whites and blacks separately. Among blacks, social differences were relatively unimportant, and we have not presented the results in our table. Like white women, black women were more likely to vote for Carter than black men. But social class, income, and educational differences were not present among the black electorate. All subsets of blacks voted heavily Democratic. Among whites, the small proportion who identified as Hispanics were much more likely to vote for Carter. As Table 5-1 shows, he received a majority of the Hispanic vote. Naturally, we can base no reliable inferences upon the 21 Hispanic voters sampled, but the CBS News/*New York Times* poll surveyed about 250 Hispanics, among whom 54 percent voted for Carter, 36 percent for Reagan, and 7 percent for Anderson.

Because of Reagan's stand against the Equal Rights Amendment, as well as his more militaristic defense policies, some experts expected women to prefer Carter. While white women were more likely to vote for Carter than white men were, and while they were less likely to vote for Reagan, they still gave a clear majority of their vote to Reagan. According to Everett Carll Ladd's analysis of the CBS News/*New York Times* surveys, the tendency of men to vote Republican was greater at higher levels of education, and a slight plurality of female college graduates voted for Carter.[5] Ladd argued that these sex differences were "substantially symbolic" and confined "to those segments of the population where there is the greatest sensitivity to the symbolic dimensions of politics."[6] However, our analysis of the SRC-CPS data revealed no tendency for sex differences in voting to increase with education, and we found that a majority of white female college graduates voted for Reagan.

Our analysis in Chapter 3 of the election results showed that the most pronounced regional differences were between the western states and the rest of the nation, with the West being more heavily Republican. When we examined regional differences among whites, it became clear that at least part of the reason the western states are more heavily Republican is because they have fewer blacks. Among whites, those in the southern and border states were actually the most likely to vote for Reagan. Ladd found a similar pattern in his examination of the ABC election day exit poll: "Closer examination of the polling data indicates that the east-west split in 1980 was a function of the contrasting ethnic makeup of these sections, rather than the emergence of new regional loyalties."[7] While our findings for 1980 resemble Ladd's, we see the movement of the western states to the Republican party as part of a long-term pattern that began in 1952. (See Chapter 3, pp. 60-66.)

Table 5-1 How Social Groups Voted for President, 1980 (Percentages Read Across)

Social Group	Reagan	Carter	Anderson	Other	Total Percent	(Number)
Electorate, by Race						
White	56	33	9	2	100%	(856)
Black	7	92	1	0	100%	(106)
Whites, by Hispanic Identification						
Identify as Hispanic	43	52	5	0	100%	(21)
Do not identify	57	32	9	2	100%	(831)
Whites, by Sex						
Male	60	30	9	1	100%	(385)
Female	53	35	9	2	99%	(471)
Whites, by Region						
New England and Mid-Atlantic	54	33	13	1	101%	(172)
North Central	55	34	10	1	100%	(240)
South	59	36	4	1	100%	(214)
Border	65	32	3	0	100%	(60)
Mountain and Pacific	54	29	12	5	100%	(170)
Whites, by Birth Cohort						
Before 1924	54	41	4	†	99%	(273)
1924-1939	60	30	8	2	100%	(199)
1940-1954	57	28	13	2	100%	(279)
1955-1962	53	30	15	2	100%	(103)
Whites, by Social Class						
Working class	54	39	5	2	100%	(323)
Middle class	58	28	13	1	100%	(437)
Farmers	61	26	9	4	100%	(23)
Whites, by Occupation of Head of Household						
Unskilled Manual	58	33	6	3	100%	(72)
Skilled, Semi-skilled Manual	53	41	5	1	100%	(251)
Clerical, Sales, Other White-Collar	58	33	8	1	100%	(114)
Self-Employed, Managerial	64	22	13	2	101%	(159)
Professional and Semi-professional	52	30	16	1	99%	(164)

Table 5-1 (Continued)

Social Group	Reagan	Carter	Anderson	Other	Total Percent	(Number)
Whites, by Annual Family Income						
Less than $5,000	41	47	6	6	100%	(49)
$5,000 to $9,999	51	43	6	0	100%	(93)
$10,000 to $14,999	51	41	8	1	101%	(133)
$15,000 to $19,999	55	33	10	2	100%	(105)
$20,000 to $24,999	63	27	9	1	100%	(147)
$25,000 to $29,999	54	33	12	1	100%	(94)
$30,000 to $34,999	68	26	6	0	100%	(66)
$35,000 to $49,999	55	33	12	1	101%	(86)
$50,000 and more	67	14	15	5	101%	(66)
Whites, by Union Membership††						
Member	47	43	9	1	100%	(215)
Nonmember	60	29	9	2	100%	(638)
Whites, by Level of Education						
Eight Grades or Less	45	52	3	0	100%	(66)
Some High School	40	58	1	1	100%	(83)
High School Graduate	61	29	9	1	100%	(301)
Some College	60	27	11	2	100%	(197)
College Graduate	57	27	13	3	100%	(206)
Whites, by Religion						
Protestant	61	31	7	1	100%	(537)
Catholic	51	40	9	0	100%	(207)
Jewish	37	47	13	3	100%	(30)
No preference	47	27	20	6	100%	(64)
Whites, by Social Class and Religion						
Middle-class Protestants	60	27	11	2	100%	(259)
Working-class Protestants	60	35	4	1	100%	(208)
Middle-class Catholics	61	29	10	0	100%	(107)
Working-class Catholics	41	53	6	0	100%	(81)

† Less than one percent.

†† Whether respondent or family member in union.

NOTE: The 24 voters for whom direction of vote was not ascertained have been excluded from these calculations.

Carter fared somewhat better among older voters, and he did best among the birth cohort born before 1924, that is those who entered the electorate before or during World War II. These findings of ours do not concur with other surveys that suggest that Carter did better among younger voters. We use somewhat different age divisions and examine the results for whites and blacks separately, yet these differences in data presentation do not account for differences between our results and other surveys. However, the SRC-CPS, CBS News/*New York Times,* ABC, and Gallup surveys all show that Anderson fared somewhat better among younger voters than among their elders. At least one reason is that young voters have weaker party loyalties. George C. Wallace, when running as the American Independent party candidate in 1968, also was more successful with young adults than with their elders.

Social Class, Occupation, Income, Education

Traditionally, the Democratic party has tended to appeal more to the relatively disadvantaged and has won the votes of persons with lower levels of formal education. These bases of support persisted in 1980, but relationships were weak. A weak relationship between social class and voting behavior may result from long-term trends that have eroded class differences, but the special circumstances of the 1980 election also tended to reduce social differences in the vote. Carter was a moderate candidate, who as president supported conservative economic policies. His administration witnessed double-digit inflation, as well as moderately high unemployment, and his economic policies were very unpopular. Reagan's past policy statements were very conservative, but he ran a middle-of-the-road campaign and sought to appeal to working-class whites. Both these short-term forces and long-term trends served to reduce the impact of traditional measures of social ranking in 1980.

When we examine the relationship of social class, occupation, income, trade union membership, and level of education to voting behavior, we find very few groups that gave Carter a plurality of their vote. Working-class whites (manually-employed workers and their dependents) gave a slight majority of their vote to Reagan. Skilled and semi-skilled manual workers (and their dependents) were more likely to vote for Carter than any other occupational group, but even among this group Reagan received 53 percent of the vote. Carter did win a plurality among whites with annual family incomes of less than $5,000 a year, but he failed to gain a majority of their vote. And while most union leaders endorsed Carter, a plurality of white union members voted for Reagan. Carter did gain a majority of the vote from whites who had not graduated from high school.

On balance, the relationship of social ranking variables to party choice was weak. However, Anderson's social support was distinctive.

Consistently, he did well among the relatively advantaged, doing best among professionals and semi-professionals, persons with family incomes above $50,000, and among college graduates. In 1968, Wallace, the most successful third-party candidate of the postwar era, did better among the relatively disadvantaged, and did especially well among whites with low levels of formal education.

Religion

Religious differences, which partly reflect ethnic differences between Catholics and Protestants, also have played a major role in American electoral politics. Roman Catholics tend to support the Democratic party, and white Protestants, especially outside the South, favor the Republicans.[8] In all of Roosevelt's elections, and in every postwar presidential election through 1976, Jews have strongly supported the Democrats. In 1980, Reagan won just over half of the white Catholic vote, although he fared about 10 points better among white Protestants. Carter even failed to gain an absolute majority of the Jewish vote, although he did gain a plurality.[9] Anderson fared better among Jews than among gentiles. He also fared relatively well among voters with no religious preferences, a finding supported by both the SRC-CPS data and the ABC exit poll.

Given the great interest in the role played by fundamentalist Christians in the 1980 election, we explored voting behavior among white Protestants in some detail, although we have not presented our results in our table. However, like Ladd and Gallup, we found little evidence that Reagan benefited from the votes of fundamentalists.[10] For example, white Southern Baptists, the most fundamentalist of the major Protestant denominations, were more likely to vote for Carter (who was a Southern Baptist) than were members of any other major Protestant denomination. Our analysis of religious views among white Protestants also found little support for the thesis that Reagan benefited from a fundamentalist vote, although Reagan did do especially well among the small number ($N=52$) who identified with evangelical groups.

When religion and social class are combined, our ability to explain how people vote is improved. Since working-class voters are more likely to vote Democratic than middle-class voters, and since Catholics are more likely to vote Democratic than Protestants, we find that the tendency to vote Democratic is highest among voters who are both working class and Catholic. As Table 5-1 shows, Carter actually gained a slight majority among working-class Catholics. That Carter's advantage was so slim among voters for whom both class and religion worked toward a Democratic vote merely serves to underscore how badly he fared among groups that the Democrats need to build winning electoral coalitions.

HOW SOCIAL GROUPS VOTED
DURING POSTWAR YEARS

Except for racial cleavages, social differences in voting behavior in 1980 were relatively small. How does this compare with other presidential elections? Were the weak relationships observed in 1980 atypical, or were they part of a long-term trend that has been eroding the impact of social forces? To answer this question we will examine the voting behavior of social groups that have been an important part of the Democratic presidential coalition during the postwar years. Our analysis begins with the 1944 presidential contest between Roosevelt and Thomas E. Dewey and uses a simple measure of social cleavages to assess the impact of social forces over time.

In his lucid discussion of the logic of party coalitions, Robert Axelrod discusses the behavior of six basic groups: the poor, blacks (and other nonwhites), union members (and members of their families), Catholics (and other non-Protestants), southerners (including border states), and residents of the 12 largest metropolitan areas.[11] John R. Petrocik's more comprehensive study identifies 15 party coalition groups and classifies seven of them as predominantly Democratic: blacks, lower-status native southerners, middle- and upper-status native southerners, Jews, Polish and Irish Catholics, union members, and lower-status border state whites.[12] Our own analysis focuses on race, region, trade-union membership, social class, and religion.[13]

The contribution that a social group can make to a party's total coalition depends upon three factors: the relative size of the group in the total electorate, its level of turnout compared with turnout among the electorate as a whole, and its relative loyalty to a party.[14] The larger a social group is the greater its total vote can be. For example, blacks now make up about 12 percent of the electorate, while the white working class makes up 37 percent. Thus, the contribution of blacks is relatively limited compared to the potential contribution of working-class whites. The electoral power of blacks is diminished further by their relatively low turnout. However, since blacks vote overwhelmingly Democratic, their contribution to the party can be greater than their 12 percent of the total size in the electorate, despite their relatively low turnout. And, their contribution grows to the extent that whites desert the Democratic party.

Race

Let us begin by examining racial divisions, which we can trace back to 1944 by using the National Opinion Research Center study for that year.[15] Figure 5-1 shows the percentage of whites and blacks among major-party voters who voted Democratic for president in each presi-

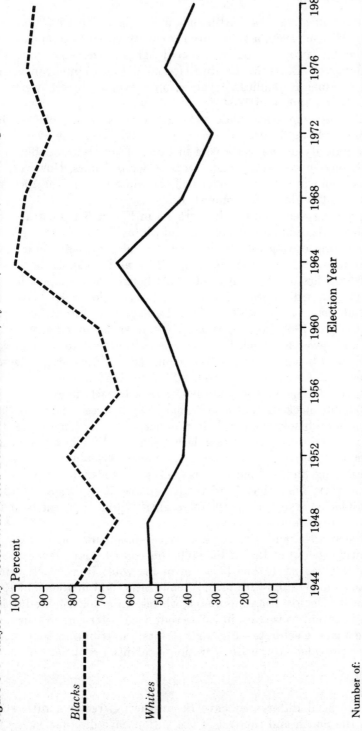

Figure 5-1 Major-Party Voters Who Voted Democratic for President, by Race, 1944-1980 (In Percentages)

Number of:

Blacks	(52)	(17)	(51)	(50)	(75)[1]	(94)	(87)	(138)	(133)[1]	(105)
Whites	(1564)	(364)	(1127)	(1213)	(1340)[1]	(1014)	(816)	(1430)	(1459)[1]	(765)

[1] Weighted Ns.

dential election since 1944. Although most blacks voted Democratic
between 1944 and 1960, a substantial minority voted Republican. The
political mobilization caused by the civil rights movement, along with
the candidacy of Barry M. Goldwater, ended this Republican voting,
and the residual Republican loyalties among older blacks were dis-
carded between 1962 and 1964.[16]

While the Democrats made substantial gains among blacks, they
lost ground among whites. Between 1944 and 1964, the Democrats
gained a majority of the white vote in three of six elections, but since
1968 they have never won a majority from white voters. However, the
Democrats can win with just under half the white vote, as the 1960 and
1976 presidential elections demonstrate.

The gap between the two line graphs in Figure 5-1 illustrates the
degree of polarization between blacks and whites. Table 5-2 shows levels
of racial voting during all 10 elections and also presents four other
measures of social cleavage. Between 1944 and 1960, racial voting
ranged from a low of 12 to a high of 40. Although black support for the
Democrats jumped in 1964, racial voting was held to 36 because a
substantial majority of whites voted Democratic. But racial voting
jumped to 56 in 1968 (to 61 if Wallace voters are included with Nixon
voters), and never fell back to the levels of the 1944 to 1960 period.
Since very few blacks voted for Anderson, racial differences are somewhat greater if Anderson voters are added to Reagan voters.

Not only did black loyalty to the Democratic party increase sharply
after 1960, but black turnout rose dramatically between 1960 and 1968,
since southern blacks (about half the black population during this
period) were enfranchised. The relative size of the black population
grew somewhat during the postwar years. Since 1960, white turnout has
been decreasing, and, as Figure 5-1 reveals, since 1964 white support for
the Democratic party has been relatively low. As a result of these
changes, blacks have become an increasingly large component of the
Democratic presidential coalition.

Between 1948 and 1960, blacks never made up more than one
Democratic vote out of 12.[17] After 1960, this contribution grew. In 1964,
Johnson received about one in seven of his votes from black voters,
while blacks made up a fifth of the Democratic total in 1968 and 1972.
In 1976, with Democratic gains among whites, the black total fell to just
over one in seven. As we saw, in 1980 about one Carter vote in four came
from the black electorate—the highest total contribution that blacks
have ever provided to the Democratic presidential coalition.[18]

Region

While racial differences have been growing, regional differences
between the South and the rest of the nation have diminished. As the

Table 5-2 Relationship of Social Characteristics to Presidential Voting, 1944-1980[1]

	Election Year									
	1944	1948	1952	1956	1960	1964	1968	1972	1976	1980
Racial Voting[2]	27	12	40	25	23	36	56	57	48	56
Regional Voting[3]										
Among Whites	—	—	12	17	6	-11	-4	-13	1	1
Among Entire Electorate	—	—	9	15	4	-5	6	-3	7	3
Union Voting[4]										
Among Whites	20	37	18	15	21	23	13	11	18	15
Among Entire Electorate	20	37	20	17	19	22	13	10	17	16
Class Voting[5]										
Among Whites	19	44	20	8	12	19	10	2	17	9
Among Entire Electorate	20	44	22	11	13	20	15	4	21	15
Religious Voting[6]										
Among Whites	25	21	18	10	48	21	30	13	15	10
Among Entire Electorate	24	19	15	10	46	16	21	8	11	3

[1] All calculations based upon major-party voters.
[2] Percentage of blacks who voted Democratic minus the percentage of whites who voted Democratic.
[3] Percentage of Southerners who voted Democratic minus the percentage of voters outside the South who voted Democratic.
[4] Percentage of members of union households who voted Democratic minus the percentage of members of households with no union members who voted Democratic.
[5] Percentage of working class that voted Democratic minus the percentage of middle class that voted Democratic.
[6] Percentage of Catholics who voted Democratic minus the percentage of Protestants who voted Democratic.

data in Figure 5-2 reveal, white southerners were more Democratic than whites outside the South in the 1952 and 1956 Eisenhower-Stevenson contests and in the 1960 Kennedy-Nixon contest.[19] But in the next three presidential elections, regional differences were reversed, with white southerners voting more Republican than whites outside the South. In 1976 and 1980, white southerners and whites outside the South voted very much alike. In the last four presidential elections, the Democrats have failed to carry a majority of either white southerners or of whites outside the South.

Levels of regional voting since 1952 are presented in Table 5-2. The negative signs for 1964, 1968, and 1972 reveal that the Republican candidate fared better among white southerners than among whites outside the South. If Wallace voters are combined with Nixon voters, regional voting in 1968 falls to -12. Including blacks in our calculations affects our results in different ways for different periods. For the first three elections, including blacks lowers regional voting because most blacks voted Democratic and cast their votes outside the South. Since 1964, including blacks in our analysis tends to increase traditional regional differences by boosting Democratic voting in the South.

The mobilization of southern blacks and the defection of white southerners from the Democratic party dramatically transformed the demographic composition of the Democratic coalition in the South. Democratic presidential candidates between 1952 and 1960 never received more than one out of 15 of their southern votes from black voters. In 1964, nearly three out of 10 of Johnson's southern votes came from black voters, and in 1968 Humphrey received nearly as many votes from southern blacks as from southern whites. In 1972, according to these data, McGovern received more of his total votes from southern blacks than from southern whites. In 1976, blacks provided Carter his margin of victory. He received about one in three of his southern votes from blacks in 1976 and again in 1980.

While regional differences between southern whites and whites outside the South have all but disappeared, other social differences have persisted throughout the postwar era. In every presidential election since 1944, union members have voted more Democratic than nonmembers, the working class has voted more Democratic than the middle class, and Catholics have voted more Democratic than Protestants. But, as we shall see, all of these group differences have diminished during the postwar years.

Union Membership

Figure 5-3 presents the percentage of union members and nonmembers who voted Democratic for president since 1944. In all six elections between 1944 and 1964, a majority of white union members

Figure 5-2 White Major-Party Voters Who Voted Democratic for President, by Region, 1952-1980 (In Percentages)

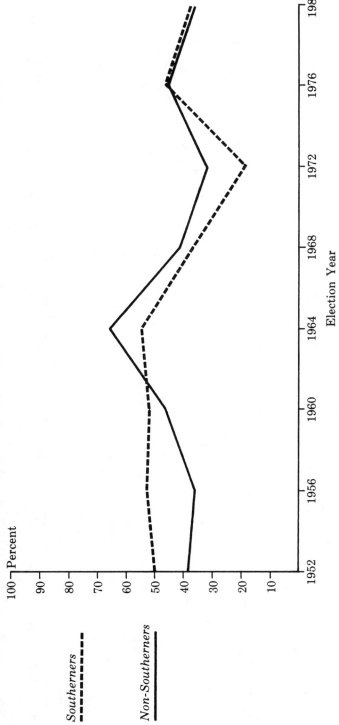

Number of:

	1952	1956	1960	1964	1968	1972	1976	1980
Southerners	(152)	(211)	(279)[1]	(163)	(124)	(267)	(266)[1]	(203)
Non-Southerners	(975)	(1002)	(1061)[1]	(851)	(692)	(1163)	(1193)[1]	(562)

[1] Weighted Ns.

Figure 5-3 White Major-Party Voters Who Voted Democratic for President, by Union Membership, 1944-1980 (In Percentages)

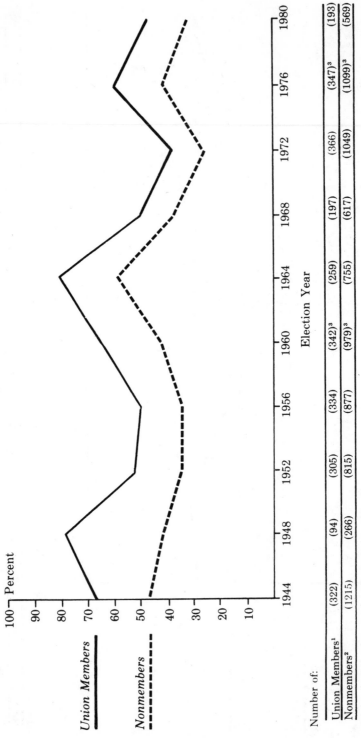

Number of:

	1944	1948	1952	1956	1960	1964	1968	1972	1976	1980
Union Members[1]	(322)	(94)	(305)	(334)	(342)[3]	(259)	(197)	(366)	(347)[3]	(193)
Nonmembers[2]	(1215)	(266)	(815)	(877)	(979)[3]	(755)	(617)	(1049)	(1099)[3]	(569)

[1] Union members or in household with union member.

[2] Not a union member and not in household with union member.

[3] **Weighted Ns.**

voted Democratic. In 1968, Humphrey received a slight majority of the major-party vote cast by white union members, but his total is cut to 43 percent if Wallace voters are included. In fact, the Democrats have failed to gain a majority of the union vote in three of the last four elections. At the same time, the Republicans have gained an absolute majority of the union vote in 1972 only.

The overall level of union voting has been relatively low in the last four elections, as Table 5-2 indicates. Union voting is even lower in 1968 (10 points) if Wallace voters are combined with Nixon voters since Wallace did better among union members than among nonmembers. On the other hand, including Anderson voters with Reagan voters has little effect on our results. We have also reported union voting for the entire electorate, but since blacks are about as likely to live in union households as whites are, including blacks has little effect on our results.

The percentage of the total electorate composed of white union members and their families has declined somewhat during the postwar years, and their turnout has declined at the same rate as that of nonunion whites. These changes have not been as dramatic as the decline in union support for Democratic presidential candidates. All the above factors, as well as increased turnout among blacks, have reduced the total contribution of white trade unionists to the Democratic presidential coalition. Through 1960, a third of the total Democratic vote came from white trade-union members. In the last five elections, only about one Democratic vote in four came from white trade unionists.

Social Class

The broad cleavage between the political behavior of manually-employed workers and their dependents and nonmanually-employed workers and theirs is especially valuable for comparative studies of voting behavior.[20] In every presidential election since 1936, the working class has voted more Democratic than the middle class. But, as Figure 5-4 shows, the percentage of the working-class whites voting Democratic has varied considerably from election to election. It fell to its lowest level in 1972. Although Carter regained a majority of the white working-class vote in 1976, he lost it four years later.

Although levels of class voting have varied since 1944, they appear to be following a downward trend, as Table 5-2 reveals. Class voting is even lower in 1968 (falling to 6) if Wallace voters are included with Nixon voters since 15 percent of the white working-class voters voted for Wallace, while only 10 percent of the white middle-class voters did. On the other hand, Anderson got relatively little support from the working class, and including Anderson voters with Reagan voters raises class voting to 11.

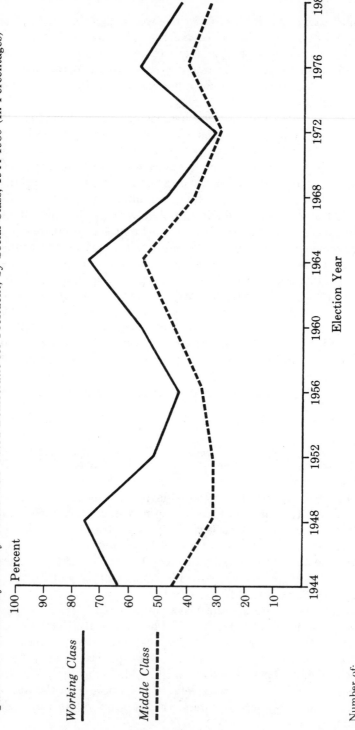

Figure 5-4 White Major-Party Voters Who Voted Democratic for President, by Social Class, 1944-1980 (In Percentages)

	1944	1948	1952	1956	1960	1964	1968	1972	1976	1980
Number of:										
Working Class	(597)	(134)	(462)	(531)	(579)[1]	(425)	(295)	(587)	(560)[1]	(301)
Middle Class	(677)	(137)	(437)	(475)	(561)[1]	(454)	(385)	(675)	(716)[1]	(376)

[1] Weighted Ns.

Class voting trends are affected substantially if blacks are included in the analysis. Blacks are disproportionately working class, and, as we have seen, they vote overwhelmingly Democratic. In three of the last four presidential elections, including blacks substantially raises class voting, and the overall trend toward declining class voting is dampened if we study the entire electorate. However, black workers voted Democratic because they were black, not because they were working class. Most blacks in the middle class also voted Democratic. It seems reasonable, therefore, to focus on changing levels of class voting among the white electorate.

During the postwar years, the proportion of the electorate made up of working-class whites has remained relatively constant, while the proportion of middle-class whites has grown. The percentage of whites in the agricultural sector declined dramatically. Since 1964, turnout has been falling faster among working-class whites than among middle-class whites, and working-class support for the Democratic party declined. Declining turnout and defections from the Democrats among the white working class, along with increased turnout among blacks, have reduced the total contribution of working-class whites to the Democratic presidential coalition.[21]

In 1948 and 1952, about half the total Democratic vote came from working-class whites, and between 1956 and 1964 over four out of 10 Democratic votes came from this social group. In 1968, the white working-class contribution fell to 35 percent, and it fell to only 32 percent in 1972. In 1976, with the rise of class voting, the white working class provided 39 percent of Carter's total vote. In 1980, the white working class provided just over a third of Carter's total support. The middle-class contribution to the Democratic presidential coalition was less than three in 10 in 1948 and 1952, just under a third in 1956, and stabilized at just over a third in the next five elections. In 1980, 33 percent of Carter's total vote came from middle-class whites.

Religion

Voting differences among religious groups also have declined during the postwar years. As Figure 5-5 reveals, in every election since 1944 Jews have been more likely to vote Democratic than Catholics, while Catholics have been more likely to vote Democratic than Protestants.[22]

Nineteen-eighty was the first presidential election since 1944 in which an absolute majority of Jews failed to vote Democratic, although a majority of their major-party vote went Democratic. A majority of Catholics voted Democratic in six of the seven elections between 1944 and 1968. The percentage of Catholics voting Democratic peaked in 1960, when the Democrats fielded a Roman Catholic candidate, but it was also very high in Johnson's landslide four years later.

Figure 5-5 White Major-Party Voters Who Voted Democratic for President, by Religion, 1944-1980 (In Percentages)

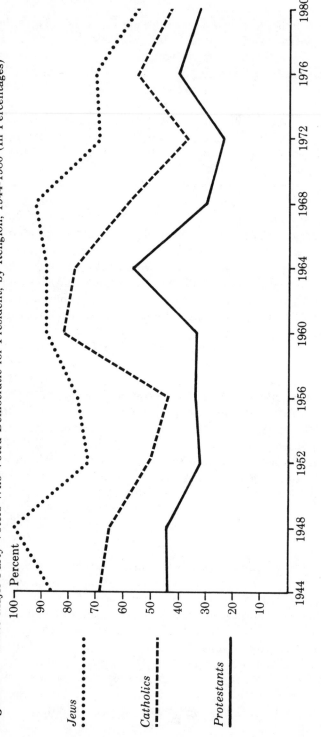

Number of:

	1944	1948	1952	1956	1960	1964	1968	1972	1976	1980
Jews	(74)	(19)	(46)	(53)	(53)[1]	(36)	(29)	(36)	(41)[1]	(25)
Catholics	(311)	(101)	(284)	(288)	(309)[1]	(267)	(206)	(384)	(378)[1]	(188)
Protestants	(1138)	(222)	(770)	(841)	(957)[1]	(674)	(553)	(938)	(959)[1]	(490)

[1] Weighted Ns.

Since then, Democratic voting declined precipitously. In 1968, a majority of white Catholics voted Democratic, although Humphrey's total is reduced from 60 percent to 55 percent if Wallace voters are included. In two of the last three elections, a majority of white Catholics voted Republican. The erosion of Democratic support between 1960 and 1980 is also documented by Gallup data.[23] As Petrocik has shown, not all Catholic subgroups have shifted away from Democratic loyalties, although the most Democratic group, Catholics with Polish and Irish backgrounds, has moved away from the Democrats.[24] White Protestants have been far less volatile in their voting behavior than Catholics. An absolute majority of white Protestants voted Republican in 9 of the 10 elections we have studied, and a majority voted Democratic only in Johnson's 1964 landslide.

Our simple measure of religious voting shows considerable change from election to election, but there appears to be a downward trend. Religious voting has been relatively low in the three most recent elections. Even though white Protestants were more likely to vote for Wallace than white Catholics were, including Wallace voters in our calculations has little effect on overall levels of religious voting. Similarly, including Anderson voters has little effect. Including blacks in our calculations, however, substantially reduces religious voting. Blacks are much more likely to be Protestant than Catholic, and to include blacks adds a substantial number of Protestant Democrats. Of course, the effect of including blacks is greater from 1964 on, since black turnout grew. In 1980, religious voting is reduced to 3 points if blacks are included.

Throughout the postwar years, the total proportion of the electorate made up of white Catholics has remained constant, but during the last two decades turnout has declined faster among Catholics than among white Protestants. In every election between 1948 and 1972 white Catholics had higher turnout than white Protestants, but the Catholic advantage was negligible in 1976 and was erased in 1980 (see Table 4-2). As we saw, Catholic support for the Democratic party has eroded. These factors, combined with change among blacks, have reduced the Catholic contribution to the Democratic presidential coalition. In 1980, only a fifth of the Democratic vote came from white Catholics, a record low. The Jewish contribution also has declined, mainly because the proportion of Jews in the electorate declined during the postwar years. In the last three elections Jews made up only about a twentieth of the Democratic presidential coalition. However, since most Jews live in a few states with a large number of electoral votes, their contribution may be more important than these numbers suggest.

As the data in Figure 5-6 reveal, the effects of social class and religion are cumulative. In every election since 1944, working-class

Figure 5-6 White Major-Party Voters Who Voted Democratic for President, by Social Class and Religion, 1944-1980 (In Percentages)

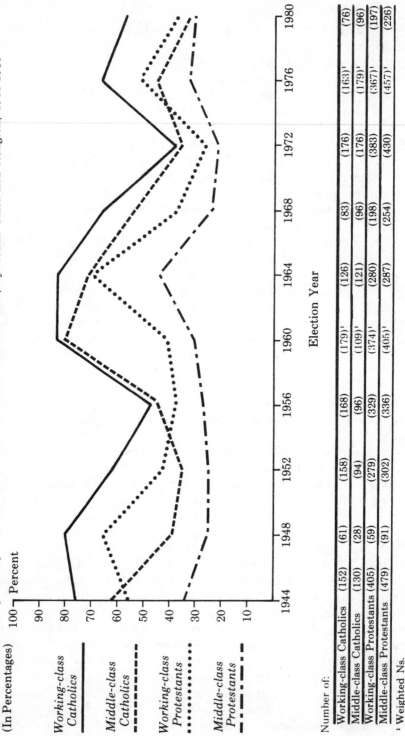

Number of:	1944	1948	1952	1956	1960	1964	1968	1972	1976	1980
Working-class Catholics	(152)	(61)	(158)	(168)	(179)[1]	(126)	(83)	(176)	(163)[1]	(76)
Middle-class Catholics	(130)	(28)	(94)	(96)	(109)[1]	(121)	(96)	(176)	(179)[1]	(96)
Working-class Protestants	(405)	(59)	(279)	(329)	(374)[1]	(280)	(198)	(383)	(367)[1]	(197)
Middle-class Protestants	(479)	(91)	(302)	(336)	(405)[1]	(287)	(254)	(430)	(457)[1]	(226)

[1] Weighted Ns.

Catholics have been more likely to vote Democratic than any other class-religion combination. In all 10 elections, white middle-class Protestants have been the least likely to vote Democratic. Of the groups we have studied, they show the most constancy in their vote. An absolute majority voted Republican in all 10 elections.

The relative impact of social class and religion can be assessed by comparing the voting behavior of middle-class Catholics with that of working-class Protestants. Religion was more important than class in 1944, 1956, 1960 (by a great margin), 1968, and 1972. Social class was more important than religion in 1948 (by a great margin), 1952, 1976, and 1980. And class and religion were equally important in 1964. However, during the last four elections all these trend lines have converged, suggesting that both social class and religion have declined in importance.

WHY THE NEW DEAL COALITION BROKE DOWN

Except for racial differences, all of the social factors we have examined—region, union membership, social class, and religion—have declined in importance during the postwar years. The decline in regional differences directly parallels the increase in racial differences. As the national Democratic party strengthened its appeal to blacks during the 1960s, party leaders endorsed policies opposed by southern whites. Several studies document the importance of issue preferences in contributing to a breakdown of Democratic support by white southerners.[25] The migration of northern whites to the South also reduced regional differences slightly.

To some extent, the Democratic party's appeals to blacks may have weakened its hold on white groups that traditionally supported it. But the erosion of Democratic support among trade union members, the working class, and Catholics results from other factors as well. During the postwar years, these groups have changed. While trade union members do not hold high-paying professional and managerial jobs, they have gained substantial economic advantages. Differences in income between the working class and the middle class have diminished. And Catholics, who often came from more recent immigrant groups than Protestants, have grown increasingly middle class as the proportion of second- and third-generation Americans grew. During the 1950s and early 1960s, white Catholics were more likely to be working class than white Protestants. This is no longer true. In 1976 and 1980 they were as likely to be middle class as white Protestants.

Not only have these groups changed economically and socially, the historical conditions that led union members, the working class, and Catholics to become Democrats have receded further into the past.

While the generational transmission of partisan loyalties gives histori-cally-based coalitions some staying power, the success of generational transmission has declined as party identification has weakened. New policy issues, sometimes unrelated to the political conflicts of the New Deal era, have tended to erode Democratic support among traditional Democratic groups. Of all these policies, race-related issues have been the most important in weakening the New Deal coalition.[26]

Our study of changing social forces suggests that the Democrats may have serious problems in future elections. While blacks vote solidly Democratic, they are a relatively small group with lower than average turnout. Blacks provide a weak base upon which to build a coalition. A coalition of minorities needs the support of many minorities, and it needs high levels of support from them. During the 10 elections between 1944 and 1980, the Democrats have never won without *at least* three-fifths of the vote of white trade union members and *at least* two-thirds of the vote of white working-class Catholics. And they have never won without an absolute majority of the white working class and of white Catholics. Moreover, the Democrats have never won an election in which blacks made up more than 15 percent of their coalition. Our own calculations suggest that it would be difficult for the Democrats to win a two-candidate election in which more than a sixth of their total vote came from blacks.

Only the future will determine if the New Deal coalition is dead. The erosion of Democratic support among southerners, union members, the working class, and Catholics could be reversed. A few years ago political scientists analyzing the 1976 election saw signs of renewed support among these groups. If Reagan's economic policies fail—especially if his policies aid the wealthy without improving economic conditions for a majority of Americans—class-based polarization could increase dramatically. But given the social changes that have occurred among the groups making up the Democratic coalition, and given the weak feelings of party identification that contribute to changes in voting preferences, it seems unlikely that the New Deal coalition will ever be restored in its previous form.

NOTES

1. We rely in this chapter and all subsequent chapters upon the way people said they voted. If we presented results only for the validated voters our analyses would not be comparable with the majority of previous election surveys conducted by the SRC-CPS. Moreover, differences between these results and the results of the voter validation study are negligible. Reagan's total vote is increased 1.5 percentage points when only validated votes are analyzed, Carter's total drops 1.8 points, and Anderson's rises .3 points. Even these differences are reduced when the white electorate is studied. Differences are also minimal when voting for Congress is studied.

2. The CBS News/*New York Times* poll is based upon an exit survey of 12,782 voters as they left the polls, and the ABC News poll is based on an exit survey of 9,341 voters. The results of the CBS News/*New York Times* survey are reported in the *New York Times,* November 9, 1980, Section 1, p. 28. See also Gerald M. Pomper, "The Presidential Election," in *The Election of 1980: Reports and Interpretations,* Gerald M. Pomper with colleagues (Chatham, N.J.: Chatham House, 1981), pp. 71-72; Everett Carll Ladd, "The Brittle Mandate: Electoral Dealignment and the 1980 Presidential Election," *Political Science Quarterly* 96 (Spring 1981): 1-25; and Steven J. Wayne, *The Road to the White House: The Politics of Presidential Elections,* postelection ed. (New York: St. Martin's Press, 1981), pp. 285-287. The basic report of the ABC News poll is presented in *The Pursuit of the Presidency 1980,* ed. Richard Harwood (New York: Berkley Books, 1980), p. 341, and some additional analyses are provided by Ladd.
3. See "Vote by Groups in Presidential Elections Since 1952," *Gallup Opinion Index,* Report No. 182 (December 1980): 6-7. The Gallup results for 1980 are based upon in-person interviews with 2,393 adults who "were considered to be likely voters." Interviews were conducted between October 30 and November 1.
4. Our estimates of the contribution that a social group makes to a party's presidential coalition is determined by dividing the total number of respondents in the group who voted for the party by the total number of respondents in the sample that voted for the party.
5. Ladd, "The Brittle Mandate," p. 16.
6. Ibid., p. 17.
7. Ibid., p. 14.
8. For a useful discussion of variations in voting behavior among Catholics, see E. J. Dionne, Jr., "Catholics and the Democrats: Estrangement But Not Desertion," in *Party Coalitions in the 1980s,* ed. Seymour Martin Lipset (San Francisco: Institute for Contemporary Studies, 1981), pp. 307-325.
9. We must be cautious about inferences drawn from the SRC-CPS study, since only 30 Jewish voters were sampled. However, Alan M. Fisher's study of the 1980 election pools the results of seven different polls and reaches similar conclusions. See Alan M. Fisher, "Jewish Political Shift: Erosion, Yes; Conversion, No," in *Party Coalitions,* p. 333.
10. See Ladd, "The Brittle Mandate," pp. 17-18; and George Gallup, Jr., "Devining the Devout: The Polls and Religious Beliefs," *Public Opinion* 4 (April/May 1981): 20, 41.
11. Robert Axelrod, "Where the Votes Come From: An Analysis of Electoral Coalitions, 1952-1968," *American Political Science Review* 66 (March 1972): 11-20.
12. John R. Petrocik, *Party Coalitions: Realignment and the Decline of the New Deal Party System* (Chicago: University of Chicago Press, 1981).
13. For a discussion of the importance of working-class whites to the Democratic presidential coalition, see Paul R. Abramson, *Generational Change in American Politics* (Lexington, Mass.: D.C. Heath & Co., 1975).
14. For a lucid discussion of the factors that determine the total contribution a social group makes to a party's presidential coalition, see Axelrod, "Where the Votes Come From."
15. The NORC survey, based upon 2,564 civilians, used a quota sample that does not follow the probability procedures employed by the SRC-CPS. Following quota procedures common at the time, southern blacks were not sampled. Because the NORC survey overrepresented upper income and

occupational groups, it cannot be used to estimate the contribution of social groups to the Democratic and Republican presidential coalitions.

16. Abramson, *Generational Change,* pp. 65-68.
17. As Note 15 explains, we cannot use the 1944 NORC study to estimate the contribution of social groups to the parties' electoral coalitions.
18. Because blacks are somewhat more likely to overreport voting than whites, we examined the racial composition of the Democratic presidential coalition using the 1964, 1976, and 1980 voter validation studies. If we calculate the composition of the Democratic coalition based only upon respondents who actually voted, we find that the black contribution drops from 13 to 11 percent in 1964, from 15 to 13 percent in 1976, and from 26 to 24 percent in 1980.
19. We define the South here as the states of the old Confederacy with the exception of Tennessee since SRC-CPS sampling procedures select respondents in Tennessee to represent the border states. In the following analysis, Alabama, Arkansas, Florida, Georgia, Louisiana, Mississippi, North Carolina, South Carolina, Texas, and Virginia are considered southern states.
20. See Robert R. Alford, *Party and Society: The Anglo-American Democracies* (Chicago: Rand McNally & Co., 1963); Paul R. Abramson, "Social Class and Political Change in Western Europe: A Cross-National Longitudinal Analysis," *Comparative Political Studies* 4 (July 1971): 131-155; Ronald Inglehart, *The Silent Revolution: Changing Values and Political Styles Among Western Publics* (Princeton, N.J.: Princeton University Press, 1977); and Seymour Martin Lipset, *Political Man: The Social Bases of Politics,* expanded ed. (Baltimore, Maryland: Johns Hopkins University Press, 1981).
21. Our calculations are based upon all respondents, except the small number for whom the head of household's occupation was not ascertained. These results therefore differ from those reported in Abramson, *Generational Change,* p. 24, where respondents are excluded if the head of household was a farmer, housewife, or student.
22. Although the number of Jews sampled is small, other surveys conducted during the postwar years also show high levels of Democratic voting. See Fisher, "Jewish Political Shift."
23. "Vote by Groups in Presidential Elections," *Gallup Opinion Index.*
24. Petrocik, *Party Coalitions,* pp. 81-83.
25. Paul Allen Beck, "Partisan Dealignment in the Postwar South," *American Political Science Review* 71 (June 1977): 477-496; and Bruce A. Campbell, "Realignment, Party Decomposition, and Issue Voting," in *Realignment in American Politics: Toward a Theory,* ed. Bruce A. Campbell and Richard J. Trilling (Austin: University of Texas Press, 1980), pp. 82-109.
26. Petrocik, *Party Coalitions,* pp. 111-153.

6

Issues, Candidates, and Voter Choice

As we have seen, the social basis of the Democratic presidential coalition all but disappeared in the 1980 presidential contest. Except for a fundamental social division between blacks and whites, the social and demographic groups that have made up the Democratic presidential coalition in the past all but deserted Jimmy Carter. Only a handful of white social groups gave him a majority of their vote. Moreover, the erosion of the Democratic presidential coalition may be part of a long-term breakup of the New Deal coalition.

Does this mean that the Republicans have the potential to forge a long-term majority coalition? It is generally argued that new political alignments are forged when a political party captures the majority position on newly emerging issues. If Ronald Reagan's election resulted from a massive movement of the American electorate to conservative economic and social policies, long-term Republican prospects may be bright. If, however, the Democratic defeat was largely a rejection of Carter, the potential for long-term Republican gains is less clear cut.

An alternate view is that enduring majority coalitions arise from the rejection of an incumbent who has been perceived as failing to solve contemporary crises. From this perspective, the 1980 presidential election may prove to be a realigning election, but only if Reagan is seen as a successful president.

In a more immediate sense, the 1980 election has led to clear-cut policy changes already. Shortly after assuming office, President Reagan launched a broad series of policy initiatives supported heavily by his fellow Republicans, and even many Democrats in Congress. By the end of spring, he had won a major legislative victory when Congress accepted his budget recommendations to reduce the rate of growth in

119

federal expenditures for domestic programs. By midsummer, Reagan's tax cut measures also had passed Congress, albeit with some compromises, and it was clear that military and defense spending would increase substantially.

Reagan and his supporters justified the dismantling of many Great Society programs in much the same terms that President Lyndon B. Johnson used when he created them. Reagan, like Johnson, saw his electoral sweep as a mandate to enact his campaign platform. In a fund-raising letter of July 8, 1981, Reagan wrote, "Throughout my campaign, I pledged to submit legislation to cut taxes, reduce the size of the federal government and restore our national defenses to assure security for us and our children. And our great Republican victory last November was an endorsement of these goals by the American people."

Clearly, Reagan made these proposals the core of his campaign platform, and clearly he won the election handily. Yet it does not follow necessarily that his supporters voted for him because they wanted to see his platform enacted. In this chapter we will examine the connection between citizens' policy preferences and evaluations and their voting choices. The 1980 election is placed in context by comparison to the 1972 and 1976 presidential elections.[1]

This chapter focuses on "prospective issue voting"—voting on the basis of how citizens view candidates' platforms and what these candidates propose to do in the coming four years. It is this form of issue voting that seems closest to the idea of an electoral mandate. The 1980 election, however, may be interpreted quite differently. The expressed mandate may be that the electorate thought that Jimmy Carter did not perform adequately as president and therefore that he should not be returned to office. "Retrospective issue voting" is based upon such evaluations of past performance, usually but not exclusively of the incumbent. Thus, the vote may express very little support for the platform enunciated by the opponent.

How much of Reagan's victory may be attributed to citizens' evaluation of his *promises* and how much to Carter's *performance* as president? Was the "mandate" (if any there be) for some kind of change or for the specific changes Reagan proposed? It is this second type of mandate, a rejection of Carter and his performance in office, that other political scientists have proposed in their interpretations of the 1980 elections.[2] We shall look at these performance evaluations in Chapter 7 as well as compare the prospective and retrospective bases for issue voting. Finally, in Chapter 8 we shall examine the basis of support for major-party candidates as party nominees and the basis of support for the independent candidacy of John B. Anderson.

THE CONCERNS OF THE ELECTORATE

The first question, then, is what sorts of concerns moved the public. Pollsters regularly ask the public a question such as "What do you personally feel are the most important problems the government in Washington should try to take care of?" In Table 6-1, we have listed the percentage of responses to what respondents claimed was the single most important problem in broad categories of concerns over the three most recent elections.[3]

In 1980, economic issues dominated the concerns of the electorate. Fifty-six percent stated this category as singularly most important, while only 32 percent considered foreign and defense matters most important. The panoply of what Richard M. Scammon and Ben J. Wattenberg termed the "social issues" (social welfare, crime and public order, labor, race, and other matters) was seen by the electorate as much

Table 6-1 Most Important Problem as Seen by the Electorate, 1972-1980

Problem	1972		1976		1980	
Economics	27%		76%		56%	
Unemployment/Recession		9%		33%		10%
Inflation/Prices		14%		27%		33%
"Social Issues"	34%		14%		7%	
Social Welfare		7%		4%		3%
Public Order		20%		8%		1%
Foreign & Defense	31%		4%		32%	
Vietnam		25%		—		—
Iran		—		—		15%
Other Foreign		4%		3%		9%
Other Defense		1%		1%		8%
Functioning of Government						
(competence, trust,	4%		4%		2%	
corruption, power, etc)						
All Others	4%		3%		3%	
Total percent	100%		100%		100%	
(Number)	(842)[1]		(2337)[2]		(1352)	
"Missing" Responses	(63)		(203)		(56)	
Percent "Missing"						
Responses	7%		7%		4%	

[1] These questions were asked of a randomly selected half of the sample in 1972.
[2] Weighted *N*.

NOTE: All of the subcategories under economics, social issues, foreign and defense, and functioning of government are not included. The total percentages for the subcategories, therefore, will not equal the percentages for the main categories.

less important.⁴ Only 7 percent felt social issues were the most important problem.

The concerns in 1980 clearly differ from those of recent prior elections. The declining interest in social issues is striking. In 1972, some kind of social problem was cited by more than one-third of the public as most important, and one-fifth felt public order (e.g., crime, civil liberties) was our most pressing political problem. By 1976, this category dropped to 8 percent, and social issues fell to less than 14 percent. By 1980, the concern about social issues was halved again, and the public order responses fell to a bare trace.

In 1972 and 1980 attention focused on a particular foreign crisis. In 1972, it was the Vietnam war that was the chief concern of 25 percent of the electorate, while 15 percent of the 1980 electorate thought the Iranian hostage crisis was the major problem. No such "hot spot" existed in 1976. Yet 1980 was distinct from the 1972 and 1976 elections in the level of concern about other foreign and defense problems. About 17 percent were so concerned in 1980, up from the near trace levels of 5 and 4 percentage points for 1972 and 1976, respectively.

Economic issues preoccupied a large segment of the public in all three elections—27 percent in 1972, 76 percent in 1976, and 56 percent in 1980. What made 1976 so distinctive in these terms was the very high level of concern about the unemployment rate and recession. One-third of the respondents mentioned this category in 1976, as compared to about one-tenth in the other two elections. The SRC-CPS data suggest that as inflation increased during the last eight years, so did the public's concern about it, from 14 to 27 to 33 percent.

These findings indicate only what problems concerned the electorate. It does not follow necessarily that concern about inflation, for example, translates into support for Reagan's anti-inflation policy, let alone a vote for him. A vote, after all, is an expression of a comparison between or among alternatives. To investigate these questions, we must look at issue preferences of voters and how they perceive the candidates on these issues.

ISSUE POSITIONS AND PERCEPTIONS

In the three most recent presidential election surveys, the SRC-CPS questionnaires included numerous issue scales designed to tap the preferences of the electorate and their perceptions of the positions the candidates took on these issues. These data will be used here for examining several questions. First, just what alternatives did voters perceive? Second, to what extent did voters meet the variety of criteria that have been advanced as being "necessary" to cast a vote on the basis of these positional issues? Finally, how strongly were voters' preferences and perceptions on these positional issues related to their choice of candidates?

The presumption that underlies this analysis is that the choice of voters is based on a comparison between or among the alternatives presented to them and their own issue preferences. For example, if a voter holds a preference for increased spending for defense, and if Reagan is the only candidate who proposes increased defense spending, then that voter will be predisposed to vote for Reagan, at least on the basis of this one issue. In this view of issue voting, it is the candidates' promises about the policies they will pursue if elected that shapes voting behavior.

While positional issue voting is "promise" oriented, there is still much room for "performance" to impinge on voters' perceptions. For example, in 1968, Vice President and Democratic presidential nominee Hubert H. Humphrey was constrained on the Vietnam war issue by the actions of the administration in which he served. While he attempted to disassociate himself somewhat from Lyndon Johnson on this issue, he personally felt constrained in the positions he could take. The electorate's perceptions of Humphrey were colored by his tie to Johnson and Johnson's escalation of the war. In short, there is no neat distinction between promise and performance, especially for the incumbent president. Even so, the seven-point issue scales we shall consider seem more nearly "promise" issues than other issues we shall analyze.

The 1980 Data

Figure 6-1 presents the text of one of the seven-point issue scale questions, along with an example of the card handed to respondents as they considered their response. Figure 6-2 places on these scales the average (median) position of the respondents and the average perception of the three major candidates in 1980. The nine issue dimensions tapped a wide variety of prominent concerns. The three major aspects of Reagan's budgetary proposals are measured: how much government spending for social services should be cut, how much federal income taxes should be cut, and how much defense spending should be increased or decreased. Other scales tap government activity on jobs, aid to minorities, women's rights, abortion, and relations with Russia. A final scale asks respondents to select their preferred balance between action against inflation and against unemployment.

What, then, of the average respondent? These issues are asked precisely because they are controversial, so it should come as no surprise that on just about every issue there is substantial support in the electorate for virtually all possible positions. As a result, the "average citizen" comes out looking moderate on most of these policies primarily because "liberals" are balanced with "conservatives." (See, for example,

Figure 6-1 An Example of a Seven-Point Issue Scale: Jobs and Standard of Living Guarantees

Interviewer begins:

"Some people feel the government in Washington should see to it that every person has a job and a good standard of living. [For the first issue scale only, the following is added: Suppose these people are at one end of the scale at point number 1.] Others think the government should just let each person get ahead on his own." [On the first issue is added: Suppose these people are at the other end, at point 7. And, of course, some people have opinions somewhere in between at points 2, 3, 4, 5, or 6.]

Interviewer hands respondent a card:

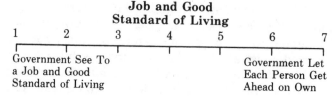

Job and Good Standard of Living

| 1 | 2 | 3 | 4 | 5 | 6 | 7 |

Government See To
a Job and Good
Standard of Living

Government Let
Each Person Get
Ahead on Own

Interviewer asks:

"Where would you place yourself on this scale, or haven't you thought much about this?"

If respondent places self on scale, the interviewer then asks:

"Where would you place _____?" [Jimmy Carter, Ronald Reagan, etc.]

SOURCE: American National Election Study, 1980, *Composite Interview Schedule,* Center for Political Studies, Institute for Social Research, University of Michigan, April 1981, p. 101.

the N's reported in Table 6-4.) This mythical average citizen is in the middle of the scale on all but two of the questions. Most respondents agreed that women should play a role equal to that of men in business, industry, and government, and people, on average, wanted to see substantial increases in spending for defense. Otherwise, the median citizen was near the center of the issue scale. Of course, since the government spending/social services scale runs from no cuts to large cuts, being in the middle of the scale means that most people wanted to see some cuts made, just as an average position to the left of the exact middle position on the abortion and tax cut scales translates into noticeable, and noticeably more conservative, changes in the status quo.

These median positions provide some evidence that the electorate wanted more conservative policies on many issues.[5] The 1980 SRC-CPS questionnaire asked respondents to place their perception of current government policy on each scale. Most citizens placed themselves on the issue scales more conservatively than they placed current government

Figure 6-2 Median Self-Placement of Electorate and the Electorate's Placement of Candidates on Issue Scales, 1980

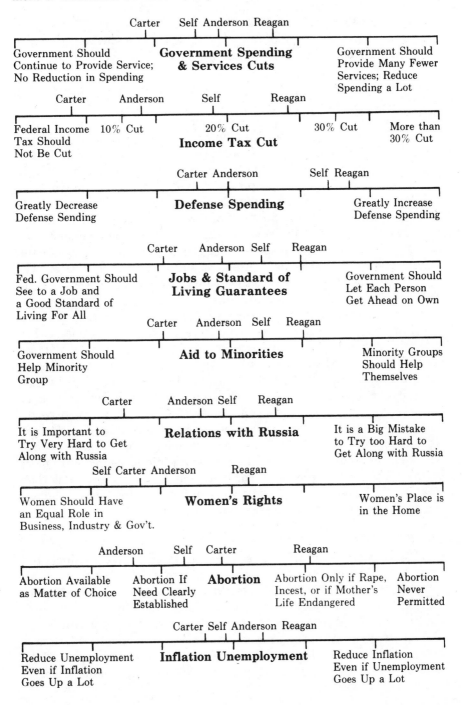

policy. The typical citizen was about a point more conservative on government spending and service cuts, abortion, and relations with Russia; about a point and a half more conservative on defense and aid to minorities; and nearly two points more conservative on jobs and standard of living and tax cuts. There was, however, virtually no difference between median citizen and current policy placements on the inflation/unemployment scale, and most people desired to see a more equal role for women in society (by about three quarters of a point).

These differences add up to an apparent desire for more conservative government policies, but they do not indicate necessarily that the typical citizen desired the policies Reagan was promising. One fact is very clear from examining the perceived candidate alternatives. People saw Carter and Reagan as proposing very different policies. On most issue scales, the typical citizen saw Carter and Reagan about two points apart out of a maximum possible difference of six points. And the average citizen, even if desiring a more conservative government, was not always very close to Reagan. Indeed, if we take the average of the distance between typical self placement and perception of Carter over all nine issues and compare it to the distance from Reagan, we find little difference. Over all nine issue dimensions, the average citizen was 1.0 units from Carter and 0.9 units from Reagan.[6]

There are, however, substantial differences from issue to issue. For example, the average citizen perceived Reagan's position on defense spending as much closer to his or her own position than Carter's. But on government spending and services cuts, most respondents placed themselves closer to what they saw Carter proposing than to Reagan's plans. And the other issue scales show a variety of such differences. A better summary, perhaps, is that on seven of the nine issue dimensions, people were in between what they saw the two party nominees proposing, while, on the women's rights and abortion questions, people were more liberal than Carter who, in turn, was seen to be more liberal than Reagan. On balance, then, people were in between the two candidates but were slightly closer to Reagan than Carter.

Comparisons with 1972 and 1976

If people saw clear differences between the two party nominees but were only slightly closer to Reagan than to Carter, how does this compare with the 1972 and 1976 elections? Although direct comparisons are limited because only three issue scales were used in all three elections (jobs, aid to minorities, and women's rights), stark differences are apparent. In 1972, the average citizen saw pronounced differences between Richard M. Nixon and George S. McGovern, differences of the same order of magnitude as 1980. Averaged over eight issue scales in

1972, the typical citizen saw Nixon and McGovern 2.0 units apart; a figure quite similar to the 1.8 of 1980. In 1976, on the other hand, the average distance separating perceptions of Carter and Gerald R. Ford (over nine scales) was only 0.8. In short, most people saw 1976 as pitting two candidates who differed relatively little on issues, while 1972 and 1980 were seen as contests between markedly different candidates.

The 1972 and 1980 elections differed substantially in a very important way. In 1980, people generally placed themselves between the two candidates and were only a little closer to Reagan than to Carter, whereas in 1972 they were very close to Nixon's policies and very far from McGovern's. On average, a typical citizen differed by less than half a point from where Nixon was perceived to stand, while McGovern was seen to be, on average, more than two points away. In 1976, even though Ford and Carter were seen as fairly similar in their policy views, the typical citizen was closer to Ford (a distance of 0.8) than to Carter (a distance of 1.1), not that much different from the figures in 1980 of .9 for Reagan and 1.0 for Carter.

In short, most people in 1972 saw McGovern as very liberal and Nixon as moderately conservative, and on average they were much closer to Nixon's positions than McGovern's. Most people saw a moderate conservative pitted against a moderate liberal in 1976, and they were slightly closer to Ford on most matters. In 1980, people perceived clear differences between the two party nominees. Most were closer to Reagan than to Carter, but not by much compared to 1972.

Table 6-2 makes more apparent the similarities and differences among these three elections, examining the three policy questions asked in all three surveys. Again, the scales range from 1, the most liberal, to 7, the most conservative option. Clearly, there was no shift to the right on jobs and standard of living, aid to minorities, and women's rights.[7] On the jobs scale, self placement changed little, on the minorities scale it became a bit more conservative, and on the women's rights scale it became steadily and substantially more liberal over the three elections. On the first two scales, the average perception of the location of the Democratic party was relatively constant and was noticeably more liberal on the women's rights scale in 1980.[8] The perceptions of the Republican party were about the same, on average, in 1972 and 1976, but became substantially more conservative on all three issues in 1980. Candidates also were perceived differently. McGovern was seen as much more liberal on the jobs and aid to minorities question than was Carter, and on all three issues, Reagan was perceived as much more conservative than Nixon or Ford.

Table 6-2   Three-Year Comparisons on Three Issue Scales, Median Placements on Seven-Point Issue Scales, 1972-1980

Issue	Self	Candidates		Party		Differences Between	
		Dem.	Rep.	Dem.	Rep.	Candidate	Party
Jobs							
1972	4.3	2.0	4.4	3.0	4.5	2.4	1.5
1976	4.4	2.9	4.3	2.7	4.5	1.4	1.8
1980	4.4	3.1	5.0	2.9	5.0	1.9	2.0
Aid to Minorities							
1972	4.2	2.4	4.1	3.2	4.1	1.7	1.0
1976	4.2	3.1	3.9	2.9	4.1	0.8	1.2
1980	4.5	3.0	5.0	2.9	5.0	2.0	2.0
Women's Rights							
1972	3.6	2.9	3.6	3.2	3.7	0.7	0.5
1976	2.9	3.2	3.5	3.2	3.8	0.3	0.6
1980	2.4	2.7	4.3	2.7	4.2	1.6	1.4

ISSUE VOTING CRITERIA

The Problem

To this point we have emphasized comparisons among the 1972, 1976, and 1980 elections at a highly aggregated level, looking only at sample-wide averages. The inference that 1980 was an election with clearly perceived differences between the two party nominees, but with people placing themselves slightly closer to Reagan than to Carter can be misleading. In fact, many people may not vote according to issue preferences, as the authors of the classic study of the American electorate, *The American Voter*, point out.[9] They argue that to vote on the basis of an issue, a voter must have an opinion on the issue, know what the government is doing about the policy, and see a difference beween the policies of the two major parties. According to their analysis, only about one-quarter to one-third of the electorate in 1956 could meet these three criteria for issue voting on a given issue. Given the changes in the SRC-CPS questionnaire, we cannot apply their procedures to the 1980 electorate. However, we begin with three similar criteria to determine whether an issue-based vote could be cast.

First, does the respondent express a personal opinion about a given issue? This is measured by the proportion of the sample who placed themselves on the scale. Obviously, one could not vote on the basis of an issue for which one had no opinion. Second, does the respondent have some perception of the positions taken by both candidates on that issue? This is measured by the percentage of the sample who could place themselves and both major-party nominees on an issue scale.[10] We will include a modified form of this criterion for the three-candidate 1980 election; specifically, could the respondent place any two candidates on the scale? Very few people who placed Anderson on any given issue dimension failed to place both Carter and Reagan on the scale as well. Moreover, many more people failed to place Anderson than failed to place Carter or Reagan. Therefore, we will focus here on the major-party candidates. Third, does the respondent see a difference between the positions of Carter and Reagan? Failing to see a difference means that the voter perceived no choice on this issue.

A voter may be able to satisfy these three criteria for casting a vote on the basis of an issue, but misperceive the offerings of the candidates. This reasoning leads us to a fourth criterion that we are able to measure more systematically than was possible in 1956. Does the respondent accurately perceive the *relative* positions of the major candidates (for example, saw Carter adopting a more "liberal" position than Reagan)? This criterion does not demonstrate that the voter accurately saw that, say, Reagan campaigned on the basis of a 30 percent cut in federal income tax rates. It demands less of the voter than that, asking only that the citizen saw that Carter desired a smaller tax cut than did Reagan.

The Data

In Table 6-3 we report the percentages of the sample meeting each of the four criteria on each issue scale in 1980. We also summarize the average proportion meeting these criteria for all nine scales.[11] As can be seen in column I, most people felt capable of placing themselves on any issue scale, and this capability was, basically speaking, common to all three election year surveys.[12]

Although most people could place themselves on the issues, many fewer could place both major-party candidates. In 1980, three out of five respondents were able to place themselves and the two candidates, a figure that corresponds closely to the two previous elections. There is substantial variation across issues, however. More than 7 out of 10 claimed to have a preference on and perceive the positions of Carter and Reagan on the issues of women's rights, defense spending, and relations with Russia. Less than half met those two criteria on the tax cut, inflation/unemployment, and abortion scales.

Note that the figures for those placing any two of the three major candidates are barely different than the figures for those placing Carter and Reagan on the scales. Few people saw a position for Anderson who

Table 6-3 Four Criteria for Issue Voting, 1980, with 1976 and 1972 Comparisons (In Percentages)

Issue Scale	I Placed Self on Scale	*Percentage of Sample Who*			
		IIa Placed Self and Any Two Candidates	IIb Placed Self, Carter and Reagan	III Placed Self and Saw a Difference Between Carter and Reagan	IV Placed Self and Saw Carter More "Liberal" Than Reagan
Government Spending/ Services Cuts	83	67	65	58	48
Income Tax Cut[1]	61	44	42	35	32
Defense Spending	86	72	71	65	56
Jobs & Standard of Living	84	70	68	57	48
Aid to Minorities	86	71	69	61	53
Relations with Russia	84	72	71	59	51
Women's Rights	94	74	72	54	47
Abortion Policy[1]	96	49	46	31	23
Inflation/Unemployment	61	48	47	39	27
Average					
9 scales, 1980	82	63	61	51	43
7 scales, 1980[2]	83	68	66	56	47
9 scales, 1976[3]	84	—	58	36	26
8 scales, 1972[4]	90	—	65	49	41

[1] Positional scales with fewer than 7 options.

[2] Does not include the abortion scale (with four points) and the income tax cut scale (with five points).

[3] Columns IIb, III, and IV compare perceptions of Carter and Ford.

[4] Columns IIb, III, and IV compare perceptions of McGovern and Nixon.

did not also perceive a Carter and a Reagan position. Indeed, relatively few perceived Anderson on issues. On average, only 42 percent placed Anderson on an issue scale, compared to 64 and 69 percent for Reagan and Carter, respectively.

More than half the sample averaged across all nine issues saw a difference between the positions of Carter and Reagan. Of those seeing a difference, more than 8 out of 10 placed the two in the "correct" order (i.e., saw Carter as more "liberal" than Reagan). In other words, a bit more than two out of every five respondents met the full set of four criteria for being able to cast a vote on the basis of a given issue.

The results for 1972 are very similar to 1980. However, in 1976, just over one-third of the electorate saw a difference between Carter and Ford, and just over one-fourth of the electorate saw Carter as more liberal.

It appears that regardless of the nature of the election, many citizens fail to meet the criteria for casting a vote on the basis of a given issue, at least in the sense of comparing the promises of the candidates with their own preferences. Yet the nature of the positions taken by the candidates influences how much issues affect voters' decisions. The more distinctive the offerings of the two candidates, the more voters perceive these differences, and the more capable they are of voting on the basis of issues. In 1972 and in 1980, the two major-party nominees were very distinctive. The differences between Nixon and McGovern and between Reagan and Carter were perceived by the electorate, and many voters met the demands for voting on the basis of an issue. In 1976, however, the differences between Ford and Carter were much less clear cut. The electorate perceived the relative similarity of the candidates, and as a result a much smaller proportion of the electorate met the issue voting criteria.[13] In sum, we support Morris P. Fiorina's argument that failure to satisfy these criteria does not reflect, exclusively, ill-formed preferences and perceptions in the electorate.[14] Rather, the "quality" of response to these issue questions is based in part on citizens' reflections of the external environment, notably the positions candidates actually adopt.

What, then, does this say about Reagan's purported mandate? First, on average, only two out of five could meet the criteria for issue voting on any given issue. Of course, many failed to vote at all, and many voted for Carter or Anderson. Second, most people were in between the two candidates and were only slightly closer to Reagan's positions than to Carter's. Third, even if all that is true, we have yet to address the central question: Did people vote on the basis of these issues? We will examine voter choice in two ways. Did people vote for the closer candidate on each issue? How strongly related to the vote is the set of all issues taken together?

APPARENT ISSUE VOTING IN 1980

Issue Criteria and Voting on Each Issue

The first question, then, is to what extent people who were closer to a candidate on a given issue actually voted for that candidate. To address this question, we examined issue by issue the respondents who placed themselves on an issue scale. In Table 6-4, we report the percentage of the two-party vote cast for Carter by those at each point along each scale. Additionally, we divided the seven points into the set of positions closer to where the average citizen saw Carter on the scale, those points closer to where Reagan was perceived to stand, and in a few cases to those who were nearly equidistant to the two candidates. (See Figure 6-2 for average perceptions.)

As can be seen in Table 6-4, there was a strong relationship between citizens' own preferences and the candidate they supported on the jobs and standard of living, aid to minorities, defense spending, government spending and services reductions, and inflation/unemployment scales. On the tax cut and relations with Russia measures, the relationship was weaker. The two scales on which the average citizen was more liberal than either candidate, women's rights and abortion, demonstrated no relationship to voter choice. Thus, apparent issue voting is strongest with the preferences on issues that tap typical Democrat-Republican cleavages and with spending measures.[15]

Another way of measuring apparent issue voting is to collapse each issue scale into the set of people whose preference on that issue puts them closer to where the average citizen saw Carter or closer to the median placement of Reagan (dropping those nearly equidistant between the two candidate placements). This measure reflects more directly the argument that issue voting involves a comparison between the two candidates' offerings. The proportion of the electorate who voted for the closer of these two candidates is reported, issue by issue, in the first column of Table 6-5. (Anderson voters are again excluded.)

If voting were unrelated to issue positions, we would expect that 50 percent would vote for the closer candidate on average. In 1980, an average of about three out of five voters who had a preference on an issue voted for the closer candidate. Yet there is substantial variation across issues. The women's rights and abortion issues, for example, are essentially unrelated to voting behavior. The three major planks of Reagan's economic platform are very much at the average, while the jobs and minorities scales are rather more strongly related to candidate choice, at about 70 percent each.

The extent of apparent issue voting is compared to that of 1972 and 1976 in Table 6-5. As we would expect, 1972 and 1980 are about comparable, with an average of two-thirds voting for the closer candi-

Table 6-4 Major-Party Voters Who Voted for Carter, by Seven-Point Issue Scales, 1980 (In Percentages)

Issue Scale	Closer to Median Perception of Carter			Equi-distant	Closer to Median Perception of Reagan			(N)
	1	2	3	4	5	6	7	
Gov't. Spending/Services Cuts[1]	74%	67%	52%	43%	24%	8%	20%	860
(N)[2]	124	109	91	149	127	99	61	
Income Tax Cut	56%	49%	35%	28%	25%			570
(N)	132	113	121	141	63			
Defense Spending	83%	94%	58%	51%	60%	30%	35%	785
(N)	18	17	41	128	190	206	185	
Jobs & Standard of Living	80%	56%	63%	50%	40%	19%	21%	760
(N)	81	57	81	153	131	155	102	
Aid to Minorities	93%	85%	55%	47%	31%	30%	29%	783
(N)	43	33	87	214	176	115	115	
Relations with Russia	61%	46%	45%	40%	32%	26%	32%	762
(N)	103	97	104	182	111	89	76	
Women's Rights	49%	39%	47%	43%	30%	25%	54%	827
(N)	275	142	92	141	68	63	46	
Abortion[1]	47%	34%	44%	48%				843
(N)	293	161	288	101				
Inflation/Unemployment[1]	78%	66%	50%	44%	28%	17%	20%	541
(N)	45	44	105	194	80	48	30	

[1] Reversed from actual scoring to make a "liberal" response closer to "1" and a "conservative" response closer to "7."

[2] Numbers are the totals upon which percentages are based.

date in 1972. And, as we also should expect by now, apparent issue voting is lower in 1976 than in 1972 or 1980. The 1976 average figure is just under three out of five or only slightly above what we would expect if issues were totally irrelevant.

In several ways the figures in the first column are misleading indicators. Many people who had a preference on an issue failed to meet the remaining issue voting criteria; they failed to perceive one or both candidate offerings, saw no difference, or thought Carter more conservative than Reagan. In the second column we report the comparable percentages for those who met all issue voting criteria on that issue, while the third column contains the percentages for those who placed themselves on an issue dimension but failed to meet some other of the criteria.[16] Obviously, so doing makes a big difference. Seven out of 10 of those meeting all the criteria voted for the closer candidate in 1980, which is the same as in 1976 (remember that far fewer met these criteria in 1976 than in 1980), and somewhat less than the three out of four in 1972. And, for those who failed to meet all of the criteria, voting was nearly random with respect to issue preference in all three elections.

Table 6-5   Apparent Issue Voting, 1980, with 1976 and 1972 Comparisons (In Percentages)

	Extent to which Voter Met Issue Voting Criteria		
Issue Scale	Placed Self on Issue Scale	Met All Four Issue Voting Criteria	Place Self on Issue Scale, but Failed to Meet Some Other Criterion
Government Spending/ Services Cuts	68	78	50
Income Tax Cut	62	71	51
Defense Spending	63	74	39
Jobs & Standards of Living	71	82	53
Aid to Minorities	71	79	51
Relations with Russia	60	70	44
Women's Rights	52	59	44
Abortion	52	37	58
Inflation/ Unemployment	68	88	44
Average			
1980	63	71	48
1976	57	70	50
1972	66	76	55

NOTE: An "apparent issue vote" is based on voting for the candidate closer to one's own position on an issue scale. The closer candidate is determined by comparing self placement to the median placement of the two candidates on the scale as a whole. Respondents who did not place themselves on the issue scale were excluded from the calculations.

Even though a substantial majority who satisfied the voting criteria voted in alignment with their preferences in all three elections, there remains considerable variation from issue to issue. In 1980, nearly 90 percent voted for the closer candidate on the basis of inflation and unemployment—the most salient issue yet one that elicited a very low proportion who met the issue voting criteria. Indeed, on most issues apparent issue voting was high. The exceptions are the women's rights scale and the abortion issue, which were essentially unrelated to voting choices.

Overall Apparent Issue Voting

The abortion issue reminds us that a single issue is only one of many factors affecting voting behavior. Few people were consistently in favor of one candidate over the other on all issues. For example, most people favored Reagan on defense spending but opposed him on abortion. So, for assessing issue voting in any election, we must consider all of the issues together. To measure this net assessment, we scored an individual as a +1 if he or she was closer to the median placement of Reagan on a given issue, −1 if closer to Carter, and 0 if equally close to both or if the respondent failed to have a preference on the issue. We then summed these scores over all issue scales yielding, for 1980, a range of −9 to +9. Minus scores indicate that, all issues considered, the individual was closer to Carter, plus scores indicate that the individual was closer to Reagan, while a sum of zero indicates that the balance of issue positions favored neither candidate for that voter.[17] In Figure 6-3 we collapsed these scales for all three elections into seven categories from strongly Democratic to strongly Republican on issues.[18] The distribution of reported voters for one of the two major-party nominees is shown. From election to election, the distributions vary, but with some similarities. More people were closer, overall, to the Republican than to the Democratic candidate. In 1972, the strength of Nixon's position vis-à-vis McGovern's is quite dramatic. Four times as many voters were closer to Nixon (or at least to the electorate's perceptions of his issue positions) than to McGovern. In 1976, nearly three times as many voters were closer to Ford than to Carter.

Nonetheless, there was considerable change from 1972 to 1976. The relatively neutral category (+1, 0, or −1) increased substantially, mostly to the detriment of the Republican candidate. In 1980, this movement increased. More than one-third of the sample's voters were in the neutral category. The rise in the neutral category comes at the expense of the pro-Republican advantage. In 1972, there were four voters closer to Nixon for every one closer to McGovern. By 1980, there were only five voters closer to Reagan for every two voters closer to Carter. In 1976, of course, most people were just slightly closer to Ford,

Figure 6-3 Distribution of Voters on Net Balance of Issues, 1972, 1976, 1980

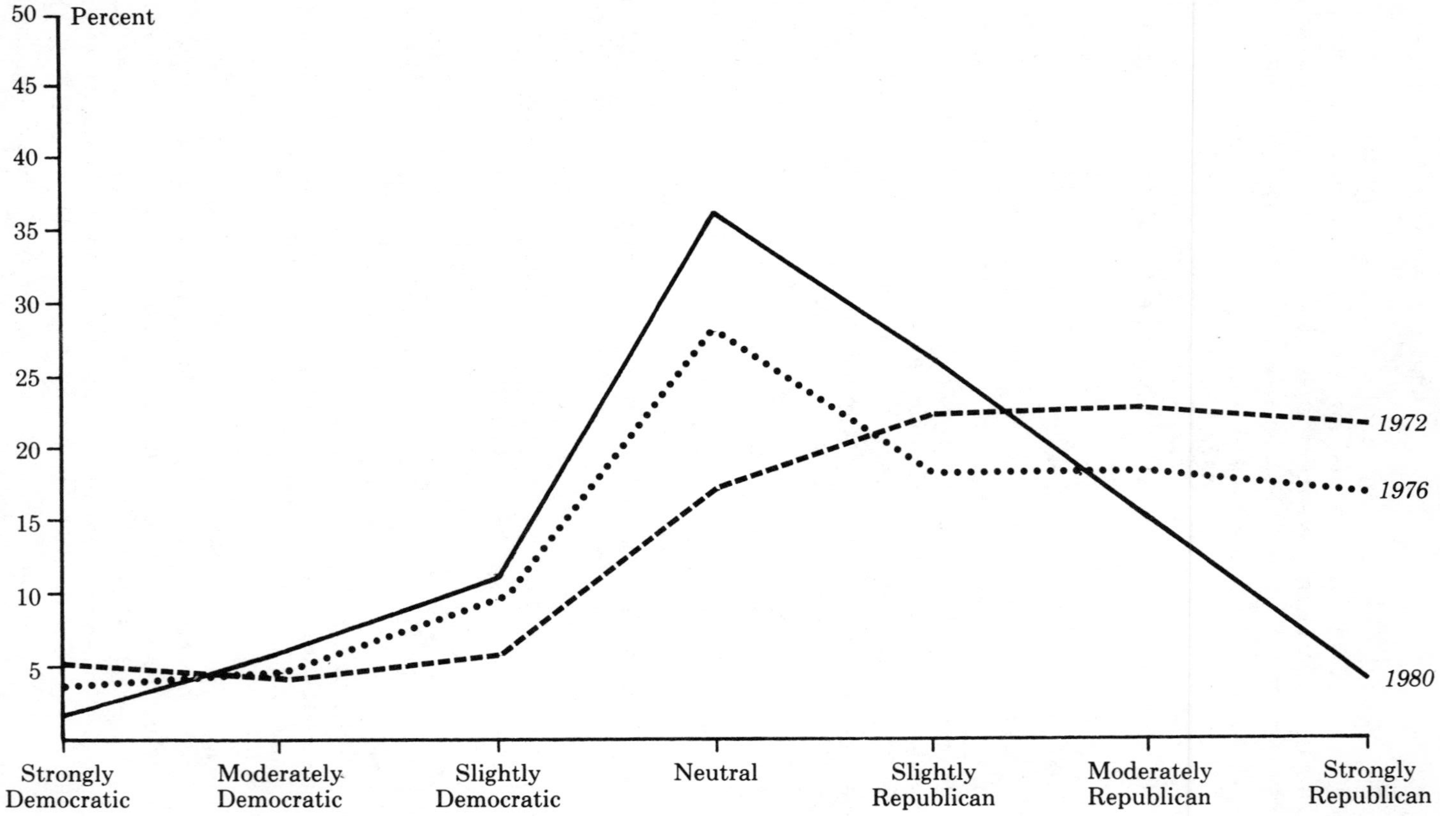

Figure 6-4 Major-Party Voters Who Voted Democratic for President, by Net Balance of Issues Measure, 1972, 1976, 1980

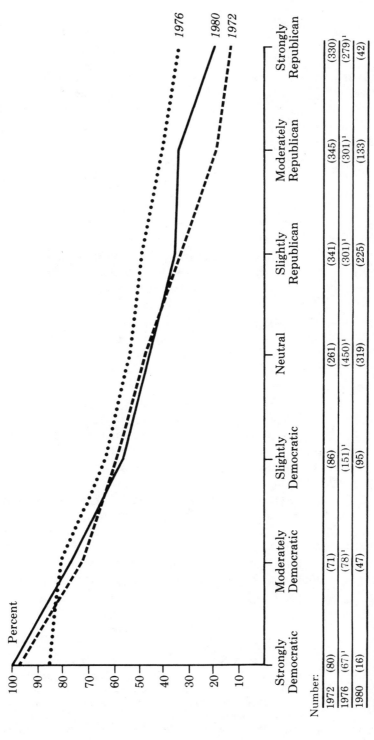

Number:	Strongly Democratic	Moderately Democratic	Slightly Democratic	Neutral	Slightly Republican	Moderately Republican	Strongly Republican
1972	(80)	(71)	(86)	(261)	(341)	(345)	(330)
1976	(67)[1]	(78)[1]	(151)[1]	(450)[1]	(301)[1]	(301)[1]	(279)[1]
1980	(16)	(47)	(95)	(319)	(225)	(133)	(42)

[1] Weighted Ns.

but tended to be so on many issues. In 1980, the mix was more substantial.

As can be seen in Figure 6-4, in all three elections the relationship between the net balance of issues measure and voting behavior was strong. Again, 1972 and 1980 are quite similar, but in 1976 the relationship is only slightly weaker. The Democrats received a substantially lower share of the major-party vote in 1972 than in 1980 mainly because voters were more Republican on the issues in the Nixon-McGovern contest.

Figures 6-3 and 6-4 together reaffirm our basic understanding of issue voting in the 1972, 1976, and 1980 elections. In 1972, most voters consistently favored Nixon's offerings to McGovern's and voted according to their policy comparisons. In 1976, voters tended to favor Ford on more issues than Carter, but Ford barely received a majority vote from those slightly pro-Republican on issues, and received only 45 percent of the vote from the largest category, the neutrals. In 1980, most voters had markedly mixed views, favoring Reagan on some measures, Carter on others, but Reagan did very well among those closer to his policies.

These data strongly suggest that Carter's loss in 1980 did not result from a major shift of the electorate on issues. The electorate was more pro-Republican on issues in 1976 when Carter won than in 1980 when he lost. Rather, Carter lost because, with the exception of voters who were strongly or moderately pro-Democratic on issues, he consistently fared worse among each balance of issues group in 1980 than four years earlier.

In short, the positional issues, while clearly related to voter choice, do not support the argument that Reagan received a mandate in favor of his particular policies. Instead, many people had quite mixed views and only slightly favored Reagan's policies over Carter's. Moreover, positional issues provide only one determinant of voter choice. Why, then, did Reagan win so handily in 1980? Indeed, why did Ford lose at all in 1976? The answer to these two questions is the same. Regardless of what the incumbent promised to do if returned to office, voters felt he had not done a very good job of managing policy during his incumbency. Our next chapter will provide the empirical evidence to support this conclusion.

NOTES

1. This chapter relies heavily upon the seven-point issue scales developed by the SRC-CPS of the University of Michigan. They are designed to locate each respondent in a "policy-space" defined by current political issues. These scales were developed in 1968, but were used extensively in presidential election surveys beginning in 1972. The issue measures analyzed in the next chapter also were used extensively beginning in the 1970s. Therefore,

in this and the subsequent two chapters we restrict out attention to the last three elections. We also include only those respondents from whom a postelection survey was obtained. For more details on measures used in Chapter 7, see Morris P. Fiorina, *Retrospective Voting in American National Elections* (New Haven: Yale University Press, 1981).

2. See Everett Carll Ladd, "The Brittle Mandate: Electoral Dealignment and the 1980 Presidential Election," *Political Science Quarterly* 96 (Spring 1981): 1-25; and Kathleen A. Frankovic, "Public Opinion Trends," in *The Election of 1980: Reports and Interpretations,* Gerald M. Pomper with colleagues (Chatham, N.J.: Chatham House, 1981), pp. 97-118.

3. Each respondent in the postelection survey is asked the question in the text and is encouraged to give up to three responses. Then, if more than one problem is raised, the respondent is asked which one is the single most important. The responses in Table 6-1 are from this latter question. Looking at the full array of as many as three responses, we find a broader range of alternatives suggested, yet the same outlines are apparent.

4. Richard M. Scammon and Ben J. Wattenberg, *The Real Majority* (New York: Coward, McCann & Georghegan, 1971).

5. The idea that the status quo policy was, on balance, too "liberal" is studied closely in Warren E. Miller, "Policy Directions and Presidential Leadership: Alternative Interpretations of the 1980 Presidential Election" (Paper delivered at the annual meeting of the American Political Science Association, New York, New York, September 3-6, 1981).

6. In calculating this measure, the four-point abortion and five-point tax cut scales were recalibrated as seven-point scales. Scales for which a low number was a conservative response (see Table 6-4) were "reflected" to reverse the direction of the scoring.

7. Other scholars document this finding. See Ladd, "The Brittle Mandate" and Frankovic, "Public Opinion Trends."

8. The question tapping party placements changed in 1980. Instead of asking respondents to place "Democrats" and "Republicans," they were asked to place their perceptions of the "Democratic Party" and "Republican Party." This change in format could affect where people placed the parties.

9. Angus Campbell, Philip E. Converse, Warren E. Miller, and Donald E. Stokes, *The American Voter* (New York: John Wiley & Sons, 1960), pp. 168-187.

10. This criterion and those following are critiqued by Fiorina in *Retrospective Voting.* Although many scholars have interpreted failure to meet this criterion as akin to failing a "test," he argues that the criteria imply no such thing. We agree. Failure to satisfy these criteria in no way impugns the citizen. The SRC-CPS interviewers did not ask those who failed to place themselves on an issue scale where they thought the candidates stood. Therefore, by definition, those who "failed" to meet the first criterion were not able to meet any of the remaining ones.

11. The abortion scale had four options, the tax cut scale five. Since these scales had fewer points, there was less room for discrimination between options. Thus, the average ability to see a difference might be affected. Therefore, we also included the averages for the seven other scales that contained a full seven points.

12. While this evidence suggests that most people *claim* to have issue preferences, it does not demonstrate that they *do.* For example, evidence indicates that some use the midpoint of the scale (4) as a means of answering the question even if they have ill-formed preferences. See John H. Aldrich,

Richard G. Niemi, George Rabinowitz, and David W. Rohde, "The Measurement of Public Opinion about Public Policy: A Report on Some New Issue Question Formats," *American Journal of Political Science,* forthcoming 1982.

13. The Vietnam war issue in 1968 and 1972 is a good illustration. In 1968, there was relatively little difference between Humphrey and Nixon on this issue, certainly in comparison to the strong anti-war stance of McGovern and the middle ground position of Nixon in 1972. Benjamin I. Page and Richard A. Brody documented the startling extent of confusion in perceptions on Vietnam in 1968 and the lack of voting on this issue even though many were concerned about the war. See "Policy Voting and the Electoral Process: The Vietnam War Issue," *American Political Science Review* 66 (September 1972): 979-995. In 1972, more than two-thirds of the public met all four criteria on this issue; candidate choice was strongly related to candidates' positions on this issue. About three-quarters of the public voted for the closer candidate, even if they failed to meet the remaining criteria besides self placement.

14. Fiorina, *Retrospective Voting.*

15. The term "apparent issue voting" is used to emphasize several points. First, there are too many factors involved to infer that closeness to a candidate on any one issue was the cause of the vote choice. In fact, the issue similarity might have been purely coincidental. Second, we use the median perceptions of the candidates rather than the individual's own reported perceptions. Third, there is a possibility of "rationalization." A voter may have decided to support, say, Reagan for entirely other reasons and may also have altered his/her own issue preference to align more closely with Reagan's positions (so-called "conversion") or have misperceived Reagan's position to be closer to the voter's preference (so-called "projection" of one's own beliefs to the candidate). See Richard A. Brody and Benjamin I. Page, "Comment: The Assessment of Policy Voting," *American Political Science Review* 66 (June 1972): 450-458. See also Page and Brody, "Policy Voting."

16. Since we are comparing self placement to the median perceptions of the candidate positions in the sample, we are able to calculate which candidate was closer to the voter, even if the voter did not report a perception of Carter or Reagan.

17. Obviously, this procedure counts every issue as equal in importance to every other issue. It also assumes that all that matters is that the voter is closer to the candidate; how much closer is not considered. Finally, it assumes that a voter with nine issue comparisons, all of them favoring one candidate, is more likely to support that candidate than a voter able to make only three comparisons, all of them also favoring that candidate.

18. Scores of +6, +7, +8, and +9 were called strongly Republican, while similar negative scores were called strongly Democratic. Scores of +4 and +5 were called moderately Republican, while similar negative scores were called moderately Democratic. Scores of +2 and +3 were called slightly Republican, while similar negative scores were called slightly Democratic. Scores of +1, 0, and −1 were called neutral.

7

Presidential Performance and Candidate Choice

Ronald Reagan's claim of a mandate for his policies is not well supported. As we have seen, there was a strong relationship between policy preferences and the choice of candidates, but strong support for precisely the platform Reagan advanced in his campaign was lacking. Most voters were torn between the offerings of the two major-party contenders and, on balance, favored Reagan's positions only slightly more than Jimmy Carter's.

To what extent did the 1980 vote represent a rejection of Carter's performance in office? Everett Carll Ladd describes Reagan's mandate as "brittle"—easily broken if he fails to quell inflation and high interest rates, or if he solves these problems only at the expense of high unemployment.[1] But even if negative evaluations of Carter were the sole source of Reagan's victory, the possibility of an "enduring" rather than a "brittle" mandate remains. Many voters did endorse Reagan's programs as well as reject Carter's conduct in office. And if Reagan produces the desired set of results, or even makes progress toward them, many might shift to endorse his methods and programs. The underlying question here is how much the public cares about outcomes, the ends of the programs candidates propose, and how much they care about the means necessary to achieve them. It is to this question we now turn.

WHAT IS "RETROSPECTIVE" VOTING?

An individual who votes against the incumbent because the incumbent failed, in the voter's opinion, to perform adequately is said to have cast a "retrospective" vote. Retrospective voting is, in effect, a referendum on the incumbent. Either the president did well during the last four years and, therefore, should be returned to office, or he performed poorly and the "rascal" should be "thrown out." V. O. Key, Jr., popularized this argument by suggesting that the voter might be a "rational god of vengeance and of reward." [2] Retrospective voting is possible only as long as the candidate of one party is identified with the actions taken by the incumbent. Obviously, the incumbent himself cannot escape such evaluations, and the incumbent vice president is often identified with the administration's performance. In 17 of the 21 presidential elections during this century (all but 1908, 1920, 1928, and 1952), an incumbent president or vice president stood for election. Since 1956, every election has provided an opportunity for voters to play the "rational god" and reward or punish the incumbent. This type of voter is outcome oriented and evaluates only the incumbent. Moreover, a "pure" retrospective voter evaluates what has been done, not what might be done.

Anthony Downs presents a different view of retrospective voting.[3] He argues that voters can look to the past to understand what an incumbent will do in the future. According to Downs, parties are basically consistent in their goals, methods, and ideologies over time. Therefore, past performance by both parties' candidates may prove relevant for projections about their conduct. Because it takes time and effort to evaluate candidates' campaign promises, it is cheaper, easier, and even less risky to use the past results of the incumbent to infer that administration's positions for the next four years. Downs emphasizes that retrospective evaluations of the incumbent (and possibly the party of the challenger) are used to make comparisons between or among the alternatives. Key's view is that of a retrospective referendum of the incumbent alone. Downs's view also emphasizes evaluating past performance as a guide to the future.

A final view of retrospective voting is that recently advanced by Morris P. Fiorina. In many respects, his effort is an elaboration and extension of the Downsian perspective. He claims that "citizens monitor party promises and performances over time, encapsulate their observations in a summary judgment termed 'party identification,' and rely on this core of previous experience when they assign responsibility for current societal conditions and evaluate ambigious platforms designed to deal with uncertain futures." [4]

Retrospective policy voting and the positional policy voting analyzed in the previous chapter differ significantly. How concerned are people with societal outcomes, and how concerned are they about the means to achieve desired outcomes? Almost everyone prefers, say, lower inflation rates to higher ones, and all candidates pledge to lower inflation. The disagreement lies in the means to do so. The real question, then, is do voters care, indeed are they even willing or able to judge, how to achieve this desired goal? Or, do they look at high unemployment in 1976 and say, "Let's try something else"? Do they look at the high inflation rate in 1980 and say, "We tried Carter's approach for four years. It failed. Let's try something else again"?

Economic policies and foreign affairs issues are often evaluated in this way and share these characteristics. First, the outcomes are clear and often affect individuals directly: unemployment, interest rates, and/or inflation are high; the U.S. is at war or at peace; the world is stable or unstable. Second, there is often near consensus on what the desired outcomes are: low unemployment, inflation, and interest rates; peace; world stability. Third, the means to achieve these ends are remarkably complex. Information is ambiguous, hard to come by and evaluate, and possibly even classified. Finally, experts in the field as well as candidates and other politicians disagree over the connection between programmatic means and the ends that would result from following the various alternative programs.

Peace and prosperity, therefore, differ sharply from policy areas in which there is vigorous disagreement over ends. The abortion issue is a prominent example, gun control another. On still other issues, people value means as well as ends. The classic cases often ask whether or not it is appropriate for government to take action at all. For instance, should the government provide national health insurance? Here, few disagree with the ends of health protection, but they do disagree over the means to achieve that protection. Or should the government in Washington guarantee a job and a good standard of living for all citizens? Civil rights provides still other examples: Does affirmative action risk "reverse discrimination," and, if so, is this acceptable or not? Will busing achieve integrated schools? The busing controversy illustrates the frequent case in which the means are valued (often negatively) as much as ends in and of themselves. Indeed, they may be seen as ends in many cases. Furthermore, the choice of means involves some of the basic philosophic and ideological differences that have divided Republican from Democrat for decades.[5]

As we saw in Table 6-1, between 1972 and 1980 the problems that concerned the electorate changed. After 1972 concern about social issues declined, while concern about economic issues rose. Since economic success is relatively easy to evaluate, we might expect more retrospective voting in 1976 and 1980 than in 1972.

Two basic conditions are necessary for retrospective evaluations. First, the individual must connect his or her concern (for example, a high inflation rate) with the incumbent and evaluate the incumbent's handling of policy germane to that concern. Second, the individual (especially in the Downs-Fiorina view) must compare that evaluation with what he or she believes the opponent or opponents would do. As to the first point, one might blame OPEC, business, consumers, or a profligate Congress for high inflation—or even believe that it is totally beyond anyone's control. If so, the incumbent president might be spared the wrath of vengeance. If not, the incumbent might be blamed wholly or only in part. As to the second point, even if a voter holds Carter responsible for high inflation, that voter might examine Reagan's programs and decide they would fare no better than Carter's and possibly even be worse.[6]

Finally, any given retrospective evaluation is but one of many conceivable factors involved in voting. The voter could decide, for example, that Carter's economic performance was alright, but vote against him because of his purportedly erratic foreign policy. We will now examine some summary retrospective evaluations, see what elements appear to go into that summary, and then study the impact of these evaluations on behavior.

EVALUATIONS OF GOVERNMENTAL PERFORMANCE

What do you consider the "most important problem" facing the country, and how do you feel the "government in Washington" has been handling this concern? Table 7-1 compares evaluations of governmental performance on most important problem in 1972, 1976, and 1980. Although the wording of the question was slightly different in 1972, the evaluation of governmental response was clearly more favorable that year. In 1976, the government was evaluated poorly, and by 1980, the evaluations were even worse. Six out of 10 thought the government was doing a poor job.[7]

If the voter is a "rational god of vengeance," we would expect a strong relationship between the evaluation of governmental performance and the vote. Such is indeed the case for all three elections, as can be seen in Table 7-1B. In 1980, Carter picked up less than a third of the major-party vote from the majority who thought the government had done poorly on the most important problem, half the vote of those who thought the government did only a fair job, and more than four out of five of the few who thought a good job had been done.[8] A similar pattern occurred in 1976. While evaluations of governmental performance were related to voting choices in 1972, Richard M. Nixon received nearly half the vote among those who thought the government was not at all helpful.[9]

According to Downs and Fiorina, it is important to measure not only how one evaluates the incumbent, but also how that evaluation compares with the evaluation of the opponent. Table 7-2 confirms their

Table 7-1 Evaluation of Governmental Performance on Most Important Problem and Major-Party Vote, 1972-1980

A. Evaluation of Governmental Performance on Most Important Problem

Government is Being	*1972*[1]	*Government is Doing*	*1976*	*1980*
Very Helpful	12%	Good Job	8%	4%
Somewhat Helpful	58	Only Fair Job	46	35
Not Helpful at All	30	Poor Job	46	61
Total percent	100%		100%	100%
(Number)	(993)		(2156)[2]	(1319)

B. Percentage of Major-Party Vote for Incumbent

	1972[1]		*1976*		*1980*	
Government is Being/Doing	Nixon	(N)	Ford	(N)[2]	Carter	(N)
Very Helpful/Good Job	85%	(91)	72%	(128)	81%	(43)
Somewhat Helpful/						
Only Fair Job	69%	(392)	53%	(695)	50%	(289)
Not Helpful/Poor Job	46%	(209)	39%	(684)	30%	(505)

[1] These questions were asked of a randomly selected half of the sample in 1972.
[2] Weighted *N*s.

NOTE: Numbers in parentheses are the totals upon which percentages are based.

view that restrospective evaluations are useful for projective comparisons. Table 7-2A shows the percentages of the electorate who felt that one party or the other would better handle the most important problem. This question is clearly future oriented, but it is also retrospective since it does not rely on evaluations of specific policies. A judgment about which party will perform better, therefore, rests partly on evaluations of past performance. About half the respondents in all three elections thought neither party would be better.

Moreover, by comparing Table 7-1A and 7-2A, we can see that nearly three times as many respondents in 1980 thought the Democratic party would be better than thought the government had done a good job on this problem. Similarly, in 1972 and 1976 more thought the incumbent party would be better than thought the incumbent government had performed well. Clearly, more is going on here than just retrospective evaluations of the V. O. Key sort. The comparative evaluations of the two parties' expected performance, while strongly related to the evaluation of the performance of the incumbent, differs from that evaluation, per se.

As Table 7-2B reveals, the relationship between the party seen as better on the most important problem and the major-party vote is very strong—stronger than just retrospective evaluations alone. (See Table 7-1B.) In all three elections, the Republican candidate received overwhelming support from those who thought the Republican party would handle the most important problem better, and even in 1972, McGovern gained three out of four votes among those who thought the Democrats would do best.[10]

The data presented in Tables 7-1 and 7-2 have two limitations. First, the problems cited by people as most important vary from respondent to respondent (a virtue as well as a problem), and some of the problems cited are less clearly retrospective than others. Comparability and interpretability problems thereby are raised. Second, the referent is to the "government in Washington" and not to the incumbent president in the first question and to the "party" and not to the candidate in the second question. Fortunately, recent surveys have included an increasing number of evaluations of the incumbent president, per se. We will build our case from the beginning, however, and focus first on economic issues.

Table 7-2 Evaluation of Party Seen as Better on Most Important Problem and Major-Party Vote, 1972-1980

A. Distribution of Responses on Party Better on Most Important Problem

Party Better	1972[1]	1976	1980
Republican	28%	14%	43%
No Difference	46	50	46
Democratic	26	37	11
Total percent	100%	101%	100%
(Number)	(931)	(2054)	(1251)

B. Percentage of Major-Party Voters Who Voted Democratic for President

Party Better	1972	(N)[1]	1976	(N)[2]	1980	(N)
Republican	6%	(207)	4%	(231)	11%	(320)
No Difference	42%	(275)	35%	(673)	57%	(391)
Democratic	75%	(180)	90%	(565)	86%	(93)

[1] These questions were asked of a randomly selected half sample in 1972.
[2] Weighted Ns.

NOTE: Numbers in parentheses are the totals upon which percentages are based.

ECONOMIC EVALUATIONS AND THE
VOTE FOR THE INCUMBENT

Economic issues have received greater attention as retrospective-type issues than any other. The impact of economic conditions on congressional and presidential elections has been studied extensively.[11] Popular evaluations of presidential effectiveness, John E. Mueller points out, are strongly influenced by the economy.[12] Edward R. Tufte suggests that because the incumbent realizes his fate may hinge on the performance of the economy, he may attempt to manipulate it, leading to what is known as the "political business cycle."[13] Perhaps as a consequence of this research, as well as the increasing dominance of economic problems in politics, the SRC-CPS surveys now measure perceptions about the economy and their political relevance.

If people are concerned about outcomes—especially those that affect them directly—a good starting point is to find out whether they consider themselves to be financially better off this year than last. Table 7-3 presents the distribution of responses. Although each year about one-third of the sample felt better off, those who felt worse off increased from 23 percent in 1972, to 31 percent in 1976, to 42 percent in 1980. This moderate drop in the average person's perception of his or her financial status is in sharp contrast to evaluations of the strength of the economy as a whole. In 1980 (the only survey with these questions), respondents were asked whether or not the economy had gotten better during the last year. Fully 84 percent said it had become worse, 13 percent said it was about the same, while barely 4 percent said it had gotten better. Clearly, perceptions of personal and aggregate financial conditions are quite different; perceptions of the nation's economy are much bleaker than perceptions of individual family finances.

The next step in the chain of reasoning is simple. Do people feel anything can be done about the economy? In 1980, 77 percent said that "something could be done about rising prices," 23 percent said nothing could be done. The comparable figures for unemployment are 81 percent yes, 19 percent no. Clearly, people felt that some of the economic outcomes could be affected, but this does not mean necessarily that they thought the government (or, specifically, the president) was to blame for poor economic conditions.

The SRC-CPS measured evaluations of governmental performance differently in all three of the last presidential election years, as Table 7-4 reveals. Respondents were asked to evaluate the government's performance on inflation and unemployment together in 1972 and separately in 1976 and 1980. Moreover, in 1980 the question shifts from governmental performance to approval of Carter's handling of these two economic outcomes.

Table 7-3 Distribution of Responses to Changes in Personal Financial Situation, 1972-1980

"Would you say that you (and your family here) are better off or worse off financially than you were a year ago?"	1972[1]	1976	1980
Better Now	36%	34%	33%
Same	42	35	25
Worse Now	23	31	42
Total percent	101%	100%	100%
(Number)	(955)	(2828)[2]	(1393)

[1] These questions were asked of a randomly selected half sample in 1972.
[2] Weighted N.

A majority of respondents in 1972 thought the government's performance on inflation and unemployment was only fair, while the rest were almost evenly divided between a favorable and an unfavorable evaluation. Four years later, the great majority remained rather neutral in their evaluations. However, many more of the remainder were negative than were positive. By 1980, almost two-thirds of the sample thought Carter had done a poor job on both inflation and unemployment. Even with the different questions asked, the summary seems clear. The evaluations of the incumbent's handling of the economy were not very positive in 1972, but were worse in 1976, and much worse in 1980.

The figures in Table 7-4B show a strong relationship between evaluations of the government's success in managing the economy and choices voters made between the two major-party candidates. Perhaps, then, the incumbents were defeated in 1976 and 1980 because they failed to produce desired outcomes, regardless of their intentions or the means they employed in their attempts to manage the economy.

An analysis of this retrospective voting, however, doesn't explain the puzzling 1972 results. Certainly, the data suggest that Nixon was seen as having done better than his successors. And yet, why did so many feel that the government had done only a fair job and still vote overwhelmingly to return the incumbent? Was it, perhaps, that the voters believed McGovern would do no better, maybe even worse? Partly so. In 1972, the SRC-CPS survey asked which party would better handle inflation and unemployment, although it did not differentiate between the two problems. The percentages seeing one or the other party as better, or saying the two parties would handle the economy about the same, are reported in the left-hand column of Table 7-5A. In 1976 and 1980, respondents were asked separate questions about which party would better handle inflation and which would better handle unemployment. The responses to the two questions are combined in the other two columns of Table 7-5A.

In 1972, 1976, and 1980, most felt that the two parties would handle the economy about equally. Of the remainder of respondents in 1972, however, more than twice as many thought the Republican party would be better. In 1976, opinion favored the Democratic party by better than a two-to-one ratio—just the reverse of 1972. The pattern shifted again in 1980; the Republican party was advantaged by better than three-to-two.[14]

While these questions about which party would handle the economy better are future oriented, we see them as basically retrospective in the way that Downs and Fiorina define retrospective voting. Respon-

Table 7-4 Combined Evaluations of Governmental Performance on Economic Outcomes, 1972-1980

A. Distribution of Responses to Governmental Performance on Inflation and Unemployment

	Governmental Performance			*Approval of Carter's Performance*	
	1972[1]		*1976*	*1980*	
Good	22%	Good on Both	5%	Approval on Both	18%
		Good on One, Fair on One	10		
Only Fair	59	Fair on Both; or Good on One, Poor on Other	45	Approve on One, Disapprove on Other	17
Poor	19	Poor on One, Fair on One	21	Disapprove on Both	65
		Poor on Both	18		
Total percent	100%		99%		100%
(Number)	(941)		(2664)[2]		(1097)

B. Percentage of Major-Party Voters Who Voted Democratic for President

1972	(N)[1]	*1976*	(N)[2]	*1980*	(N)
Good	9% (149)	Good on Both	13% (75)	Approve on Both	88% (130)
		Good, Fair	24% (172)		
Only Fair	32% (401)	Fair on Both or Good/Poor	43% (688)	Mixed	60% (114)
Poor	70% (122)	Poor, Fair	64% (317)	Disapprove on Both	23% (451)
		Poor on Both	86% (280)		

[1] Question was asked of a randomly selected half sample in 1972.
[2] Weighted Ns.

NOTE: Numbers in parentheses are the totals upon which percentages are based.

Table 7-5   Distribution of Responses and Major-Party Vote by Which Party Would Better Handle Inflation and Unemployment, 1972-1980

A. Distribution of Responses

Which Party Would Better Handle Inflation and Unemployment Combined 1972[1]		Which Party Would Better Handle Inflation and Which Unemployment	1976	1980
Republicans	31%	Republicans on both concerns	8%	21%
		Republicans on one, same by both on other	7	12
Same by both	54	Same by both on both concerns, or Republicans on one, Democrats on other	46	47
		Democrats on one, same by both on other	15	10
Democrats	15	Democrats on both concerns	23	10
Total percent	100%		99%	100%
(Number)	(930)		(2497)[2]	(1275)

B. Percentage of Major-Party Voters Who Voted Democratic

	1972[1] (N)		1976 (N)[2]	1980 (N)
Republicans	9% (206)	Republicans on both concerns	3% (149)	3% (211)
		Republicans on one, same by both on other	7% (130)	14% (103)
Same by both	39% (358)	Same by both on both concerns, or Republicans on one, Democrats on other	36% (635)	53% (321)
		Democrats on one, same by both on other	82% (219)	87% (84)
Democrats	84% (100)	Democrats on both concerns	96% (330)	96% (97)

[1] Question asked of a randomly selected half sample in 1972.
[2] Weighted Ns.

NOTE: Numbers in parentheses are the totals upon which percentages are based.

dents are not asked about specific economic programs and in their comparisons of the parties probably draw heavily from the evaluations of the prior performance of these parties while in office. Downs argued, after all, that prior performance is a reliable guide to the future.

In any event, as Table 7-5B shows, the comparative evaluation of parties on these two concerns was very closely related to voter choice. If we consider the middle category as neutral, 9 out of 10 major-party voters who favored one party over the other voted consistently with that preference in all three elections. Clearly, this relationship between comparative evaluation of anticipated economic performance and choice of major-party candidates is powerful, so powerful that, except for the middle category, it overwhelms all else. Those who fell in the middle category split their votes much more evenly than those who favored one party. In all three elections, the incumbent did somewhat better in that category, which indicates a tendency to stay with the incumbent unless the opponent appears to be able to do better. The similarities between comparative assessment and voter choice in each election suggest that the very different outcomes in 1972, 1976, and 1980 must be attributed to the behavior of the relatively constant proportion of neutrals and to the wide swings in perceptions among the rest about which party appears to be the better one for handling the economy.

OTHER RETROSPECTIVE EVALUATIONS

Even though the economy has dominated the concerns of the electorate in recent years, other concerns have been voiced that are consistent with the retrospective view of voting behavior. Respondents in several surveys were asked whether there is a greater chance of war now than in the last few years (or a greater chance of an even bigger war during the Vietnam and Korean eras). They also were asked which party is better at avoiding war (or a bigger war). The relationships of these measures to voting behavior are very similar to those of the economic variables.[15] The retrospective evaluation is clearly related to the vote, but the comparative assessment of parties is related even more strongly. Thus, these questions about war show the same basic patterns as those about the economy.[16]

In 1980, respondents were asked to rate Carter's handling of the Iranian hostage seizure and the Soviet invasion of Afghanistan. A similarly specific question was asked about Ford in 1976: Should he have pardoned former President Nixon? As Table 7-6A demonstrates, opinion on the pardon, Iran, and Afghanistan questions was more evenly divided than on the economic outcomes questions. Forty-two percent agreed that Ford should have pardoned Nixon, 35 percent approved of Carter on Iran, and 49 percent thought his response to the Soviet invasion of Afghanistan was neither too weak nor too strong. As Table 7-6B shows, for all three questions, evaluation of the incumbent was related to voting choices, with relationships the weakest for the Afghanistan question.

Given the high degree of concern about Iran, the effect of this issue on the vote is significant. Opinion was running against Carter in the fall (unlike in the winter and spring), and most people voted in line with their evaluation of him on this issue. Clearly, Iran hurt Carter's reelection chances.[17] While opinion was more evenly divided on Ford's pardon of Nixon, once again this act appears to have harmed his reelection bid. Given the closeness of his loss, the pardon might have been just enough to cost Ford the presidency.

Table 7-6   Distribution of Responses and Major-Party Vote on Various Retrospective Issues, 1976, 1980

A. Distribution of Responses

1976		*1980*		*1980*	
Should Ford have pardoned Nixon?		Do you approve of Carter's handling of the Iranian hostage crisis?		How has Carter responded to the invasion of Afghanistan?	
Yes	42%	Approve	35%	About Right	49%
No	58	Disapprove	65	Too Strongly	5
				Not Enough	47
Total percent	100%		100%		101%
(Number)	(2579)[1]		(1301)		(1306)

B. Percentage of Major-Party Voters Who Voted for Carter

Should Ford have pardoned Nixon?			Do you approve of Carter's handling of the Iranian hostage Crisis?			How has Carter responded to the invasion of Afghanistan?		
Yes	24%	(667)[1]	Approve	75%	(312)	About Right	60%	(389)
No	75%	(830)[1]	Disapprove	24%	(515)	Too Strongly	42%	(33)
						Not enough	27%	(403)

[1] Weighted *N*s.

NOTE: Numbers in parentheses are totals upon which percentages are based.

EVALUATIONS OF THE INCUMBENT

Thus far we have considered two kinds of retrospective evaluations. Personal effects of social outcomes (one's financial status this year compared to last, for example) and perceptions of these outcomes in general can be understood as "simple retrospective evaluations," according to Fiorina. Specific evaluations and comparisons of the president, government, and the handling of these outcomes by political parties are "mediated retrospective evaluations"—evaluations mediated through perceptions of political actors and institutions.[18]

As we have seen, the more politically "mediated" the question, the more closely responses align with voting behavior. Perhaps the ultimate in mediated evaluations is the so-called (and misnamed) "presidential popularity" question: "Do you approve or disapprove of the way [the incumbent] is handling his job as President?" From a retrospective voting standpoint, this evaluation is a summary of all aspects of the last term in office. Table 7-7 reports the distribution of these evaluations and their relationship to major-party voting for the last three elections.

As can be seen in Table 7-7A, the Republican incumbents in 1972 and 1976 enjoyed widespread approval whereas only four in ten approved of Carter's handling of the job. Carter's dilemma is even clearer if we look at Table 7-7B, in which the very strong relationship to the vote is evident. Like previous incumbents, Carter held the support of those who approved. Indeed, if anything, he did as well among approvers and better among disapprovers than previous incumbents. There were just too few who approved. Ford, in 1976, was the anomaly. A clear majority approved of his job, yet he was unable to hold that support as well as the other incumbents, and he received negligible support from the disapprovers.

If presidential approval does stand as a summary of other, more specific evaluations, then it ought to be strongly related to those evaluations. It is. For example, in 1980, 86 percent of those who

Table 7-7 Distribution of Responses and Major-Party Vote on President's Handling of Job Measure, 1972-1980

A. Distribution of Responses

Do you approve or disapprove of the way [the incumbent] is handling his job as president?	Election Year		
	1972[1]	*1976*	*1980*
Approve	71%	63%	41%
Disapprove	29	37	59
Total percent	100%	100%	100%
(Number)	(1215)	(2439)[2]	(1279)

B. Percentage of Major-Party Voters Who Voted for the Incumbent for President

Do you approve or disapprove of the way [the incumbent] is handling his job as president?	Election Year					
	1972	(N)[1]	*1976*	(N)[2]	*1980*	(N)
Approve	83%	(553)	74%	(935)	81%	(315)
Disapprove	14%	(203)	9%	(522)	18%	(491)

[1] Presidential approval question was asked of a randomly selected half sample in 1972.
[2] Weighted *N*s.
NOTE: Numbers in parentheses are the totals upon which percentages are based.

approved of Carter in general approved of his handling of inflation in particular. And only 24 percent of those who disapproved of Carter's incumbency approved of his handling of inflation. In other words, if you approved of Carter's presidency in general, you also were very likely to approve of his incumbency in particular areas, while if you disapproved in general, you were quite likely to disapprove of the particulars. There are similarly strong relationships between presidential approval and evaluation of governmental performance on the most important problem and between presidential approval and the party seen as better at handling that problem. Finally, the same type of relationships can be produced for 1972 and 1976. In sum, presidential "popularity" serves as a summary of respondents' retrospective evaluations and comparative assessments.

CONCLUSION

Our evidence is strong; retrospective voting appears to be widespread. Moreover, the evidence is clearly on the side of the Downs-Fiorina view. Retrospective evaluations appear to be used to make comparative judgments. Presumably, voters find it easier, less costly, and less risky to evaluate the incumbent on what he has done in the past than on his promises for the future. And yet, that evaluation is not used as a referendum, but for comparisons. When the incumbent's performance in 1976 and 1980 was compared with the anticipated performance of the opponent, most felt that the incumbent had not done very well, but a surprisingly large number of those believed that his opponent would do worse.

What does retrospective voting imply about Reagan's "mandate" and a possible Republican majority for years to come? The answer, unfortunately, awaits two developments. How will Reagan's performance be seen in 1984? And how will the Democratic nominee, whomever that might be, be evaluated? If Reagan is seen as making progress on major concerns like the economy and does not preside over some new, major problem (e.g., threats to peace), he will be difficult to stop, and so might another Republican candidate. And yet, he could be stopped if a sufficiently attractive opponent emerges.

A second major question concerns how this view of retrospective evaluations for comparative projections compares to issue-based voting decisions. If voters were rational gods of "vengeance and of reward," they could be sharply distinguished from voters who were comparative weighers of campaign pledges. However, both retrospective and prospective voters make comparative assessments. The evaluation of the opponent presumably is the same under either view. Moreover, the "projective" issue questions are not clearly distinguishable from retrospective evaluations. For example, a voter's perception of Carter on defense spending may be informed by both what he said in the campaign and what he actually spent while in office.

Nonetheless, by pitting the retrospective against the prospective measures, we are able to get some sense of their relative contribution to major-party voting. We will use the best measure of each type of evaluation. Prospective voting will be tapped by our "balance of issues measure," developed in Chapter 6 and collapsed in Table 7-8 into five categories. This measure captures each respondent's preferences for the candidate offerings on nine spatial-type policy questions in both the 1976 and 1980 elections. To measure the impact of retrospective evaluations, we use the respondents' perceptions of which party would handle inflation and unemployment better, because this measure involves a comparative assessment of the two parties and focuses on the concerns that dominated the last two elections.

Table 7-8 compares the relative impact of prospective and retrospective evaluations. By reading across each row, we can see that in both 1976 and 1980, retrospective evaluations were always related to electoral choice regardless of prospective attitudes. When we read down each column, we can see that in both 1976 and 1980, prospective issue preferences appear to have no effect on candidate choice among respondents who have clearly pro-Democratic or clearly pro-Republican evaluations of party performance. In 1976, prospective evaluations were unrelated to voting choices among voters with slightly Republican retrospective evaluations, were weakly related among those who were slightly pro-Democratic, and were clearly related to candidate choice only among voters who were neutral in their retrospective comparisons. In 1980, prospective comparisons were related to voting choices among all three of these groups. On balance, prospective comparisons had a much more independent impact on voting choices in 1980 than in 1976. The retrospective comparisons had a strong and independent impact on voting choices in both elections.

We can summarize retrospective and prospective voting in the last three elections roughly as follows. In 1972, prospective-based comparisons were strongly related to the vote.[19] The impact of these positional type issues appears to be due to the electorate's perception of the clear differences between Nixon and McGovern and to the relative satisfaction with Nixon's performance in office. In 1976, the weakening economy concerned many, people were dissatisfied with Ford's performance, and the candidates' stands on the issues were not perceived as very distinctive. Thus, retrospective comparisons were more substantial than the prospective comparisons. In 1980, both measures were important, although retrospective evaluations appear somewhat more important. While the candidates were seen to promise very different policies,

Table 7-8 Percentage of Major-Party Voters Who Voted for Carter in 1976 and 1980, by Prospective and Retrospective Comparisons

Prospective-Based Comparisons[1]	Retrospective-Based Comparisons[2]					
	Clearly Democratic	Slightly Democratic	Neutral	Slightly Republican	Clearly Republican	Total
1976[3]						
Clearly Democratic	98% (49)	88% (26)	63% (39)	— (1)	— (4)	84% (119)
Slightly Democratic	98% (51)	87% (23)	46% (69)	7% (15)	— (1)	65% (159)
Neutral	96% (106)	81% (69)	38% (169)	7% (29)	0% (36)	55% (409)
Slightly Republican	96% (72)	79% (57)	35% (188)	13% (32)	6% (32)	49% (381)
Clearly Republican	94% (52)	77% (44)	23% (169)	4% (53)	4% (76)	32% (394)
Total	96% (330)	82% (219)	36% (634)	7% (130)	3% (149)	51% (1462)
1980						
Clearly Democratic	100% (17)	92% (13)	88% (17)	[3] (7)	— (3)	82% (57)
Slightly Democratic	94% (18)	[7] (9)	65% (40)	[2] (8)	0% (14)	58% (89)
Neutral	94% (31)	97% (29)	58% (126)	14% (40)	4% (74)	46% (300)
Slightly Republican	94% (17)	85% (20)	43% (84)	9% (22)	3% (65)	35% (208)
Clearly Republican	100% (14)	69% (13)	39% (54)	8% (26)	4% (55)	30% (162)
Total	96% (97)	87% (84)	53% (321)	15% (103)	3% (211)	44% (816)

[1] Prospective-based comparisons based on the balance of issues measures. The "clearly" category is formed by combining the "strongly" and "moderately" categories used in the last chapter.

[2] Based on the party better on inflation and on unemployment questions.

[3] Weighted Ns.

NOTE: Numbers in parentheses are the totals upon which percentages are based. Numbers in brackets are the number voting for Carter in cases where the total N is less than 10.

most voters had mixed feelings, supporting Reagan on some issues and Carter on others. Many voters leaned toward Reagan out of disenchantment with Carter's performance. In short, 1972 was a prospective voting election, 1976 was a retrospective-comparison based election, and 1980 was both.

What is the origin of retrospective-type comparisons? In part, they come from observations of real events. Certainly, the shifts from 1972 to 1980 in evaluations of the government's handling of economic issues are based in large part on the worsening U.S. economy. But voters may interpret real events—inflation and unemployment or foreign crises, for example—according to different criteria. As we shall see in the next chapter, partisan loyalties appear to influence both prospective and retrospective evaluations.

NOTES

1. Everett Carll Ladd, "The Brittle Mandate: Electoral Dealignment and the 1980 Presidential Election," *Political Science Quarterly* 96 (Spring 1981): 1-25. See also Kathleen A. Frankovic, "Public Opinion Trends," in *The Election of 1980: Reports and Interpretations,* Gerald M. Pomper with colleagues (Chatham, N.J.: Chatham House, 1981), pp. 97-118; and Warren E. Miller, "Policy Directions and Presidential Leadership: Alternative Interpretations of the 1980 Presidential Election" and Arthur H. Miller and Martin P. Wattenberg, "Policy and Performance Voting in the 1980 Election" (Papers delivered at the annual meeting of the American Political Science Association, New York, New York, September 3-6, 1981).
2. V. O. Key, Jr., *Politics, Parties, and Pressure Groups,* 5th ed. (New York: Thomas Y. Crowell Co., 1964), p. 568.
3. Anthony Downs, *An Economic Theory of Democracy* (New York: Harper & Row, 1957).
4. Morris P. Fiorina, *Retrospective Voting in American National Elections* (New Haven, Conn.: Yale University Press, 1981), p. 83.
5. See Benjamin I. Page, *Choices and Echoes in Presidential Elections: Rational Man and Electoral Democracy* (Chicago: Chicago University Press, 1978). He argues that "party cleavages" distinguish the two parties at the candidate and mass levels.
6. Carter and Democrats generally wanted to make Reagan's advocacy of supply-side economics a campaign issue. They tried to transform an evaluation of the incumbent into a comparison between alternatives by debating means as well as ends.
7. Such a negative evaluation is not surprising. After all, if you thought the government had done a good job with the problem, then it probably would not be your major concern.
8. Anderson received about 8 percent of the "only fair job" vote and about 10 percent of the "poor job" vote. None of his voters thought a good job had been done.
9. Nixon scored higher in each category than his counterparts in 1976 and 1980, possibly because of the different question formats and possibly because of other factors affecting behavior. As we will argue later, the 1972 election appears to have been less a pure "retrospective" election than those in 1976 and 1980.

10. These responses might be subject to "rationalization." For example, a Democrat in 1980 might have thought that Carter had done poorly but that Reagan would do worse—because the voter was a Democrat. Of course, the evaluation of the incumbent's performance may have been rationalized as well. For a discussion of rationalization by voters, see Richard A. Brody and Benjamin I. Page, "Comment: The Assessment of Policy Voting," *American Political Science Review* 66 (June 1972): 450-458.

11. See Gerald H. Kramer, "Short-Term Fluctuations in U.S. Voting Behavior, 1896-1964," *American Political Science Review* 65 (March 1971): 131-143; Morris P. Fiorina, "Economic Retrospective Voting in American National Elections: A Micro-Analysis," *American Journal of Political Science* 22 (May 1978): 426-443; Fiorina, *Retrospective Voting*; and M. Stephen Weatherford, "Economic Conditions and Electoral Outcomes: Class Differences in the Political Response to Recession," *American Journal of Political Science* 22 (November 1978): 917-938.

12. John E. Mueller, *War, Presidents and Public Opinion* (New York: John Wiley & Sons, 1973).

13. Edward R. Tufte, *Political Control of the Economy* (Princeton, N.J.: Princeton University Press, 1978).

14. A close relationship exists between approval of governmental performance and view of which party is likely to do better on that problem. Those who thought the incumbent had done well are much more likely to say his party would be better in handling that concern than are those who thought the incumbent had done poorly. Nonetheless, as the overall distribution of responses makes clear, the relationship is less than perfect. In 1980, for example, more thought the Democrats would handle inflation better than approved of Carter's handling of inflation, and such examples are found across policy domains and in all elections.

15. Fiorina, *Retrospective Voting*. Fiorina also shows that these variables have an effect on the vote independent of the economic measures.

16. In 1980, survey respondents were asked, "Which party would better handle keeping us out of war in the next four years?" Twenty-eight percent said the Democrats, 18 percent the Republicans, and 54 percent said neither would be better. This variable was strongly related to the vote. Of the major-party voters, Carter received 80 percent saying Democrats, 39 percent saying "same", and only 10 percent saying Republicans would do better.

17. Pollsters and others speculated that the last-minute surge to Reagan, making a predicted close race one-sided, was due to the last-minute machinations over the Iranian hostage crisis. Our data do not speak to the question of this last minute surge, but are not inconsistent with this view.

18. Fiorina, *Retrospective Voting*.

19. Table 7-8 does not include data for 1972 because the single economic comparison question is not wholly comparable. Although we don't have as good a set of retrospective measures for 1972 as for 1976 and 1980, the prospective measures appear more dominant in 1972 than in the other elections.

8

Party Loyalties, an Independent Candidate, and the Vote

Political parties are central institutions in our political and electoral system. Most citizens identify with a political party, and this identification influences their political attitudes and, ultimately, their behavior. In the fifties and sixties the authors of *The American Voter* along with other scholars began to emphasize the importance of party loyalties.[1] Although today few would deny that partisanship is central to political attitudes and behavior, many scholars have begun to question the interpretation of the evidence gathered during the last three decades. Indeed, what is party identification, and how does it actually structure other attitudes and behavior? We will try and answer these questions before examining the role that party identification played in the 1980 presidential election.

PARTY IDENTIFICATION: THE STANDARD VIEW

According to the authors of *The American Voter*, party identification is "the individual's affective orientation to an important group-object in his environment," in this case the political party.[2] In other words, an individual sees that there are two major political parties that play significant roles in elections and develops an affinity for one of them. Most Americans develop a liking for either the Republican or Democratic party. The remainder are mostly Independents, who are not only unattached to a party, but also relatively unattached to politics in general.[3] They are less interested, informed, and active than their attached peers. Partisanship is, therefore, an evaluation of the two parties, but its implications extend to a wider variety of political phenomena. Angus Campbell and his colleagues measured partisanship simply by asking with which party an individual identifies and how strongly that identification is held.[4] If the individual does not identify with either party, they may "lean" towards a party or, if not, be "purely" independent. The small percentage who could not relate to the party identification questions were labeled "apolitical."

Partisan identification in this view becomes an attachment or loyalty not unlike that observed between the individual and other groups or organizations in society, such as a religious body, social class, or even a favorite ball team. As with loyalties to many of these groups, partisan affiliation often begins early. One of the first political attitudes children develop is party identification, and it develops well before they acquire policy preferences and many other political orientations. Furthermore, as with other group loyalties, once an attachment to a party develops, it tends to endure. Some people do switch parties, of course, but they usually do so only if their social situation changes, if there is an issue of overriding concern that sways their loyalties, or if the political parties themselves change substantially.

Party identification, then, stands as a base or core orientation to electoral politics. It is often formed at an early age and endures for most people throughout their entire lives. Once formed, this core, predicated on a general evaluation of the two parties, affects many other specific orientations. Democratic loyalists tend to evaluate Democratic candidates and officeholders more highly than do Republicans, and vice versa. In effect, one is predisposed to evaluate the promise and the performance of one's party leaders relatively higher. It follows, therefore, that Democrats are more likely to vote for Democratic candidates than are Republicans and vice versa.

PARTY IDENTIFICATION: AN ALTERNATIVE VIEW

In *The Responsible Electorate* published in 1966, V. O. Key, Jr., argued that party loyalites contributed to electoral inertia with many partisans voting as "standpatters" from election to election.[5] That is, in the absence of any information to the contrary, or if the attractions and disadvantages of the candidates are fairly evenly balanced, partisans are expected to vote consistently with their loyalty to a political party. In recent years, scholars have re-examined the reasons for such behavior. In this new view, a citizen has a standing decision to vote for the Democratic nominee because of the past positions of Democrats compared to Republicans and because of their comparative past performances while in office. In short, this view of party identification presumes that it is a "running tally" of past experience (mostly in terms of policy and performance), a sort of summary expression of one's political memory.[6]

Furthermore, when in doubt about what, say, a Democratic candidate is likely to do on civil rights in comparison to the Republican opponent, it is reasonable to assume the Democrat would be more liberal than the Republican—at least unless the candidate indicates otherwise. Since the political parties tend to be consistent on the basic historical policy cleavages for lengthy periods of time, summary judgments of parties and their typical candidates will not change radically or often.[7] As a result, one's running tally serves as a good first approximation, changes rarely, and can be an excellent device for saving time that would be spent gathering information in the absence of this "memory."

Many of the major findings used in support of the conventional interpretation of party identification are completely consistent with this more policy-oriented view. We do not have the evidence to assert one view as superior to the other. Indeed, the two interpretations are not mutually exclusive and to choose between them calls for a very different sort of empirical research than is available at the present time. What is important is that, while party identification can be understood differently, both views emphasize the central role of party identification in shaping voters' decisions.

PARTY IDENTIFICATION IN THE ELECTORATE

If partisan identification is a fundamental orientation for most citizens, then the distribution of party loyalties among the electorate is of crucial importance. As Table 8-1 shows, the Democratic party enjoyed a clear edge in loyalty over the Republican party in 1980. Before

Table 8-1 Party Identification, 1980

Party Identification	Pre-election Survey	Postelection Survey
Strong Democrat	18%	17%
Weak Democrat	24	24
Independent, Leans Democratic	12	11
Independent, No Partisan Leanings	13	12
Independent, Leans Republican	10	12
Weak Republican	14	14
Strong Republican	9	10
Total percent	100%	100%
(Number)	(1577)	(1376)
Apolitical	2	2
(Number)	(35)	(26)

the election, there were twice as many strong Democrats as strong Republicans. If we compare respondents who claim to be partisans (strong plus weak party identifiers), we see that the Democratic advantage is reduced somewhat. If Independents who lean toward a party are assumed to have some partisan loyalties, the Democratic advantage is further reduced, but the Democrats still enjoy a three-to-two advantage.

As we saw in Chapter 5, the fundamental social division in U.S. electoral politics is race. This division is sharply reflected in partisan affiliations. In Table 8-2 we report the identification of whites between 1952 and 1980, while in Table 8-3 we report the affiliation of blacks. Not only are the racial divisions apparent in these tables, but so is the relative stability of this core orientation (or running tally of past experiences), especially among white Americans.

Let us look first at the remarkable stability of partisanship among whites. From 1952 to 1964—what Philip E. Converse refers to as the "steady-state" period—the distribution of partisan loyalties changed very little.[8] Less than 10 percent were "pure" Independents, and about 15 percent were Independents who "leaned" either Democratic or Republican. Strong and weak Democrats outnumbered strong and weak Republicans by a ratio of about three to two throughout this period.

Between 1964 and 1966, systematic, but hardly overwhelming, changes in partisan loyalties began to occur among the white electorate. The proportion claiming to be "pure" Independents increased from 8 percent in 1964, to 12 percent in 1966, to 14 percent in 1980. At the same time, the proportions of strong partisans declined from more than one-third in the steady-state period to less than one-quarter in 1980. Less strongly identified partisans have remained at about the same proportions, but independent leaners have increased to about one-quarter of the white population. Interestingly enough, this movement towards the more independent categories has not changed the balance of loyalties between the two parties much at all. Democrats still outnumber Republicans among whites by a ratio of about three to two; there are, simply, proportionately fewer of both.

Party identification among blacks changed substantially since 1952, as Table 8-3 makes clear. Equally importantly, it has been distributed in a much more Democratic fashion. Between 1952 and 1962, the Democratic party received greater loyalty from blacks than did the Republican party, although about one out of seven blacks still supported the Republicans.

The 1964 election marked a point of rapid growth of Democratic loyalty among blacks; 52 percent of the black electorate considered themselves strong Democrats. Since then, around 70 percent have identified, either strongly or weakly, with the Democratic party. At the

Table 8-2 Party Identification Among Whites, 1952-1980

Party Identification[1]	Survey Year														
	1952	1954	1956	1958	1960	1962	1964	1966	1968	1970	1972	1974	1976	1978	1980
Strong Democrat	21%	22%	20%	26%	20%	22%	24%	17%	16%	17%	12%	15%	13%	12%	14%
Weak Democrat	25	25	23	22	25	23	25	27	25	22	25	20	23	24	23
Independent, Leans Democratic	10	9	6	7	6	8	9	9	10	11	12	13	11	14	12
Independent, No Partisan Leanings	6	7	9	8	9	8	8	12	11	13	13	15	15	14	14
Independent, Leans Republican	7	6	9	5	7	7	6	8	10	9	11	9	11	11	11
Weak Republican	14	15	14	17	14	17	14	16	16	16	14	15	16	14	16
Strong Republican	14	13	16	12	17	13	12	11	11	10	11	9	10	9	9
Apolitical	2	2	2	3	1	3	1	1	1	1	1	3	1	3	2
Total percent	99%	99%	99%	100%	100%	101%	99%	101%	100%	99%	99%	99%	100%	101%	101%
(Number)	(1615)	(1015)	(1610)	(1638)[2]	(1739)[2]	(1168)	(1394)	(1131)	(1387)	(1395)	(2397)	(2246)[2]	(2490)[2]	(2006)	(1405)

[1] The percentage supporting another party has not been presented; it usually totals less than one percent and never totals more than one percent.
[2] Weighted Ns.

same time, Republican identification fell to a near trace. The jump in support for the Democratic party in 1964 can be attributed to the two presidential nominees. Lyndon B. Johnson's advocacy of civil rights legislation appealed directly to black voters, and his Great Society programs in general made an only slightly more indirect appeal. The Republican nominee, Barry M. Goldwater, voted against the 1964 Civil Rights Act in the Senate, a vote criticized even by his Republican peers. Party stances have not shifted since then, although the percentage of blacks who were strong Democrats declined somewhat after 1968.

The other notable change in black partisanship concerned the apolitical category. Between 1952 and 1962, 14 percent or more could not relate to the questions used to measure party identification. In 1964, this percentage plummeted to four percent and has hovered at the one to four percent range since then, quite comparable to the percentages of apoliticals among whites. This shift also can be attributed directly to the civil rights movement and the Johnson-Goldwater contest. Civil rights activism stimulated many blacks, especially in the South, to become politically active. And the Voting Rights Act of 1965 enabled many blacks to vote for the first time.

The number of Independents among blacks grew slightly in the post-1964 period, but this seems to represent more of a shift away from the apolitical and Republican categories. While the percentage of pure Independents increased in 1966 (it fell massively in 1968, probably in response to George Wallace's American Independent party candidacy), it declined between 1976 and 1980. Today there are about one-half to two-thirds as many Independents among blacks as among whites.

In short, the Democratic character of black partisanship is unmistakable. There are virtually two electorates in America, a white majority that is somewhat more Democratic than Republican and a black minority that is overwhelmingly Democratic. While some recent surveys, which we will discuss in Chapter 11, suggest that a Republican surge has eroded the Democratic advantage, the overall evidence from recent polls is mixed, and it would be premature to conclude that a long-term shift toward the Republicans has occurred. In Table 8-1 we reported the partisanship of the electorate as gathered in the postelection survey conducted in November and December of 1980. No Republican shift of any magnitude is evident. If there is such a shift, it must be attributed to factors relevant after Reagan's inauguration rather than between his victory and incumbency.

PARTY IDENTIFICATION AND THE VOTE

As we saw in Chapter 4, partisanship is related to turnout. Strong partisans of either party are more likely to vote than weak partisans,

Table 8-3 Party Identification Among Blacks, 1952-1980

Party Identification[1]	Survey Year														
	1952	1954	1956	1958	1960	1962	1964	1966	1968	1970	1972	1974	1976	1978	1980
Strong Democrat	30%	24%	27%	32%	25%	35%	52%	30%	56%	41%	36%	40%	34%	37%	45%
Weak Democrat	22	29	23	19	19	25	22	31	29	34	31	26	36	29	27
Independent, Leans Democratic	10	6	5	7	7	4	8	11	7	7	8	15	14	15	9
Independent, No Partisan Leanings	4	5	7	4	16	6	6	14	3	12	12	12	8	9	7
Independent, Leans Republican	4	6	1	4	4	2	1	2	1	1	3	—[2]	1	2	3
Weak Republican	8	5	12	11	9	7	5	7	1	4	4	—[2]	2	3	2
Strong Republican	5	11	7	7	7	6	2	2	1	0	4	3	2	3	3
Apolitical	17	15	18	16	14	15	4	3	3	1	2	4	1	2	4
Total percent	100%	101%	100%	100%	101%	100%	100%	100%	101%	100%	100%	100%	99%	100%	100%
(Number)	(171)	(101)	(146)	(161)[3]	(171)[3]	(110)	(156)	(132)	(149)	(157)	(267)	(224)[3]	(290)[3]	(230)	(187)

[1] The percentages supporting another party has not been presented; it usually totals less than one percent and never totals more than one percent.

[2] Less than one percent.

[3] Weighted Ns.

and Independents who lean towards a party are more likely to vote than Independents without partisan leanings. Republicans are somewhat more likely to vote than Democrats. While partisanship influences whether or not people go to the polls, it is more strongly related to *how* people vote.

Table 8-4 reports the percentage of white, major-party voters who voted for the Democratic candidate across all categories of partisanship since 1952. Clearly, a strong relationship exists between partisan affiliation and candidate choice. With the single exception of the 1972 election, the Democratic nominee has received more than 80 percent of the vote of strong Democrats and majority support among both weak Democratic partisans and Democratic leaners. The picture is even clearer among Republicans. Since 1952, strong Republicans have given the Democratic candidate less than one vote in 10, even in the face of the massive Democratic landslide in 1964. The other two Republican categories are also more loyal than their Democratic counterparts. The pure Independent vote, which fluctuates substantially, tends to be Republican, with the exception of 50 percent for John F. Kennedy in 1960 and 75 percent for Johnson in 1964. In strong Republican years, their vote is clearly Republican.

Among whites, then, partisanship leads to loyalty in voting. Note, however, that in recent elections the relationship between partisanship and the vote has weakened slightly. This is particularly evident in the landslide elections of 1964 and 1972, as weak partisans of the losing side were distinctly less loyal than usual. This pattern is not apparent at all in 1976 and less clear but still existent in 1980. Weak and Independent leaning Democrats gave less than 60 percent of their vote to Jimmy Carter. However, in both 1968 and 1980, the relationships between partisanship and voting choices are reduced if Anderson and Wallace voters are included in the analysis. (See Table 8-8.) The weakened relationship is clearer if John Anderson votes are included as votes not given to Carter, for Anderson received disproportionate support from Democratic leaning Independents.

As we saw in Chapter 5, blacks have voted overwhelmingly Democratic since 1964. Because of this near unanimity, the relationship between party identification and the vote is not meaningful since even the very few black Republicans voted Democratic. Prior to 1964, however, more blacks identified with the Republican party. Nevertheless, the relationship between partisanship and the vote was weak because even blacks who said they were Republicans often voted Democratic.

Partisanship is related to the way people vote, but why do partisans support their party's candidates? As we shall see, party identification affects behavior because it helps structure the way voters view candidates and policies.

Table 8-4 White Major-Party Voters Who Voted Democratic for President, by Party Identification, 1952-1980 (In Percentages)

Party Identification	Survey Year							
	1952	1956	1960	1964	1968	1972	1976	1980
Strong Democrat	82	85	91	94	89	66	88	87
Weak Democrat	61	63	70	81	66	44	72	59
Independent, Leans Democratic	60	65	89	89	62	58	73	57
Independent, No Partisan Leanings	18	15	50	75	28	26	41	23
Independent, Leans Republican	7	6	13	25	5	11	15	13
Weak Republican	4	7	11	40	10	9	22	5
Strong Republican	2	—¹	.2	9	3	2	3	4

¹ Less than one percent.

NOTE: To approximate the numbers upon which these percentages are based, see Table 8-2. Actual Ns will be smaller than those that can be derived from Table 8-2 since respondents who did not vote (or who voted for a minor party) have been excluded from these calculations. Numbers also will be lower since the voting report is provided in the postelection interviews that usually contain about 10 percent fewer respondents than the pre-election interviews in which party identification is measured.

POLICY PREFERENCES AND
PERFORMANCE EVALUATIONS

In their study of voting in the 1948 presidential election, Bernard R. Berelson, Paul F. Lazarsfeld, and William N. McPhee discovered that Democratic voters attributed to their nominee, incumbent Harry S Truman, positions on key issues that were consistent with their own beliefs—whether they were liberal, moderate, or conservative.[9] Similarly, Republicans tended to see their nominee, Governor Thomas E. Dewey, taking whatever positions they preferred. Since then, research has emphasized the roles of party identification in this "projection" on the preferred candidate of positions similar to the voter's own views and in influencing policy preferences in the public.[10] Here we will use three examples to illustrate the strong relationship between partisan affiliation and perceptions, preferences, and evaluations of candidates and other election-specific factors.

First, most partisans evaluate a president of their party as having done a better job than partisans of the other party evaluate that incumbent. This is clearly revealed in Figure 8-1, which shows the percentage of each of the seven partisan groups who approve of the way that the incumbent has handled his job as president (as a proportion of those approving or disapproving) in the 1972, 1976, and 1980 presidential elections. Strong partisans regularly approve of an incumbent of their party and disapprove of one from the other party, weak partisans and Independents with partisan leanings fall in between, and "pure" Independents give something near an average evaluation (which, of course, was more positive for both Republicans than was the average evaluation of Carter). Obviously, some presidents are more popular at re-election time than others. Strong and weak Democrats were the only groups giving majority approval of Carter's handling of the presidency, while every partisan category but strong Democrats gave majority approval to both Nixon and Ford. Clearly, partisanship is not directly translated into approval or disapproval, but it is closely related to it.

Second, partisans' policy preferences tend to put them closer to the policy positions of their party's nominee. In Table 8-5 we have collapsed into three categories—pro-Democratic, neutral, and pro-Republican—our "balance of issues" measure (the number of issues on which a respondent reports a policy preference closer to where the sample as a whole saw the Democratic candidates compared to the number of issues on which the respondent is closer to the average placement of the Republican candidate). We then compare the proportion of strong Democratic identifiers, who are, on balance, pro-Democratic on these positional issues, and so on across all categories. In the three most

Figure 8-1 Partisan Groups Approving of Incumbent's Handling of Job, 1972, 1976, 1980

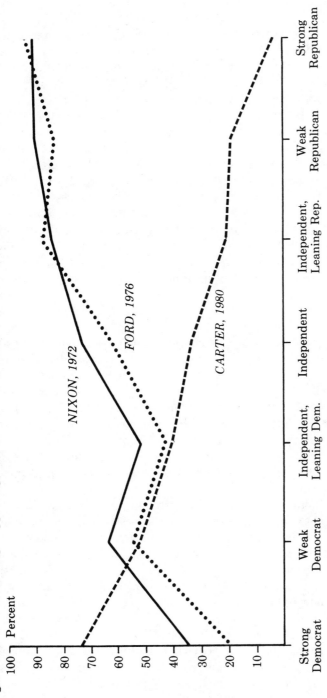

Number:

	Strong Democrat	Weak Democrat	Independent, Leaning Dem.	Independent	Independent, Leaning Rep.	Weak Republican	Strong Republican
1972	(151)	(323)	(127)	(142)	(137)	(177)	(137)
1976[1]	(359)	(608)	(282)	(325)	(253)	(358)	(235)
1980	(214)	(291)	(148)	(163)	(144)	(193)	(119)

[1] Weighted Ns.

recent presidential elections, few strong Republicans were closer to the Democratic candidate whereas strong Democrats were more widely split. As we saw in Chapter 6, the advantage has been held by the Republicans in all three elections, and this advantage is evident even among Democrats.

Why is the relationship between partisan affiliation and positions on issues clearer among Republicans? For the most part, the Republicans' ideology is more sharply defined than the Democrats', perhaps because they are a smaller and more cohesive political party.[11] This Republican advantage is balanced against the advantage enjoyed by the Democratic party—more identifiers. Note also that "leaners" often are at least as close or even closer to their party's nominee on issues than are weak identifiers of that party. A relationship does exist between partisan affiliation and positions on issues, but it is not overwhelming, which suggests that the effect of particular candidates and their policy promises on voting behavior is quite important relative to partisanship alone.

Finally, the relationship between partisanship and the party seen to be better at handling economic issues depicted in Table 8-6 is much closer than the tie between partisanship and the balance of positional issues measure. This can be seen by using a comparative measure drawn from the study of retrospective evaluations in Chapter 7. The measure is based on a summary of which party the respondent thinks would better handle inflation and which party would better handle unemployment (in 1972, the two performance measures were combined into a single question). Again, we report this summary in a three-party categorization: pro-Democratic, neutral, and pro-Republican. Table 8-6 shows the distribution of responses over all categories of partisan identification.

The relationship between partisanship and party seen to be better on the economic issues appears to be at least as strong as and probably stronger than that between partisans' evaluations of the incumbent's performance. Part of the close tie may be due to the cueing of partisanship in asking the question ("Which party would ..."), but the relationship is nonetheless real. Here, however, we are confronted with the problem of how to interpret partisanship. According to the standard view, partisans believe their party would do better because they are loyal to their party and because they are likely to be more receptive to their party's successes and less forgiving of the opposition's failures. According to the more recent interpretation of Fiorina and others, partisans are partisans because they believe one party has been better at handling these and other problems. Either way, we find a strong tie between party loyalties and evaluations of the parties among the American electorate.

Table 8-5 Balance of Positional Issues Among Partisan Groups, 1972-1980

	Party Identification							
Positional Issues, Closer to	Strong Democrat	Weak Democrat	Independent, Leans Democratic	Independent	Independent, Leans Republican	Weak Republican	Strong Republican	*Total*
1972								
Dem. candidate	23%	17%	32%	12%	8%	8%	4%	15%
Neutral	25	19	15	20	13	19	10	18
Rep. candidate	52	64	52	68	78	73	86	67
Total percent	100%	100%	99%	100%	101%	100%	100%	100%
(Number)	(308)	(563)	(235)	(272)	(235)	(304)	(237)	(2154)
1976[2]								
Dem. candidate	28%	27%	22%	15%	12%	9%	3%	18%
Neutral	32	26	37	29	27	23	27	29
Rep. candidate	39	47	40	55	61	67	69	53
Total percent	99%	100%	99%	99%	100%	99%	99%	100%
(Number)	(422)	(655)	(336)	(416)	(277)	(408)	(254)	(2778)
1980								
Dem. candidate	26%	23%	27%	20%	12%	10%	9%	19%
Neutral	34	37	33	43	40	43	31	37
Rep. candidate	40	40	40	37	48	48	60	43
Total percent	100%	100%	100%	100%	100%	101%	100%	99%
(Number)	(245)	(317)	(161)	(176)	(150)	(202)	(127)	(1378)

[1] The neutral category consists of those who were scored as 0 on the balance of issues measure or as 1 in a pro-Democratic or pro-Republican direction. A score of more than 1 in a pro-Democratic direction is considered as closer to the Democratic candidate, while more than 1 in a pro-Republican direction is considered as closer to the Republican candidate.

[2] Weighted Ns.

In sum, partisanship appears to affect the way voters evaluate incumbents and their performance. Moreover, the projective inference about likely future performance on economic and, presumably, other issues is intimately bound up in party loyalties. Positional issues are rather different. While partisans are likely to be closer to their party's nominee and his policy platform, the connection between party identification and comparisons between partisans' preferences and candidates' positions on issues is less clear cut. Policy-related evaluations in general are partly influenced by history and political memory and partly by the candidate's campaign rhetoric. Partisan attachments, then, are constraints placed on the ability of candidates to fully control their fate in the electorate, but they are not entirely rigid constraints. Candidates may be fairly tightly constrained by prior performance of the incumbent, as seen in partisan terms, but they are less constrained by partisanship in their ability to receive support based on positional issues.

John B. Anderson campaigned for the presidency as an Independent candidate. To be successful, he had to rely on this flexibility to attract the support of partisans, but he also had to count on attracting heavy support from the newly increased number of Independents. Anderson's candidacy presented citizens with a reasonably serious third alternative—one that could not be evaluated fully in partisan terms. Just how, then, did voters evaluate Anderson, and who in the electorate actually voted for him? We turn now to these questions.

THE ANDERSON CANDIDACY

Anderson's candidacy was not unlike other third-party candidacies that had an appreciable level of success in this century. Theodore Roosevelt in 1912, Robert M. LaFollette in 1924, J. Strom Thurmond in 1948, and George C. Wallace in 1968 were notable figures within the two-party system before they launched independent presidential campaigns. Like Roosevelt, LaFollette, and Wallace, Anderson earlier had sought his party's nomination, and it was feared his third-party presidential bid could jeopardize the fortunes of the major-party nominees. Consequently, Ronald Reagan and Jimmy Carter, who was suspected to be the more seriously affected, tried to minimize Anderson's influence. Ultimately, Anderson's support was too low to alter the outcome of the 1980 election. His popular showing of nearly 7 percent, however, was sufficient to generate greatly needed campaign funds from the government (although after the election and in proportion to his showing) and raised the possibility, in some minds at least, that he could form a third party that could have an enduring impact on our electoral system.

Table 8-6 Party Better on Inflation and Unemployment Among Partisan Groups, 1972-1980

Party Better	Strong Democrat	Weak Democrat	Party Identification Independent, Leans Democratic	Independent	Independent, Leans Republican	Weak Republican	Strong Republican	Total
1972[1]								
Democrats	59%	31%	29%	15%	6%	4%	4%	23%
Neutral	37	57	60	72	61	62	45	56
Republicans	4	12	10	13	33	33	50	20
Total percent	100%	100%	99%	100%	100%	99%	100%	99%
(Number)	(165)	(362)	(136)	(151)	(138)	(177)	(139)	(1268)
1976[2]								
Pro-Democratic	83%	55%	49%	15%	10%	10%	5%	38%
Neutral	16	38	48	78	56	61	36	46
Pro-Republican	2	6	3	6	34	28	58	16
Total percent	101%	99%	100%	99%	100%	99%	99%	100%
(Number)	(386)	(638)	(296)	(329)	(256)	(349)	(225)	(2479)
1980								
Pro-Democratic	57%	27%	24%	6%	1%	3%	3%	21%
Neutral	37	57	63	72	35	35	21	47
Pro-Republican	6	16	13	22	65	62	75	33
Total percent	100%	100%	100%	100%	101%	100%	99%	101%
(Number)	(228)	(286)	(147)	(149)	(139)	(191)	(118)	(1258)

[1] In 1972 a random half sample were asked the question.

[2] Weighted Ns.

NOTE: A single question was asked in 1972; in 1976 and 1980 a two-question measure was used.

To understand the nature of the Anderson constituency, let us begin by looking at general evaluations of the three candidates. The SRC-CPS surveys use a so-called "thermometer" scale that runs from 0 through to 100 degrees. A zero rating indicates "very cold" or negative feelings about the candidate, 50 indicates neutral feelings, and 100 indicates the "warmest" possible evaluation. In the pre-election survey, roughly three times as many respondents were unable to rank Anderson on this scale (about 14 percent) as failed to rank Carter or Reagan. In the postelection survey, only about 9 percent felt unable to rank Anderson, but only about 2 percent failed to rank Reagan and even fewer Carter. Furthermore, many repondents ranked Anderson at the neutral 50 point (27 and 34 percent, respectively) about two times as many as so evaluated Reagan (with Carter attracting even fewer neutral evaluations). In short, voters knew less about Anderson than about Carter and Reagan.

Most respondents that evaluated Anderson in the pre- and post-election surveys gave him lukewarm ratings. The median response was very close to the neutral position (50.4 and 50.1), which contrasts with the more favorable median evaluations of Carter (60.1 and 59.8) and Reagan (59.9 and 60.1). The average respondent "liked" both major-party nominees, at least giving them slightly positive evaluations, but evaluated Anderson neutrally.

The comparative rankings of the candidates on these measures is usually an accurate reflection of voter behavior. Candidate thermometers have been used by the SRC since 1968, and voters are overwhelmingly likely to vote for a major-party candidate if they rank him highest. Minor-party candidates do not fare as well. Table 8-7 reports the candidate ranked highest by voters in the 1980 postelection survey and the candidate they actually supported.[12] For comparison, we include the three-candidate election of 1968. Of the 12 percent of the sample who ranked Anderson first, only 57 percent actually voted for him. In both 1968 and 1980, however, more than 95 percent of those ranking a major-party candidate first voted for him. Wallace fared better among his supporters than Anderson; 85 percent of those who preferred Wallace backed him at the polls. The few respondents who ranked Wallace first but voted for Nixon were found in non-southern states in which he lost big.

The most obvious problem facing an Independent or third-party candidate is how to attract a more popular following, but a second obstacle appears to be just this: people find it hard to justify voting for their preferred candidate if they believe the candidate has very little chance to win. Most people are unwilling to "waste" a vote.[13] Many seemed swayed by that reasoning in 1980 and some in 1968. And few thought Wallace and Anderson could win. Only seven respondents in

Table 8-7 Candidate Thermometer Rankings and the Vote, 1968 and 1980

First Place in Thermometer Rankings	Voted for in 1968				
	Nixon	Humphrey	Wallace	Total percent	(Number)
Nixon	96%	2	2	100%	(322)
Humphrey	2%	97	1	100%	(272)
Wallace	14%	1	85	100%	(79)
N-H tie	45%	53	2	100%	(51)
W-N tie	[4]	—	[4]	—	(8)
W-H tie	—	[3]	—	—	(3)
3-way tie	[3]	[4]	—	—	(7)

	Voted for in 1980				
	Reagan	Carter	Anderson	Total percent	(Number)
Reagan	97%	2	1	100%	(409)
Carter	3%	97	0	100%	(253)
Anderson	18%	25	57	100%	(111)
R-C tie	40%	60	0	100%	(40)
A-R tie	88%	3	9	100%	(34)
A-C tie	7%	67	26	100%	(27)
3-way tie	24%	64	12	100%	(25)

NOTE: Postelection survey thermometer rankings were used. Numbers in brackets indicate the total N is less than 10.

the pre-election survey felt Anderson would win, or one half of one percent of those hazarding a guess. (Carter led Reagan by 55 to 45 percent by this set of prognostications.) Indeed, 75 percent claimed he would "trail behind the other candidates," while another 21 percent picked him to finish a close third.[14]

The reasons behind this lack of faith in Anderson's chances illustrate the rationale of the wasted vote thesis, as exacerbated by our two-party system. For example, in the pre-election survey about 27 percent who claimed they would vote for some other candidate also claimed they had "considered" supporting Anderson. About 45 percent of those who considered Anderson said they decided not to vote for him because they felt he had no chance of winning. Nearly 55 percent of them agreed with Carter's campaign argument that a vote for Anderson would "help elect another candidate I dislike more." About 26 percent claimed to feel uneasy about voting for a candidate not backed by a major party, but 46 percent considered voting for him "as a way of protesting the choice of presidential candidates from the major parties." Of course, that 46 percent had changed their minds by the time of the pre-election survey and supported one of the major-party nominees.

For the candidate with little chance of victory, the wasted vote logic becomes a self-fulfilling prophecy. Because people perceive the candidate unlikely to win, they don't vote for him. Consequently, the candidate cannot win. Potential contributors perceive the candidate's inability to generate support and, unwilling to waste their money, decide not to give. Raising large sums of money is extremely difficult for a third candidate. His major-party opponents, on the other hand, receive full federal funding—if they choose to accept it—by virtue of their major-party nomination. Thus, they can launch expensive campaigns that he cannot match, and he becomes even less competitive. It is not surprising, therefore, that Anderson's support in the polls, like Wallace's, peaked early in the general election campaign and then receded.

The brute fact of third-party candidates is that they do not bear the imprimatur of one of the two major political parties, with the web of support that endorsement entails. Major-party nominees are guaranteed federal financing; third-party candidates must raise money themselves during the campaign and almost certainly will wind up with fewer federal dollars. Major-party nominees invariably are supported by prominent politicians of their party; third-party candidates often have difficulty even locating a well-known running mate who is willing to face the stigma among "faithful" Democrats or Republicans of being a defector. Major-party nominees can count on the support of strong party identifiers; third-party candidates cannot rely on a core of supporters.

What support can major-party candidates expect? If we assume that only three-fifths of the strong Democrats really vote and that only 7 of 10 of these voters support the Democratic nominee (a smaller percentage than have ever actually supported any Democrat), these voters would provide the Democratic candidate with nearly 12 million votes. If we assume that two-thirds of the strong Republicans turn out and that 9 out of 10 of them vote for the Republican candidate (since 1952, no Republican candidate received less support), then the Republican nominee would be assured more than 8 million votes. In other words, just by receiving the Republican nomination, Reagan was assured of 2 million more votes than Anderson ultimately received. The core of support for party candidates due to partisanship in the electorate is very large relative to the near zero "core" guaranteed a third-party or independent candidate such as Anderson.

And yet, partisanship has changed. While the numerical advantage of Democrats over Republicans is about the same, the proportion of Democrats and Republicans together has declined as the number of

Table 8-8 How Whites Voted for President Among the Three Major Candidates in 1968 and 1980, by Party Identification

Party Identification	Voted for in 1968					Voted for in 1980				
	Humphrey	Wallace	Nixon	Total percent	(Number)	Carter	Anderson	Reagan	Total percent	(Number)
Strong Democrat	80%	10	10	100%	(164)	84%	3	12	99%	(129)
Weak Democrat	55%	17	28	100%	(212)	54%	9	38	101%	(173)
Independent, Leans Democratic	51%	18	31	100%	(89)	44%	23	33	100%	(93)
Independent, No Partisan Leanings	23%	20	57	100%	(84)	20%	13	67	100%	(79)
Independent, Leans Republican	4%	14	82	100%	(101)	11%	10	78	99%	(106)
Weak Republican	9%	8	83	100%	(163)	5%	9	87	101%	(151)
Strong Republican	3%	2	96	101%	(117)	4%	4	93	101%	(110)

Independents has increased. The proportionately smaller core of support for major-party nominees boosts the chances of independent candidates, many suggest.

In fact, Anderson and Wallace had limited success at attracting Independent voters to their camps, as Table 8-8 reveals.[15] Anderson did best among Independents who leaned toward the Democratic party, receiving somewhat less than one vote in four. He received about one vote in eight from pure Independents and about one in ten from all other groups except the strongest partisans. Wallace's support was strongest among pure Independents, with weak Democrats and Independents with Democratic leanings voting for him in about equal proportions. Anderson and Wallace both drew disproportionate support from Independents first and Democrats second (Wallace doing much better among Democratic identifiers, especially in the South). Yet neither Independent candidate came close to gaining a plurality of the Independent vote.

Partisanship by itself, however, can be misleading. For example, the social characteristics of Anderson and Wallace voters differed considerably, as we saw in Chapter 5. Wallace voters also had distinctive, and distinctly conservative, issue preferences.[16]

Table 8-9 reports some general characteristics of Anderson voters in comparison to the full electorate on the seven-point issue scales. Looking first at self-placement, we see that on many issues Anderson voters are similar to the full sample. For example, the median preference on the scales for jobs and standard of living, government services and spending cuts, inflation and unemployment, and relations with Russia was essentially the same, while the typical Anderson voter was only somewhat more in favor of government aid to minority groups and less for increases in defense spending. Anderson voters, however, strongly endorsed the most liberal position on women's rights and abortion and favored a less substantial tax cut than the full sample.

As should be expected, Anderson voters were more likely to know where their candidate stood on the issues than the electorate as a whole. However, this is damning with faint praise. Less than half the electorate, on average, could place Anderson on an issue scale, far less than could place Carter or Reagan. Anderson voters failed to perceive his position on the average issue almost one-third of the time, and they, too, were more likely to place Carter and Reagan than the candidate they supported. In general, there were relatively few differences between Anderson voters and the full electorate in terms of placement of Anderson on these issue scales. The only real differences came on women's rights, abortion, and the tax cut measure. On these scales, Anderson voters saw Anderson as more liberal—that is closer to their own preferences as well as to Anderson's campaign planks.

Table 8-9 Some Comparisons Between Anderson Voters and the Full Sample on Seven-Point Issue Scales, 1980

Issue Scale	Median Self-Placement		Median Perception of Anderson		Percentage Not Rating Anderson	
	Anderson Voters	Full Sample	Anderson Voters	Full Sample	Anderson Voters	Full Sample
Government Spending/Services Cuts[1]	3.7	3.7	3.9	3.9	30%	57%
Tax Cut[2]	2.8	3.8	2.3	3.0	47%	74%
Defense Spending	4.8	5.4	4.3	4.0	36%	56%
Jobs and Standard of Living	4.4	4.4	3.7	3.9	21%	50%
Aid to Minorities	4.0	4.5	3.8	3.9	15%	48%
Relations with Russia	3.8	3.9	3.7	3.8	26%	53%
Women's Rights	1.4	2.4	2.6	3.1	17%	50%
Abortion[3]	1.4	3.4	1.7	2.6	47%	68%
Inflation/Unemployment[1]	4.2	3.9	4.1	4.1	53%	69%

[1] Reversed so that 1="Liberal," 7="Conservative" response.
[2] Reversed and expanded to seven-point spread (1=7; 2=5; 3=3; 4=1).
[3] Expanded to seven-point spread (1=1; 2=2.5; 3=4; 4=5.5; 5=7).

The differences on these three scales could be attributed to most voters' uncertainty about the third-party candidate. The electorate as a whole was much more likely to place Anderson in a middle position on these scales than were Anderson voters. Anderson voters, however, placed their candidate at the "4" midpoint on the scales more often than any other position, further indicating that on many issues they were almost as unsure as other voters of his positions. Nonetheless, Anderson voters were more likely to hear their candidate, at least on some key issues—those that differentiated most clearly Anderson and his supporters from the general public.

In Table 8-10 we compare Anderson voters to Carter and Reagan supporters in two basic ways: their respective views on Carter's job as incumbent and on party differences concerning key retrospective evaluations. Turning first to evaluations of the incumbent, we can see that Anderson voters usually have even more negative views of Carter as incumbent than other voters. On the general approval item, for example, only about half as many Anderson voters approved of Carter's handling of the presidency. The exceptions are on energy, with Anderson voters giving the president only slightly lower marks, and on Afghanistan, with Anderson voters being slightly more positive about Carter's reactions.

Most Anderson voters were first Independents and only secondly partisans. This independence of party ties is evident in Table 8-10B. On the most important problem and inflation, the Anderson voter gave the Republican party much better marks than the Democrats. But on avoiding war, the Democrats were scored higher. Although Anderson voters perceived some differences between the parties, they were consistently more likely than major-party voters to say that neither party would be better at dealing with the nation's problems.

The views of Anderson voters were somewhat paradoxical. They stood on issues much like the electorate as a whole, except for being more liberal on social issues. Carter did a rather poor job, they thought, but they had little confidence that the Republicans would do much better. In general, they had even less sanguine views of the Republican party, even given their low opinion of Carter's performance. Two final issue variables illustrate the nature of opinions held by Anderson voters. About 71 percent of them believed we should not relax government regulations concerning environmental protection, compared to 62 percent of Carter voters and 42 percent of Reagan voters. But like Reagan voters, Anderson voters favored continued government control of oil and gas prices (59 percent for both candidates' supporters compared to 83 percent of Carter voters).

In other words, Anderson's voters were more like Carter's in favoring government activity on social issues, yet more like Reagan's on economic activity. Voters most torn between the principles of the two

Table 8-10 Distribution of Anderson Voters Compared to Major-Party Voters on Selected Retrospective Issues, 1980

A. Approve of Carter's Handling of

Voted For	Presidency		Inflation		Unemployment		Energy		Iranian Hostages		Afghanistan†	
	Anderson	Major Party	Anderson	Major Party	Anderson	Major Party	Anderson	Major Party	Anderson	Major Party	Anderson	Major Party
Approve	20%	39%	12%	24%	20%	31%	35%	39%	21%	38%	53%	49%
Disapprove	80	61	88	76	80	69	65	61	79	62	47	51
Total Percent	100%	100%	100%	100%	100%	100%	100%	100%	100%	100%	100%	100%
(Number)	(78)	(806)	(78)	(775)	(70)	(732)	(75)	(763)	(76)	(827)	(79)	(825)

B. Which Party Would Better Handle

Voted For	Most Important Problem		Inflation		Unemployment		War/Peace	
	Anderson	Major Party	Anderson	Major Party	Anderson	Major Party	Anderson	Major Party
Republican	42%	49%	35%	38%	17%	29%	9%	24%
Same by Both	46	40	55	46	67	51	56	49
Democratic	12	12	11	16	16	21	35	27
Total percent	100%	101%	101%	100%	100%	101%	100%	100%
(Number)	(78)	(804)	(75)	(842)	(76)	(838)	(79)	(831)

† Respondents were asked if Carter's handling of the Afghanistan crisis was "just right," "too strong," or "not enough." The disapprove category in the table includes "too strong" or "not enough" responses.

parties were the most likely to support Anderson. In contrast, Wallace was endorsed by strong conservatives who were Democrats in identification but closer to Republican policies on many of the most salient issues in that campaign (in fact, typically more conservative than most Republicans in 1968).

Table 8-11 presents another way of summarizing the differences among supporters of Reagan, Carter, and Anderson. There we report the distribution of the voters for each of the three candidates on the summary prospective-based and retrospective-based comparison measures, discussed in Chapters 6 and 7. With so few Anderson voters in the sample, we collapsed both summary scales into the pro-Democratic, neutral, and pro-Republican categories.

Obviously, the issue preferences of supporters of the three candidates are quite distinct. Reagan voters typically favored his party on both measures. Carter voters were widely split on prospective issues. More were neutral than anything else, but more favored Reagan than favored their own candidate. Few, however, favored the Republican party on retrospective, economic issue-based comparisons, and there was about an even split between those being neutral and those favoring the Democratic party.

Anderson voters present a distinct, third pattern. Few favored Reagan on prospective issues. Most were neutral, but, on balance, they were more in favor of Carter's positions than Carter's own voters! Retrospective comparisons tended to favor the Republican party over the Democratic party, but a clear majority were neutral. In large part, then, Anderson picked up voters that were somewhat more liberal than Reagan and Carter supporters, yet who felt that the Democrats had done poorly—and that the Republicans would do little better.

Do these findings suggest the potential for formation of a new party (or reordering of one or both current parties)? Only possibly. Anderson did draw from the recently increased number of self-proclaimed Independents. And those voters tended to have a different issue orientation than traditional Democratic or Republican platforms. In fact, Anderson received more of the vote from those who felt as he did about policy. But more importantly, Anderson demonstrated the extreme difficulty facing the candidate running independent of either major party. First, people discounted his chances—and did so on quite reasonable grounds. Thus, his support, never as high as Wallace's in 1968, halved between August and November. Second, he was unable to convey his views effectively to most of the electorate. Even his own voters had hazy ideas of his position on all but a few key issues. Third, he faced a rather good opportunity. It does not seem likely that a third-party candidate will be faced with an electorate rejecting the performance of the incumbent and, simultaneously, not very strongly in favor of the policy positions

Table 8-11 Distribution of Voters for the Three Major Candidates in 1980 on the Prospective-Based and Retrospective-Based Summary Comparisons Issue Scales (In Percentages)

	Retrospective-Based Comparisons											
Prospective-Based Comparisons	*Carter Voters*				*Anderson Voters*				*Reagan Voters*			
	Pro-Dem.	Neutral	Pro-Rep.	Total	Pro-Dem.	Neutral	Pro-Rep.	Total	Pro-Dem.	Neutral	Pro-Rep.	Total
Pro-Dem.	15	11	1	28	9	18	7	34	1	3	6	10
Neutral	16	20	2	39	4	26	15	45	1	12	23	35
Pro-Rep.	16	16	2	34	3	8	11	22	2	18	35	54
Total percent	46	48	6	100%	16	51	32	100%	3	33	64	100%
(Number)				(358)				(74)				(458)

advocated by his major-party opponent. Finally, his constituency had a strong mixture of policy positions, favoring government activity in some areas, but not in others. One could well imagine a strong Democratic candidate advocating such issue positions in 1984. And one could equally as well imagine that if the Reagan administration is successful, the resultant positive retrospective evaluations, especially on economic issues, would make the Republicans unstoppable. In sum, while there was discontent with both major-party nominees in 1980, Anderson's campaign platform and independent status left little room for developing broad support in the electorate.

Anderson's showing in 1980 demonstrated the resiliency of our two-party system. Even if parties as organizations are in decline, and even if the proportion of citizens strongly attached to political parties is substantially smaller than a decade or two ago, political parties maintain strong barriers against electoral incursions from third-party candidates. Many in the electorate still identify with one party or the other. Partisan attachments remain entwined with voters' evaluations of the candidates themselves, their performance in office, and their promises for the future. And, even if less strongly, they affect the proximity of a typical partisan to candidates on positional issues. As objects of attachment or repositories of citizens' political "memories," parties still remain important by hindering third-party candidates and by providing a core of support for the nominees of the two major parties.

NOTES

1. Angus Campbell, Philip E. Converse, Warren E. Miller, and Donald E. Stokes, *The American Voter* (New York: John Wiley & Sons, 1960).
2. Ibid., p. 121. See also Morris P. Fiorina, *Retrospective Voting in American National Elections* (New Haven, Conn.: Yale University Press, 1981), pp. 85-86.
3. A very few identify with another political party, while only somewhat more are so uninvolved or even excluded from electoral politics that they are entirely apolitical.
4. For the full wording of the party identification questions, see Chapter 4, note 14.
5. V. O. Key, Jr., *The Responsible Electorate* (Cambridge, Mass.: Harvard University Press, 1966), p. 52.
6. See Morris P. Fiorina, "An Outline for a Model of Party Choice," *American Journal of Political Science* 21 (August 1977): 601-625; and Fiorina, *Retrospective Voting.*
7. Benjamin I. Page, *Choices and Echoes in Presidential Elections: Rational Man and Electoral Democracy* (Chicago: University of Chicago Press, 1978).
8. Philip E. Converse, *The Dynamics of Party Support: Cohort-Analyzing Party Identification* (Beverly Hills, Calif.: Sage Publications, 1976). Of course, many individuals may have changed their partisan loyalties as panel

studies that interview the same respondents more than once demonstrate. See Edward C. Dreyer, "Change and Stability in Party Identifications," *The Journal of Politics* 35 (August 1973): 712-22; and Richard G. Niemi, Richard S. Katz, and David Newman, "Reconstructing Past Partisanship: The Failure of the Party Identification Recall Questions," *American Journal of Political Science* 24 (November 1980): 633-651. However, studies of individual-level change also demonstrate that party identification is more stable than other political attitudes. See Philip E. Converse and Gregory B. Markus, "Plus ca change...: The New CPS Election Study Panel," *American Political Science Review* 73 (March 1979): 32-49.

9. Bernard R. Berelson, Paul F. Lazarsfeld, and William N. McPhee, *Voting: A Study of Opinion Formation in a Presidential Campaign* (Chicago: The University of Chicago Press, 1954).

10. See Richard A. Brody and Benjamin I. Page, "Comment: The Assessment of Policy Voting," *American Political Science Review* 66 (June 1972): 450-458; and Benjamin I. Page and Richard A. Brody, "Policy Voting and the Electoral Process: The Vietnam War Issue," *American Political Science Review* 66 (September 1972): 979-995.

11. Sidney Verba and Norman H. Nie, *Participation in America: Political Democracy and Social Equality* (New York: Harper & Row, 1972).

12. Anderson's support in the pre-election survey was dispersed greatly by election day. Anderson received a bare plurality of 40 percent among those who ranked him first before the election. In particular, 20 percent became Reagan supporters. On the other hand, he picked up 12 percent of his supporters from erstwhile Carter backers and another 8 percent came from those who originally tied Carter and Anderson for first place. By comparison, Reagan received 98 percent of the vote from those who ranked him first before the election, and Carter received the votes of 87 percent of his pre-election supporters.

13. For a rational-choice based analysis of this problem, see Richard D. McKelvey and Peter C. Ordeshook, "A General Theory of the Calculus of Voting," *Mathematical Applications in Political Science*, ed. J. F. Herndon and J. L. Bernd (Charlottesville, Va.: University of Virginia Press, 1972), pp. 32-78; John H. Aldrich, "Some Problems in Testing Two Rational Models of Participation," *American Journal of Political Science* 20 (November 1976): 713-33; and Jerome H. Black, "The Multicandidate Calculus of Voting: Application to Canadian Federal Elections," *American Journal of Political Science* 22 (August 1978): 609-638.

14. Only 1 percent believed Anderson would carry their home state. Surely, many more would have felt Wallace would carry their state in 1968, had such a question been asked.

15. To maintain comparability with Table 8-4, Table 8-8 presents the results for whites. As we saw in Chapter 5, very few blacks voted for Anderson. The Michigan SRC survey in 1968 found no blacks who voted for Wallace.

16. See Philip E. Converse, Warren E. Miller, Jerrold G. Rusk, and Arthur C. Wolfe, "Continuity and Change in American Politics: Parties and Issues in the 1968 Election," *American Political Science Review* 63 (December 1969): 1083-1105.

PART III

The 1980
Congressional Election

The focus of this book so far has been the presidential contest, the major event of interest in the 1980 elections. The president, however, does not govern alone; he shares responsibility and power with the Congress, which must approve his major appointments and enact his legislative program. Having concluded our analysis of the election of Ronald Reagan as president, it is appropriate to turn our attention to the selection of the Congress that serves with him. In Part III we will consider the similarities and differences in the selection processes of these offices and the policy implications of the electorate's choices.

Nineteen-eighty witnessed many elections. Even if we exclude the 13 gubernatorial contests, and the thousands of lesser state and local races, the electorate chose 34 United States senators and 435 members of the House of Representatives. Indeed, of all the electoral surprises of 1980, the most dramatic was the Republican gain of 12 seats in the Senate, the largest gain for any party since 1958 when the Democrats took over 15 seats. The Republicans thus won control of the Senate for the first time since 1952—a victory even Republican optimists did not anticipate. The Democrats retained control of the House in 1980, but they lost 33 seats.

Explaining these Republican gains is crucial; if the Republicans had not won the Senate, and if they had not made major inroads in the House, the policy consequences of Reagan's victory would have been less significant. In the post World War II period, Republicans had won four presidential elections, but they had gained control of the House and the Senate only once (1952). Moreover, Republicans failed to make gains in Congress during their two most dramatic presidential land-slides. In 1956, Eisenhower defeated Stevenson by 15 percentage points in the popular vote, but the Republicans actually lost one seat in both the House and the Senate. In 1972, Nixon scored the most impressive electoral vote landslide in postwar history, defeating McGovern by 23 percentage points in the popular vote. Nevertheless, the Republicans lost two seats in the Senate, while gaining only 12 in the House. Although Reagan's victory aided the Republicans, it alone cannot account for their success in 1980. We must examine other political changes that have made the Republicans a more competitive party.

The discussion of congressional elections in Part III is divided into two parts. Chapter 9 examines the candidates' decisions and their effect upon electoral outcomes. The most crucial factor in congressional elections is incumbency. In recent years the re-election margins of incumbents in the House have increased, and we will evaluate alternative explanations for this growing success. Our own explanation stresses the importance of campaign funding, which can account not only for the re-election success of incumbents, but for the successes of their challengers when they attain adequate funding. Republicans' ability to raise money has contributed greatly to their victories in recent congressional elections. Chapter 9 also shows how the changed composition of the House and Senate has contributed to Reagan's early legislative victories. Finally, we will speculate on the effects of changes in the patterns of congressional elections upon the 1982 contests.

Chapter 10 explores the way voters make congressional voting choices—one of the most exciting and rapidly growing areas of research since the University of Michigan's Survey Research Center-Center for Political Studies introduced new survey questions in 1978 on congressional voting behavior. Because the composition of the Senate's electorate changes more radically from election to election, our analysis will focus on voting for the House. Chapter 10 examines how voters' race, sex, age, income, union membership, and religion influence their choice of representatives and compares the relationship of these social forces in congressional and presidential voting. The effects of issue preferences, partisan loyalties, and incumbency on congressional voters' decisions also are assessed. As we will see, issues are important, but only for a small subset of the electorate, and the influence of partisan loyalties on congressional voting has declined dramatically since 1964. Finally, we will consider the thesis that congressional voting choices are a referendum on the performance of individual members of Congress, as well as on the president.

9

Candidates and Outcomes

By any standard, the outcome of the 1980 congressional election was significant: for the first time in more than a quarter of a century, the Republicans controlled one house of Congress—the Senate—and made substantial gains in the other house.[1] Measuring these changes against the balance of power in Congress just before the election, the Republicans gained a net of 12 seats in the Senate (for a 53 to 47 majority) and 33 seats in the House (cutting the Democratic margin to 243 to 192). What made the Republican takeover of the Senate even more remarkable was that it was unexpected, even by Republican campaign officials. Most observers expected some Republican gains, but the predictions were on the order of three to five seats. Instead the 12-seat gain gave the Republicans the largest number of Senate seats they had held in 50 years, since the 71st Congress (1929-1931) when they held 56.

In our analysis in this chapter of the 1980 congressional candidates and the election results, we will consider how that year's events fit into the pattern of post-World War II elections. Chapter 10 looks at the voters in the congressional electorate, examining the patterns of their responses to the congressional candidates of 1980.

ELECTION OUTCOMES

Changing Patterns of Incumbent Success

One of the most salient features of congressional elections is that the overwhelming majority of them involve incumbents, and the overwhelming majority of these incumbents are re-elected. Table 9-1 presents the election outcomes for House and Senate races involving incumbents between 1954 and 1980.[2] During this period, an average of 92 percent of House incumbents and 80 percent of Senate incumbents were successful in their bids for re-election. Most of the incumbents who were defeated met their fate in a general election rather than in a primary, although in the last decade an increasing number of incumbents have been defeated in Senate primaries. Not only have House members been more successful at getting re-elected since 1954, but there also has been a divergence over time between the two houses in the rates of re-election. For the House, the average proportion of incumbents re-elected increased slightly from 90.9 percent between

Table 9-1   House and Senate Incumbents and Election Outcomes, 1954-1980

Year	Incumbents Running	Primary Defeats		General Election Defeats		Re-elected	
	(N)	(N)	%	(N)	%	(N)	%
House							
1954	(407)	(6)	1.5	(22)	5.4	(379)	93.1
1956	(410)	(6)	1.5	(15)	3.7	(389)	94.9
1958	(394)	(3)	0.8	(37)	9.4	(354)	89.8
1960	(405)	(5)	1.3	(25)	6.7	(375)	92.6
1962	(402)	(12)	3.0	(22)	5.5	(368)	91.5
1964	(397)	(8)	2.0	(45)	11.3	(344)	86.6
1966	(411)	(8)	1.9	(41)	10.0	(362)	88.1
1968	(409)	(4)	1.0	(9)	2.2	(396)	96.8
1970	(401)	(10)	2.5	(12)	3.2	(379)	94.5
1972	(392)	(13)	3.3	(13)	3.3	(366)	93.4
1974	(391)	(8)	2.0	(40)	10.2	(343)	87.7
1976	(383)	(3)	0.8	(12)	3.1	(368)	96.1
1978	(382)	(5)	1.3	(19)	5.0	(358)	93.7
1980	(398)	(6)	1.5	(31)	7.8	(361)	90.7
Senate							
1954	(27)	(0)	—	(4)	17	(23)	83
1956	(30)	(0)	—	(4)	13	(26)	87
1958	(26)	(0)	—	(9)	35	(17)	65
1960	(28)	(0)	—	(1)	4	(27)	96
1962	(30)	(0)	—	(3)	10	(27)	90
1964	(30)	(0)	—	(2)	7	(28)	93
1966	(29)	(2)	7	(1)	3	(26)	90
1968	(28)	(4)	14	(4)	14	(20)	71
1970	(28)	(1)	4	(3)	11	(24)	86
1972	(26)	(1)	4	(5)	19	(20)	77
1974	(26)	(1)	4	(2)	8	(23)	88
1976	(25)	(0)	—	(9)	36	(16)	64
1978	(22)	(1)	5	(6)	27	(15)	68
1980	(29)	(4)	4	(9)	31	(16)	55

1954 and 1966 to 93.3 percent between 1968 and 1980; the corresponding figures for the Senate were 86.3 percent and 72.7 percent, respectively. Representatives have become marginally more successful at getting re-elected; senators significantly less so. Indeed, the success rate for senators in the last three elections has fallen to 62 percent.

From Figure 9-1, which shows the partisan representation in the House and Senate since World War II, we can see that the Democratic level of representation in both houses has fallen to as low a level as at any time since the mid-1950s. Furthermore, as we will demonstrate later in this chapter, the Democrats are unlikely to see any significant rebound in seats in the near future, particularly not in the Senate. These substantial shifts in political power have had, and will continue to have, a significant impact on the internal politics of the Congress.

The specific interaction between party and incumbency in 1980 is shown in Table 9-2. The Democrats won 56 percent of the seats in the House, and the Republicans won 65 percent of the Senate seats at stake. (Of course, only about a third of the Senate seats are contested in any one election, so the overall Republican margin of control in the Senate is a much narrower 53 percent.) The Republicans were extremely successful in both the House and Senate in retaining previously Republican seats, both those with incumbents and those without. They did not lose a single previously held seat in the Senate, and only four seats out of 159 in the House, three held by incumbents seeking re-election. (Two of these three involved difficult situations for the Republicans: the Maryland first district in which the incumbent, Robert E. Bauman, was involved in a homosexual scandal, and the California eleventh district, a Democratic district normally, which was won by a Republican in a special election in 1979 because of a split in the Democratic party.) Overall, the Republicans' level of success in retaining their seats is remarkable.

The Democrats were much less successful in retaining what they had previously held. In the Senate, they barely kept a majority of the seats in which incumbents were seeking re-election (losing 9 of 19), and they lost three of their five seats with no incumbent. In the House, the Republicans took almost two-fifths of the open Democratic seats. Eighty-nine percent of the Democratic House incumbents survived, which reflects the higher rates of incumbency survival in that body.

Regional Bases of Power

The geographic pattern of 1980 election outcomes can be seen in the partisan breakdowns by region for the House and Senate presented in Table 9-3.[3] The greatest proportional Republican gains in the House were in the East and West: 10 percent in each. They gained almost as much (8 percent) in the South and border states. Paradoxically, the

Figure 9-1 Democratic Share of Seats in the House and Senate, 1947-1981

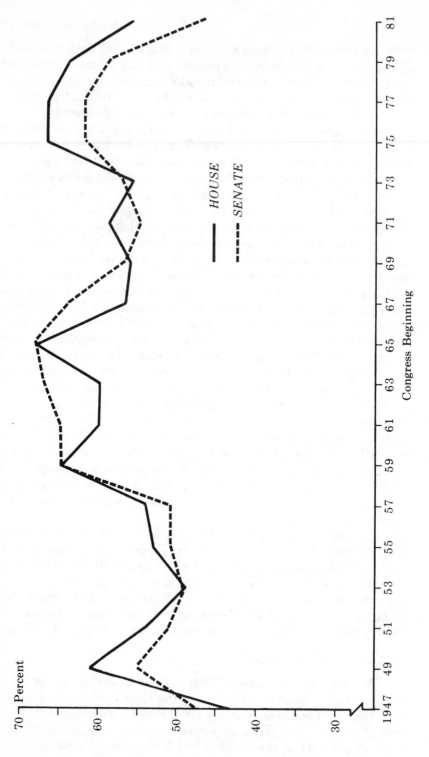

Table 9-2 House and Senate Election Outcomes, by Party and Incumbency, 1980

1980 Winners	*1980 Candidates*				
	Democratic Incumbent	No Incumbent (Seat Was Democratic)	No Incumbent (Seat Was Republican)	Republican Incumbent	*Total*
House					
Democrats	89%[1]	63%	6%	2%	56%
Republicans	11	37	94	98	44
Total percent	100%	100%	100%	100%	100%
(Number)	(249)	(27)	(16)	(143)	(435)
Senate					
Democrats	53%	40%	0%	0%	35%
Republicans	47	60	100[2]	100	65
Total percent	100%	100%	100%	100%	100%
(Number)	(19)	(5)	(4)	(6)	(34)

[1] Includes two districts in which Democratic incumbents were defeated by Democrats.
[2] Includes New York in which the Republican incumbent was not the Republican candidate, but did run as the Liberal party candidate.

Republicans made the fewest gains in the Midwest, historically the Republican heartland. Although the Democrats' margin of control in the House was reduced in 1980, they still retained majorities in four of the five regions shown in Table 9-3, and they were near an even share in the fifth.

The pattern in the Senate was different, reflecting the greater Republican gains there. After the 1980 elections, the Democrats retained majorities only in the South and border states. The greatest Republican gains were in the South and the Midwest: 18 percent each. They gained 11 percent in the West and 5 percent in the East. There was no change in the border states. In both houses, the Republicans in 1981 were strongest in the West and Midwest, and weakest in the South and border states.

It is also interesting to view the regional breakdowns from a historical perspective. Table 9-3 includes regional breakdowns for the opening of the 83rd Congress in 1953, the last time the Republicans controlled the House and the Senate. The regional power bases of both parties in Congress have shifted significantly during the last three decades, but the most obvious change has occurred in the South. The percentage of southern seats in the House held by Democrats declined from 94 percent in 1953 to 64 percent in 1981. In 1953, the Democrats

Table 9-3 Party Shares of Regional Delegations in the House and Senate, 1953, 1980, 1981

Region	1953 % Dem.	1953 % Rep.	(N)	1980 % Dem.	1980 % Rep.	(N)	1981 % Dem.	1981 % Rep.	(N)
House									
East	35	65	(116)	66	34	(105)	56	44	(105)
Midwest	23	76	(118)[1]	50	50	(111)	47	53	(111)
West	33	67	(57)	61	39	(76)	51	49	(76)
South	94	6	(106)	72	28	(108)	64	36	(108)
Border	68	32	(38)	77	23	(35)	69	31	(35)
Total	49	51	(435)	63	37	(435)	56	44	(435)
Senate									
East	25	75	(20)	55	45	(20)	50	50	(20)
Midwest	14	86	(22)	59	41	(22)	41	59	(22)
West	45	55	(22)	46	54	(26)	35	65	(26)
South	100	0	(22)	73	27	(22)	55	45	(22)
Border	70	30	(10)	70	30	(10)	70	30	(10)
Total	49	51	(96)	59	41	(100)	47	53	(100)

[1] Includes one Independent.

NOTE: The 1980 figures are for immediately before the election; the 1953 and 1981 figures are for the opening of the Congress that year.

held all the Senate seats from the South, but in 1981 they controlled only 55 percent. The South is no longer a Democratic stronghold for presidential or congressional candidates.

This change in the partisan share of the South's seats in Congress has had an important impact on that region's influence within the two parties. The South used to be the backbone of Democratic congressional representation. This, and the corresponding seniority its members built up, gave southerners disproportionate power within the Democratic party in Congress. That numerical strength, however, has waned. In 1947, with the Republicans in control of both houses of Congress, southerners accounted for about half of the Democratic seats in the House and Senate. During the late 1940s and the 1950s, southern strength was fairly stable at something over 40 percent. It then began to decline, and by the 1970s it stabilized again at about one-fourth of the Democratic seats in Congress. An examination of the South's share of Republican congressional representation would present the reverse picture. Miniscule or nonexistent at the end of World War II, it steadily began to grow, reaching about 20 percent in 1981. As a consequence of these changes, southerners' influence has declined in the Democratic party and grown in the GOP.

Other regional changes since 1953, while not as striking as those in the South, also are significant. In the 1953 House, the Republicans controlled the East and West by two-to-one margins, and the Midwest by a margin of three-to-one; in 1981, they controlled only the Midwest, but partisan control in all three regions was about even. In the 1953 Senate, the Republicans had a massive lead in the East and Midwest, and a slight lead in the West; by 1981, their lead in the East was eliminated, their hold on the Midwest reduced, and their lead in the West had increased somewhat. On balance, what we have witnessed in the last three decades is the "deregionalization" of congressional elections. While some regional variations are still apparent, the Congress of 1981 was regionally homogeneous compared to that of 1953.

CANDIDATES' RESOURCES

Political Backgrounds

What resources are available to congressional candidates, and how do these resources influence election results?[4] One major resource available to many candidates is the visibility and reputation for performance that usually accompany public office. For example, a state legislator running for a House seat can appeal to the electorate on the basis that the candidate's prior experience was good preparation because of the similarities between the two offices. Furthermore, a state legislator would have previously constructed a successful electoral organization that would be of some use in the campaign. For these and other reasons, such a candidate would presumably have an electoral advantage over another candidate who had held no previous elective office. In general, candidates with a greater "investment" in political office—that is, candidates who, relative to others, have achieved higher offices—would be more successful than those with a lesser "investment."

Table 9-4 presents 1980 House and Senate winners, controlling for office background, party, and incumbency. In House races, the Republicans were more successful than the Democrats in the case of every office background. Moreover, candidates with greater office investment usually were more successful than those with lesser office investment, particularly in races without incumbents. In those no-incumbent races, for both Democrats and Republicans, state legislators were markedly more successful than candidates with other elective backgrounds. The Senate races, with the smaller number of candidates, present less clear patterns. Nevertheless, those candidates with the greatest office investments (U.S. representatives and state-wide officeholders) were in gen-

Table 9-4   House and Senate Winners, Controlling for Office Background, Party, and Incumbency, 1980

Candidate's Last Office	Opponent of Democratic Incumbent		No Incumbent Democratic Candidate		No Incumbent Republican Candidate		Opponent of Republican Incumbent	
	%	(N)	%	(N)	%	(N)	%	(N)
House								
State Legislature	24	(21)	58	(19)	85	(13)	5	(20)
Other Elective Office	29	(17)	27	(11)	67	(6)	0	(11)
No Elective Office	10	(173)	23	(13)	46	(24)	2	(97)
Senate								
U.S. Representative	100	(5)	50	(2)	100	(1)	—	(0)
State-Wide Elective	67	(3)	33	(3)	50	(2)	—	(0)
Other Elective Office	0	(5)	0	(3)	100	(3)	0	(4)
No Elective Office	40	(5)	0	(1)	67	(3)	0	(2)

NOTE: Percentages show the proportion of candidates in each category who won; numbers in parentheses are the totals upon which the percentages are based.

eral more successful than those candidates with lesser office investments. Clearly, previous office achievements are a useful resource in House and Senate elections.

Incumbency

Another major resource we will consider is incumbency. Actually, incumbency is not a single resource, but rather a status that usually conveys to a candidate a variety of benefits. In some respects, incumbency works to a candidate's advantage automatically. For example, incumbents tend to be more visible to voters and to be more favorably viewed by them than are their challengers.[5] Moreover, incumbents' districts or states frequently contain an electorate that is biased in their favor in terms of party identification. In other respects, incumbents can *use* their status to gain advantages. For example, incumbents usually raise and spend more campaign funds than challengers, and they usually have a more developed and experienced campaign organization. Because of advantages in terms of these important resources, incumbents historically have been more successful getting elected than their opponents.

As we saw in Table 9-1, in the last decade the success rate of House incumbents has increased slightly while that of Senate incumbents has decreased. Other research has shown that the margins by which incumbents won election to the House and Senate during the 1970s increased,[6] although since 1976 this trend has reversed for senators. What explains these changes in the rate of incumbent success? This is an important question to consider if we are to understand the "mechanisms" that govern the pattern of outcomes in congressional elections and anticipate the shape of congressional membership in the years to come.

One of the first explanations of increased incumbent success was offered by Edward R. Tufte. He argued that "redistricting—particularly 'bipartisan' redistricting—was making a substantial contribution to the recent decline in political competition and increase in the tenure of incumbents. . . ."[7] This seemed to be a plausible argument, since the decline in competition in House elections occurred about the same time as the massive redistricting brought about by the Supreme Court voting rights decisions in the early 1960s. Others argued that while House incumbents did indeed become safer in the mid-1960s in redistricted states, this was also the case in states that did not redraw House districts and for Senate seats.[8]

Another explanation involves the perquisites members of Congress enjoy, such as the frank (free mailings by members of Congress for official business), congressional staff, and travel allowances. In recent years the number of congressional staff members has increased dramatically, and evidence suggests that the franking privilege has been used more extensively by incumbents.[9] Morris P. Fiorina emphasizes specific ways some of these resources have helped incumbents.[10] During the post-New Deal period, the level of federal services and the bureaucracy that administers them has grown tremendously. Along with this growth, people began to experience more problems with the delivery of government services. These problems are frequently brought to the attention of members of Congress who act as ombudsmen for their constituents and intervene on their behalf with the bureaucracy. Fiorina contends that in the mid-1960s the congressmen who replaced senior members put more emphasis on constituency service than did their predecessors. Voters thus concluded that it was to their advantage to support incumbents because they could help them untangle red tape. Although it is difficult to demonstrate that constituency services yield significant electoral benefits, it is likely that they may account in part for the changes in incumbency success and safeness.

A third explanation of the increased advantage of incumbents is a change in the way individual voters decide how to cast their ballots. Until the mid-1960s, the standard description of American voting behavior was party voting; as we saw in Chapter 8, three out of four Americans identified with one of the two major parties, and the great majority of those identifiers supported their chosen party at election time. Since the mid-1960s, however, voters have relied less on party as a determinant of their vote. John A. Ferejohn, in his analysis of national survey data, concludes that voting behavior within party identification categories has changed.[11] Albert D. Cover shows that there has been a steady increase in defections by voters who identify with the party of challengers of House incumbents between 1958 and 1974, while there has been no such increase in defections by voters who identify with the party of incumbents.[12]

Campaign Spending

Increased incumbency resources and a changes in voter behavior contribute to the greater electoral safety of incumbents. There is another factor, however, which helps account not only for the increasing advantage for members of both houses in the 1960s and early 1970s, but also for the divergence between the House and Senate in this regard in more recent years. That factor is campaign spending. None of the major studies of the growth of the advantage of incumbents has devoted any extensive attention to relative campaign spending.[13] It is, however, reasonable to assume that campaign spending has an effect on candidate performance, and data on congressional campaign expenditures

Table 9-5   Average Congressional Campaign Spending and Interyear Increases, 1972, 1976

	House	*Senate*
1972		
Incumbents	$ 50,978	$495,424
Challengers	31,941	244,126
Open Seats	90,052	469,820
1976		
Incumbents	$ 79,837	$677,278
Challengers	48,945	440,460
Open Seats	114,869	768,956
1972-1976 Increases		
Incumbents	+56.6%	+36.7%
Challengers	+53.2%	+80.4%
Open Seats	+27.6%	+63.7%

SOURCE: All data are from *Congressional Quarterly Weekly Reports* as follows: 1972 House and Senate, December 1, 1973, p. 3130; 1976 House, October 29, 1977, p. 2301; 1976 Senate, June 25, 1977, p. 1294. The House figures for 1972 and the Senate open seat figures for 1972 are averages of Democratic and Republican average spending figures.

Table 9-6 Election Outcomes in House Races Involving Incumbents, Controlling for Campaign Spending by Challengers, 1976 (Percentages Read Across)

Challenger Spent	Incumbent's Percentage of the Vote				Total Percent	(N)
	Less than 55%	55-59.9%	60-69.9%	70+%		
$0 - $9,999	0%	2	29	69	100%	(109)
$10,000 - $29,999	3%	12	43	42	100%	(74)
$30,000 - $89,999	7%	35	51	7	100%	(81)
$90,000+	52%	29	19	0	100%	(73)
All Races	14%	18	35	33	100%	(337)

show that incumbents have a considerable monetary advantage. Table 9-5 presents spending data for 1972 and 1976, the period in which the divergence between the houses on incumbency success began. In both years, for both houses, on average incumbents spent more than challengers—at least 50 percent more in all four comparisons, and as much as 100 percent more for the 1972 Senate races. One also can see that expenditures increased over time, but at different rates. House incumbents and challengers increased spending by about the same percentage between 1972 and 1976, but in Senate races the increase for challengers was much greater than for incumbents, which may explain the diverging trends in incumbents' safety.

Beginning in the mid-1960s, election campaigns began to rely more heavily on those aspects of campaign strategies that cost money (for example, media time, campaign consulting, direct mailing, and computers), and these items became more and more expensive. Consequently, the gap in campaign spending between incumbents and challengers became more important, and the re-election success and election margins of incumbents increased. Most challengers were unable to raise sufficient funds to compete. This, we believe, is more important than the mere fact that challengers were outspent. For example, in 1976, 54.3 percent of the challengers of House incumbents spent less than $30,000; indeed, 32.3 percent spent less than $10,000. Incumbents have many inherent advantages in terms of name recognition and resources that a challenger must spend money to overcome if he hopes to win. The available data on campaign spending support these arguments. Table 9-6 presents data on 1976 House election outcomes, controlling for campaign expenditures by the challenger.[14] Clearly, a strong negative relationship exists between how much challengers spend and how well incumbents do at the polls. For example, when challengers spent less than $10,000, not a single incumbent received less than 55 percent of the vote, and over two-thirds received at least 70 percent of the vote. When, on the other hand, challengers spent $90,000 or more, no incumbent received 70 percent of the vote and over half won less than 55 percent.

Challengers who are expected to do well find it easier to raise money than challengers whose chances of election are doubtful. Thus, the reader might argue, what we are seeing may be simply a reflection of expected performance, rather than performance influenced by spending. Other research, however, indicates that this is probably not the case. In an analysis of 1972 and 1974 congressional elections, Gary C. Jacobson concludes:

> our evidence is that campaign spending helps candidates, particularly nonincumbents, by bringing them to the attention of voters; it is *not* the case that well known candidates simply attract more money; rather, money buys attention.[15]

Similar conclusions can be drawn from the data on Senate elections shown in Table 9-7. Given the small number of cases, we want to present a comparison of the results in Senate races between challengers and incumbents, attempting to control for whether the challenger spent an adequate amount of money. There are two difficulties with such a comparison. First, states vary substantially in population and thus a budget that would be adequate in a small state would be hopelessly inadequate in a large state. Therefore, in estimating the adequacy of a budget, state size must be considered. However, it is also likely that the political productivity of money does not increase in a linear fashion with population, and so a pure "dollars per vote" comparison is also insufficient.

The second obvious problem is to determine what is the "adequate" amount for the challenger to spend. For this analysis, we divided states into four categories depending on the number of their representatives: those states with one or two representatives in the first category, states with three to six in the second, seven to 10 representatives in the third, and more than 10 in the fourth. Then for each category, we established a "minimum" spending figure for the challengers based on a number of

Table 9-7 Election Outcomes in Senate Races Involving Incumbents, Controlling for Campaign Spending by Challengers, 1972-1978

Incumbent's Percentage of the Vote	Did Challenger Spend Minimum Amount?		
	Yes	No	All Races
Less than 55%	74%	19%	46%
55-59%	14	17	16
60% or more	12	64	39
Total percent	100%	100%	101%
(Number)	(43)	(47)	(90)

NOTE: A "minimum" expenditure is defined above.

cents per voter: 20 cents per voter for states in the first category (one or two representatives), 15 cents for the second, 10 cents for the third, and 5 cents for the fourth. This controls for the population variations we discussed earlier. Finally, for each Senate race we ascertained whether the challenger spent more than the minimum amount per voter and what the outcome of the race was in terms of the percentage of the two-party vote received by the incumbent. The results presented in Table 9-7 are striking.

In those races where the challenger was not able to spend the minimum amount deemed necessary for effective competition, only 19 percent of the outcomes were in the marginal category (less than 55 percent of the vote), and almost two-thirds of the incumbents received more than 60 percent of the vote. On the other hand, in those races in which the challenger did spend at least the minimum amount per voter, almost three-fourths of the outcomes were in the marginal category and only 12 percent of the incumbents received more than 60 percent of the vote.

In short, without adequate campaign funding, challengers cannot compete effectively with incumbents. Our evidence also suggests that campaign funding of challengers in Senate elections between the early and late 1970s has increased relative to incumbents—a plausible explanation for the decline in the frequency of re-election of Senate incumbents. As funding for challengers increased, more of those challengers were able to spend the minimum amount necessary to compete effectively. Once this spending "threshold" was passed, elections turned on other factors than simple incumbency advantage or how much money was spent. Those incumbents who were vulnerable on a variety of grounds were vulnerable to defeat, and many of them were defeated.

This explanation, then, helps to account for the different patterns of incumbency success in Senate and House elections in recent years. While Senate incumbents have been less successful, House incumbents have maintained their previously high success rates. With regard to campaign spending, no significant change in the relative positions of House incumbents and challengers has been exhibited. Most Senate challengers in recent years have been adequately funded while House challengers have not. This helps, in turn, to explain differences in visibility and ability to contact voters on the part of the two groups of challengers. In 1978, for example, 86 percent of survey respondents were able to recognize and place on thermometer scales Senate challengers, but the same was true in the case of House challengers for only 44 percent of the sample. In the case of Senate challengers, 63 percent of the sample read about them in newspapers or magazines and 70 percent saw them on television. The corresponding figures for House challengers were 32 percent and 24 percent, respectively.[16]

THE 1980 ELECTION: THE IMPACT ON CONGRESS

Election analysis is interesting in and of itself, but what makes it important are the consequences of elections: the selection of persons who will make governmental policy. The most immediate and obvious consequence of the 1980 congressional elections was the transfer of control of the Senate from the Democrats to the Republicans. When it comes to controlling the formal institutional levers of power, partisan control of the chamber is everything. Thus with the election, Republicans gained control of the Senate majority leadership posts, committee and subcommittee chairmanships, and the staff resources that go with these positions. Republicans are now able to determine the legislative agenda of committees and decide what bills are considered on the Senate floor and when. This shift of institutional control has important implications for policy outcomes in the Congress. Ideas favored by the Republicans have greater chances of success, while the chances of Democratic proposals are diminished, although the Democrats still retain control of the House.

The 1980 elections also produced a significant shift in the ideological complexion of the Congress. Table 9-8 presents data on the average conservative coalition support ratios of departing and remaining members of the House and Senate in 1980.[17] (Higher support ratios indicate greater conservatism.) Examining the House data first, we see that there are no substantial differences between departing and remaining members except among southern Democrats. Here the retainees are much more conservative than the departures. Thus the main ideological consequence of the elections in the House stems from the net replacement of 33 Democrats by Republicans. The difference between the average support ratios of Democrats and Republicans in the House is large, so this replacement produces a significant ideological shift within the body.

The picture in the Senate is somewhat different. For all three groups—northern Democrats, southern Democrats, and Republicans—those members departing were more liberal than those remaining. In the Senate the ideological center of gravity of *both* parties was shifted to the right. Moreover, the proportional replacement of Democrats by Republicans was greater in the Senate than in the House. Thus the liberals in the Democratic party in the Senate were damaged in three ways: their party lost control, their party became noticeably more conservative, and the Republican conservatives were substantially strengthened. In the House, only the last of these changes occurred.

With the Republicans taking control of the White House and the Senate, the main arena of combat for Republican programs has become the House of Representatives. At the beginning of the 97th Congress,

Table 9-8 Conservatism of Departures and Retainees in the House and Senate Elections, 1980

	1980 Mean Conservative Coalition Support Ratios					
	Departures		*Retainees*		*Total*	
	%	(N)	%	(N)	%	(N)
House						
Northern Democrats	29	(42)	29	(156)	29	(198)
Southern Democrats	55	(13)	71	(65)	69	(78)
All Democrats	36	(55)	41	(221)	40	(276)
Republicans	84	(19)	81	(140)	81	(159)
All Members	48	(74)	56	(361)	55	(435)
Senate						
Northern Democrats	18	(10)	32	(33)	29	(43)
Southern Democrats	68	(4)	75	(12)	73	(16)
All Democrats	33	(14)	43	(45)	41	(59)
Republicans	68	(4)	77	(37)	74	(41)
All Members	42	(18)	58	(82)	55	(100)

NOTE: The ratios are based on the percentage of all roll call votes on which a majority of voting southern Democrats and a majority of voting Republicans opposed the stand taken by a majority of voting northern Democrats. Numbers in parentheses are the totals upon which the mean conservative coalition support ratios are based.

the Democrats held only a 51-seat margin over the Republicans, a comparatively narrow edge. (If everyone were to vote, and all Republicans were to vote together, the Republicans needed only a net gain of 26 Democratic votes to win.) Political conflict on the House floor has become a battle for the support of members whose ideological positions place them closest to the opposite party: conservative southern Democrats and moderate Republicans or—as they have come to be known—the "Boll Weevils" and the "Gypsy Moths," respectively.

The "Boll Weevils" is the informal name given to a group of mostly southern House Democrats who have joined together to influence House Democratic policy in a conservative direction. They have established a formal organization for this purpose called the Conservative Democratic Forum with more than 40 members.[18] These conservative Democrats along with virtually all House Republicans formed the basis on which President Reagan's string of 1981 legislative victories was built. Much has been made in the press of the outpouring of public pressure in support of the Reagan program, so one might expect that it is fear of electoral defeat in 1982 that has provided the impetus for southerners to support the president. Analysis shows, however, that the situation is not so simple. To illustrate, we will consider the House vote on July 29, 1981, on the president's tax bill.[19]

Seventy southern Democrats cast votes on the tax bill, with slightly less than half (32) supporting Reagan's plan.[20] Electoral vulnerability, however, seems to provide little explanation for this support. Eleven of these southerners were elected with less than 60 percent of the vote; only three supported the president. Of the 11, five received less than 55 percent of the vote; of these only one voted with Reagan. On the other hand, 29 of the 59 who received more than 60 percent of the vote in 1980 supported the Reagan plan.

The degree of support for the president can be explained instead by a mixture of personal ideology and length of service of the southern Democrats. Table 9-9 breaks down the votes of southern Democrats on the tax bill, controlling for length of service and whether they were members of the Conservative Democratic Forum. As can be seen, both of these elements had an independent impact, although forum membership seems more important. Reagan received the support of about five-sixths of the most junior members of the forum, but only about one-sixth of those senior southerners who were not forum members voted with him.[21] Conservatives were more in sympathy with the policies of President Reagan than those of the House Democratic leadership. Junior members had weaker, more short-lived personal ties with the more senior Democratic leaders, thus these ties were less effective in overcoming ideological predispositions.

This pattern emphasizes the importance of congressional elections as a selection mechanism as well as a control mechanism. That is, it is easier to use elections to select a legislator with a given ideological view

Table 9-9   Voting of Southern House Democrats on 1981 Tax Bill, by Seniority and "Boll Weevil" Membership

Elected	Yes %	Yes (N)	No %	No (N)	Total %	Total (N)
Before Nov. 1974	57	(14)	17	(18)	34	(32)
Nov. 1974-Oct. 1978	50	(12)	38	(8)	45	(20)
Nov. 1978 and Later	85	(13)	20	(5)	67	(18)
Total	64	(39)	23	(31)	46	(70)

NOTE: Percentages show the proportion of members in each category that supported President Reagan's tax bill instead of the Democratic plan; numbers in parentheses are the totals upon which percentages are based.

that he will follow than it is to use them as a future threat to persuade a member to deviate from his personally held views. Popular pressure, however, can be important in buttressing a legislator's resolve to resist countervailing pressure from the leadership or elsewhere.

The "Gypsy Moths" are a coalition of 20 to 30 eastern and midwestern Republican representatives. Many of them are from urban areas or areas with significant academic concentrations—districts that offer ripe opportunities for Democrats to build competing coalitions.[22] Thus they could experience significant electoral pressure from siding with the president. Unlike southern Democrats, however, they have remained united on most issues. On the early budget votes they were unanimous, on the final budget vote only two defected, and on the tax bill only one voted with the Democrats. They have negotiated concessions helpful to their districts from the administration. An "inside" approach to dealing with the conservative policies of President Reagan, they believe, has been successful so far.

Because of the importance of elections as a selection mechanism, the future of policymaking in Congress will depend heavily on the 1982 elections. Therefore, we will conclude this chapter by looking at the likely pattern of those outcomes.

THE 1982 CONGRESSIONAL ELECTION

Democrats were at a disadvantage in the 1980 Senate elections because they had more than twice as many seats at stake than did the Republicans (24 to 10). Unfortunately for them, they will be at almost as great a disadvantage in this regard in 1982: of 33 seats at stake, 21 now are held by Democrats.[23] Beyond noting this numerical disparity, it is difficult to predict with any certainty precisely which seats will be in the greatest jeopardy in 1982. We can discuss, however, certain systematic elements and some relevant individual circumstances that are apparent a year before the elections.

In terms of election margins, the Democrats have a larger number (but a smaller proportion) of seats that were won by less than 55 percent of the vote—seven versus five for the Republicans. In addition, George J. Mitchell, D-Maine, was appointed to his seat and is therefore at least as vulnerable as a marginally elected senator. Seventeen of the senators were first elected in 1976 and one in 1978. Senators seeking their first re-election tend to be more vulnerable than those who have had more time to solidify their position. Combining the two elements, seven of the nine Democratic first-termers were elected with less than 55 percent of the vote; this is true of only four of the nine Republicans. Thus there is a marked situational bias in favor of the Republicans in the Senate races of 1982. Individual circumstances also reinforce this. Four Democratic retirements seem possible: Harry F. Byrd, Jr., of Virginia (who already has announced his retirement in 1982), John C. Stennis of Mississippi and Quentin N. Burdick of North Dakota because of age, and Harrison A. Williams, Jr., of New Jersey because he was caught in the FBI's Abscam operation. Among Republicans, S. I. Hayakawa of California has announced his retirement, and there will probably be no others. As we have seen, vacant seats are more likely to change partisan control than those seats with incumbents, thus Democrats are disadvantaged in this respect, too.

In the House, redistricting probably will hurt the Democrats slightly. The most visible population losses have occurred in urban areas dominated by Democrats, and the greatest gains have occurred in the Sun Belt where the Republicans are advantaged. Almost certainly, this will produce some Republican gains. Democrats, on the other hand, will have the greater number of incumbents running, producing a distinct bias in their favor. Probably the most important factor in the House races will be whether the Reagan administration can produce a positive change in the nation's economic fortunes by the fall of 1982.

Campaign financing will play a significant role in the mid-term congressional elections. Although many more Democratic incumbents ran in House races than Republicans in 1980, the aggregate expenditures were equal: $58.4 million for each party.[24] This suggests that Republicans are accelerating their congressional fund raising and that they may be able to use money to neutralize to a substantial degree the Democratic incumbency advantage in the House—something they already appear to have accomplished in Senate races.

In short, the Republicans appear to have an advantage in the 1982 Senate races, and they may even add to their majority. If that happens, the Democrats probably will not be able to regain control of the Senate until 1986 at the earliest. Historically, the party of the president loses seats in mid-term elections. Nevertheless, the Republicans may be able to make some gains in the House if economic conditions improve and if the Republicans are able to maintain their fund-raising advantage. On the other hand, if the economy worsens and the Democrats can compete successfully for funds, we would anticipate a standoff or Democratic gains.

NOTES

1. Split control of Congress is a particularly rare event. The last time it occurred was in the 72nd Congress (1931-1933) when the Republicans lost control of the House but kept the Senate.
2. The definition of incumbent here is limited to *elected* incumbents. This includes all members of the House, since the only way to become a representative is by election. In the case of the Senate, however, vacancies may be filled by appointment. These senators are not counted as incum-

bents. There is no obvious ground on which to choose a beginning date for the study of congressional change. We will use one of two in this chapter: 1946, because the war years produced many unique events rendering data from that period imperfectly comparable to those from later years, and 1954, because beginning with that year more reliable data are available and it is the first opportunity for re-election for members elected after the first postwar reapportionment of congressional seats.

3. The regional breakdowns used in this chapter are as follows: *East:* Connecticut, Delaware, Maine, Massachusetts, New Hampshire, New Jersey, New York, Pennsylvania, Rhode Island, Vermont; *Midwest:* Illinois, Indiana, Iowa, Kansas, Michigan, Minnesota, Nebraska, North Dakota, Ohio, South Dakota, Wisconsin; *West:* Alaska, Arizona, California, Colorado, Hawaii, Idaho, Montana, Nevada, New Mexico, Oregon, Utah, Washington, Wyoming; *South:* Alabama, Arkansas, Florida, Georgia, Louisiana, Mississippi, North Carolina, South Carolina, Tennessee, Texas, Virginia; *Border:* Kentucky, Maryland, Missouri, Oklahoma, West Virginia. This classification differs somewhat from the one we use in other chapters, but it is fairly standard for congressional analysis.

4. See Gary C. Jacobson and Samuel Kernell in *Strategy and Choice in Congressional Elections* (New Haven: Yale University Press, 1981), especially Chapters 2 through 4, for corroborating analysis.

5. See also Thomas E. Mann and Raymond E. Wolfinger, "Candidates and Parties in Congressional Elections," *American Political Science Review* 74 (September 1980): 617-632.

6. See David R. Mayhew, "Congressional Elections: The Case of the Vanishing Marginals," *Polity* 6 (Spring 1974): 295-317; Robert S. Erikson, "The Advantage of Incumbency in Congressional Elections," *Polity,* 3 (Spring 1971): 395-405; Robert S. Erikson, "Malapportionment, Gerrymandering and Party Fortunes in Congressional Elections," *American Political Science Review* 66 (December 1972): 1234-1245; and Warren Lee Kostroski, "Party and Incumbency in Postwar Senate Elections: Trends, Patterns and Models," *American Political Science Review* 67 (December 1973): 1213-1234.

7. Edward R. Tufte, "Communication," *American Political Science Review* 68 (March 1974): 211-213. The communication involved a discussion of Tufte's earlier article, "The Relationship Between Seats and Votes in Two-Party Systems," *American Political Science Review* 67 (June 1973): 540-554.

8. See John A. Ferejohn, "On the Decline of Competition in Congressional Elections," *American Political Science Review* 71 (March 1977): 166-176; Albert D. Cover, "One Good Term Deserves Another: The Advantage of Incumbency in Congressional Elections," *American Journal of Political Science* 21 (August 1977): 523-541; and Albert D. Cover and David R. Mayhew, "Congressional Dynamics and the Decline of Competitive Congressional Elections," in *Congress Reconsidered,* 2d ed., edited by Lawrence C. Dodd and Bruce I. Oppenheimer (Washington, D.C.: Congressional Quarterly Press, 1981), pp. 62-82.

9. On the frank, see Mayhew, "Congressional Elections," p. 312.

10. Morris P. Fiorina, *Congress: Keystone of the Washington Establishment* (New Haven: Yale University Press, 1977), especially Chapters 4-6.

11. Ferejohn, "On the Decline in Competition," p. 174.

12. Cover, "One Good Term," p. 535.

13. A number of studies, however, deal with the impact of spending on congressional elections. See Gary C. Jacobson, "Practical Consequences of

Campaign Finance Reform: An Incumbent Protection Act?" *Public Policy* (Winter 1976): 1-32; Jacobson, "Campaign Spending and Voter Awareness of Congressional Candidates" (Paper presented at a meeting of the Public Choice Society, New Orleans, Louisiana, May 11-13, 1977); Jacobson, "The Effects of Campaign Spending in Congressional Elections," *American Political Science Review* 72 (June 1978): 469-491; and Jacobson, *Money in Congressional Elections* (New Haven: Yale University Press, 1980).

14. Unfortunately, the 1980 campaign spending data were not available at the time this was written. Therefore we use data on the 1976 presidential election. For the Senate, because of the small number of cases, we use data on all available years: 1972-1978.

15. Jacobson, "Campaign Spending and Voter Awareness," p. 16.

16. See Mann and Wolfinger, "Candidates and Parties," pp. 624, 627.

17. This is the standard measure of ideological views in congressional research. The conservative coalition is the voting coalition of a majority of Republicans and a majority of southern Democrats. The ratio is a measure of how frequently a member supports this coalition. It is computed by dividing the frequency of support by the sum of the frequency of support and the frequency of opposition. These figures are published annually in the *Congressional Quarterly Almanac.*

18. For a list of members, see *Congressional Quarterly Weekly Report,* June 13, 1981, p. 1026. The boll weevil is an insect that destroys cotton crops in the South by boring within the cotton balls. The analogue is to the southern conservatives "boring within" the Democratic party. Gypsy moths are a northern crop parasite.

19. The vote appears in the *New York Times,* July 30, 1981, p. D21.

20. See our definition of the South in note 3.

21. It is also important to note that junior members were more likely to be members of the forum than were senior members.

22. See David Broder, "The Gypsy Moths," *Washington Post,* July 27, 1981, p. A1.

23. Harry F. Byrd, Jr., of Virginia was elected as an Independent, but caucuses with the Democrats. He is, therefore, counted as a Democrat.

24. Federal Election Commission press release, March 29, 1981.

10

The Congressional Electorate

In this chapter we move from a consideration of the 1980 congressional election results to the behavior of individual voters as sampled by the University of Michigan's Survey Research Center-Center for Political Studies. We examine how social forces, issues, partisan loyalties, incumbency, and evaluations of congressional and presidential performance influence congressional voters' decisions. Where possible, we will compare the impact of these factors on both presidential and congressional voting.

SOCIAL FORCES AND THE CONGRESSIONAL VOTE

In general, social forces relate to the congressional vote much the same way that they do to the presidential vote, although Democratic congressional candidates in 1980 did better in virtually all of the social categories depicted earlier in Table 5-1.[1] For example, with respect to voting by race, Democratic House candidates ran 3 percent better among blacks and 17 percent better among whites than did Jimmy Carter. For both electorates, race produces the most fundamental social division in voting. Indeed, blacks were 45 percentage points more likely to vote Democratic than whites.

One explanation for Democratic congressional candidates' substantially better performance among white voters is that individual Democratic House incumbents were more popular than Carter, as we will see. Furthermore, many more Democrats ran for re-election to the House in 1980 than Republicans. Table 10-1 shows House and Senate voting in 1980, controlling for the incumbency of the respective candidates.[2] The Democratic candidates did the best when they were incumbents and the worst when they were running against Republican incumbents. Furthermore, both Republican and Democratic incumbents did better in House than in Senate elections.

After looking at Table 10-1, the reader might wonder how the Democrats could have done about the same in the proportion of the Senate vote as in the proportion of the House vote, and yet fared so much worse on election day. The explanation lies in the electoral consequences of our federal structure. The populations of all House districts are roughly the same at the beginning of any decade. By the end of the decade, district populations vary substantially, but they do not approach the wide variations in population among the states. As we saw in the last chapter, district populations during the 1970s grew by the greatest margins in the Sun Belt, a Republican region, and declined the most in Democratic urban areas. On the other hand, population among the Senate "districts" varies enormously. In 1980, the Democrats won Senate elections by comfortable margins in California, Ohio, and Illinois and ran very close races in New York and Pennsylvania—all large states. Meanwhile, they lost a string of close contests in the smaller states. Thus Democrats compiled 3 million more popular votes than Republicans, but lost 22 of the 34 Senate races.

Presidential and congressional voting patterns are similar not only with respect to race, but for other social categories, including occupation, family income, education, union membership, and religion. Among whites, union voting registered 15 percentage points, while Catholics were 12 points more likely to vote Democratic than Protestants. Union membership and religion were related to party differences more strongly than any other social characteristics among the white electorate. A few differences from the presidential patterns are particularly worth noting.

The partisan pattern of voting when controlling for sex is reversed from the presidential results. While women were more likely to vote for Carter than men, men were somewhat more likely than women to vote for Democratic House candidates. Military issues and the Equal Rights

Table 10-1   House and Senate Voting, Controlling for Incumbency, 1980

Incumbency Status	Percentage Voting Democratic			
	House		Senate	
Democratic Incumbent	75%	(497)	59%	(310)
No Incumbent	40%	(53)	49%	(232)
Republican Incumbent	23%	(293)	38%	(58)
Total	54%	(843)	53%	(600)

NOTE: Numbers in parentheses are the totals upon which percentages are based.

Amendment (ERA) may not have influenced the congressional vote as they did the presidential vote. Several commentators have suggested that women who thought Ronald Reagan was too hawkish or who disagreed with him on ERA disproportionately voted against him. The absence of this influence on the congressional vote may account for the different pattern. In any event, the differences in voting by sex are not large in either case.

Comparing the impact of region on voting, we find almost a complete reversal of the presidential pattern. Reagan received his greatest voting support among whites from voters living in southern and border states. No other regional variations were apparent. In House voting, however, it was the Democrats who received the greatest support in the South and border states; Republicans received a majority in the other regions. We believe these results reflect the influence of ideology on voting patterns. Southern and border state voters, most of whom have historical loyalties to the Democratic party and share conservative political views, were willing to stick with relatively conservative Democratic congressional candidates, but deserted the top of the ticket which they regarded as too liberal and too unsuccessful.

We found relatively weak relationships between major-party presidential voting and age, although all surveys agree that John B. Anderson fared better among younger voters. There was no relationship between congressional voting and age.

Finally, unlike the presidential vote, the congressional vote was scarcely related to social class. As we saw in Chapter 5, Carter received more support from working-class whites than from middle-class whites. While class voting for president was low (only 9 points), it was still present. But class voting for Congress registered a scant 2 points among the white electorate. As with presidential voting in 1980, the impact of most social forces on the congressional vote was relatively weak. We will have to seek other factors to explain how congressional voters make up their minds.

ISSUES AND THE CONGRESSIONAL VOTE

Although data on perceptions of candidates and voter preferences are much less extensive in congressional elections than in presidential contests, it is possible to look at issues and the congressional vote from several interesting perspectives. One approach is to ask whether groups of voters' varying positions on an issue are related to variations in the proportion of the vote going to one party or another. Figure 10-1 depicts party voting for the House and Senate in 1980, controlling for party identification and positions on the liberal-conservative issue scale.[3] In general, as conservatism increases, the proportion voting Democratic

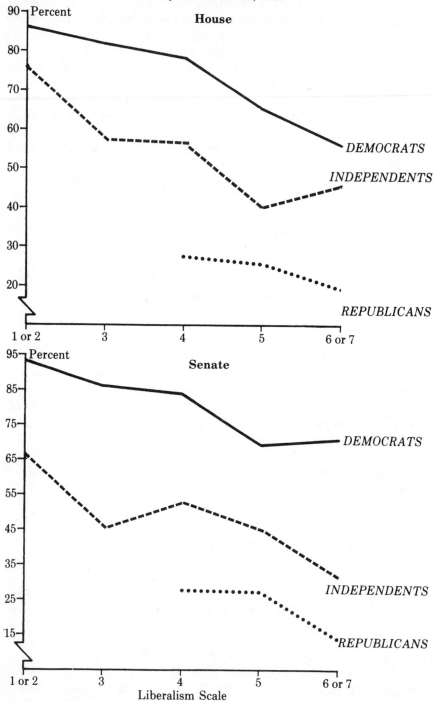

Figure 10-1 Percentage Voting Democratic for House and Senate, by Position on Liberalism Scale and Party Identification, 1980

NOTE: A score of "1" indicates the most liberal response; a score of "7" indicates the most conservative response.

declines, although the relationship is not completely consistent. For both the House and Senate, the patterns are similar. Although party identification accounts for larger variations in the vote than positions on the liberal-conservative scale, the data show a systematic relationship between issue positions and the vote.

Another perspective on issues and the congressional vote is to ask whether a voter casts his or her ballot according to which candidate is closer to the voter's own position on the issues. This is the strictest and most direct test of whether issues matter in congressional voting. In 1980, the Survey Research Center-Center for Political Studies asked respondents not only their position on the liberal-conservative scale, but also their perception of where on this scale the Republican and Democratic House candidates stood.

Before presenting these findings, however, a warning is appropriate. When testing for the impact of issues, the results are always biased in favor of finding an effect. Bear in mind that we will be running our tests on a relatively small subset of voters. To be included, a voter must be able to place himself on the issue. Furthermore, in the situation we are about to consider, the voter must be able to place both candidates on the issue and must perceive a difference on the issue between the candidates. In the analysis below, only about 20 percent of those respondents who voted for the House met all of these conditions. Thus even if we find an effect below, it may not be present (at least to the same degree) among a large majority of the electorate.

With that caveat in mind, Table 10-2 details the proportion of the sample that cast their vote for the candidate that they perceived was

Table 10-2 Proportion of House Voters Who Voted "Correctly" on the Liberalism Issue, 1980

Position on Liberalism Scale	*Voter "Should Have" Voted* Democratic		Republican		*Total*	
1 (Most Liberal)	[1]	(1)	—	(0)	[1]	(1)
2 (Liberal)	94%	(16)	[2]	(2)	94%	(18)
3 (Slightly Liberal)	82%	(17)	[2]	(4)	76%	(21)
4 (Moderate, Middle of the Road)	82%	(28)	71%	(17)	78%	(45)
5 (Slightly Conservative)	[3]	(5)	70%	(37)	69%	(42)
6 (Conservative)	[2]	(3)	82%	(50)	81%	(53)
7 (Extremely Conservative)	—	(0)	[5]	(5)	[5]	(5)
Total	83%	(70)	77%	(115)	79%	(185)

NOTE: Numbers in parentheses are the totals upon which percentages are based. Numbers in brackets are the number who voted "correctly" in cases where the total N is less than 10.

closest to them on the liberal-conservative scale. The results are fairly impressive. About four-fifths of the respondents voted "correctly" (i.e., in accord with their positions and perceptions). As one would expect, the results are somewhat stronger at the extremes of the scale, since voters who are less sure of their positions are more likely to place themselves toward the center.

In summary, issues have some direct impact on the congressional vote, although this impact may be felt only among a subset of the electorate. Clearly, issues do not account for all of the variation in voting, and we must consider other determinants of voting behavior as well.

PARTY IDENTIFICATION AND THE CONGRESSIONAL VOTE

As we have seen, party identification strongly influences voters' decisions, although less so today than in the past. Table 10-3, which corresponds to Table 8-4 on the presidential vote, reports the percentage of whites voting Democratic for the House, across all categories of partisanship from 1952 through 1980. Even a casual inspection of the data will reveal that the proportion of voters casting ballots in accordance with their party identification has declined substantially over time.

Consider first the strong identifier categories. In every election between 1952 and 1964 at least 9 out of 10 strong party identifiers supported the candidate of their party. After that, the percentage dropped, falling to 4 out of 5 in 1980. Similar patterns of defection are found among weak partisans, although defection rates are always higher. In 1966, defections by Independent leaners of both parties increased. (The Independents with no party leanings exhibit more erratic behavior.) Despite this increase in defections from party identification since the mid-1960s, strong party identifiers are more likely to vote in accord with their party than weak identifiers, who, in turn, are usually more likely to remain loyal to their party than Independents with partisan leanings. As we know, however, the proportion of the electorate that falls in the strong party identification categories has declined. Thus strong Democrats, for example, are not only less likely to vote Democratic than before, but fewer voters identify themselves as strong Democrats. The impact of party on voting, therefore, has suffered a double weakening.

If party identifiers have been defecting more frequently in House elections, to whom have they been defecting? As one might expect from the preceding chapter, the answer is: to incumbents.

Table 10-3 Percentage of White Major-Party Voters Who Voted Democratic for the House, by Party Identification, 1952-1980

Party Identification	Election Year														
	1952	1954	1956	1958	1960	1962	1964	1966	1968	1970	1972	1974	1976	1978	1980
Strong Democrat	90	97	94	96	92	96	92	92	88	91	91	89	86	83	82
Weak Democrat	76	77	86	88	85	83	84	81	72	76	79	81	76	79	66
Independent, Leans Democratic	63	70	82	75	86	74	78	54	60	74	78	87	76	60	69
Independent, No Partisan Leanings	25	41	35	46	52	61	70	49	48	48	54	54	55	56	57
Independent, Leans Republican	18	6	17	26	26	28	28	31	18	35	27	38	32	36	32
Weak Republican	10	6	11	22	14	14	34	22	21	17	24	31	28	34	26
Strong Republican	5	5	5	6	8	6	8	12	8	4	15	14	15	19	22

NOTE: To approximate the numbers upon which these percentages are based, see Table 8-2. Actual Ns will be smaller than those that can be derived from Table 8-2 since respondents who did not vote (or who voted for a minor party) have been excluded from these calculations. Numbers also will be lower for the presidential election years since the voting report is provided in the postelection interviews that usually contain about 10 percent fewer respondents than the pre-election interviews in which party identification was measured. The 1954 survey measured voting intention shortly before the election. Except for 1954, the off-year election surveys are based only upon a postelection interview.

INCUMBENCY AND THE CONGRESSIONAL VOTE

Albert D. Cover's analysis of congressional voting behavior between 1958 and 1974 compared the party defection rates for voters who were of the same party as incumbents (e.g., Democrats in a district with a Democratic incumbent) and those who were of the same party as challengers.[4] He found no systematic increase over time in defections among those who shared party identification with incumbents (the proportions varied between 5 and 14 percent). Among those voters who shared identification with challengers, however, the rate of defection (that is, the proportion voting with the incumbent instead of the candidate of their own party) increased steadily from 16 percent in 1958 to 56 percent in 1972, and then dropped to 49 percent in 1974. The decline in voting in accord with party identification appears to be attributable largely to increased support for incumbents.

Table 10-4 presents the data for 1980 on the percentage of respondents who voted Democratic for the House and Senate, controlling for party identification and incumbency. House voting continues the pattern we have been discussing. The proportion of voters defecting from their party identification is low when that identification is shared by the incumbent (11 percent for Democrats and 7 percent for Republicans). However, the rates are much higher when the incumbent is of the other party (55 percent for Democratic identifiers and 35 percent for Republicans). Note also that the difference in the proportion of Independents voting Democratic is much greater when the incumbent is a Democrat.

The Senate data present a similar pattern, although the impact of incumbency is far weaker. Again the defection rates are low when party identification is shared with the incumbent, but much higher when the incumbent is of the other party. Note, however, that the proportions of pro-incumbent defections are lower in the Senate voting: 33 percent among Democratic identifiers and 27 percent among Republicans. Also the proportion of Independents voting for Democratic incumbents is substantially lower than in House voting. These factors, plus the structural differences between House and Senate voting we discussed earlier in this chapter, help to explain the differences in the success of Senate and House incumbents in achieving re-election in 1980.

THE CONGRESSIONAL VOTE AS A REFERENDUM

In Chapter 7 we discussed the impact of perceptions of presidential performance on the presidential vote, in effect viewing this vote as a referendum. A similar conception can be applied here. First, and most obviously, a congressional election can be considered as a referendum on

Table 10-4 Percentage Voting Democratic for House and Senate, by Party Identification and Incumbency, 1980

Incumbency	Party Identification					
	Democratic		Independent		Republican	
House						
Democrat	89%	(183)	68%	(123)	35%	(98)
None	71%	(17)	29%	(21)	20%	(15)
Republican	45%	(87)	22%	(85)	7%	(114)
Senate						
Democrat	89%	(130)	47%	(95)	27%	(84)
None	78%	(92)	44%	(61)	18%	(79)
Republican	67%	(21)	29%	(17)	16%	(19)

NOTE: Numbers in parentheses are the totals upon which percentages are based.

the performance of the congressional incumbent in office. Second, it can be viewed as a referendum on the performance of the president. We will consider both aspects.

In a thought-provoking article published in 1975, Richard F. Fenno, Jr., discussed an interesting phenomenon he had noticed while travelling with incumbents in their districts.[5] The people he encountered overwhelmingly approved of the performance of their own congressmen, although, according to poll data, the public generally disapproves of the job performance of the U.S. Congress. This paradox, Fenno argued, helps to explain why individual members are electorally successful while the Congress as a whole is unpopular. Congressmen run *against* the Congress when they seek re-election, differentiating themselves from the institution.

SRC-CPS data verify the existence of this phenomenon. Among respondents with an opinion, only 41 percent approved of the job the Congress was doing, while an overwhelming 88 percent approved of the job their own representative was doing.[6] As Table 10-5 indicates, this proportion varies somewhat according to the party of the incumbent and that of the respondent, but even when party allegiances are different, the *lowest* proportion approving of their representative's performance is 74 percent!

The evidence indicates, moreover, that Fenno was correct in seeing this phenomenon as electorally consequential. Table 10-6 shows the proportion of voters who supported their incumbent, controlling for attitude toward the congressman's job performance and incumbent-voter partisan agreement or disagreement. When voters are of the same party as the incumbent and approve of the incumbent's performance, the rate of defection from party identification is only 3 percent. For the same type of voters who *disapprove* of the incumbent's performance,

Table 10-5 Percentage Approving of Representative's Performance, by Party Identification and Incumbency, 1980

Party Identification	Incumbent is Democrat		Republican		Total	
Democrat	93%	(194)	85%	(88)	90%	(272)
Independent	78%	(137)	90%	(105)	83%	(242)
Republican	74%	(81)	93%	(115)	85%	(196)
Total	84%	(402)	90%	(308)	86%	(710)

NOTE: Numbers in parentheses are the totals upon which percentages are based.

however, the rate of defection is 71 percent. Conversely, if voters who are of the opposite party from the incumbent disapprove of the incumbent's job, the rate of defection from party identification is zero. If, however, that type of voter approves of the performance of the incumbent, the rate of defection is 68 percent. Since the overwhelming majority of voters approve of their representatives' performance, the amount of support that accrues to incumbents because of this phenomenon is tremendous.

The other type of referendum that may be operative in congressional elections is a referendum on the president's performance. Edward R. Tufte and others have argued that the outcomes of House elections in non-presidential election years are strongly influenced by public perceptions of the job performance of the president.[7] If a voter thinks that the president is doing a good job, he is more likely to support the congressional candidate of the president's party. Not much attention has been paid to this relationship in presidential years, but the survey data in 1980 would lead one to conclude, at first glance, that presidential performance evaluations are important in this as well. Among voters

Table 10-6 Percentage of Voters Supporting Incumbents in House Voting, by Party and Attitude toward Incumbent's Performance, 1980

Incumbent is	Attitude Toward Congressmen's Job Performance Approve		Disapprove	
Same Party as Voter	97%	(198)	29%	(14)
Opposite Party	68%	(94)	0%	(27)

NOTE: Numbers in parentheses are the totals upon which percentages are based.

who approved of Carter's performance, 70 percent voted for Democratic House candidates; among those who disapproved of the president's performance, only 45 percent voted Democratic.

Further analysis, however, indicates that this initially positive conclusion is largely incorrect. Table 10-7 presents data on this relationship, controlling for the voter's party identification and the party of the congressional incumbent. What seemed to be a direct effect of evaluation of the president's performance was largely the effect of party identification. Democrats were much more likely to approve of Carter's performance and to vote for Democratic candidates; the reverse was true among Republicans. When controlling for incumbency and party, we see that positive evaluation of the president's performance has a small positive effect on the Democratic congressional vote among Democrats and Republicans, but none among Independents.

In summary, then, we can conclude that in 1980, at least, evaluation of the congressional incumbent's job performance had a substantial impact on the congressional vote, but evaluation of the president's performance had little effect.

PRESIDENTIAL COATTAILS AND THE CONGRESSIONAL VOTE

The final factor we want to consider in relation to the congressional vote is the impact of the voter's presidential voting decision, or the "length" of a presidential candidate's "coattails." Specifically, the question is whether a voter's decision to support a presidential candidate makes him more likely to support a congressional candidate of that

Table 10-7 Percentage Voting Democratic for the House, Controlling for Attitude Toward Carter's Job, Party Identification, and Incumbency, 1980

| Party Identification | Attitude Toward Carter's Job | | | |
| | Incumbent is Democrat | | Incumbent is Republican | |
	Approve	Disapprove	Approve	Disapprove
Democrat	93% (97)	80% (69)	45% (47)	37% (30)
Independent	69% (36)	67% (82)	19% (16)	25% (59)
Republican	[3] (7)	36% (86)	12% (16)	7% (88)

NOTE: Numbers in parentheses are the totals upon which percentages are based. Numbers in brackets are the number voting Democratic for the House in cases where the total N is less than 10.

presidential candidate's party, permitting the congressional candidate (as the saying goes) to ride into office on the presidential candidate's coattails. The problem is that this is a difficult phenomenon to test. Most observers assume that the directionality of the effect is from presidential choice to congressional choice. We also make this assumption, but it is hard to prove that a voter cast his congressional ballot because of his presidential choice rather than the other way around.

Table 10-8 presents the data on the percentage of respondents who voted Democratic for the House and Senate, controlling for their presidential vote and their party identification. For both congressional offices, a strong relationship is apparent. In each party identification group, the proportion of Carter voters who voted Democratic for Congress is substantially higher than the proportion of Reagan voters who voted that way. The support levels of Anderson voters vary.

Unlike the case of presidential approval analyzed earlier, respondents' presidential voting preferences appear to have a major impact on their congressional voting choices even when we control for both party identification and incumbency. Table 10-9 presents these data and corresponds to Table 10-7 which showed the comparable data related to presidential approval. In every category, Reagan voters support Democratic candidates at a substantially lower rate than do Carter voters. These data suggest that Reagan was a significant asset to Republican congressional candidates in 1980.

Table 10-8 Percentage of Respondents Voting Democratic for House and Senate, Controlling for Party Identification and Presidential Vote, 1980

Presidential Vote	*Party Identification*			
	Democrat	Independent	Republican	*Total*
House				
Reagan	55% (67)	43% (146)	22% (217)	34% (430)
Carter	83% (246)	80% (61)	40% (10)	81% (317)
Anderson	90% (21)	53% (34)	25% (12)	60% (67)
Senate				
Reagan	56% (48)	31% (100)	21% (165)	29% (313)
Carter	89% (170)	71% (41)	[4] (8)	84% (219)
Anderson	88% (17)	56% (25)	[1] (6)	62% (48)

NOTE: Numbers in parentheses are the totals upon which percentages are based. Numbers in brackets are the number voting Democratic for the House and Senate in cases where the total N is less than 10.

Table 10-9 Percentage of Respondents Voting Democratic for the House, Controlling for Presidential Vote, Party Identification, and Incumbency, 1980

Party Identification	Presidential Vote			
	Incumbent is Democrat		Incumbent is Republican	
	Carter	Reagan	Carter	Reagan
Democrat	93% (130)	67% (33)	52% (60)	15% (20)
Independent	94% (35)	56% (66)	43% (14)	19% (54)
Republican	— (1)	34% (93)	[2] (6)	5% (97)

NOTE: Numbers in parentheses are the totals upon which percentages are based. Numbers in brackets are the number voting Democratic for the House in cases where the total N is less than 10.

SUMMARY

We have examined a variety of factors that one might expect to be related to the congressional vote, with mixed results. By and large, social forces are weakly related to the vote, although race, union membership, and religion were significantly related to voter choice. Party identification also continues to have an effect, but that effect is substantially less than in the past.

Issue positions appear to affect congressional voting choice to some degree over and above the impact of party identification. Congressional voters also are influenced by their evaluations of their representatives' job performance, although a similar evaluation of the president's performance seems to have little effect. The presidential vote decision, on the other hand, exhibited a substantial impact.

Finally, throughout this analysis the impact of incumbency on congressional voting has been demonstrated. Voters overwhelmingly approve of the job performance of their House incumbents, and those who do approve tend to vote disproportionately for those incumbents when they seek re-election. This tendency is maintained across party identification categories and presidential voting choices. In short, the advantage of incumbency is maintained no matter what other political variables we control for. If we recall our analysis of campaign spending in Chapter 9, only time will tell whether sufficient funding of challengers will successfully neutralize this advantage.

NOTES

1. We will confine our attention in this section to voting for the House since this group of voters is more directly comparable to the presidential electorate. Except for our comparison of whites and blacks, our social comparisons refer to white voters only. We here employ the same definitions for social and demographic categories used in Chapters 4 and 5.
2. A significant portion of our analysis will deal with the incumbency status of the districts in which voters reside. Therefore, with the exception of the data presented in Table 10-3, we eliminate from consideration those voters who voted in a congressional district different from the one in which they were interviewed. To simplify the presentation, we also have eliminated from consideration votes for minor-party candidates.
3. We used the seven-point liberal-conservative scale because it exhibited the strongest relationship to the vote of the issues we examined. (Jobs and government spending were related almost as strongly.) We used the postelection scale because a larger proportion of the sample was able to place themselves than on the pre-election scale. The portion of the scale for Republicans is truncated because there were fewer than 10 respondents at the missing scale points.
4. Albert D. Cover, "One Good Term Deserves Another: The Advantage of Incumbency in Congressional Elections," *American Journal of Political Science* 21 (August 1977): 535. Cover includes in his analysis not only strong and weak partisans, but also Independents with partisan leanings.
5. Richard F. Fenno, Jr., "If, as Ralph Nader says, Congress is 'The Broken Branch,' How Come We Love Our Congressmen So Much?" in *Congress in Change*, ed. Norman J. Ornstein (New York: Praeger Publishers, 1975), pp. 277-287. This theme is expanded and analyzed in Fenno, *Home Style: House Members in Their Districts* (Boston: Little, Brown & Co., 1978).
6. It should be noted that 18 percent of the respondents did not know whether to approve or disapprove of Congress's performance, and that 35 percent did not know whether to approve or disapprove of their representative's performance. (Only 5 percent failed to rate Carter.) Since persons who failed to rate their representative are excluded from our analyses, the Ns in Table 10-5 are lower than those in most other tables. The N in Table 10-6 is reduced further since it is based only upon Democratic and Republican identifiers who voted for Congress in a district in which an incumbent stood for re-election.
7. Edward R. Tufte, "Determinants of the Outcomes of Midterm Congressional Elections," *American Political Science Review* 69 (September 1975): 812-826. See also Barbara Hinckley, *Congressional Elections* (Washington, D.C.: Congressional Quarterly, 1981), pp. 113-132.

PART IV

The 1980 Elections in Perspective

11

The 1980 Elections and the
Future of American Politics

What does the Republican triumph in 1980 mean for the future of American politics? For the short-term at least, it has led to the greatest change in social policy since the New Deal reforms of the mid-1930s. Despite Ronald Reagan's pronouncements before the election, these policy consequences were largely unexpected. Presidents are seldom successful in implementing large-scale changes in domestic policy, constrained as they usually are by a recalcitrant Congress and an entrenched federal bureaucracy.

But Reagan succeeded in implementing a large part of his economic program within six and a half months of his inauguration. These legislative triumphs have been compared with Woodrow Wilson's successful introduction of tariff reforms in 1913, Franklin D. Roosevelt's "hundred days" in 1933, and Lyndon B. Johnson's Great Society proposals in 1965. Reagan's achievements are all the more remarkable since Wilson, Roosevelt, and Johnson worked with Congresses in which both houses were controlled by their own party, whereas Reagan scored his victories even though Democrats controlled the House of Representatives.

POLICY CHANGES OF THE REAGAN ADMINISTRATION

While Reagan addressed a wide range of foreign and domestic issues during the campaign, his major focus was the Carter administration's economic failures. Once elected, he made cutting government spending and federal taxes his top priorities. Reagan did not accomplish all he wanted in either area during the first session of the 97th Congress, but he was highly successful.

Domestic Spending Cuts

Since Reagan had promised to provide "real-dollar" increases in defense spending, most budget cuts were made in domestic programs. He instituted a "needs test" for college loans and substantially cut federal aid for elementary and secondary education and aid to schools in "impacted" areas that enroll large numbers of children of government personnel.[1] Reduced funding for food stamps disqualified a million persons with incomes just above the poverty line, and cuts in school nutrition programs made it more difficult for children to get free or reduced-priced meals. Fees paid by patients for Medicare were increased, and federal aid for medical payments for the poor were reduced gradually. In addition, most federal health programs were cut back.

Public service employment through the Comprehensive Employment and Training Act (CETA) was eliminated, and spending for other job training programs was reduced. Child abuse programs and community services for the elderly lost considerable funding. Public housing funds were cut almost in half. Urban development action grants (UDAGs) and programs to help low-income families weatherize their homes also were cut somewhat, and subsidies for solar energy units and other conservation measures were reduced by 60 percent. Cuts in funding for the National Endowment for the Arts and the National Science Foundation were not as extensive as Reagan proposed, and Congress reduced dairy price supports by only half the amount the administration had requested. User fees were imposed for federal inspection of many agricultural products, while interest rates were increased on farm loans.

The Reagan budget cuts affect Americans of all income groups, but the burden falls most heavily on the relatively disadvantaged. And while these cuts were not aimed at any racial or ethnic group, blacks will suffer disproportionately. At least one black leader, the Reverend Jesse L. Jackson, is convinced of "an element of racism in the budget cuts." [2] On the other hand, Reagan's supporters argue that blacks stand to benefit more if his programs are successful. According to Edwin L. Dale, Jr., speaking on behalf of the Office of Management and Budget, "Blacks benefit even more than the rest of the population when the economy performs properly." [3]

The Tax Cuts

Congress put up more of a fight over the Reagan tax plan than over his budget reductions. Many conservative Democrats favored cutting social programs, but they feared that the administration's proposal to reduce federal income taxes 10 percent a year for three consecutive years would lead to huge federal deficits and worse inflation. "Supply-side" economists disagreed. According to the "Laffer curve," developed by conservative economist Arthur Laffer, reduced taxes would stimulate productivity and investment, thus increasing federal revenues.

As with his budget package, Reagan did not get all the tax cuts he requested. He won a 5 percent cut in federal income taxes on October 1, 1981, another 10 percent on July 1, 1982, and a final 10 percent on July 1, 1983. In addition, Congress passed a significant tax reform that was not part of the original Reagan proposal. Beginning in 1985, the income tax schedule will be indexed to inflation. Thus, taxpayers will not move automatically into higher and higher tax brackets solely due to increased income that merely keeps up with inflation. This so-called "bracket-creep" was a hidden source of federal revenues every year, and its elimination has major policy consequences. According to *Newsweek,* indexing is a "formula consciously designed to bleed old social programs and to discourage new ones forever." [4]

Many features of the Reagan tax plan benefit the well-to-do. The 1982 federal income tax schedule provides greater savings for persons with higher incomes. The top rate on federal income taxes for persons in the upper-income brackets was cut from 70 percent to 50 percent, perhaps the most important goal of the entire tax reform package.[5] Capital gains taxes were reduced from 28 percent to 20 percent, and new tax breaks for reinvesting dividends from utility stocks were introduced. The "all-savers" certificate, which allows interest earnings free of federal taxes, primarily benefits persons in upper-income brackets. Similarly, increased opportunities to establish tax-deferred retirement accounts assist persons who can save part of their current income. Businesses will directly gain through faster depreciation allowances and investment tax credits.

The logic of this tax cut is not that the rich are more deserving than the poor, but that people with higher incomes are more likely to invest their tax savings in ways that will increase productivity. Presumably, improved productivity will aid everyone by increasing the supply of goods, thus lowering the inflation rate. According to this reasoning, increased investment also will generate new jobs, thus benefiting lower-income groups. The well-to-do are more likely to invest their tax savings than the less affluent, but economists cannot predict to what extent these tax savings will be used for investment or for consumption. Nor can economists accurately predict the extent to which new investments will stimulate capital formation.

Within a month of Reagan's major tax cut victories on Capitol Hill in late July 1981, economic forecasters were projecting far greater budget deficits than Reagan claimed. In September, when Reagan proposed additional cuts for most federal agencies—with the exception of the Department of Defense—serious opposition developed, even from Republicans in Congress. By November 1981, the president acknowledged that a balanced budget was unlikely by the end of his term, and by early 1982 budget deficits of more than $100 billion were projected for the 1983 fiscal year. Despite pressures within his administration, Reagan opposed new taxes and resisted calls to reduce defense spending. His proposed budget for fiscal year 1983 called instead for further reductions in domestic programs. Congressional opposition to additional cuts will be great. But even if Reagan doesn't achieve more cuts in federal domestic spending, he already has set in motion the most radical changes in domestic policy since the New Deal.

Block Grants to States

Not only did Reagan cut spending, but he also altered the way federal money will be spent. Monies that in the past went directly from the federal government to localities will now go from the federal government to the states. These "block grant" policies are designed to give states greater autonomy in establishing specific spending priorities. According to *New York Times* reporter Steven V. Roberts, "The block grant strategy flows partly from a deeply-held Republican belief that Washington contains a powerful network of liberal power centers— lobbyists and bureaucrats, congressional staff members and national news reporters. Dispersing decision-making responsibility to the states ... would undermine such forces, and thus change the basic priorities of government." [6] Political scientist Richard P. Nathan confirms this view that the block grant strategy will alter federal-state relationships: "Cuts in domestic spending made in 1981, combined with efforts to shift the control of many programs from the federal government to the states, will have ... important repercussions for American federalism." [7]

These changes, however, are not as far-reaching as those Reagan proposed in the State of the Union message on January 26, 1982. Under his "new federalism" program, the federal government would assume the responsibility for Medicaid programs that now cost the states $19 billion annually. By 1984, the states also would assume responsibility for Aid to Families with Dependent Children (AFDC), food stamps, as well as 40 other domestic programs that now cost about $47 billion. The difference would be made up by a "grass roots trust fund" that would be phased out by 1991. Since these changes need congressional approval, we cannot tell whether or to what extent they will be implemented. Opponents have argued that the poor will be less well protected by the states than by current federal programs. [8]

Presidential Appointments

The Reagan administration has taken other steps to reduce federal involvement in the economy, many of them designed to aid the business community. Through appointments to key federal positions, Reagan has sought to reverse government policies for dealing with business. According to *New York Times* reporter Howell Raines, "This reversal would consist mainly of lifting restrictions on business while playing down the Government's activist role as a protector of workers, consumers and minorities." [9] The most conspicuous pro-business appointment has been Secretary of the Interior James G. Watt, who strongly favors the development of federal lands and is opposed to "environmental extremists." According to one White House adviser, Reagan's devotion to pro-business appointments "reflects the belief that an election occurred in November, and the President was elected with a clear promise that he would appoint people in the regulatory and environmental areas that favor less regulation. He believes he had a mandate to appoint people like that." [10]

Economic Outlook

The future of American politics depends heavily on the success of Reagan's economic reforms. This is consistent with our conclusion that the 1980 presidential election signaled more a rejection of the incumbent than a mandate for Reagan's policies. Most voters felt Carter was unsuccessful in handling the two basic economic issues—inflation and unemployment. And most of those who judged Carter a failure voted for Reagan. Similarly, the electorate will hold the Reagan administration responsible for its success or failure in solving these same two basic problems.

While most professional economists are skeptical about Reagan's supply-side policies, economists have been as notoriously unsuccessful in predicting economic trends as political scientists have been in predicting political developments. Although we cannot predict the future course of American politics, we can see at least four possibilities: a realignment that clearly establishes the Republicans as the majority party, a restoration of the Democratic party to a dominant position, the emergence of new political parties that offer alternatives to the present party system, and continued electoral volatility in support for the two major parties.

A PRO-REPUBLICAN REALIGNMENT

One could argue that a pro-Republican realignment has occurred already. Today the West, a Democratic stronghold between 1932 and

1948, is a heavily Republican region, while the South, the mainstay of the Democratic coalition, is electorally competitive. Republicans have won five of the last eight presidential elections, as well as three of the last four, and they now have won the United States Senate for the first time since 1952. Nevertheless, they are not yet a majority party. To attain this status, they must capture the House of Representatives and stay in power for several elections. Some would argue that a basic shift in partisan loyalties among the electorate is another prerequisite of majority status, but we view such a shift as less important than the actual election results.

The House is not beyond the Republicans' reach, however. They are better at raising campaign funds than the Democrats and have developed a more professional national organization that can target funds in marginal Democratic districts. The Republican party also has demonstrated more skill at using public opinion data to aid their campaigns. The Democrats recognize these advantages and may in time successfully imitate Republican techniques. Although the Democrats certainly can improve their fund-raising efforts, they do not have the potential number of wealthy contributors that the Republicans can rely upon.

Some recent evidence suggests that the Republicans have benefited from shifts in partisan loyalties. The 1980 SRC-CPS postelection interviews conducted in November and December did not reveal a shift toward the GOP, but a shift may have been under way by early 1981. Republican pollster Richard B. Wirthlin claims that the Democratic edge in partisan loyalties has been eliminated. As of May 1981, he argues, some 40 percent of the electorate were either Democrats (or Independents who leaned Democratic), while 39 percent were Republicans (or Republican leaners).[11] According to Richard Richards, chairman of the Republican National Committee, these results demonstrate that "the Republican Party is on the verge of majority party status for the first time in generations."[12]

Other polls indicate that the Democrats still enjoy a decided edge but that the Republicans are catching up. Results of the CBS News/*New York Times* poll show definite gains by the Republican party. If Independent leaners are classified as partisans, the Democrats' 53 to 34 percent margin over the Republicans from January through September 1980 fell to a 49 to 41 percent margin in April 1981.[13] Moreover, as Adam Clymer and Kathleen Frankovic report, the biggest shift toward the Republicans was among the baby-boom cohort between the ages of 25 and 34: "The potential impact of the electorally inactive members of this age cohort is immense. With just a little more movement and a higher rate of voting, they could cement a Republican plurality for a generation."[14]

When Independents who lean toward a party are considered as Independents, the shift toward the Republicans revealed by these data appears far less impressive. The Democratic margin drops from 42 to 22 percent over the Republicans in 1980 to 34 to 26 percent in April 1981. The Democrats do show a marked drop in support, but the Republicans' gains are only modest. The proportion of Independents actually increases from 36 percent in 1980 to 40 percent in April 1981. Thus, as Paul Allen Beck argues, the CBS News/*New York Times* data could be taken to indicate continued dealignment—a further breakdown of partisan loyalties, rather than the movement toward a new alignment.[15]

Gallup poll data, which do not distinguish between Independents who lean toward a party and those who do not, also show a shift toward the Republicans. In early 1980, the Democrats held a 47 to 21 percent lead over the GOP; in polls conducted between March and June 1981, this margin narrowed to 42 to 28 percent.[16] Clearly, none of these polls, even Wirthlin's, shows the Republicans as the majority party. Although there has been a shift to the GOP, these changes merely show the possibility of a pro-Republican realignment and do not confirm its presence. Indeed, by late 1981, some evidence indicated that the shift toward the Republicans had been stopped or even reversed.[17]

In their attempts to become the dominant party, the Republicans face two major obstacles: increased turnout among social groups that support the Democratic party and divisions within their own party over social issues. As we saw in Chapter 4, overall turnout in postwar presidential elections has been declining since 1960. By 1980, 47 percent of the adult population failed to vote.[18] Since 1966, turnout also has been falling in off-year congressional elections. Sixty-five percent of the adult population failed to vote in 1978. Nonvoters are disproportionately found among the young, and increased turnout may help the Republicans if the CBS News/*New York Times* polls were correct in detecting a shift toward the Republicans among the baby-boom generation.

Nonvoters also are concentrated among disadvantaged Americans—the blacks, the poor, and persons with little formal education. While we found negligible differences in policy preferences between voters and nonvoters, Reagan's policies may bolster turnout among the social groups most threatened by his economic policies. There is also the danger that, even if Reagan's policies are moderately successful, they will sharpen income differentials between the well-to-do and "middle-Americans," leading to a resurgence in Democratic voting by trade union members and members of the white working class.

Because the decline in electoral participation results from long-term shifts in attitudes toward the political system, a substantial increase in turnout is unlikely. Nonetheless, it is possible. For example, there was a surge in black voting in the Virginia gubernatorial election of November 1981 that helped Charles S. Robb (Lyndon B. Johnson's son-in-law) become the first Democrat elected to the Virginia governorship in 16 years. Several commentators attribute this increase in black turnout to anti-Reagan sentiments.[19] If turnout in national elections were to increase among the disadvantaged, Republican prospects could be damaged.

A second danger to the Republicans is that they may lose support if they begin to push for reforms on social or moral issues, such as a tougher national criminal code, strong anti-abortion legislation, or attempts to legalize school prayer. If these issues are raised, the Republican party itself will be divided, just as the Democratic party was in the sixties. Moreover, despite the claims of the Moral Majority and of single-issue groups, the electorate holds fairly moderate positions on most of these issues.

In the first session of the 97th Congress, Reagan steered clear of controversies over social reforms, but whether he will continue to avoid these issues remains to be seen.[20] Moreover, there is no assurance that Reagan, who would be 73 by the 1984 election, will be the next Republican presidential candidate. If Reagan chooses not to run, the Republican party nomination will be hotly contested. Even if George Bush becomes president, through Reagan's resignation or death, he may not have a firm hold on the party's nomination.

A struggle over the nomination would not necessarily harm Republican prospects, but it might prove costly, especially if it divided Republicans who emphasized controversial social issues from those who focused on economic problems. And if Republicans in 1984 select a nominee who emphasizes such issues at the expense of economic goals, they might destroy their prospects for attaining majority-party status. On the other hand, if Reagan's policies reduce inflation without increasing unemployment, and if the Republicans avoid partisan-related conflicts over so-called "moral" issues, the shift toward the Republican party among the electorate might continue. Clearly, the Republicans now have a chance to become the dominant party for the first time in over half a century.

A RESURGENT DEMOCRATIC PARTY

The Democratic party has survived since 1828, when Andrew Jackson defeated the incumbent president, National Republican John Quincy Adams, and it would be foolish to ignore its chances to return to dominance. Even though the Democrats have lost three of the last four presidential elections and have now lost control of the Senate, they still have certain advantages. Despite the decline in party loyalties in recent years, almost all polls show that there are more Democrats than

Republicans. At the opening of the 97th Congress, the Democrats held a 51-seat majority in the the House of Representatives (243 Democrats, 192 Republicans) and will have the decided advantage of fielding more incumbents in the 1982 off-year elections.

The greatest Democratic chances lie in the failure of the Reagan administration's economic policies or in a widespread perception that, whatever their benefits, they place too great a burden on middle- and low-income Americans. Reagan's success in winning passage of his budget cuts, especially his tax cuts, may prove to be an advantage for the Democratic party. Had the House Democratic leadership succeeded in blocking Reagan's economic reforms, the Republicans could claim that they never had the opportunity to implement their own policies. Indeed, some Democrats made precisely this argument, maintaining that it was a mistake to attempt to prevent Reagan's tax cuts from becoming law. Passage of the tax cut, which was opposed by the House Democratic leadership, and which four out of five House Democrats voted against, could be a blessing in disguise for the Democrats—if these tax cuts lead to massive government deficits, with increased government borrowing pushing interest and/or inflation rates upward.

Since Reagan's cuts in social programs will hurt the poor disproportionately and since the tax benefits are greater for the well-to-do, the Democrats can hope that at least some elements of the New Deal coalition can be restored. The Democrats also may regain some of their traditional sources of support if the elimination of federal jobs and job training programs contributes to increased unemployment. As we have seen, Democrats win presidential elections only when they can mobilize substantial support from members of their electoral coalition. As a coalition of minorities, they must attain high levels of electoral participation from the groups that favor them. Of all the major groups that have made up the Democratic presidential coalition since 1948, only white southerners no longer are part of the overall alliance. Even in 1980, there were traces of union voting, class voting, and religious voting. And the Democrats gained the massive support of black Americans.

The social groups that support the Republican party have been remarkably consistent. In the 10 presidential elections since 1944, there has been only one election, 1964, in which a majority of whites from non-union families, a majority of the white middle-class, and a majority of white Protestants failed to vote for the Republican party. In all 10 elections, a majority of white middle-class Protestants voted Republican.[21] Democratic successes, then, depend upon substantial levels of voting support from members of their traditional coalition, since they rarely pick up much support from the social groups that favor the Republicans.

As we saw earlier, however, restoring the traditionally pro-Democratic groups to the Democratic presidential coalition would be difficult. Not only have these groups changed, but, except for blacks, the political conditions that forged the ties between group membership and Democratic loyalties occurred nearly half a century ago. Even so, the Democrats may be able to restore the loyalties of traditional social groups, and they could gain majority support from previously Republican groups. Whether or not they succeed, however, is primarily dependent upon social and political conditions. Political fallout from Reagan's economic policies may help the Democrats retain high levels of black support while regaining support from the white working class.

Of course, the future of the Democratic party is not tied only to what the Republicans accomplish. It also depends upon the Democrats' own leadership skills. Jimmy Carter is still the titular leader of the Democratic party, but he remains too discredited to assume an active leadership role. Thomas P. (Tip) O'Neill, Jr., as Speaker of the House, holds the highest national office of any Democrat, but his leadership in the House has been largely ineffectual.[22] It is difficult to predict who will be the Democratic standard-bearer for 1984, but a June 1981 Harris poll (which provided respondents with a list) presents a string of likely possibilities. Respondents were asked, "If you had to choose right now, which *one* of these candidates would be your *first* choice for the Democratic nomination for president in 1984?" Among Democrats, Ted Kennedy was the first choice with 35 percent, former Vice-President Walter Mondale scored 24 percent, while Governor Jerry Brown of California scored 8 percent.[23] Also included on the list, in order of popularity, were Senators John Glenn (Ohio), Robert Byrd (West Virginia), Pat Moynihan (New York), Sam Nunn (Georgia), Gary Hart (Colorado), Dale Bumpers (Arkansas), and Ernest Hollings (South Carolina), who ranged from 7 percent down to 1 percent. Governor Hugh Carey (New York), who has since announced that he will not seek a third term, received 2 percent. While this poll confirms the conventional wisdom that Kennedy and Mondale will be the top contenders, it is possible that the future Democratic standard-bearer was not even listed.

More important than the Democrats' choice for 1984 is the quality of leadership the party demonstrates in the meantime. For the moment, the Democrats seem to lack new ideas and have been reduced to reacting to Republican policy initiatives. We cannot predict whether the Democrats will adopt a centrist strategy of offering minor modifications of Reagan's proposals, or whether they will be driven to the left by the social polarization that Reagan's policies could create. The overwhelming response of the Democratic National Convention to Kennedy's speech endorsing traditional Democratic principles strongly suggests that considerable sympathy still exists for a left-of-center Democratic candidate among party activists. If the Democrats do nominate a left-of-center candidate, the 1984 election could emerge as one of the most socially polarizing elections in American history.

A NEW POLITICAL PARTY

The political struggle need not be confined to the Republican and Democratic parties. The great hope for third parties is the large percentage of the electorate (roughly one-third) who claim to have no party ties. Perhaps more importantly, only one-fourth of the electorate claims to be strongly committed to either of the two major parties. In principle, then, a massive number of voters might support a third-party candidate. Clearly, a new political party could emerge, but how likely is such a development, and what would be such a party's ideological stripe?

The only parties since World War II that have gained a single electoral vote have been parties on the political right—the States' Rights Democrats in 1948 and the American Independent party in 1968—with all these votes coming from states of the old Confederacy. While conservatives may be disappointed with Reagan's failure to push for conservative social legislation, and while many objected to his appointment of Supreme Court Justice Sandra Day O'Connor, at present a new party on the American political right has little room to succeed. As we saw in our analysis of policy preferences in Chapter 6, the electorate in 1980 was actually more liberal than their perception of Reagan on all nine of the issue scales we considered. For a party to the right of the Republicans to be successful, the Republican party first would have to move closer to the political center—a move that seems possible only if Bush, who is relatively moderate, succeeds Reagan as president. For the moment at least, new conservative parties will languish.

John B. Anderson's candidacy clearly illustrates the problems with a centrist third party. According to Anthony Downs, the "center" is the logical place for each party to strive, yet at least one of the two major parties is likely to hold that space already.[24] A party of the center thus finds it difficult to present a distinctive policy agenda. Since most voters do not want to "waste" their vote, most people who consider voting for a third party eventually move toward one of the two major parties. The prospects for a third party of the center would brighten if the Republicans persisted with conservative policies to such an extent that they could not move to the center at election time and if the Democratic party moved to the left. The recent successes of the new Social Democratic party in Britain, for example, result from Margaret Thatcher's Conservative party government moving to the right while the Labour party was moving to the left. If both major American parties abandoned the political center, the prospects for a centrist party would improve, but such a party would still need effective leadership that offered attractive policy alternatives.

A left-wing third party has plenty of room on the American political landscape and could draw voters from the disadvantaged social groups that have had very low turnout in recent elections. (It could lose some of this room, however, if the Democrats nominated Kennedy or another left-of-center candidate in 1984.) However, a party of the left faces severe organizational difficulties. To be successful, it must appeal not only to upper-middle class environmentalists, as the Citizens party under Barry Commoner may have done, but also must win the confidence of the poor, the blacks, and the white working class.

In his study of social welfare and the 1980 election, Ira Katznelson refers to arguments advanced by the sociologist C. Wright Mills. As Katznelson reminds us, "Over three decades ago . . . Mills observed that the only mass, multiracial, progressive organizations in the United States were trade unions; and that the future of social policy depended heavily on the zeal of their members and the choices of their leaders." [25] Mills was pessimistic about the prospects for unions taking a lead in social reforms, and we have even less reason today to expect unions to seize an active political role. As Katznelson concludes, "Organized labor has become increasingly disinclined to engage in larger political battles." [26]

It seems unlikely that anything more than a small segment of American trade union leadership will support a new or existing party of the left. While Reagan's firing of striking Federal Air Traffic Controllers alienated union leaders, and while the Solidarity Day demonstrations on September 19, 1981, underscored union opposition to the Reagan administration, it remains to be seen whether such protests will lead to broader union political activity. In electoral terms, union opposition almost certainly will be confined to supporting Democratic candidates. In fact, in January 1982, 20 major labor unions officially established ties with the Democratic National Committee. [27]

To be taken seriously by the media, a third-party candidate must get on the ballot in all (or nearly all) 50 states and have a chance of winning the 270 electoral votes needed to be elected president. In 1980, the Libertarian party attained this goal (but still received little media attention), and through last minute efforts Anderson's name appeared on the ballot in all 50 states, plus the District of Columbia.

Getting on the ballot is much less difficult than raising money, however, and it is here that federal election laws place an additional burden on third-party candidates. Democratic and Republican nominees are guaranteed full federal funding merely by gaining their party's nomination, but third-party candidates can receive funding only if they obtain 5 percent of the total vote in November. Thus Anderson was forced to ask supporters to lend money with no guarantee when—and if—they would be repaid.[28] Given the importance of money for organizational, travel, and media expenses, the built-in federal funding for major-party nominees is a tremendous advantage. Moreover, nomination by either major party provides another huge bonus—millions of voters. According to our estimates, the Democratic party nomination virtually assures a candidate nearly 12 million votes, while the Republican party nomination is worth more than 8 million votes.[29]

Lastly, the very weakness of the current party structure dictates that most candidates who wish to become president will seek their goal by first earning either the Democratic or the Republican party nomination. The party reforms introduced by the Democrats between 1968 and 1972 made it far more difficult for elected political leaders to influence the choice of nominee. Perhaps this is why George C. Wallace, who had earned nearly 10 million votes as the American Independent party candidate in 1968, decided four years later to seek the Democratic party nomination. The nomination of George S. McGovern in 1972 and the nomination of Jimmy Carter in 1976 attest to the openness of the system. While the Republican party did not engage in similar reforms, it was affected by many of the changes wrought by the Democrats, and two-thirds of the Republican delegates are now selected through primaries.

Wresting a party's nomination away from an incumbent president is still a formidable task. Even an unelected president, Gerald R. Ford, was able to hold off Reagan in 1976, and four years later Carter was able to outrun Kennedy. But at least one party's nomination is always open, and sometimes both will be. The very weak structure of the two major parties makes aiming at a major-party nomination the most reasonable strategy for any presidential candidate and contributes to an absence of attractive candidates to lead third-party movements.[30]

CONTINUED ELECTORAL VOLATILITY

As we have seen, the election of Ronald Reagan may lead to a pro-Republican realignment of the American electorate, a resurgence of the Democratic party, or the emergence of a new political party. More likely than these possibilities, however, is continued electoral volatility. Since 1952, neither major party has been able to win more than two presidential elections in a row and support for the major parties has swung widely from election to election. Several factors suggest that the electorate may continue to be volatile.

First, the weakness of party loyalties today favors this possibility. While claiming to be an Independent does not necessarily signify a positive commitment to "Independence," as a principle, it does reveal a lack of commitment to either of the major parties.[31] Moreover, a majority of Democrats are weak Democrats and a majority of Republicans are weak Republicans, and partisans who claim to be "not very strong" supporters of their party are much more unpredictable in their voting than individuals who claim "strong" partisan ties. Second, social variables (other than race) have less and less influence on voting behavior—a trend that is likely to contribute to electoral volatility. Today, fewer voters are bound to a particular party by class, ethnic, or religious ties. This increases the proportion of the electorate that is likely to switch parties from election to election.

Reagan's election is another sign of the volatility of the American electorate. It was less an endorsement of new conservative principles than a rejection of Jimmy Carter's performance as president. Voters were closer to Reagan than to Carter on most issues, but they voted for Reagan largely because of retrospective evaluations of the incumbent's handling of inflation and unemployment. Similarly, voters who merely voted *against* Carter in 1980 may feel relatively free to vote against Reagan (or another Republican nominee) in 1984. Will the electorate judge Reagan's performance in office more favorably than Carter's? We remain fairly pessimistic about the success of his economic policies, although we hope that our pessimism is unfounded.

Today, voters seem to give the incumbent party little time to get the nation's economic house in order. The primary cause of Ford's narrow loss in 1976 was a negative evaluation of his handling of the economy, and similar criticisms led to Carter's more crushing defeat four years later. And 1980 witnessed the first election in this century in which the incumbent party lost the White House in two successive elections. V. O. Key, Jr., once argued that the American voter might be a "rational god of vengeance and of reward." [32] This characterization may well be correct. Today that god has little patience.

NOTES

1. The summary of Reagan's budget cuts is condensed from a more detailed report in the *New York Times*, August 2, 1981, p. E3.
2. David E. Rosenbaum, "Blacks Would Feel Extra Impact From Cuts Proposed by President," *New York Times*, June 2, 1981, p. A1.
3. Ibid.
4. "Rest in Peace, New Deal," *Newsweek*, August 10, 1981, p. 16. *Newsweek* was not suggesting, however, that this was the major motivation behind the support for indexing.

5. In his famous interviews with *Washington Post* editor William Greider, David A. Stockman, Director of the Office of Management and Budget, stated, "The hard part of the supply-side tax cut is dropping the top tax rate from 70 to 50 percent—the rest of it is a secondary matter." According to Stockman, the Kemp-Roth tax reform plan "was always a Trojan horse to bring down the top tax rate." See William Greider, "The Education of David Stockman," *Atlantic Monthly* 248 (December 1981): 46. Greider's article provides an excellent account of the political process through which the budget cutting and tax reforms were formulated and approved.
6. Steven V. Roberts, "Budget Ax Becomes a Tool of Social Change," *New York Times,* June 21, 1981, p. E4.
7. Richard P. Nathan, "The Nationalization of Proposition 13," *PS* 14 (Fall 1981): 755.
8. "President's Plan Must Quiet Doubts Concerning Fairness," *New York Times,* January 31, 1982, section 4, p. 1.
9. Howell Raines, "Reagan Reversing Many U.S. Policies," *New York Times,* July 3, 1981, p. A1.
10. Ibid., p. A8.
11. "Closing the Historic Party Identification Gap," *National Journal,* June 13, 1981, p. 1081.
12. Ibid, p. 44.
13. Adam Clymer and Kathleen Frankovic, "The Realities of Realignment," *Public Opinion* 4 (June/July 1981): 42-47.
14. Ibid., p. 44.
15. Paul Allen Beck, "Realignment Begins? The Republican Surge in Florida" (Paper delivered at the annual meeting of the American Political Science Association, New York, New York, September 3-6, 1981), p. 10. However, Beck suggests that there may be evidence of a pro-Republican realignment beginning in Florida.
16. The Gallup Poll, July 16, 1981.
17. According to *Washington Post* writer Barry Sussman, surveys conducted by the *Washington Post*/ABC News polls in late November 1981 show a slight increase in support for the Democrats and suggest that movement toward the Republican party was ending. Sussman also reports that both the Gallup and CBS News/*New York Times* polls reveal a similar pattern. See Barry Sussman, "Shift by Voters to GOP Ending, Poll Finds," *Washington Post,* December 16, 1981, p. A2. A CBS News/*New York Times* poll conducted in mid-January 1982 found a slight shift away from the Republicans and an even smaller shift toward the Democrats. Thirty-seven percent called themselves Republicans (including Independent leaners), while 51 percent were Democrats (including leaners). See Adam Clymer, "Poll Finds Reagan's Program Raises Hope Despite Losses," *New York Times,* January 19, 1982, p. A20. However, Louis Harris claims that support for the Democratic party was still declining. See Louis Harris, "Democratic Ranks Still Dwindling," *Detroit Free Press,* January 14, 1982, p. B5.
18. For somewhat different estimates of turnout, see Walter Dean Burnham, "The 1980 Earthquake: Realignment, Reaction, or What?" in *The Hidden Election: Politics and Economics in the 1980 Presidential Campaign,* ed. Thomas Ferguson and Joel Rogers (New York: Pantheon Books, 1981), p. 101.
19. Adam Clymer, "A Warning to the GOP," *New York Times,* November 5, 1981, p. B18. Ken Bode of NBC News reaches similar conclusions. For election reports that discuss black turnout, see Glenn Frankel and Celestine

Bohlen, "How the Battle Was Lost," *Washington Post,* November 5, 1981, pp. A1-A2; and David S. Broder, "Message From Election '81 Far From Clear," *Washington Post,* November 5, 1981, p. A2.

20. Nadine Cohodas, "Emphasis on the Economy Kept Divisive Social Issues on a Back Burner in 1981," *Congressional Quarterly Weekly Report,* January 2, 1982, pp. 3-5.
21. Nixon gained a majority of all these groups in 1968 even when Wallace voters are included in the analysis.
22. Martin Tolchin, "The Troubles of Tip O'Neill," *New York Times Magazine,* August 16, 1981, p. 30.
23. The Harris Survey, July 13, 1981.
24. Anthony Downs, *An Economic Theory of Democracy* (New York: Harper & Row, 1957).
25. Ira Katznelson, "A Radical Departure: Social Welfare and the Election," in *The Hidden Election,* p. 331.
26. Ibid., p. 332.
27. Robert S. Greenberger, "Democrats, 20 Labor Unions, Forge Ties They Hope Will Yield '82 Election Gains," *Wall Street Journal,* January 6, 1982, p. 6.
28. Anderson received 4.2 million dollars in federal funds after the election, and he may be entitled to some federal funding if he were to run for president in 1984. See Adam Clymer, "Anderson is Moving to Form New Party," *New York Times,* May 12, 1981, p. A16.
29. See Chapter 8, p. 176 for these estimates.
30. We are grateful to Joseph A. Schlesinger for this insight. Proposed reforms for the Democratic party under which elected officials would make up about one-seventh of the Democratic delegates would only slightly strengthen the present party structure. However, since these elected officials would be unpledged delegates, the chance of the convention actually choosing the party nominee would be increased somewhat.
31. This is our reading of the extensive analyses of new questions on party identification introduced by the SRC-CPS in 1980. See Jack Dennis, "On Being an Independent Partisan Supporter" (Paper delivered at the annual meeting of the Midwest Political Science Association, Cincinnati, Ohio, April 15-18, 1981). For further evidence that Independent leaners may be less partisan than weak partisans, see W. Phillips Shively, "The Nature of Party Identification: A Review of Recent Developments," in *The Electorate Reconsidered,* ed. John C. Pierce and John L. Sullivan (Beverly Hills, Calif.: Sage Publications, 1980), pp. 232-235.
32. V. O. Key, Jr., *Politics, Parties, and Pressure Groups,* fifth ed. (New York: Thomas Y. Crowell Co., 1964), p. 568.

PART V

1982 Election Update

The American midterm election is a curious political animal. Unlike legislative elections in parliamentary democracies, it does not affect the term of service of the executive or, as in France, imperil his leadership by threatening constitutional deadlock. The American president, elected for a four-year term, will serve regardless of legislative support. Yet the very system of biennial elections for all the members of the House and one-third of the Senate often reduces the capacity of the president to govern.

V. O. Key, Jr., thus explains the role of the electorate at midterm:

> Since the electorate cannot change administrations at midterm elections, it can only express its approval or disapproval by returning or withdrawing legislative majorities. ... The President's party, whether it basks in public favor or is declining in public esteem, ordinarily loses House strength at midterm—a pattern that, save for one exception, has prevailed since the Civil War.[1]

The single exception was the election of 1934 during President Franklin D. Roosevelt's first term—a period when America was moving toward a long-term Democratic realignment. Between 1858 and 1982, the president's party gained power in the House in that midterm contest alone.

Although, in line with precedent, the Republicans lost House seats in 1982 (26 seats to be exact), they maintained their 54-46 majority in the Senate. Thus the meaning of the 1982 elections is ambiguous. Both parties could justly claim substantial successes. Moreover, the policy implications of the elections were not immediately apparent. Almost certainly the elections did not provide a mandate for President Ronald Reagan to "stay the course." Neither did they show, as Senator Ted Kennedy had hoped, that Reagan had "flunked the course."

Part V, 1982 Election Update, analyzes the results of the election. In Chapter 12 we describe the pattern of outcomes and consider the basic question: "Who won?" Reapportionment and redistricting and the reasons why the Republicans failed to capitalize upon these processes—despite their (and our) expectations that they would—also are discussed. We then consider the way strategic advantages minimized

245

Republican losses. Chapter 12 concludes with an assessment of the impact of the election on Congress although in early 1983 it was too soon to know what the specific policy consequences of Democratic House gains would be.

Chapter 13, "1984 and Beyond," explores what may happen in future elections in light of the events of 1982. We begin by examining the ways in which rules changes adopted by the Democratic National Committee in 1982 will affect the Democratic nomination struggle in 1984. By looking at how political opportunities are structured, we then show why some politicians are more likely than others to seek the presidency. Finally, we discuss the 1984 general election and show why the prospects for a pro-Republican realignment have dwindled.

NOTES

1. V. O. Key, Jr., *Politics, Parties and Pressure Groups,* 5th ed. (New York: Thomas Y. Crowell Co., 1964), pp. 567, 568.

12

The 1982 Congressional Election

Unlike the 1980 elections, with the resounding victory by Ronald Reagan and the Republican sweep of the Senate, the 1982 midterm elections failed to provide any dramatic surprises. In the House the Democrats won 269 seats and the Republicans 166, a 26-seat gain for the Democrats that almost enabled them to reclaim the 275 seats they had held before the 1980 elections.[1] If there was anything remarkable in the elections, it was the small turnover in the Senate. When the 98th Congress convened on January 3, 1983, the composition of the Senate was identical to the composition at the close of the 97th: 54 Republicans and 46 Democrats. There were, however, some interesting variations on the themes discussed in Chapter 9 that will become apparent as we consider the 1982 outcomes in detail. First we will discuss the effects of incumbency and party. Then the regional composition of the new Congress will be examined.

THE PATTERN OF OUTCOMES

Incumbency

Table 12-1, House and Senate Incumbents and Election Outcomes, 1982, updates the data provided in Table 9-1. The House results resemble those for 1980: in 1982 about the same number of incumbents sought re-election, a somewhat larger percentage were defeated in primaries (due mainly to reapportionment and redistricting), and a slightly smaller percentage were defeated in the general election. If general election contests alone are considered, 92.4 percent of incumbents were re-elected in 1982 compared with 92.1 percent in 1980.

Table 12-1   House and Senate Incumbents and Election Outcomes, 1982

	Incumbents Running (N)	Primary Defeats		General Election Defeats		Re-elected	
		(N)	%	(N)	%	(N)	%
House	(393)	(10)	2.5	(29)	7.4	(354)	90.1
Senate	(30)	(0)	—	(2)	6.7	(28)	93.3

NOTE: For results between 1954 and 1980, see Table 9-1, p. 192.

For senators, however, the 1982 results differed significantly from recent elections. Thirty incumbents sought re-election, and 28 won—the highest numbers in each category since 1965. The 7 percent defeat rate was less than one-fourth of the average rate for the three preceding elections.

Table 12-2 shows the interaction between party and incumbency in the 1982 elections. In the House races the Democrats fared very well but not as well as the Republicans did in 1980. Only one Democratic incumbent, Bob Shamansky of Ohio, was defeated by a nonincumbent Republican challenger. Shamansky defeated a Republican incumbent in 1980, but redistricting hurt his re-election chances. The Democrats did well holding their vacant districts (districts in which the incumbent Democratic member of Congress was not running in the general election), won a narrow majority of the new districts created by redistricting, and took more than one-fourth of the vacant Republican districts.

The Democrats in 1982 did fare a little better than the Republicans in 1980 in defeating their opponents' incumbents. Democratic challengers defeated 13 percent of the Republican incumbents (compared with 11 percent of the Democratic incumbents defeated two years before). This increase resulted from the vulnerability of first-term Republican incumbents. Of the 50 first-term Republicans who ran in the general election, 13 were defeated, and of the 26 who entered the House in 1980 by defeating a Democratic incumbent, 9 were defeated. On the other hand, more senior Republicans were far more successful in gaining re-election. Of the 118 who served more than one term, only 13 lost in the 1982 general election.

Republicans were vulnerable because the president's party almost always loses ground in midterm elections and also because of the high level of unemployment in the fall of 1982. But the heavy losses among Republican first termers represents a marked departure from the pattern of recent elections in which House freshmen have been very successful at being re-elected. In 1980 no Democrat who had been

Table 12-2 House and Senate Election Outcomes, by Party and Incumbency, 1982

1982 Winners	Democratic Incumbent	1982 Candidates				Total
		No Incumbent (Seat Was Democratic)	No Incumbent (New Seat)	No Incumbent (Seat Was Republican)	Republican Incumbent	
House						
Democrats	99%	86%	55%	29%	13%	62%
Republicans	1	14	45	71	87	38
Total percent (Number)	100% (213)[1]	100% (22)	100% (22)	100% (14)	100% (164)[2]	100% (435)
Senate						
Democrats	95%	0%	—	50%	9%	61%
Republicans	5	100	—	50	91	39
Total percent (Number)	100% (19)	100% (1)[3]	—	100% (2)	100% (11)	100% (33)

[1] Excludes two Democratic incumbents who were defeated by Republican incumbents.

[2] Excludes four Republican incumbents who were defeated by Democratic incumbents.

[3] Harry F. Byrd, Jr., an Independent senator from Virginia, is counted here as a Democrat because he caucused with that party.

NOTE: For results for 1980, see Table 9-2, p. 195.

elected to a first term in 1978 was defeated. Even in the large class of
Democrats elected in 1974 (sometimes known as the Watergate class
because they came into office shortly after President Richard M.
Nixon's forced resignation), only one member was defeated in 1976. In
1982, 13 of the 26 Republican incumbents who lost were freshmen. The
Democrats had targeted some of these unsuccessful Republicans for
defeat in the redistricting process, and as we will see this contributed to
the Democrats' success.

One of the reasons for the low rate of incumbent defeats in Senate
races in 1982 is apparent from Table 12-2. Although economic conditions made the Republicans vulnerable, only 13 of the 33 seats at stake
were held by Republican senators. It was a "structural" advantage for
the Republicans that the many Republican first-term senators who first
had won election in 1980 did not have to seek re-election in 1982.
Instead, relatively senior colleagues, who had more time to build ties to
the voters, faced the electorate, and they were universally successful.

In 1982 as in 1y80, the Republicans were often lucky. In 1980
almost all of the close races swung toward the GOP; Republicans that
year defeated nine Democratic incumbents, giving them control of the
Senate. In 1982 almost all of the close races again went to the
Republicans, but this time the outcomes favored Republican incumbents who had been in trouble. Of the nine races involving incumbents
that were won by less than 55 percent of the vote, Republicans won
seven. Indeed, the net result of 1982 easily could have been much worse
for the GOP. In the 19 races with Democratic incumbents, the incumbent received less than 55 percent of the vote in only two races and less
than 60 percent in only four more; the average (mean) Democratic vote
was 62.9 percent. On the other hand, among the 11 Republican
incumbents, seven received less than 55 percent and not one received 61
percent of the vote; the average percent of the vote was 52.5. A small
shift in favor of the Democrats might have turned into a Republican
rout in the Senate, returning control to their opponents.

The Regional Pattern

Table 12-3 updates Table 9-3, Party Shares of Regional Delegations
in the House and Senate in 1953, 1980, and 1981. The 1982 House
elections largely reinstated the pattern that existed in 1980. The largest
Democratic gain in percentage terms was in the Midwest, the former
Republican heartland where the Democrats now hold a majority of
seats. In 1953 the Democrats had only 23 percent of the House seats
from the Midwest. A significant source of the percentage shift in 1982
was the decline in the number of Midwest seats due to reapportionment.
The Democrats held a larger share of a smaller base; they actually
gained only four seats while the Republicans lost nine.

The continuation of the shift of seats from the Northeast to the South and West becomes apparent when Table 9-3 and Table 12-3 are compared. In 1953 the East and Midwest combined had 234 House seats; 30 years later they had only 200 seats. During the same period the South gained 10 seats, the West 28. The partisan pattern of Senate seats by region is virtually identical to the pattern in 1981. The only net change is a one-seat Republican gain in the South. This shift, albeit tiny, is significant. The Republicans now hold precisely half of the Senate seats from the South. As recently as 1960, the Democrats held all 22 Senate seats from the South. Clearly, Democratic dominance of the South has been broken.

WHO WON? THE CHOICE OF A YARDSTICK

Having reviewed the pattern of outcomes in 1982, we now will consider which party won. Trying to answer "Who won?" is a bit like trying to answer "How high is up?" To make a sensible response one needs a standard of comparison, some sort of yardstick against which to measure the observed outcomes.

Historical Standards

The first obvious yardstick is history, measuring results against what has happened before. Table 12-4 presents House seat losses by the

Table 12-3 Party Shares of Regional Delegations in the House and Senate, 1983

	House			Senate		
Region	% Dem.	% Rep.	(N)	% Dem.	% Rep.	(N)
East	61	39	(96)	50	50	(20)
Midwest	54	46	(104)	41	59	(22)
West	54	46	(85)	35	65	(26)
South	71	29	(116)	50	50	(22)
Border	76	24	(34)	70	30	(10)
Total	62	38	(435)	46	54	(100)

NOTE: Figures reflect composition of the House and Senate when the 98th Congress convened on Jan. 3, 1983. See Chapter 9, note 3, p. 209, for explanation of regional breakdown used here. See Table 9-3, p. 196, for party shares of regional delegations in the House and Senate in 1953, 1980, and 1981.

party of the president in the post-World War II midterm elections. The first section of the table shows all midterm elections together. This is the standard usually employed by journalists when discussing the historical pattern of midterm elections. The average number of seats lost by the president's party between 1946 and 1978 was 29.6, with the losses ranging from 4 seats in 1962 to 55 seats in 1946. The performance of the Republicans in 1982—a net loss of 26 seats—was slightly better than this, so one might argue from this perspective that the two parties roughly broke even.

Such a conclusion is somewhat bothersome, however, because of the great range in historical outcomes—losses from 4 to 55 seats. Analyzing

Table 12-4   House Seat Losses by Party of the President in Midterm Elections, 1946-1978

All Elections

1946:	55 Dem.		1966:	47 Dem.
1950:	29 Dem.		1970:	12 Rep.
1954:	18 Rep.		1974:	43 Rep.
1958:	47 Rep.		1978:	11 Rep.
1962:	4 Dem.			

Average: 29.6

By Term of President

First Term

1946:	55 Dem.
1954:	18 Rep.
1962:	4 Dem.
1966:	47 Dem.
1970:	12 Rep.
1974:	43 Rep.
1978:	11 Dem.

Average: 27.1

Later Term

1950:	29 Dem.
1958:	47 Rep.

Average: 38.0

By Term of Administration

First Term

1954:	18 Rep.
1962:	4 Dem.
1970:	12 Rep.
1978:	11 Dem.

Average: 11.2

Later Term

1946:	55 Dem.
1950:	29 Dem.
1958:	47 Rep.
1966:	47 Dem.
1974:	43 Rep.

Average: 44.2

these data from another perspective permits us to sharpen our interpretations and narrow the range of anticipated outcomes. The second section of Table 12-4 divides midterms into two types, the first term under a particular president and then a later term. The logic of this division rests on the idea, discussed in Chapter 10, of a midterm election as a referendum on the president's performance. How effective were President Reagan's appeals in 1982 to "stay the course" or "give us a chance"? As the table suggests, during the first two years of a president's first term, voters are likely to make allowances on the grounds that some problems were inherited. Four years later, after the president has been in office for nearly six years, they are not so tolerant. During the postwar period, only two midterm elections (1950 and 1958) occurred during a president's second term. The average seat turnover in these two elections was higher than in the other elections—38.0 versus 27.1. Thus, viewing House seat losses from this perspective appears to have merit.

There is, however, a third way of looking at these data that will sharpen our expectations further. Table 12-4 also divides the midterm elections into those that were in the first term of an administration and those that were in a later term. Three of the postwar presidents assumed office because their predecessors did not complete a term: Harry S Truman and Lyndon B. Johnson because Franklin D. Roosevelt and John F. Kennedy died in office, and Gerald R. Ford because Nixon resigned. When these presidents faced their first midterm, they carried with them the record of their predecessor with whom they had served and whose policies they had supported. Thus, in a sense, the first midterm election for Truman could be viewed as the fourth midterm of the Roosevelt-Truman era; the first midterm election for Johnson and Ford could be viewed as the second midterm of the Kennedy-Johnson and the Nixon-Ford administrations.

House seat losses by term of administration reveal two fairly homogeneous sets of outcomes that are sharply different from one another. In the four elections that were in the first term, the president's party lost between 4 and 18 seats, with an average loss of 11.2; in the five elections after the first term, the range of losses was between 29 and 55 seats, with an average loss of 44.2. These results are rather "neat." There is no overlap between the two sets, the difference between the averages is large (33 seats), and the variation within each set is comparatively small (only a 14-seat range in the first midterm set and 26 seats in the second set). Most importantly, we have provided a sound explanation for the differences between these two types of elections.

It would seem reasonable to use this concept of midterm elections as our historical yardstick in comparing the outcome of the 1982 House elections with other midterm elections. We therefore compare 1982 with other elections held during the first term of an administration. Clearly, the performance of the Republican party was poor. The 26-seat loss in 1982 more than doubled the average loss for other similar elections. It was almost 50 percent larger than the previous maximum loss in the set of first-term midterm elections. By this historical standard, the 1982 House elections can only be called a significant Republican setback.

Politicians' Expectations

Another yardstick is the expectations of the parties and of other observers before the elections. Even if a party loses ground, it frequently will try to claim victory (at least a "moral victory") if it did significantly better than expected. Of course, expectations will change over time. For example, in 1981 the Republicans were optimistic about their chances in 1982 because they thought that reapportionment and redistricting would work to their advantage and economic conditions would be relatively favorable. By the time the elections drew near, however, they realized that redistricting would not be the boon they had hoped for. Rising unemployment further dampened their hopes while fueling Democrats' optimism.

The summer before the campaign the Republicans were sanguine, both publicly and in private, about their prospects. Nancy Sinnott, executive director of the National Republican Congressional Committee, said she expected little loss below the 192 seats Republicans then held, and an anonymous Republican strategist expected House losses below 20 and a likely gain of a seat or two in the Senate. These expectations were based on Republican advantages in money and direct mail, strong candidates, a weak Democratic campaign program, Reagan's ability to blame the Democrats for the nation's economic problems, and predictions of low voter turnout.[2]

Republicans remained optimistic through September and early October, but by the middle of the month their sights had lowered considerably. The announcement in early October of double-digit unemployment dampened hopes. One Republican campaign consultant privately made this assessment:

> If we had had the election on October 18 ... we would have had a severe jolt to the Republican party. We had already had a pretty strong body blow. It was a delayed reaction to unemployment reaching 10.1 percent and strong Democratic attacks on our candidates.[3]

As a result of these devastating economic conditions, the Republican party strategists adopted a defensive posture, concentrating most of their efforts on maintaining incumbents rather than winning open or Democratic seats. Richard Bond, deputy chairman of the Republican National Committee, said at the time: "We are doing more for incumbents that we've ever done in history."[4] The Republicans privately feared the loss of as many as 40 House seats. By the end of October, however, Republican optimism again increased because district-level polls showed that losses of this magnitude were unlikely.

Democratic expectations during the campaign fairly well mirrored those of Republicans. Early in the campaign there was little realistic hope for major gains. By October hopes had risen substantially, yet strategists in both parties had difficulty naming more than 15 specific House districts that were likely to switch from Republican to Democrat. As election day neared, attention shifted to the Senate where Democrats seemed to be making late gains in a number of races. Some began to hope that the Democrats would retake control of the Senate.

By the end of October, the parties were making public predictions of the outcome that were substantially different, but these were for political effect. The private projections were for gains of 20 to 30 House seats for the Democrats plus a number of governorships, and for the Senate gain to be a seat or two either way. Thus, by this yardstick, the actual outcome fell close to expectations, and neither party did significantly worse than anticipated. On election day the electorate did not provide any major surprises, although the Democratic gubernatorial gain—a net of seven—was somewhat higher than most predictions.[5]

Academic Models

Academic models of elections, such as Edward R. Tufte's model discussed in Chapter 10, are a third means of evaluating who won. Tufte views midterm elections as a referendum on the president's performance. While academic modelers realize that local conditions affect individual races, they assume that there are so many House races that national political and economic conditions can be used to predict the overall outcome. Most of these models use the president's approval rating in the Gallup polls, national economic conditions, or a combination of both, to predict the proportion of the vote that each of the two major parties will receive.

Collectively, the models did quite well at predicting the partisan division of the aggregate national House vote.[6] Tufte predicted that the Democrats would receive 57 percent of the national vote; they received 56 percent. Most of the models, however, did not do well when it came to predicting the number of House seats each party would win. Tufte's model indicates that 57 percent of the vote for the Democrats should have translated into a gain of 40 to 45 seats; another model constructed by Douglas A. Hibbs, Jr., predicted a 39-seat Democratic gain.[7] While both Tufte's and Hibbs's models were "wrong," they illustrate a very important result: the Republicans did better than one would have predicted given the poor economic conditions in the fall of 1982.

THE IMPACT OF REAPPORTIONMENT
AND REDISTRICTING

Article I, Section 2, of the U.S. Constitution mandates that a census of the population be conducted every 10 years:

> Representatives and direct Taxes shall be apportioned among the several states which may be included within this Union, according to their respective Numbers.... The actual Enumeration shall be made within three Years after the first Meeting of the Congress of the United States, and within every subsequent Term of ten Years, in such Manner as they shall by Law direct.

When the results of the decennial census are known, the Congress uses a formula to determine the number of House seats to which each state is entitled. This redistribution of House seats is called *reapportionment.* Once a state knows the number of House seats it will have, it can begin *redistricting,* the process of drawing the boundary lines of those districts. For most of American history, states that neither gained nor lost representatives could choose whether or not to redistrict. Since 1964, however, redistricting after every census has been mandated by U.S. Supreme Court decisions that require every congressional district in a state to be as close to equal in population as possible with every other district.[8] While only those states that gain or lose representatives are affected by reapportionment, nearly all 44 states with more than one representative will be affected by redistricting.

Reapportionment: The Republicans Lose Out

Reapportionment and redistricting usually have a substantial political impact, and 1982 was no exception. After the 1980 census results became known, the Republicans had great hopes that the reapportionment process would help to neutralize their normal midterm losses in the House. Why they were so optimistic becomes obvious when one considers where seats were lost or gained. New York lost five seats; Illinois, Ohio, and Pennsylvania lost two; and Indiana, Massachusetts, Michigan, Missouri, New Jersey, and South Dakota each lost one. Florida gained four seats; Texas gained three; California gained two; and Arizona, Colorado, Nevada, New Mexico, Oregon, Tennessee, Utah, and Washington each gained one.

Thus most of the shift was from the industrial states of the Northeast and Midwest (the Frost Belt where the Democrats were relatively strong) to the Sun Belt states of the South and West (where Republicans had been doing relatively well). This pattern of seat losses and gains seemed to portend a Republican advantage. Moreover, the reasons for the shifts appeared to favor Republican prospects. The Frost

Belt losses were caused primarily by declining populations in major cities where the congressional districts were virtually all Democratic. The Sun Belt gains were mainly due to substantial population gains in suburban areas where the districts were largely Republican. Strategists for the Republican party could be pardoned for hoping that the reapportionment process would directly transform Democratic seats in the North into Republican seats in the South and West.

Like so many political hopes, however, these were not to be realized. The Republicans were at a political disadvantage in some states, and luck worked against them in others. To be sure, things went as planned in a few cases in the North. In Indiana, Republicans controlled the governorship and both houses of the state legislature. Indiana lost one congressional seat, and the Republicans eliminated a Democratic district so that this seat loss would be borne by the Democrats. In Michigan, where control of the government was divided, the seat of a suburban Democrat who had announced for governor was eliminated because both parties found this an acceptable compromise. In other states, however, the seats lost were not those that had been anticipated.[9] In New Jersey, on the last day before the Republicans took over the statehouse in 1982, the Democrats rushed through a partisan plan that eliminated a Republican seat. In South Dakota, the two old districts were merged into one state-wide district with a Democratic and a Republican incumbent. The Democrat, Thomas A. Daschle, had been first elected in 1978; his opponent, Clint Roberts, entered the House in 1980. Knowing that the state would be reduced to a single district, Daschle advertised as much in South Dakota's other district as in his own in his first re-election campaign in 1980 and afterward. In 1982 these tactics paid off. He won despite South Dakota's Republican leanings.

In Massachusetts, two incumbents—Republican Margaret M. Heckler and Democrat Barney Frank—were placed in a district that many observers thought favored the Republican candidate. Frank won, however. In Ohio, the seats of two retiring Republicans were eliminated. Perhaps the unkindest cut of all for the Republicans came in Illinois. Illinois's two-seat loss was due to a major decrease in Chicago's population. Because all the House seats in Chicago were Democratic, the Republicans anticipated that the Democrats would lose two seats. Control of the state government was divided, with Republicans holding the house of representatives and governorship and the Democrats controlling the senate. A stalemate resulted over redistricting, and a federal court took jurisdiction. The court adopted a computer-generated Democratic plan that made all districts almost identical in population. The plan also worked to the Democrats' advantage. Instead of eliminating their districts in the city, it extended the city districts into the

Republican suburbs, taking in enough people to equalize the districts in terms of population. To compensate for the maintenance of the city districts, two pairs of Republican incumbents were put in the same districts, and thus two suburban Republican members were forced out of office.

Of the 17 seats lost by states in the East and Midwest, only seven belonged to Democrats in the 97th Congress, and 10 were Republican. Furthermore, the Republicans did not fare much better in the Sun Belt states to which these seats were transferred. The same combination of political disadvantages and bad fortune befell them. For example, Florida gained four seats, but because the Democrats controlled the government only two seats were targeted for the Republicans. In Texas, the conservative Republican governor struck a deal with conservative Democrats in the legislature to produce a plan that helped the Republicans. Because of racial patterns, however, a federal court intervened and redrew the lines of six districts. As a result, only one of the three new seats was targeted for a Republican.

The worst situation for the Republicans in the Sun Belt developed in California, where both houses of the legislature and the governorship were in Democratic hands. Rep. Phillip Burton—the leader of the Democratic House delegation from California, a political power in the San Francisco area, and a former state legislator—instigated a redistricting process that resulted in one of the most blatant, and most effective, gerrymanders of modern times. Both of the new seats allocated to California were targeted for Democrats even though the state's main population gains were in Republican areas such as Orange County.

What was the overall result of reapportionment in 1982? Of the 17 new seats, eight were prospectively Democratic, and nine were likely to be Republican. Yet even this was not the end of Republican woes. When the election was held the Republicans won one seat that was slated to be Democratic (in Tennessee), but the Democrats won two seats targeted for Republicans (in Arizona and Texas). The Democrats took the Sun Belt seats nine to eight. In short, the reapportionment process that Republicans had hoped would yield them significant gains to neutralize midterm losses instead produced victory for their opponents. Democrats lost seven seats in the Frost Belt through reapportionment and won nine in the Sun Belt for a net gain of two.

Redistricting: The Democratic Advantage

While the reapportionment process affected only a minority of states, redistricting had an impact almost everywhere. The important question, however, is whether redistricting had a discernible political impact beyond the simple rearrangement of boundaries. In Chapter 9 we indicated that there was no evidence that redistricting caused the increase in incumbents' success in the 1960s and 1970s. One might anticipate, therefore, that there would be little effect on incumbents' fortunes in 1982. We think, however, that the summary judgment on the earlier effects of reapportionment may have been premature. In 1982 there were clearly some contexts in which the net effect of redistricting was to harm Republican incumbents.

Before the advent of the rise of ticket splitting and the weakening of the link between party identification and voting, most states usually had a governor and a state legislature of the same party.[10] When the opportunity for redistricting presented itself, there was nothing to prevent state political leaders from turning the opportunity to partisan advantage. Since the 1960s, however, divided party control of state governments has become more frequent. Divided party control often leads to court-imposed redistricting. In 21 of the 39 states that redistricted after the 1980 census, party control was divided. One branch of the government blocked other branches controlled by the opposite party from gaining partisan advantage through redistricting. In seven of these states (as well as one state with one party control), jurisdiction over the state's redistricting was taken over by a federal court.

The three possible redistricting contexts—one party control, split party control, and court control—differ sharply and produce differing effects. In one party situations there often occurs a partisan gerrymander in which the dominant party tries to gain House seats through the redistricting process. The standard practice is to concentrate the opposing party's voting strength in as few districts as possible, making a few opposing incumbents very safe. Then the voting strength of the party in power is added to the districts of the remaining opposing incumbents, weakening their electoral chances severely. Gaining this advantage is risky, however; the voting strength used to weaken opponents usually must be obtained by reducing the partisan advantage of some of one's own incumbents. Thus the net result of such a design (if it works as planned) is to make some incumbents of both parties less safe, and some incumbents of the opposing party much safer.

The context of split party control produces quite different expectations. Since it is unlikely that one party can persuade members of the opposition to go along with a plan that puts them at a disadvantage (an exception was the Texas case mentioned earlier), one of two outcomes usually will occur. The first is a bipartisan gerrymander in which the incumbents of both parties are made as safe as possible, preserving the status quo. Such a plan increases incumbent safeness generally. The alternative is a deadlock that persists until a federal court takes jurisdiction.

When the courts take control of redistricting, no general prediction can be made about the outcome. The impact of court-ordered redistricting depends on the type of plan the court chooses to impose. The court may ask various political parties as well as other interested actors to submit proposed plans and then choose among them. (In these situations a very partisan plan may be enacted even though the party control of the state is split.) It may impose its own bipartisan gerrymander, thus preserving the status quo as much as possible. Or it may want to have a plan drawn up independently and may completely disregard existing political patterns. Such a plan was imposed on California in 1974, and it played havoc with the interests of representatives of both parties all over the state (although because of the Watergate landslide in 1974, its impact was felt almost exclusively by Republicans). The uncertainty of court-ordered redistricting often motivates parties in split situations to reach a compromise.

In 1982 the prototypes of the partisan gerrymander were the California case mentioned earlier and the Republican redistricting in Indiana. The California redistricting was one of the most determined partisan gerrymanders on record and also one of the cleverest.[11] The Democrats began with a margin of 22 to 21 in the House delegation, and two new seats were to be added by the reapportionment. Even though most of the population gain occurred in Republican areas, the Democrats crafted the districts to their advantage. Three Republican districts were carved up into a number of pieces, eliminating them and putting their incumbents in the same districts with other Republicans. The Democrats took the three resulting surplus seats and the two new ones and created five new districts without incumbents, most with a Democratic bias and designed for specific political allies of Rep. Burton. A few other Republican incumbents were weakened, and certain weak Democrats were shored up at the expense of safe ones. When the 1982 election was held, the Democrats beat one opposition incumbent and took four of the five new districts plus one vacant Republican district. Their margin of advantage in the California delegation then became 28 to 17.

The Indiana redistricting had just as partisan a complexion as the redistricting in California, albeit on a smaller scale. The Republicans controlled the governorship and both legislative houses, and Indiana lost a seat in the reapportionment (from 11 seats to 10). The Republicans produced a plan that jeopardized three of the six Democratic representatives. Two Democratic districts were cut up four ways, which persuaded one of the incumbents to retire from the House and run for the Senate. The other challenged a fellow Democrat for the nomination in another district and lost. A third Democratic incumbent was seriously weakened, a marginal Republican was strengthened, and a new and overwhelmingly Republican district was created. In the election, however, the plan did not work out entirely as designed. The weakened Democratic incumbent won, and the strengthened Republican incumbent lost. The postelection partisan division of the delegation was 5 to 5 rather than the 6 to 4 or 7 to 3 advantage the Republicans had hoped for.

Many states with split delegations produced neutral or incumbent protection plans. This was particularly true in smaller states. Arkansas strengthened its four incumbents, two from each party. Louisiana advanced the re-election prospects of all eight incumbents, two Republicans and six Democrats. In Oregon, the Democrats in the legislature strengthened their three incumbents at the price of strengthening one Republican and giving the new fifth district a pro-Republican bias in order to gain the agreement of the Republican governor.

The 1982 court-ordered redistrictings exhibit the anticipated variety. In Colorado, the Republican-controlled legislature passed three plans drawn to their advantage, and Democratic Governor Richard D. Lamm vetoed all three. A federal court took jurisdiction and substantially redrew the district lines. The districts were drawn to the advantage of the five incumbents (three Democrats and two Republicans), with the new sixth district given a pro-Republican bias. The Texas plan, after the intervention of the courts, had a similar pro-incumbent character.

The Illinois situation illustrates the opposite extreme. The courts adopted a Democratic plan that was shaped to that party's advantage. The courts seemed to have chosen this plan partly because it preserved the black majority in Chicago districts. Minority-group representation seemed to have been of general interest to many courts participating in redistricting.[12] The Illinois plan forced the Republicans to bear the cost of the two seats lost in the reapportionment. The Democrats won a vacant Republican seat and defeated a Republican incumbent (Paul Findley), whose district was redrawn to his disadvantage.[13] Finally, in Minnesota and Missouri, courts imposed plans that disrupted the interests of incumbents of both parties, although Republicans suffered most of the damage in the elections.

Table 12-5 summarizes the results for the 39 states in 1982 with districts that were redrawn by either the state government or the courts. Results are arranged according to who controlled the redistricting process in each state. The Republicans practically broke even in the states that they controlled and in the states with split control. The Democrats fared well in the states in which they controlled the redistricting process. They also did well in the states in which a court redrew the district lines, although most of this advantage stemmed from three states (Illinois, Minnesota, and Texas) where the combined results were +7 for the Democrats and −6 for the Republicans.

Table 12-5 Representation in the House Before and After the 1982 Elections, Controlling for Who Redrew the Districts

| | Party Division | | | | | |
| | Before Election | | After Election | | Change | |
	Dem.	Rep.	Dem.	Rep.	Dem.	Rep.
State Government Redrew Districts						
Democrats Controlled	83	51	98	41	+15	−10
Republicans Controlled	26	26	26	24	0	− 2
Split Control	62	58	63	56	+ 1	− 2
Court Redrew Districts	56	45	65	36	+ 9	− 9

NOTE: Excluded from this table are three states that were redrawn by an independent commission (Connecticut, Hawaii, and Maryland), six states that did not redraw because they had only one representative (Alaska, Delaware, North Dakota, South Dakota, Vermont, and Wyoming), and two states with small population variances that will not redistrict until 1983 (Maine and Montana). All of the eight states in which a court imposed a plan had split party control except one (South Carolina); the other seven were Colorado, Illinois, Kansas, Michigan, Minnesota, Missouri, and Texas. Twelve states were in Democratic hands (Alabama, California, Florida, Georgia, Kentucky, Massachusetts, New Jersey, New Mexico, North Carolina, Oklahoma, Rhode Island, and West Virginia). The Republicans controlled five states (Indiana, Iowa, Nebraska, Pennsylvania and Washington). Fourteen additional states were split (Arizona, Arkansas, Idaho, Louisiana, Mississippi, Nevada, New Hampshire, New York, Ohio, Oregon, Tennessee, Utah, Virginia, and Wisconsin).

Table 12-6 indicates the region of the country of the 26 Republican incumbents defeated in 1982 and shows whether or not they were harmed by redistricting. As the table indicates, redistricting hurt half of them. (It also hurt all three Democratic incumbents defeated in 1982.)

Table 12-6 Defeated Republican Incumbents, Controlling for Region and Redistricting Damage, 1982

| Region | Was The Incumbent Hurt By Redistricting? | | |
	Yes	No	Total
East	4	5	9
Midwest	5	2	7
West	2	0	2
South	1	5	6
Border	1	1	2
Total	13	13	26

NOTE: See Chapter 9, note 3, p. 209, for explanation of regional breakdown used here.

Eleven of the 13 defeated Republican incumbents that were *not* hurt by redistricting were from regions of traditional Democratic strength— the East, South, and Border states. Only two were from the Midwest (the traditional Republican heartland), and none were from the West (the core of support for Reagan's brand of Republicanism). This regional breakdown offers an opportunity for an interesting characterization of the election. Once we remove those cases where Republican incumbents were hurt by redistricting, we see at least a temporary reassertion of the old regional basis of the Democratic coalition.

REPUBLICAN STRATEGIC ADVANTAGES

Academic models that viewed the 1982 midterm elections largely as a referendum on the performance of the president and the economy generally predicted larger Republican losses than actually occurred. As we pointed out earlier in this chapter, Republican candidates were partly insulated from the negative effects of the national shift against them in the congressional vote. Our discussion of redistricting and reapportionment reinforces this conclusion. Without the effects of that process, Republican House losses almost certainly would have been even smaller in 1982. What then were the factors that served to protect Republican candidates?

One strategic advantage of the Republicans was in the area of *campaign financing.* New data from the 1980 elections and early indications from 1982 show a major Republican advantage in this area. As we indicated in Chapter 9, most challengers must be able to spend a certain minimum amount of money to get their message to the voters and compete effectively with incumbents, who usually are better known. Data on campaign spending in 1980 show that Republican challengers were much more likely to be able to spend adequately. In 1980 incumbents of both parties spent about the same amount (an average of $159,382 for Democrats, $175,771 for Republicans). Estimated figures for challengers, however, indicate a much larger disadvantage for Democrats relative to their opponents than for Republicans.[14] (Republican challengers averaged $114,958, while Democrats averaged $76,361.) Thus Democratic incumbents in 1980 outspent their challengers by only 39 percent, while Republicans outspent theirs by 130 percent!

In early 1983 similar data were not yet available for 1982, but several reports indicated that the GOP spending advantage continued unabated. Figures covering the period through September 30, 1982, showed Republican incumbents had spent $118,379 while all nonincumbent Democratic candidates spent an average of $53,882.[15] Since this last figure combines spending by candidates for open seats with that of challengers of incumbents, it almost certainly underestimates the challengers' disadvantage.

Campaign strategists of both parties support this view. Rep. Tony Coelho, chairman of the Democratic Congressional Campaign Committee in 1982, commented on the importance of having money to spend at the end of the campaign: "The money Republicans could spend in the last two weeks in close races was the most crucial, and it saved them at least 10 seats." Nancy Sinnott seemed to agree: "We think quality of campaigns made the difference ... and money is certainly one way to measure the quality of a campaign." [16]

A second resource that appears to have helped the Republicans in 1982 was *candidate quality,* usually indicated by a solid political background. As Gary C. Jacobson and Samuel Kernell point out, Republicans recruited their congressional candidates for 1982 in 1981, when Reagan was dominating Congress and was relatively popular.[17] Although economic conditions had deteriorated by the summer of 1982, and although Reagan's popularity had slipped, most of these high quality Republican candidates were committed, and they did not change their minds.

A third major Republican advantage was *national party organization.* As Jacobson and Kernell wrote, "If 1982 is not a Republican disaster, national-level Republican party committees will be the reason." [18] This factor partly is linked to the Republicans' financial advantage. The National Republican Senatorial Committee budgeted $26 million while the House counterpart, the National Republican Congressional Committee, budgeted $37 million. The Democratic Senatorial Campaign Committee and the Democratic Congressional Campaign Committee spent perhaps one-tenth of these amounts.[19] Some of these funds are money contributions to candidates reflected in the figures cited earlier, and the promise of such major funding certainly is an advantage in recruiting strong candidates. Some of the money, however, goes to pay candidates' bills. In the last month of the campaign, the National Republican Congressional Committee paid $2 million in bills for candidates, and that money is not included in candidate-reported expenditures.[20]

The national organization benefited GOP candidates in other ways as well. The Republican national-level committees provided training programs for candidates and their staffs and tactical advice during the campaign. They also ran national advertising campaigns designed to advance the cause of all Republican contenders. It appears that the Democrats recognized these advantages in 1982 and began to take steps to imitate the Republican pattern.[21] Until they are successful, however, the Republicans have significant strategic advantages that magnify their gains or minimize their losses.

THE 1982 ELECTION: THE IMPACT ON CONGRESS

To assess the impact of the 1982 congressional election on Congress, it is simplest to begin with the Senate, where the direct effects were minimal. Only three senators retired and two incumbents were defeated. The entering class of five freshman senators was the smallest since 1913, when the Seventeenth Amendment to the Constitution provided for popular election of senators. Because the party balance in the Senate remained the same, few significant shifts in the makeup of Senate committees took place. It also was not expected that the five new senators in the 98th Congress would alter in any important way the chamber's ideological balance. The Democrats probably will gain about one net vote on most issues as a result of the election.

In the House, with a net gain there of 26 seats for the Democrats and a total of 81 freshman representatives (57 Democrats and 24 Republicans), there probably will be significant changes, some of which were visible in the first months of the new Congress. Most obviously, President Reagan will find it more difficult to produce a majority for his programs on the floor of the House. Before the election, the party-regional balance was 173 Northern Democrats, 70 Southern Democrats, and 192 Republicans. The Republicans then tended to vote as a cohesive block, and they found it fairly easy to get the relatively small number of Democratic votes needed to pass Reagan's initiatives or defeat Democratic ones (although producing these votes got noticeably more difficult as election day drew near).

After the election, the balance became 187 Northern Democrats, 82 Southern Democrats, and 166 Republicans. The Republicans thus needed to get many more votes to construct a floor majority, and even the greater number of Southern Democrats did not offer much hope because many of the 20 freshman Southern Democrats and 37 Northern Democrats campaigned explicitly against Reagan's economic programs. With more votes needed and fewer "boll weevil" Democrats to get them from, the Republican leadership in the House will have difficulty winning floor votes.

Less obvious than the problems confronting the Republicans on the floor, but probably more significant in determining the character of national policy, were the changes that occurred in the makeup of House committees in the 98th Congress. Because of their numerical gain in House seats, the Democrats got a larger share of seats on standing committees than they had in the 97th. Additional vacancies were created on committees by the 31 Democratic representatives who did not return when the new Congress convened on January 3, 1983. These departure-caused vacancies did not affect all committees equally. Five Democratic vacancies were created on Armed Services, two on Agriculture, six on Government Operations, and none on District of Columbia. Thus one might expect more continuity in the policies of the Agriculture Committee than in the policies of the Armed Services Committee. Frequently, the particular committee members are more important than the number of vacancies created. For example, two new subcommittee chairmen on Armed Services were Les Aspin of Wisconsin, who has often criticized the Pentagon, and Ronald V. Dellums of California, a black radical who was first elected on an anti-Vietnam War platform and has been a persistent opponent of the committee leadership. These two changes portend significant difficulties for the Reagan administration's military policies.[22]

Reflecting the growth in Democratic numbers on the floor and in committees, and the increased resources these provide in combatting the administration's programs and providing alternatives, are a series of rules and procedural changes for the House as a whole and for the House Democratic caucus. Overall, the 1982 election strengthened Democratic leadership in the House, increased party cohesion, and weakened the influence of conservative Democrats. For example, changes in House rules will make it more difficult to pass riders to appropriations bills and to bring proposed constitutional amendments to a floor vote.

New Democratic caucus rules also prohibit members from participating in campaign activities on behalf of Republicans; offenders will be expelled from the caucus. Departing from recent practice, Democratic leaders warned freshmen that they should not expect appointments to the four most important House committees (Appropriations, Budget, Rules, and Ways and Means), although ultimately one freshman, Representative Robert J. Mrazek (D-N.Y.), was appointed to Appropriations. The attitudes of Democratic freshmen on matters of party loyalty were reflected in their unanimous vote to drop Rep. Phil Gramm of Texas (a leader of the "boll weevils") to the bottom of the Democratic seniority list because of his consistent support for Reagan's economic program. In response, Gramm resigned from the House January 5, 1983, and returned to Texas to run for re-election as a Republican. He won the special election on February 12, 1983, with 55 percent of the vote.

In summary, little change in the behavior of the Senate is expected as a result of the 1982 elections (although the atmosphere probably will get more combative with the approach of the 1984 elections and the presence of a number of Democratic presidential candidates). In the House, however, the level of interparty conflict should increase, and we should see more willingness by the president to compromise on his programs, or more consistent defeat of those programs and the substitution of Democratic initiatives.

NOTES

1. Phil Duncan, "House Vote: Major Midterm Setback for the Republicans," *Congressional Quarterly Weekly Report,* Nov. 6, 1982, p. 2780. Unless otherwise indicated, election data used in this chapter are from *Congressional Quarterly Weekly Reports.*
2. James R. Dickenson, "GOP Planners See Fall Elections as the Little Truck That Could," *Washington Post,* August 14, 1982, p. A12.
3. Hedrick Smith, "Republicans Shift from Defensive to Bold Strategy," *New York Times,* October 30, 1982, p. 1. All citations in this chapter are to the Midwest edition.
4. Ibid.
5. *Congressional Quarterly Weekly Report,* November 6, 1982, p. 2806.
6. Evans Witt, "A Model Election?" *Public Opinion* 5 (December/January 1983): 46-49. Witt provides an excellent description of four academic models and their predicted results for the 1982 elections.
7. Ibid. Estimates by Gary C. Jacobson and Samuel Kernell suggested that the Democrats would gain between 45 and 55 seats, but they argued that strategic Republican advantages would substantially reduce these expected gains. One model proved more accurate than the rest; Richard A. Brody predicted a 1-seat Democratic gain in the Senate and an 18-seat Democratic gain in the House.
8. *Wesberry* v. *Sanders* (376 U.S. 1 (1964).
9. In some instances it could not be determined which party was likely to be harmed in a district until the election was actually held. For more information, see *State Politics and Redistricting,* part 1 (Washington, D.C.: Congressional Quarterly, 1982).
10. This discussion is part of a larger study by David W. Rohde on "The Electoral Effects of Redistricting and Reapportionment, 1952-1982."
11. For a detailed account by a participant in the California redistricting, see Bruce E. Cain, "The Reapportionment Puzzle," unpublished manuscript, California Institute of Technology, 1982.
12. Charles S. Bullock, III, "The Inexact Science of Congressional Redistricting," *PS* 15 (Summer 1982): 431-438.
13. Otis Pike, "Artful Democrats Excel at Redrawing Districts," *Detroit Free Press,* November 18, 1982, p. A9.
14. Norman J. Ornstein et al., eds., *Vital Statistics on Congress, 1982* (Washington, D.C.: American Enterprise Institute for Public Policy Research, 1982), pp. 60-61. Figures for challengers are estimates because many candidates with low-budget campaigns are exempt from filing reports of expenditures. The cited figures use the actual amounts for candidates that filed and assume an expenditure of $5,000 for those that did not.
15. Adam Clymer, "GOP Candidates Leading in Fund Raising," *New York Times,* October 30, 1982, p. 33.
16. Adam Clymer, "Campaign Funds Called a Key to Outcome of House Races," *New York Times,* November 5, 1982, pp. 1, 11.

17. Gary C. Jacobson and Samuel Kernell, "Strategy and Choice in the 1982 Congressional Elections," *PS* 15 (Summer 1982): 428-429.
18. Ibid., p. 428.
19. Ibid.
20. Clymer, "Campaign Funds Called a Key."
21. David Hoffman, "Rep. Coelho: Democrat Fund-Raiser Extraordinaire," *Washington Post*, August 26, 1982, p. A2.
22. We are grateful to Kenneth A. Shepsle for providing insights about the consequences of these committee changes.

13

1984 and Beyond

By early 1983, potential contenders for the 1984 presidential nomination, especially on the Democratic side, had begun laying plans, developing strategies, and courting grass-roots support. This chapter begins with an examination of two aspects of the unfolding nomination campaigns: changes in the rules for selecting delegates to the conventions and the field of likely contenders. We then consider prospects for the 1984 general election and the future of American politics in light of the November 1982 elections. Thus, from the vantage point of early 1983, we re-evaluate the long-term impact of the 1980 elections.

DELEGATE SELECTION REFORMS

As we noted in Chapter 1, the method of selecting presidential nominees has changed considerably since 1968 when a series of Democratic party reforms led to a resurgence in the use of the primary. These reforms made the states' primary or caucus proceedings for selecting convention delegates the crucial phase in determining the party's nominee. Although most of the reforms were initiated by various commissions within the Democratic National Party, they affect both parties since state laws often are required to implement them.

The commission appointed in 1980 by the Democratic party (the Hunt Commission chaired by North Carolina Governor James B. Hunt, Jr.) made its recommendations to the Democratic National Committee in January 1982. With some modifications, these reforms were approved by the DNC in March 1982 and became effective for the 1984 campaign. In this section we will consider three particularly important rules changes: the creation of "superdelegates," shortening of the primary season, and the recreation of the "Democratic loophole" provision.

"Superdelegates"

Did the Democratic party reforms of the 1970s take too much political power out of the hands of elected officeholders and party officials? Some fear that they did. Today the public effectively chooses the presidential candidate, and even the highest elected officeholders in the party find it difficult to attend the convention as delegates. In 1968, 68 percent of Democratic senators and 39 percent of Democratic representatives were delegates. By 1980, the percentages had fallen to 15 percent and 14 percent, respectively. To increase the attendance of top Democratic officials—and to give them more influence over the presidential nomination—the Hunt Commission recommended that they be given a significant number of delegate seats at the convention and that they be free to support the candidate of their choice, regardless of the sentiment expressed by the public in the primaries and caucuses. This recommendation was adopted. Approximately one-seventh of all delegates are now appointed. Generally, they will be Democratic senators, representatives, governors, and party officials. The press dubbed these appointed, uncommitted delegates "superdelegates."

What are the effects of this rules change? First, top leaders of the Democratic party are assured a vote at the convention. Second, these delegates have a chance to influence the selection of the nominee. Because superdelegates are free to support the candidate of their choice, they may have the deciding vote in a close nomination campaign. To win the presidential nomination, a candidate still needs 50 percent of the total number of delegates (plus one). To win a majority of all delegates through primaries and caucuses alone, a candidate now needs to win more than 58 percent of all delegates selected in that fashion.

Just how important these superdelegates will prove to be is unclear. In three of the six nomination campaigns in 1972, 1976, and 1980, the nominee won easily, and the new rules would not have affected the outcome. In the other three campaigns, the victor won by an amount closer to the 58 percent mark. The two key votes in Gerald R. Ford's nomination (one over rules, the other over the nomination itself) were won by him with less than 53 percent of the vote. The key votes in George S. McGovern's nomination suggested that he was just short of the 58 percent figure. The first vote for the nomination gave him 57.3 percent; shifts before the first ballot was finalized raised his victory total to 61.8 percent. The key vote in the 1980 contest between Jimmy Carter and Edward M. Kennedy was over rules binding the delegates. On that vote Carter forces received 58.133 percent of the vote! In these latter three contests, superdelegates could have been decisive had they all been truly uncommitted and had they been acting as a cohesive group. Such cohesiveness, however, is unlikely.

By changing the rules in 1982 and allowing for the appointment of superdelegates, the Hunt Commission was not trying to recreate a system dominated by political "bosses." Rather, it wanted to give leaders increased influence when the primary process was not decisive. Under the new rules, the Democratic nominee could win even without the support of the superdelegates. It probably would be difficult, however, for political leaders to refuse to nominate a candidate who won a majority of the delegates during the primaries and caucuses but failed to win enough to enter the convention with the absolute majority of delegates needed to win the nomination. After all, most alternatives to the frontrunner probably would be active candidates themselves—candidates who must have done less well than the frontrunner.

Pressures on the superdelegates to back the frontrunner are likely to be great. But because the superdelegates represent a large number of votes, all candidates will try to win the support of as many of them as they can, quite possibly *before* the convention. This is, perhaps, the key aim of the reform. Under the new rules, candidates will be more attuned to party leaders' concerns. While an outsider, such as Jimmy Carter in 1976, would not be denied the nomination, the outsider probably would make a greater effort to respond to the major concerns of the leadership, at least if the contest were close.

The Primary Season: Five Weeks Shorter

In 1980 as in 1976, delegate selection to the Democratic National Convention began in Iowa in mid-January and continued until the early weeks of June. In response to concerns that this six-month campaign was simply too long and unwieldy, the Democratic party has tried to shorten the delegate selection period.

The basic change for 1984 concerns the timing of the Iowa caucuses and the New Hampshire primary. Ever since 1920, New Hampshire has conducted the first primary, which it always held in March. After 1972, when Massachusetts and Vermont decided to hold their primaries the first Tuesday in March, New Hampshire moved its primary up to February to maintain first place. In 1984 the New Hampshire primary will be moved back to the first week in March and the other two New England primaries will follow. As in 1976 and 1980, the Iowa caucuses will precede the New Hampshire primary, but by no more than eight days.

In sum, the primary and caucus season, at least on the Democratic side, has been shortened by about five weeks. The 1984 Republican primary in New Hampshire will be held at the same time as the Democratic one, and it is likely that the Republican and Democratic caucuses in Iowa also will be held at the same time.

Rules created by one national party often affect state parties and even legislatures as well as the other national party. While parties have declined in strength since the late 1960s, a trend toward strengthening the power of the national party at the expense of the state and local party organizations is emerging.[1] In this case, the national Democratic party is imposing its will on the Iowa Democratic party and on the entire New Hampshire state political system to try to make the current jumble of primaries and caucuses at least a bit more coherent.

This 1984 reform also makes it more difficult for a relative unknown, such as Carter in 1976 or George Bush in 1980, to capitalize on an early primary win, build momentum, and make effective use of their new-found resources before too many primaries pass. Carter and Bush generated a great deal of media attention and financial contributions from their early victories in Iowa. Yet it took them time to translate publicity, money, and other resources into votes later on. Thus the "longshot" candidates are seemingly at a disadvantage.

The Democratic Loophole

One concern of Democratic reformers has been how votes cast in a primary or caucus should be translated into delegate support at the convention. Three basic rules have been used in presidential primaries: the so-called "winner-take-all" or WTA rule, the "Democratic loophole" provision which has several variations, and the "proportional representation" or PR rule. The WTA rule awards all delegates to the candidate who wins the most votes in a state primary. The PR rule awards delegates to candidates in rough proportion to the popular vote they received. For example, Jimmy Carter won 51 percent of the vote in the 1980 Ohio primary. Because the PR rule was being used, he received 52 percent of the delegates. Under WTA he would have received 100 percent of the delegates.

Until 1976, states could use any rule they wanted in Democratic primaries. In the 1972 Democratic primary in California, McGovern won 43.5 percent of the vote and Hubert H. Humphrey 38.6 percent. Because WTA was the rule, McGovern won all 271 California delegates, just enough, it appeared, to give him the nomination. The anti-McGovern forces challenged the WTA in attempting to block seating of the California delegation and to block McGovern's nomination. While McGovern's side won, the Democratic party subsequently ruled that no state could use WTA in 1976. The Republican party, however, continued to allow the WTA rule.

Despite strong sentiment in favor of requiring the use of PR, the Democratic party eventually compromised by allowing the "loophole" rule. Thus, a state with two congressional districts could allocate one-third of its delegate seats to one district, another third to the other district; the remaining third would be determined by the state-wide vote. While all state-wide seats had to be allocated according to PR, all district-wide seats could go to the candidate who carried that district. Many of the large, industrial states adopted the loophole rule. Ohio used the "loophole" in 1976 and the PR in 1980. In 1976, Carter won 52 percent of the Ohio vote and 83 percent of the delegates; four years later, a nearly identical share of the popular vote yielded Carter a bare majority of Ohio's delegates.

The Democratic party required all states to use PR in 1980. In 1984, however, states can choose either the PR or the loophole rule. Many of the larger states probably will use the loophole rule as they did in 1976 because the results of a loophole primary tend to give a much bigger block of delegates to the winner than under PR. Thus the impact of that state on the nomination, especially if the state has a large delegation, would be increased.

Some think the PR requirement in 1980 helped Carter since Kennedy did best in the large industrial states. Under PR—even with a relatively poor showing of, say, 40 percent of the vote— Carter picked up large numbers of delegates. Kennedy was unable to catch up once Carter jumped off to an early lead, a problem that some claim was compounded by the use of PR.

The creation of superdelegates can be undermined by the way the loophole rule works. A candidate who comes in first in many primaries will win more delegates under the loophole provision than under the PR rule. Thus the frontrunner coming out of the primary season could have a bigger lead in delegates than if the PR requirement were in effect for all primaries.

The overall impact of these rules changes seems to be more "fine tuning" of the 1980 system rather than major revamping. The Hunt Commission upheld the Democratic party's commitment to popular participation in delegate selection as well as affirmative action provisions for women, blacks, and Hispanics. Nevertheless, these changes somewhat increase the influence of elected officials and may somewhat reduce the chances of a relative unknown winning the Democratic nomination.

While Democratic candidates face a somewhat altered system in 1984, the Republican candidates face a system only slightly changed. In all probability their primary season, like the Democrats', will be shortened by five weeks. Some of their primary elections also may be decided by "loophole" rules since most legislatures enact a single law governing the primary. Not all do, however. For example, not all Republican primaries in 1980 were decided by PR. Finally, there is no reason to believe that the Republican party will be affected in 1984 by the Democrats' creation of superdelegates, since the Republicans did not introduce reforms to increase the representation of their elected officials.

1984 PRESIDENTIAL CANDIDATES

The effects of rules changes on the 1984 presidential contest are much easier to predict than who will run. Politicians' decisions are often shaped by unpredictable personal factors. Senator Kennedy's decision not to seek the Democratic presidential nomination resulted largely from family pressures, and his decision changed dramatically the prospects for other Democratic hopefuls. Likewise, President Ronald Reagan's decision whether to run for a second term may be influenced by personal considerations and will affect, even more profoundly, the field of contenders from his party.

To the casual observer, the entire nomination struggle may look like a series of idiosyncratic events that defies systematic explanation. But, in fact, there are regularities in the political process that explain why some people choose to run and others do not. In this section we will focus on the Democratic nomination process, since the shape of the Republican nomination contest will depend very largely upon the decision of a single individual: the president.

Democratic Candidates

In all post-1968 nomination campaigns and in many prior ones, few have challenged an incumbent president seeking renomination, while many have contended for the "out" party's nomination. There are many reasons to believe 1984 will follow this pattern.

Not every Democrat who would like to be president will run, however. Serious contenders emerge primarily from highly visible elective offices that provide a strong electoral base for a presidential bid. These offices, in 1984 as in the past, will include state governorships, the Senate, and, to a lesser extent, the House. Given the lengthy pre-convention campaign, former officeholders—especially those in good standing who have left office fairly recently—enjoy certain advantages. They have the benefits of visibility and political experience without the constraints of public duties. Former Vice President Walter F. Mondale meets most of these conditions, as does another contender, former Governor Reubin Askew of Florida.

Some politicians may have a strong electoral base but because of their sex, race, ethnic background, or religion may not run for president. Women, blacks, Hispanics, Jews, and Asian-Americans might have considerable difficulty gaining support. Similarly, those who have not demonstrated a strong commitment to their political party or whose ideological beliefs are out of the mainstream often find it hard to convince party regulars to back them.

These constraints do not mean that a campaign is impossible. They do mean, however, that such candidates would be at a competitive disadvantage. These candidates must prove their credentials as serious contenders to an often inattentive or skeptical public and persuade key activists, leaders, and groups to support them, which is no easy task. Like potential contenders without a strong electoral base, they simply may decide not to run. The basic point, of course, is that many would like to be president (for reasons discussed in Chapter 1), but only one will actually be chosen. Since many candidates are likely to try for the nomination, all hopefuls recognize the difficulty and relative improbability of their success. Only the few with a relatively good chance and little to lose are likely to make the effort.

Since the 1984 Democratic nomination struggle will be highly competitive, even small liabilities may discourage possible candidates from seeking their party's nomination. To show how these forces work, we will examine such "liabilities" among a set of potential candidates who all have a strong electoral base—the 46 Democrats in the United States Senate when it convened on January 3, 1983. Table 13-1 presents these senators and enables us to evaluate the likelihood of their presidential candidacies.

Unlikely Contenders. We will begin by considering the senators whose political disadvantages make them unlikely presidential candidates. Quentin N. Burdick, Jennings Randolph, and John C. Stennis are unlikely to run because they are too old. Burdick, the youngest, will be over 75 by election time. In 1972, Thomas F. Eagleton won the Democratic vice-presidential nomination, but a few days later it was revealed that he had received electro-shock treatment for mental health problems and he was forced to step down. Eagleton's candidacy is therefore improbable. Because Spark M. Matsunaga and Daniel K. Inouye are Asian-Americans their candidacies are also unlikely. Frank R. Lautenberg, Carl Levin, Howard M. Metzenbaum, and Edward Zorinsky, four Jewish Democratic senators in the 98th Congress, probably will not run as well. We also can consider the candidacies of Lloyd Bentsen, Robert C. Byrd, and Henry M. Jackson quite unlikely. They ran for the Democratic presidential nomination one or more times and were easily defeated.[2] Thus 13 Democrats can be considered burdened by factors that make their presidential candidacies improbable. Senators with these "liabilities" are listed under the "Other Factors" column in Table 13-1.

Of the remaining 33 Democratic senators, 12 are up for re-election in 1984. If they remain in the nomination contest, they will face the

Table 13-1 Democratic Senators in the 98th Congress

Name	State	First Termer	Up for Re-election	Other Factors	Total Political Disadvantages	Proven Risk Taker
Baucus, Max	Mont.	x			2	No
Bentsen, Lloyd	Texas		x	x[1]	1	Yes
Biden, Joseph R., Jr.	Del.		x		1	Yes
Bingaman, Jeff	N.M.	x			1	Yes
Boren, David L.	Okla.	x	x		2	No
Bradley, Bill	N.J.	x	x		2	Yes
Bumpers, Dale	Ark.				0	Yes
Burdick, Quentin N.	N.D.			x[2]	1	No
Byrd, Robert C.	W.Va.			x[3]	1	Yes
Chiles, Lawton	Fla.				0	No
Cranston, Alan	Calif.				0	Yes
DeConcini, Dennis	Ariz.				1	No
Dixon, Alan J.	Ill.	x			1	No
Dodd, Christopher J.	Conn.	x			1	No
Eagleton, Thomas F.	Mo.			x[4]	1	Yes
Exon, J. James	Neb.	x	x		2	No
Ford, Wendell H.	Ky.				0	Yes
Glenn, John	Ohio				0	Yes
Hart, Gary	Colo.				0	Yes
Heflin, Howell	Ala.	x	x		2	No
Hollings, Ernest F.	S.C.				0	Yes
Huddleston, Walter D.	Ky.		x		1	Yes
Inouye, Daniel K.	Hawaii			x[5]	1	No
Jackson, Henry M.	Wash.			x[6]	1	Yes
Johnston, J. Bennett	La.		x		1	No
Kennedy, Edward M.	Mass.				0	No
Lautenberg, Frank R.	N.J.	x		x[7]	2	No

Name	State					Risk taker
Leahy, Patrick J.	Vt.			0		Yes
Levin, Carl	Mich.		x	3	x[8]	Yes
Long, Russell B.	La.			0		No
Matsunaga, Spark M.	Hawaii			1	x[9]	No
Melcher, John	Mont.					No
Metzenbaum, Howard M.	Ohio			1	x[10]	Yes
Mitchell, George J.	Maine	x[11]		1		No
Moynihan, Daniel Patrick	N.Y.			0		Yes
Nunn, Sam	Ga.		x	1		No
Pell, Claiborne	R.I.		x	1		No
Proxmire, William	Wis.			0		No
Pryor, David	Ark.	x	x	2		Yes
Randolph, Jennings	W.Va.		x	2	x[12]	Yes
Riegle, Donald W., Jr.	Mich.			0		No
Sarbanes, Paul S.	Md.			0		Yes
Sasser, Jim	Tenn.			0		Yes
Stennis, John C.	Miss.			1	x[13]	No
Tsongas, Paul E.	Mass.	x		2		Yes
Zorinsky, Edward	Neb.			1	x[14]	Yes[14]
Total		13	14	17 total zero	13	24 proven risk takers

NOTE: Included here are the 46 Democratic senators in the 98th Congress when it convened Jan. 3, 1983.

[1] Bentsen ran poorly for the Democratic presidential nomination in 1976.

[2] Burdick was born June 19, 1908.

[3] Byrd ran poorly for the Democratic presidential nomination in 1976.

[4] Eagleton was forced to resign as George S. McGovern's vice-presidential running mate in 1972 subsequent to revelations that he received electro-shock therapy.

[5] Inouye is an Asian-American.

[6] Jackson ran poorly for the Democratic presidential nomination in 1972 and 1976.

[7] Lautenberg is Jewish.

[8] Levin is Jewish.

[9] Matsunaga is an Asian-American.

[10] Metzenbaum is Jewish.

[11] Mitchell was appointed in 1980 to fill the seat of Edmund S. Muskie. Although Mitchell won election in 1982, he will have served less than a full six-year term in 1984.

[12] Randolph was born March 8, 1902.

[13] Stennis was born Aug. 3, 1901.

[14] Zorinsky is Jewish. In 1975 he switched from the Republican to the Democratic party, prior to his run for the Democratic nomination for the Senate. He replaced retiring Republican Roman L. Hruska. At the time, the state had been giving Republican senatorial candidates an average vote of 57.05 percent.

unenviable dilemma of choosing between a relatively safe run for their Senate seat or a much riskier race for the presidency. These 12 (along with two of the senators with "liabilities," Levin and Randolph) are listed under the "Up for Re-election" column in the table. Of course, being up for re-election does not rule out a candidacy. Arizona Senator Barry M. Goldwater was up for re-election in 1964 but chose to run for president. He lost the presidency and had to forego defending his Senate seat, reinforcing our argument that seeking the White House can be extremely costly.

Of the remaining 21 Democrats, four will be in their first six years in the Senate in 1984. These four (and nine others with additional disadvantages) are listed under the "First Termer" column. While first termers may hold an office that provides a strong base for running for president, they have not yet had sufficient time to capitalize fully on the advantages of that office. Therefore, first termers generally can be considered improbable presidential candidates.

Thus, of the 46 Democrats in the Senate, 17 are situated more favorably to contend for the presidency than the remainder. As we have seen, particular circumstances have reduced the number of possible presidential candidates by almost two-thirds.

Potential Candidates. Although 17 senators are in a better position to run than the rest, only a few will enter the fray. Probable candidates are likely to be proven risk takers. Of course, all elected officials face a risky situation every time they run for office. The presidency, however, is by far the most competitive office, both for nomination and for election. Since senators already hold a powerful office, it is not surprising that few are willing to jeopardize their position by trying for the presidency. But a presidential bid is risky even for those who are not up for re-election. Influential officeholders suffer political embarrassment when they perform poorly.

We can look at the past electoral behavior of the Democratic senators in the 98th Congress to get an indication of those who are risk takers. Table 13-1 describes as risk takers those who challenged an incumbent the first time they ran for a Senate seat or who ran for re-election in a relatively "safe" Republican state, defined here as a state that gave Republicans an average of at least 57 percent of the vote in the last four Senate elections. Democratic senators who did not seek office facing such obstacles may or may not be risk takers, but those who did run under such adverse conditions clearly have demonstrated risk-taking tendencies.[3]

Thus, of the 46 Democrats in the Senate, 24 are risk takers. Fourteen of the 24 have one or more political liabilities. This leaves 10 who are optimally situated to run for their party's presidential nomination. These are senators who are not disadvantaged by circumstances (age, re-election status, etc.) and who have demonstrated a willingness to take risks. They are Dale Bumpers, Alan Cranston, Wendell H. Ford, John Glenn, Gary Hart, Ernest F. Hollings, Patrick J. Leahy, Daniel Patrick Moynihan, Paul S. Sarbanes, and Jim Sasser. Of course, not all of these men will run for president, but five of them—Bumpers, Cranston, Glenn, Hart, and Hollings—addressed the California state convention in January 1983, which gave some indication that they might be potential "hopefuls." Mondale and Representative Morris K. Udall (D-Ariz.) also spoke.

In early 1983, six of the seven who addressed the convention remained probable candidates. The exception, Udall, announced on February 9, 1983, that he would not run. In the 1976 Democratic presidential nomination contest, Udall had the distinction of being the only one to survive the full campaign in the primaries against Carter. When Kennedy withdrew from the race on December 1, 1982, Udall, a particular favorite among liberals, emerged as a possible candidate. But he faced three problems. Udall finished second seven times in 1976 but failed to win a single primary. He was up for re-election to the House in 1984. And he did not start his presidential bid soon enough. For good or ill, late 1982 was too late to begin a serious campaign, especially against a number of strong and already well-organized contenders.

After Kennedy withdrew, Mondale became the "frontrunner" according to most analysts. Glenn, who had been viewed as the most likely "dark horse," then became perceived as Mondale's strongest competitor. Kennedy's withdrawal, by removing a strong candidacy, opened up the competition. The chances of such "long shots" as Cranston and Hart improved. Bumpers also began to consider a candidacy more seriously.

In early 1983, the course of the quickly unfolding nomination campaign could not be predicted. Prior campaigns demonstrate that presumed frontrunners may fail and lesser known hopefuls may succeed. Nevertheless, we can anticipate the general shape the contest for the nomination will take. Only a very few candidates will do well enough in the early primaries and caucuses to obtain the resources, popularity, and media attention needed to remain viable. The crowded field will narrow to two or three serious competitors. It is likely that the nominee will emerge from this small set of "survivors." The candidate who beats the other "survivors" in the primary season probably will be nominated.

In sum, there is little reason to believe that the Hunt Commission reforms will change the general direction of the Democratic presidential nomination campaign of 1984. More likely than not, the primary campaign will prove to be the decisive phase once again.

Republican Candidates

If President Reagan chooses to run for renomination, few, if any, Republicans are likely to stand in his way. Traditionally, an incumbent president's party fields few candidates. If a challenge to the incumbent is mounted, the challenger is likely to be an unusually strong candidate—one able to imagine unseating his party's president. In 1976, Reagan campaigned against President Ford for the Republican presidential nomination, and four years later Ted Kennedy took on President Carter in a race to become the Democratic nominee. Both challenges were unsuccessful. Since even strong candidates are unlikely to wrest the party nomination away from an incumbent president, politicians with lesser credentials are unlikely to try.

President Reagan is likely to see little competition in 1984 for two reasons. First, he has strong support within the Republican party. Admittedly, by January 1983 Reagan had slipped seriously in the polls. Head-to-head preference polls showed that both Mondale and Glenn led Reagan, whereas in early 1979 Jimmy Carter led his potential Republican opponents. Moreover, Reagan's presidential approval ratings were lower at midterm than were ratings for Dwight D. Eisenhower, John F. Kennedy, Richard M. Nixon, or Jimmy Carter at similar points in their presidencies. Nevertheless, Reagan's approval among Republicans was still favorable in early 1983. A Gallup Poll conducted in mid-January 1983 showed that 68 percent of the Republicans approved of Reagan's performance as president. Because the nomination contest is fought mainly for the support of Republicans, Reagan's overall weakness in the polls does not necessarily affect his chances for renomination.

In many respects, previous postwar presidents who faced serious challenges from within their own party were more vulnerable than Reagan. By the summer of 1979, only 34 percent of the Democrats endorsed Carter's presidency, which, as Everett Carll Ladd points out, "was the lowest proportion endorsing a president of their own party since Gallup began using this measure during the second term of Franklin Roosevelt."[4] In 1976, Ford had the unique status of never having been elected president or vice-president. In 1968, incumbent President Lyndon B. Johnson was challenged by Eugene J. McCarthy, a Democratic senator from Minnesota. McCarthy's surprisingly close finish in the New Hampshire primary may have swayed Johnson's decision not to seek re-election. But despite Johnson's weaknesses, he was able to see his vice-president, Hubert H. Humphrey, win the hotly contested nomination. For all the heat, the outcome was not very close. Even though Johnson, Ford, and Carter were vulnerable in one respect or another, each was able to see himself or his chosen successor nominated.

The second reason Reagan is unlikely to be challenged is that in early 1983 there were no Republicans with the credentials needed to mount a strong fight against him. Serious challenges to incumbent presidents usually have been launched by candidates with particularly impressive credentials of their own, credentials that would make them likely nominees if there were no incumbent in their own party. McCarthy was an exception, but he was able to challenge Johnson on an extremely salient issue—the Vietnam War. But in early 1983 there was no Republican with the credentials of Reagan in 1976 or Kennedy in 1980.

It is possible, of course, that Reagan may choose to retire at the end of his first term or that George Bush may assume office through the resignation or death of the president. If Reagan were not a candidate in 1984, for whatever reason, the Republican nomination probably would become a wide open affair, attracting the usual array of contenders. The general principles we discussed in our analysis of Table 13-1 could then be used to specify which Republicans were the most likely to throw their hats into the ring. If Vice President Bush were to assume the presidency in 1983 or 1984, he would have the opportunity to capitalize on the great political resources of incumbency. But his incumbency advantage would be less than Ford's was in 1976, because Ford, after all, had been the incumbent president for nearly two years by the time he was nominated.

In sum, if Reagan chooses to seek renomination in 1984 he is likely to be unopposed. If opposed, he will be challenged by few contenders. Given the advantages of an incumbent president, he is unlikely to be defeated if he is challenged. The Republican party simply does not have a strong alternative to Reagan waiting in the wings. While incumbent presidents have lost the last two general election contests, it is difficult to imagine a Republican defeating Reagan and then winning in November.

Conclusion

Barring dramatic and unexpected developments, the 1984 presidential campaign probably will follow historical lines and be a contest between the two major-party nominees. Although a third-party candidate may emerge, such as John B. Anderson in 1980, there is little reason to believe that such a candidate will be more successful in 1984 than in 1980. A centrist candidate like Anderson will have the greatest chance if the Democrats nominate someone clearly left-of-center, allowing that candidate to capture the middle ground. But the chances of the Democrats choosing a candidate clearly identified with the left were reduced when Kennedy bowed out of the race.

The outcome of the contest will largely depend upon the state of the economy. Reagan's 1980 victory was basically a rejection of Carter—especially his economic performance—and Reagan will be judged by similar criteria. If Reagan seeks re-election, the contest will be an essentially retrospective election in which votes are heavily influenced by perceptions of his handling of economic problems. If Bush is the Republican nominee, it will be difficult for him to avoid blame for Reagan's shortcomings, although it is less clear that a sitting vice-president can gain credit for his president's successes. If the Republicans choose a candidate not identified with the Reagan administration, he may be held somewhat less accountable for the president's failures, while gaining even less credit for his accomplishments. In such a case, prospective evaluations may become more important. Of course, the importance of issues also will depend upon the extent to which the Democratic nominee offers clear policy alternatives.

The Republicans' chances will be better with Reagan as the standard-bearer rather than with a nonincumbent. Admittedly, two incumbent presidents, Ford and Carter, have lost in successive elections—a pattern found only once before in American history. (Presidents Grover Cleveland and Benjamin Harrison lost in 1888 and 1892, respectively.) Defeat of the incumbent president, however, is the exception. Following Andrew Jackson's election in 1828, the incumbent party has nominated its incumbent president 21 times; it won 14 of these elections. During this period the party holding the White House did not run the incumbent president in 17 elections; it won only seven of these contests. The last time the party holding the White House has won without running its incumbent president was in 1928. All three subsequent attempts to win with nonincumbents (1952, 1960, and 1968) ended in defeat.[5]

Of course, a Republican other than Reagan (or an incumbent Bush) could win. If the economy improves markedly by election time, a Republican candidate could argue that Republican policies should be continued under the leadership of another Republican president. A candidate clearly associated with supply-side policies, such as Representative Jack F. Kemp of New York, might best be able to capitalize upon economic improvement. But if unemployment remains high, the GOP may be better off with a candidate not directly associated with the Reagan administration and supply-side economics.

WANING REPUBLICAN PROSPECTS?

The 1982 elections cast the results of the 1980 elections in an altered light. Part IV presented four main possibilities for the future of American politics as of early 1982: a pro-Republican realignment that established the Republicans as the majority party, a restoration of the Democratic party to a dominant position, the emergence of new political parties that offered alternatives to the current party system, and continued electoral volatility in support for the two major parties.

In early 1983, the last of these alternatives continued to be the most likely. And we still see little reason to believe that a third party would be successful. However, the events of 1982 have led us to reassess the likelihood of the first two possibilities. A pro-Republican realignment seems less likely than it did a year ago; the prospects for a resurgent Democratic party seem somewhat more likely.

There are six basic reasons why the prospects for a pro-Republican realignment have declined. First, America's economic problems continue. Second, since mid-1981, fewer voters have identified with the Republican party. Third, the 1982 House races did not signal a pro-Republican realignment. Fourth, the Democrats appear to have made gains among some of the traditional groups of the New Deal coalition. Fifth, increased turnout by blacks and Hispanics has jeopardized Republican prospects. Lastly, the growing "gender gap" could harm the Republicans.

Continuing Economic Difficulties

The nation's economic woes are the greatest obstacle to a pro-Republican realignment, and they may contribute to the five remaining problems. Figure 13-1 shows the annual average rates of inflation and unemployment from 1974 through 1982. Inflation dropped markedly during Reagan's first term, and in 1982 the Consumer Price Index increased at an annual rate of only 3.9 percent. Unfortunately for the Republicans, unemployment by the end of 1982 reached 10.8 percent, with 12 million Americans out of work and seeking employment. For all of 1982, unemployment averaged 9.7 percent, the highest level since 1941.

While the "misery index" (the sum of the inflation rate and the unemployment rate) was down in early 1983, concern about unemployment was up. More people considered unemployment the most important national problem. At the mid-point of Reagan's first term, the nation was in the midst of a 17-month recession. Although some indicators pointed toward recovery, and although unemployment dipped slightly in early 1983, the Reagan administration's own forecasts predicted high levels of unemployment through 1983.

Reagan claimed credit for reduced inflation and substantially lower interest rates, but most economists believed these outcomes resulted primarily from the recession—not from Reagan's economic policies. Moreover, Reagan's campaign goal of simultaneously lowering taxes, increasing defense spending, and balancing the budget seemed unattainable. Perhaps those goals could have been attained if his policies had stimulated economic growth, thus increasing federal rev-

Figure 13-1 Annual Rates of Inflation and Unemployment, 1974-1982

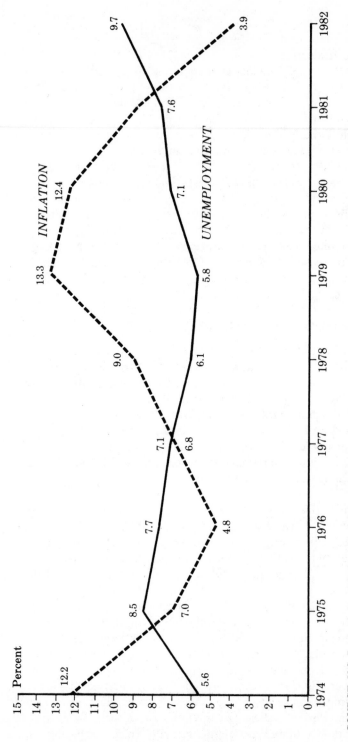

SOURCE: U.S. Department of Labor, Bureau of Labor Statistics, *Handbook of Labor Statistics* (Washington, D.C.: U.S. Government Printing Office, 1980), p. 62; Council of Economic Advisors, *Economic Indicators* (Washington, D.C.: U.S. Government Printing Office, December 1982), pp. 12, 24, 1982 averages are from figures released by the Bureau of Labor Statistics in January 1983.

enues despite lower tax rates. But in an economic downturn, these policies produced unprecedented deficits in the federal budget. By May of 1982, the projected deficit for fiscal year 1983 reached $105 billion. Since deeper cuts in domestic spending could not substantially reduce such a deficit, Reagan reluctantly supported a series of tax increases. In August 1982, Congress, with the active support of the Democratic leadership, approved tax changes designed to increase federal revenues by $98 billion over the next three years. Despite this policy reversal, the tax increase was viewed as a major legislative victory for Reagan.

After cooperating with Reagan to increase taxes, congressional Democrats opposed additional cuts in domestic spending. When Reagan vetoed a $14 billion supplemental appropriation in September 1982, claiming it was a "budget buster" with too much spending for domestic programs, both the Democratic-controlled House and the Republican-controlled Senate mustered the two-thirds vote necessary to override a presidential veto. The congressional override of September 10, 1982, was Reagan's first major congressional defeat and marked the end of a remarkable string of legislative successes. Within a month, the House defeated a balanced budget amendment.

During the "lame duck" session following the November 1982 elections, the 97th Congress continued to balk at Reagan's proposals. Congress refused to appropriate money for the production of the MX missile, and it refused to even reconsider the balanced budget amendment. By the time Reagan proposed his 1984 fiscal year budget in late January 1983, the projected deficit for fiscal year 1983 had reached $208 billion. His proposed deficit for fiscal year 1984 was $189 billion, spelling further trouble for the Reagan White House.

In its first weeks the 98th Congress was even less willing than its predecessor to go along with the Reagan administration on additional domestic cuts or defense increases. Moreover, the president's proposals to give the states more responsibility for domestic programs faced strong opposition. The Democrats' gain of seven governorships and strengthened position in many state legislatures made it more difficult for Reagan to implement his New Federalism policies.

Fortunately for Reagan, most of his economic recovery program was in place before the November 1982 elections. If Reagan vetoes any delay or curtailment of the scheduled income tax cuts, they will go into effect unless Congress can muster the votes necessary to override a veto. Since Reagan cannot force Congress to appropriate money for the projects he favors, Congress has considerable bargaining power. Still it seems likely that the Reagan reforms already in place before the off-year elections will stay in place. New initiatives could prove difficult to implement.

While Reagan may be unable to introduce new reforms, his administration is still likely to get most of the credit if the economy improves, and most of the blame if it founders. Reagan's mandate, if he had one, was to improve the faltering economy, not to introduce specific economic policies. As Douglas A. Hibbs, Jr., has written, "If the Reagan program does eventually generate higher growth, lower unemployment, and lower inflation, or is at least correlated in time with a sharp improvement in America's macroeconomic performance, the president probably will succeed in crystallizing a popular base for 'Reaganomics' that might well last a generation or more." [6] But, Hibbs concludes, "if the economy does not register dramatic improvement over the next two years, Reaganism and Reaganomics will no doubt be interpreted, in hindsight, not as a reflection of a fundamental 'shift to the right' but as a one-term political aberration." [7] In February 1983 prospects for "dramatic improvement" were bleak.

Changing Party Identifications

Perhaps the strongest sign of waning Republican prospects comes from public opinion polls that monitor feelings of party identification. Many political scientists argue that partisan realignments occur not only when voting patterns shift, but when the partisan affiliations of the electorate change. Thus the poll evidence summarized in Chapter 11 was heartening to the Republicans because it suggested that they had made sizable inroads in reducing the Democratic lead in party identification. These Republican gains, however, appear to have been short-lived. Public opinon polls in mid-1982 showed a major Democratic rebound, almost totally erasing earlier Republican gains.[8]

We can compare 1982 poll results with the 1980 and 1981 polls reviewed on pages 232 and 233. Richard B. Wirthlin's data was the most encouraging for the Republicans. According to his polls before the 1980 election, 51 percent of the electorate was Democratic, 35 percent was Republican (with Independent leaners classified as partisans). By May 1981, this 16-point Democratic advantage had declined to a single point. In his post-1982 election polls, however, Wirthlin found that the Democrats had widened their lead to 17 points.[9] CBS News/*New York Times* polls conducted in April 1982 showed that 52 percent of the electorate was Democratic, while 36 percent was Republican (with Independent leaners classified as partisans).[10] In CBS News/*New York Times* polls conducted in June 1982, 40 percent were Democrats, while 29 percent were Republicans (with Independent leaners classified as Independents).[11] And Gallup Polls conducted in June 1982 showed that 48 percent identified with the Democrats and only 26 percent with the Republicans.[12]

These pro-Democratic shifts do not mean that the Democrats will win in 1984; after all, Reagan won in 1980 despite a substantial Democratic lead in partisan loyalties. But these shifts make a pro-

Republican realignment appear less likely than it did after the 1980 elections.

Republican House Losses

The results of the 1982 elections are ambiguous. They do not clearly point to a resurgence of the Democratic party or a decline in the Republican party's fortunes. As we saw in Chapter 12, the question "Who won?" can be answered in several ways, depending upon the yardstick used for comparison. But the election results clearly provided no evidence to suggest that a pro-Republican realignment is under way; the Republicans lost 26 seats in the House. House gains, on the other hand, would have signalled a significant shift in the electorate. Consider the historic evidence.

The party holding the White House has lost House seats in all postwar midterm elections, as Table 12-4 on page 252 indicates. In fact, the party holding the White House has lost House seats in 30 of the 32 midterm elections between 1858 and 1982,[13] and one of the two exceptions, 1902, resulted from an increase in the total number of representatives after the 1900 census. The only true exception was 1934, during Franklin D. Roosevelt's first term. The Democrats gained nine House seats in that election. In retrospect, the 1934 gain can be seen as a clue that a pro-Democratic realignment was under way. No other partisan realignment, however, has been accompanied by a similar midterm clue.

Shifts by Social Groups

Preliminary analyses of the 1982 election results suggest that Democratic gains partly resulted from increased Democratic voting among groups that traditionally have supported the Democrats. CBS News/*New York Times* exit polls strongly indicate that income differences in voting behavior sharpened. Between 1978 and 1982, lower income voters appear to have become more Democratic, while upper income voters actually voted more Republican.[14] Likewise, exit polls conducted by NBC and ABC showed sharp income differentials.

"The significant gains made by the Democrats in the House reflect the intense disillusionment of traditional Democratic voter groups with Reaganomics," wrote Andrew Kohut, president of the Gallup organization.[15] Gallup data reveal that blacks, manual workers, low-income families, and trade union members have been "coalescing in opposition to the administration." According to Kohut, "The Democratic party owes its strong showing in the House and gubernatorial races to the solid support and turnout of old-line Democrats." [16]

As we discussed on pages 212 and 213, the SRC-CPS data for 1980 revealed that, apart from race, social forces were only weakly related to the way people voted for Congress. We expect the 1982 SRC-CPS surveys to reveal stronger relationships between social forces and the vote.

Increased Turnout

Increased turnout may also jeopardize Republican prospects for becoming the major party—especially if turnout increases most among traditionally Democratic social groups. Like turnout in presidential elections, turnout in off-year elections has declined. Although turnout was low in 1946 (only 37.1 percent of the voting-age population voted for Congress), it grew to 41.1 percent in 1950, 41.7 percent in 1954, 43.0 percent in 1958, and 45.4 percent in 1962 and 1966.[17] In the next three off-year elections, however, turnout fell, dropping to 43.5 percent in 1970, 36.2 percent in 1974, and 35.5 percent in 1978—a 10-point drop in only 12 years. Preliminary estimates suggest that turnout rose in 1982 by about 3 percentage points.[18]

While the overall increase in turnout was moderate, "selective but significant increases" were noticeable.[19] Many commentators point to the importance of increased turnout among black voters. According to Congressional Quarterly reporter Rhodes Cook, heavy black turnout in Alabama aided George C. Wallace in his bid to gain a fourth term as governor, since Wallace was more liberal than his Republican opponent, Montgomery Mayor Emory Folmar. Cook also cites black turnout as a factor helping Ben Erdreich defeat incumbent Republican Albert Lee Smith, Jr., in the Alabama 6th congressional district and Norman Sisisky defeat incumbent Republican Robert W. Daniel, Jr., in the Virginia 4th.[20]

Curtis B. Gans, director of the Committee for the Study of the American Electorate, points to black support for Democrat Bill Clinton who defeated incumbent Republican Governor Frank D. White in Arkansas.[21] The Joint Center for Political Studies, a research institute that studies black politics, claims that increased black turnout helped Democrat Charles Robin Britt defeat Republican incumbent Eugene Johnston in the North Carolina 6th and Robert M. Tallon, Jr., defeat Republican incumbent John L. Napier in the South Carolina 6th.[22] The president of the center, Eddie N. Williams, explains: "There was an almost unprecedented dislike and concern about Reaganomics. . . . And that caused a great deal of ferment in the black community."[23]

Republicans acknowledge that increases in minority turnout aided their opponents. Vince Breglio, director of the National Republican Senatorial Committee, argues that blacks and low-income voters also hurt the Republicans in two Senate races. They helped Frank R. Lautenberg defeat Millicent Fenwick in New Jersey, and heavy Hispanic voting helped Jeff Bingaman unseat incumbent Harrison "Jack" Schmitt in New Mexico.[24] According to Democratic pollster Peter Hart, Democratic Senator Lloyd Bentsen's get-out-the-vote drive in Texas aimed especially at urban blacks and Hispanics aided Mark White, the Democratic candidate for governor, in his upset win over incumbent Republican William Clements.[25]

Some of these claims about the impact of increased minority turnout may not bear close scrutiny. The Democratic margins of victory were fairly large in some of these elections; differential increases in turnout do not completely explain them. And while increased turnout in 1982 aided the Democrats in some contests, it may only be a short-term reaction to high unemployment. In future elections, increased turnout will not necesssarily help the Democrats. Turnout is so low in the United States that it is fairly low even among advantaged Americans. Even so, a pro-Republican realignment will always be a precarious proposition if it depends upon low turnout by minorities and low-income voters.

The "Gender Gap"

While gender differences in voting behavior have been pronounced in some European countries, they have been relatively negligible in American politics. Survey research in this country demonstrates that gender has been only weakly and inconsistently related to voting behavior or party identification.[26]

In House contests in 1980 women were slightly more likely to vote Republican. Moreover, gender differences were only weakly related to partisan loyalties. Neither the fall 1980 pre-election surveys by the SRC-CPS nor the postelection surveys conducted in November and December revealed meaningful differences in party identification.

In 1980, however, surveys indicated that women were less likely to vote for Reagan than men were. (See Table 5-1 on pages 98 and 99 for our analysis of SRC-CPS data for 1980.) Moreover, men's and women's attitudes about Reagan during his first term were not the same. Gallup presidential approval polls conducted in July 1982 revealed that women were 12 percentage points less likely than men to approve of his performance, whereas evaluations of Eisenhower, Kennedy, Nixon, and Carter at similar points in their presidencies revealed negligible gender differences.[27] The negative attitudes of women toward Reagan may contribute to gender differences in party identification. CBS News/*New York Times* polls show that in 1980 women were only three points more likely than men to identify with the Democratic party; in early 1982 this difference widened to eight percentage points.[28] Moreover, gender differences were greatest among young adults.[29]

In November 1982, gender differences in voting behavior were discovered by numerous exit polls. In 73 of the 85 state-wide exit polls conducted in 1982 by the three television networks, women were more likely to have voted Democratic than men.[30] The CBS News/*New York Times* polls show that the heaviest Democratic voting was among unmarried women. In House races, 64 percent voted Democratic, while only 33 percent voted Republican.[31]

What causes this "gender gap" in voting behavior? Some argue that it results from Reagan's opposition to such "women's issues" as the Equal Rights Amendment or abortion, although little evidence appears to support this conclusion. Kathleen A. Frankovic attributes the gender gap to women's greater fear of nuclear war, opposition to aggressive American foreign policy, and concern for protection of the environment.[32] A White House study by Ronald H. Hinckley emphasizes economic factors: "Fear of losing government benefits appears to be causing women to oppose the administration." [33] And Ann Hulbert claims that the impact of foreign policy matters on the gender gap has diminished. The gap, she argues, mainly reflects the self-interest of women who have been hurt by Reagan's economic policies.[34]

The gender gap hurts the Republicans, it is usually assumed. For example, the Hinckley White House report concludes:

> It is clear that the gender gap as measured in terms of public opinion differences during 1981 and 1982 is being translated into electoral differences. Continued growth of the gender gap in its current form could cause serious trouble for the Republicans in 1984. [35]

But a gap can be caused in several ways. The CBS News/*New York Times* data show that between 1980 and early 1982 women actually became one percentage point less Democratic; this gap developed because men had become six points less Democratic. The bulk of the change resulted from a seven percentage point increase in the number of Independent identifiers among men.[36] A gap in voting behavior may have no effect on electoral outcomes, or it may prove decisive. The gender gap cannot affect the outcome where either the Democratic or Republican candidate receives a plurality of both the male and female vote. The gap can affect the outcome where the Democrat receives a plurality of the female vote, while the Republican receives a plurality of the male vote. In cases where the Democrat wins, the gender gap may be said to have hurt the Republicans. But if the Republican wins, the gender gap has hurt the Democrats.

Adam Clymer argues that the gender gap appears to have provided the margin of victory for the Democrats in two gubernatorial races: Mario M. Cuomo's defeat of Lew Lehrman in New York and White's defeat of Clements in Texas.[37] The gap may have provided the Democrats with the margin of victory in two other gubernatorial contests: Michigan (where James J. Blanchard defeated Richard H. Headlee) and Connecticut (where incumbent Democrat William A. O'Neill defeated Lewis B. Rome). Clymer, however, also believes the gap helped the Republicans in the California gubernatorial race (where George Deukmejian defeated Tom Bradley by a single percentage point) and in two Senate races: Connecticut (where incumbent Lowell P. Weicker, Jr., defeated Toby Moffett) and Virginia (where Paul S. Trible, Jr., defeated Richard J. Davis).[38] The White House report, while concerned with the tendency of women to favor the Democrats, claims that the only state-wide loss suffered by the Republicans due to the gap was Lehrman's defeat by Cuomo.[39]

Although the gender gap caused few Republican losses and resulted more from the movement of men away from the Democrats than from women toward them, it represents a lost opportunity for the Republicans. They would be stronger today if men manifested their present level of Republicanism and if women, as in times past, voted as men did. In the long run it is difficult to see how a pro-Republican realignment can be built without substantial support from women voters.

Conclusion

All six factors (with the possible exception of the gender gap) signal problems for the Republicans. Given continued competition between the Republican and Democratic parties, these factors make a resurgent Democratic party somewhat more likely than in early 1982. The prospects for the Democrats have improved, but many obstacles still may prevent them from becoming the dominant party as they were between 1932 and 1964. To again become dominant the Democrats will need to regain the presidency and hold it for a series of elections, as well as to regain control of the Senate. The shift to the Democrats of blacks, low-income voters, the working class, and union members in the November 1982 midterm elections does not mean that the traditional New Deal coalition has been restored. It remains to be seen whether this coalition can be brought together—and held together—over a series of presidential elections. Another unknown is whether the Democrats will be able to implement successful policies if they do regain the White House in 1984.

Although united in their opposition to Reagan, the Democrats have seldom offered clear alternatives to the administration's policies. Despite the Philadelphia convention in the summer of 1982 on Goals and Principles, and despite specific proposals by the House Democratic caucus, no set of policy alternatives became the center for debate during the 1982 campaign. But is it reasonable to expect clear choices

292   1982 Election Update

from 435 separate House contests, 33 separate Senate elections, and 36 gubernatorial contests? Many would agree with Leon Billings, director of the Democratic Senatorial Campaign Committee:

> No party out of power can come up with a unified set of alternatives, and especially not in a congressional campaign where dozens of candidates are running in different places. A unified set of positions must await the presidential campaign.[40]

The Democrats did advance some specific policy alternatives in their nationally televised response to Reagan's State of the Union message on January 25, 1983. But it will be difficult for them to sustain a set of coherent proposals as a focus of debate. As the pace of the presidential nominating campaign quickens, media attention will focus more on Democratic presidential contenders, and they are likely to advance proposals that distinguish them from other Democrats.

During 1982 the prospects for a pro-Republican realignment diminished, while the prospects for a Democratic return to dominance increased. But both parties must confront a volatile electorate with weak party loyalties. Thus the 1984 presidential election easily could be won by either of the major parties.

If the Democrats win, the incumbent party will have lost the White House for three elections in a row. As Table 3-2 on page 58 indicates, similar stretches of incumbent party losses (1840-1844-1848-1852; 1884-1888-1892-1896) have been followed by a realignment favoring a single party. Ultimately, America may again have a clear majority party. But the nation's current economic difficulties probably cannot be solved in a single presidential term. For the remainder of this century electoral volatility is likely to continue.

NOTES

1. Austin Ranney, *Curing the Mischiefs of Faction: Party Reform in America* (Berkeley, Calif.: University of California Press, 1975), pp. 180-187.
2. Kennedy was, of course, a defeated candidate for the 1980 presidential nomination. He was not defeated as soundly as Bentsen, Byrd, or Jackson. In fact, his loss was one of the closer ones in recent decades. Moreover, his convention speech was considered to have "revived" his future potential. That even a close loss requires one to "revive" one's credentials indicates that a losing bid is, indeed, a liability under most circumstances.
3. David W. Rohde, "Risk-Bearing and Progressive Ambition: The Case of Members of the United States House of Representatives," *American Journal of Political Science* 23 (February 1979): 1-26. A similar formulation was used in studying the U.S. Senate as source of Democratic candidates for the 1976 presidential nomination. See John H. Aldrich, *Before the Convention: Strategies and Choices in Presidential Nomination Campaigns* (Chicago: University of Chicago Press, 1980).
4. Everett Carll Ladd, "The Brittle Mandate: Electoral Dealignment and the 1980 Presidential Election," *Political Science Quarterly* 96 (Spring 1981): 6.

5. Dwight D. Eisenhower, the incumbent president in 1960, was barred from seeking re-election by the 22nd Amendment. He was the only incumbent at election time who was constitutionally ineligible to run.
6. Douglas A. Hibbs, Jr., "President Reagan's Mandate from the 1980 Elections: A Shift to the Right?" *American Politics Quarterly* 10 (October 1982): 408.
7. Ibid., p. 413.
8. For a compilation of mid-1982 results from eight polling organizations, see "Opinion Roundup," *Public Opinion* 5 (August/September 1982): 29.
9. Hedrick Smith, "Aides Trying to Nudge Reagan Toward '84 Bid," *New York Times,* December 4, 1982, p. 8. All *New York Times* citations in this chapter are from the Midwest edition.
10. "Democratic Rebound," *New York Times,* April 25, 1982, p. E4.
11. "Opinion Roundup," *Public Opinion* 5 (August/September 1982): 29.
12. Ibid. Gallup surveys do not distinguish between Independents who lean toward a party and those who do not.
13. Except for 1982, all midterm results reported in this paragraph are from "Election Results, Congress and the Presidency, 1854-1980," *Congressional Quarterly Weekly Report,* October r3, 1982, p. 2742.
14. "Opinion Roundup," *Public Opinion* 5 (December/January 1983): 28-29.
15. Andrew Kohut, "Ambivalent Election Results Mirror Equivocal Opinion at Reagan Program," *Poll Watch,* November 10, 1982, p. 1.
16. Ibid.
17. All estimates of turnout between 1946 and 1978 are based upon U.S. Department of Commerce, Department of the Census, *Statistical Abstract of the United States, 1981* (Washington, D.C.: U.S. Government Printing Office, 1981), Table 824, p. 496. This source accords perfectly with our own estimate of 1980 presidential turnout, although the 1980 result is still considered preliminary.
18. For purposes of historical comparison, midterm turnout is based upon the number of voters for House contests. Since there are always some uncontested House seats, and since some voters do not vote in House races, the actual percentage voting is always somewhat higher than the official turnout estimate. Other turnout estimates differ somewhat from those reported by the Census Bureau. Curtis B. Gans, director of the Committee for the Study of the American Electorate, estimates that turnout was 37.9 percent in 1978 and 40.3 percent in 1982. When all votes are counted, according to Gans, 1982 turnout might rise to 41 percent. See Hedrick Smith, "Big Voter Turnout Laid to 3 Factors," *New York Times,* November 10, 1982, pp. 1, 10. According to Congressional Quarterly estimates, turnout was 34.5 percent in 1978 and 37.7 percent in 1982 after absentee and third-party ballots were counted. (Before counting these ballots, Congressional Quarterly had estimated the 1982 turnout to be 35.7 percent.) See Rhodes Cook, "The 1982 Turnout Question: Voters Angry or Depressed?" *Congressional Quarterly Weekly Report,* October 30, 1982, pp. 2748-2749; Cook, "Rise in Voter Participation: Democrats Reap the Benefits," *Congressional Quarterly Weekly Report,* November 13, 1982, pp. 2850-2851; and *Congressional Quarterly Weekly Report,* "Final, Official Election Returns for 1982," February 19, 1983, pp. 386-394.
19. Jack Germond and Jules Witcover, "White House Got Poor Voter Data," *Lansing State Journal,* November 10, 1982, p. A4.
20. Cook, "Rise in Voter Participation."
21. Smith, "Big Voter Turnout."

22. Kenneth B. Noble, "This Time Out, Black Voters Got Their Message Across," *New York Times,* November 14, 1982, p. E6.
23. Ibid.
24. Smith, "Big Voter Turnout."
25. Ibid.
26. For data on both voting behavior and party identification, see Warren E. Miller, Arthur H. Miller, and Edward J. Schneider, *American National Election Studies Data Sourcebook, 1952-1978* (Cambridge, Mass.: Harvard University Press, 1980). See also "Vote by Groups in Presidential Elections Since 1952," *Gallup Opinion Index,* Report No. 183 (December 1980): 6-7.
27. George Gallup, "Reagan Popularity Unchanged Despite Recent Events," *The Gallup Poll,* July 8, 1982, p. 2.
28. Kathleen A. Frankovic, "Sex and Politics—New Alignments, Old Issues," *PS* 15 (Summer 1982): 439-448. The full results are as follows. The combined results of polls conducted throughout 1980 show that 23 percent of the men were Republicans, 38 percent Independents, and 39 percent were Democrats; among women, 22 percent were Republicans, 36 percent Independents, and 42 percent were Democrats. In the combined results of polls conducted in January, March, and May 1982, 22 percent of the men were Republicans, 45 percent were Independents, and 33 percent were Democrats; among women, 23 percent were Republicans, 36 percent Independents, and 41 percent were Democrats. Independent leaners are classified as partisans in all of these results.
29. Among men between the ages of 18 and 24, 31 percent were Republicans, 45 percent Independents, and 24 percent were Democrats; among young women, 21 percent were Republicans, 46 percent Independents, and 33 percent were Democrats.
30. Adam Clymer, "G.O.P. Is Disturbed by Women's Role in Election," *New York Times,* November 18, 1982, p. 16.
31. Ibid.
32. Frankovic, "Sex and Politics."
33. Adam Clymer, "Warning on 'Gender Gap' From the White House," *New York Times,* December 3, 1982, p. 12.
34. Ann Hulbert, "What Gender Gap?" *New York Times,* December 10, 1982, p. 31.
35. Clymer, "Warning on 'Genger Gap.'"
36. Frankovic, "Sex and Politics." See note 28 for the full distribution of partisanship among men and women.
37. Clymer, "G.O.P. Is Disturbed."
38. Ibid.
39. Hulbert, "What Gender Gap?"
40. Saul Friedman, "Democrats Consider Anti-Reagan Ideas But Agree on Few," *Detroit Free Press,* October 28, 1982, p. B7.

Suggested Readings

(Starred readings include discussions of the 1980 elections.)

Chapter 1: The Nomination Struggle

Aldrich, John H. *Before the Convention: Strategies and Choices in Presidential Nomination Campaigns.* Chicago: University of Chicago Press, 1980.

Brams, Steven J. *The Presidential Election Game.* New Haven, Conn.: Yale University Press, 1978, pp. 1-79.

Ceaser, James W. *Presidential Selection: Theory and Development.* Princeton, N.J.: Princeton University Press, 1979.

Davis, James W. *Presidential Primaries: Road to the White House.* New York: Thomas Y. Crowell Co., 1967.

*Drew, Elizabeth. *Portrait of an Election: The 1980 Presidential Campaign.* New York: Simon & Schuster, 1981, pp. 11-260.

*Harwood, Richard, ed. *The Pursuit of the Presidency 1980.* New York: Berkley Books, 1980, pp. 65-203.

*Jones, Charles O. "Nominating 'Carter's Favorite Opponent': The Republicans in 1980." In *The American Elections of 1980,* edited by Austin Ranney, pp. 61-98. Washington, D.C.: American Enterprise Institute for Public Policy Research, 1981.

Keech, William R., and Matthews, Donald R. *The Party's Choice.* Washington, D.C.: The Brookings Institution, 1976.

*Moore, Jonathan, ed. *The Campaign for President: 1980 in Retrospect.* Cambridge, Mass.: Ballinger Publishing Co., 1981, pp. 1-182, 278-288.

*Polsby, Nelson W. "The Democratic Nomination." In *The American Elections of 1980,* edited by Austin Ranney, pp. 37-60. Washington, D.C.: American Enterprise Institute for Public Policy Research, 1981.

——, and Wildavsky, Aaron. *Presidential Elections: Strategies of American Electoral Politics.* 5th ed. New York: Charles Scribner's Sons, 1980, pp. 79-155.

*Pomper, Gerald M. "The Nominating Contests." In *The Election of 1980: Reports and Interpretations,* Gerald M. Pomper with colleagues, pp. 1-37. Chatham, N.J.: Chatham House, 1981.

*Wayne, Stephen J. *The Road to the White House: The Politics of Presidential Elections.* postelection ed. New York: St. Martin's Press, 1981, pp. 81-151, 257-275.

Chapter 2: The Campaign

Asher, Herbert B. *Presidential Elections and American Politics: Voters, Candidates, and Campaigns since 1952.* rev. ed. Homewood, Ill.: Dorsey Press, 1980, pp. 215-344.

Brams, Steven J. *The Presidential Election Game.* New Haven, Conn.: Yale University Press, 1978, pp. 80-133.

*Caddell, Patrick H. "The Democratic Strategy and Its Electoral Consequences." In *Party Coalitions in the 1980s,* edited by Seymour Martin Lipset, pp. 267-303. San Francisco, Calif.: Institute for Contemporary Studies, 1981.

*Drew, Elizabeth. *Portrait of an Election: The 1980 Presidential Campaign.* New York: Simon & Schuster, 1981, pp. 261-347.

*Germond, Jack W., and Witcover, Jules. *Blue Smoke and Mirrors: How Reagan Won and Why Carter Lost the Election of 1980.* New York: Viking Press, 1981.

*Harwood, Richard, ed. *The Pursuit of the Presidency 1980.* New York: Berkley Books, 1980, pp. 275-321.

*Hunt, Albert R. "The Campaign and the Issues." In *The American Elections of 1980,* edited by Austin Ranney, pp. 142-176. Washington, D.C.: American Enterprise Institute for Public Policy Research, 1981.

Kessel, John H. *Presidential Campaign Politics: Coalition Strategies and Citizen Response.* Homewood, Ill.: Dorsey Press, 1980, pp. 47-170.

*Moore, Jonathan, ed. *The Campaign for the President: 1980 in Retrospect.* Cambridge, Mass.: Ballinger Publishing Co., 1981, pp. 183-259.

Polsby, Nelson W., and Wildavsky, Aaron. *Presidential Elections: Strategies of American Electoral Politics.* 5th ed. New York: Charles Scribner's Sons, 1980, pp. 156-209.

*Wayne, Stephen J. *The Road to the White House: The Politics of Presidential Elections.* postelection ed. New York: St. Martin's Press, 1981, pp. 275-283.

*Wirthlin, Richard B. "The Republican Strategy and Its Electoral Consequences." In *Party Coalitions in the 1980s,* edited by Seymour Martin Lipset, pp. 235-266. San Francisco, Calif.: Institute for Contemporary Studies, 1981.

Chapter 3: The Election Results

America Votes 14: A Handbook of Contemporary American Elections Statistics, compiled and edited by Richard M. Scammon and Alice V. McGillivray. Washington, D.C.: published for the Elections Research Center by Congressional Quarterly, 1981.

Burnham, Walter Dean. *Critical Elections and the Mainsprings of American Politics.* New York: W. W. Norton & Co., 1970.

———. "The United States: The Politics of Heterogeneity." In *Electoral Behavior: A Comparative Handbook,* edited by Richard Rose, pp. 653-725. New York: Free Press, 1974.

*———. "The 1980 Earthquake: Realignment, Reaction, or What?" In *The Hidden Election: Politics and Economics in the 1980 Presidential Campaign,* edited by Thomas Ferguson and Joel Rogers, pp. 98-140. New York: Pantheon Books, 1981.

Clubb, Jerome M.; Flanigan, William H.; Zingale, Nancy H. *Partisan Realignment: Voters, Parties, and Government in American History.* Beverly Hills, Calif.: Sage Publications, 1980.

Key, V. O., Jr. *Southern Politics in State and Nation.* New York: Alfred A. Knopf, 1949.

*Pomper, Gerald M. "The Presidential Election." In *The Election of 1980: Reports and Interpretations,* Gerald M. Pomper with colleagues, pp. 65-96. Chatham, N.J.: Chatham House, 1981.

Presidential Elections Since 1789. 2d ed. Washington, D.C.: Congressional Quarterly, 1979.

*Schneider, William. "Democrats and Republicans, Liberals and Conservatives." In *Party Coalitions in the 1980s,* edited by Seymour Martin Lipset, pp. 179-231. San Francisco, Calif.: Institute for Contemporary Studies, 1981.

*———. "The November 4 Vote for President: What Did It Mean?" In *The American Elections of 1980,* edited by Austin Ranney, pp. 212-262. Washington, D.C.: American Enterprise Institute for Public Policy Research, 1981.

Sundquist, James L. *Dynamics of the Party System: Alignment and Realignment of Political Parties in the United States.* Washington, D.C.: The Brookings Institution, 1973.

Chapter 4: Who Voted

Aldrich, John H. "Some Problems in Testing Two Rational Models of Participation." *American Journal of Political Science* 20 (November 1976): 713-733.

Brody, Richard A. "The Puzzle of Political Participation in America." In *The New American Political System,* edited by Anthony King, pp. 287-324. Washington, D.C.: American Enterprise Institute for Public Policy Research, 1978.

Burnham, Walter Dean. "The 1976 Election: Has the Crisis Been Adjourned?" *American Politics and Public Policy,* edited by Walter Dean Burnham and Martha Wagner Weinberg, pp. 1-25. Cambridge, Mass.: The M.I.T. Press, 1978.

Cavanagh, Thomas E. "Changes in American Voter Turnout, 1964-1976." *Political Science Quarterly* 96 (Spring 1981): 53-65.

Ferejohn, John A., and Fiorina, Morris P. "The Paradox of Not Voting: A Decision Theoretic Analysis." *American Political Science Review* 68 (June 1974): 525-536.

Hadley, Arthur T. *The Empty Polling Booth.* Englewood Cliffs, N.J.: Prentice-Hall, 1978.

Riker, William H., and Ordeshook, Peter C. "A Theory of the Calculus of Voting." *American Political Science Review* 62 (March 1968): 25-42.

Shaffer, Stephen D. "A Multivariate Explanation of Decreasing Turnout in Presidential Elections, 1960-1976." *American Journal of Political Science* 25 (February 1981): 68-95.

*U.S., Department of Commerce, Bureau of the Census. *Voting and Registration in the Election of November 1980 (Advance Report).* Washington, D.C.: U.S. Government Printing Office, 1981.

Wolfinger, Raymond E., and Rosenstone, Steven J. *Who Votes?* New Haven, Conn.: Yale University Press, 1980.

Chapter 5: Social Forces and the Vote

Abramson, Paul R. *Generational Change in American Politics.* Lexington, Mass.: D. C. Heath & Co., 1975.

Alford, Robert R. *Party and Society: The Anglo-American Democracies.* Chicago: Rand McNally & Co., 1963.

Axelrod, Robert. "Where the Votes Come From: An Analysis of Electoral Coalitions, 1952-1968." *American Political Science Review* 66 (March 1972): 11-20.

*Dionne, E. J., Jr. "Catholics and the Democrats: Estrangement but Not Desertion." In *Party Coalitions in the 1980s,* edited by Seymour Martin Lipset, pp. 307-325. San Francisco, Calif.: Institute for Contemporary Studies, 1981.

*Fisher, Alan M. "Jewish Political Shift? Erosion, Yes: Conversion, No." In *Party Coalitions in the 1980s,* edited by Seymour Martin Lipset, pp. 327-340. San Francisco, Calif.: Institute for Contemporary Studies, 1981.

Hamilton, Richard F. *Class and Politics in the United States.* New York: John Wiley & Sons, 1972.

*Ladd, Everett Carll. "The Brittle Mandate: Electoral Dealignment and the 1980 Presidential Election." *Political Science Quarterly* 96 (Spring 1981): 1-25.

*Lipset, Seymour Martin. *Political Man: The Social Bases of Politics.* expanded ed. Baltimore: Johns Hopkins University Press, 1981.

Petrocik, John R. *Party Coalitions: Realignment and the Decline of the New Deal Party System.* Chicago: University of Chicago Press, 1981.

*"Vote by Groups in Presidential Elections Since 1952." *Gallup Opinion Index,* Report No. 183, December 1980, pp. 6-7.

Chapter 6: Issues, Candidates, and Voter Choice

Asher, Herbert B. *Presidential Elections and American Politics: Voters, Candidates, and Campaigns since 1952.* rev. ed. Homewood, Ill.: Dorsey Press, 1980, pp. 95-211.

Brody, Richard A., and Page, Benjamin I. "Comment: The Assessment of Policy Voting," *American Political Science Review* 66 (June 1972): 450-458.

Campbell, Angus; Converse, Philip E.; Miller, Warren E.; and Stokes, Donald E. *The American Voter.* New York: John Wiley & Sons, 1960, pp. 168-265.

*Frankovic, Kathleen A. "Public Opinion Trends." In *The Election of 1980: Reports and Interpretations,* Gerald M. Pomper with colleagues, pp. 97-118. Chatham, N.J.: Chatham House, 1981.

Kessel, John H. *Presidential Campaign Politics: Coalition Strategies and Citizen Response.* Homewood, Ill.: Dorsey Press, 1980, pp. 173-221.

Margolis, Michael. "From Confusion to Confusion: Issues and the American Voter." *American Political Science Review* 71 (March 1977): 31-43.

Page, Benjamin I. *Choices and Echoes in Presidential Elections: Rational Man and Electoral Democracy.* Chicago: University of Chicago Press, 1978.

*Plotkin, Henry A. "Issues in the Presidential Campaign." In *The Election of 1980: Reports and Interpretations,* Gerald M. Pomper with colleagues, pp. 38-64. Chatham, N.J.: Chatham House, 1981.

Pomper, Gerald M. *Voters' Choice: Varieties of American Electoral Behavior.* New York: Dodd, Mead & Co., 1975.

Scammon, Richard M., and Wattenberg, Ben J. *The Real Majority.* New York: Coward, McCann & Georghegan, 1971.

Chapter 7: Presidential Performance and Candidate Choice

Downs, Anthony. *An Economic Theory of Democracy.* New York: Harper & Row, 1957.

Fiorina, Morris P. *Retrospective Voting in American National Elections.* New Haven, Conn.: Yale University Press, 1981.

Hibbs, Douglas A., Jr. "Political Parties and Macroeconomic Policy." *American Political Science Review* 71 (December 1977): 1467-1487.

Key, V. O., Jr. *The Responsible Electorate: Rationality in Presidential Voting, 1936-1960.* Cambridge, Mass.: Harvard University Press, 1966.

Kramer, Gerald H. "Short-Term Fluctuations in U.S. Voting Behavior, 1896-1964." *American Political Science Review* 65 (March 1971): 131-143.

*McDonald, Stephen L. "Economic Issues in the Campaign." In *A Tide of Discontent: The 1980 Elections and Their Meaning,* edited by Ellis Sandoz and Cecil V. Crabb, Jr., pp. 139-156. Washington, D.C.: Congressional Quarterly Press, 1981.

Mueller, John E. *War, Presidents and Public Opinion.* New York: John Wiley & Sons, 1973.

Riker, William H. *Liberalism Against Populism: A Confrontation Between the Theory of Democracy and the Theory of Social Choice.* San Francisco, Calif.: W. H. Freeman & Co., 1982.

Tufte, Edward R. *Political Control of the Economy.* Princeton, N.J.: Princeton University Press, 1978.

Weatherford, M. Stephen. "Economic Conditions and Electoral Outcomes: Class Differences in the Political Response to Recession." *American Journal of Political Science* 22 (November 1978): 917-938.

Chapter 8: Party Loyalties, an Independent Candidate, and the Vote

Abramson, Paul R. "Generational Change and the Decline of Party Identification in America: 1952-1974." *American Political Science Review* 70 (June 1976): 469-478.

Asher, Herbert B. *Presidential Elections and American Politics: Voters, Candidates, and Campaigns Since 1952.* rev. ed. Homewood, Ill.: Dorsey Press, 1980, pp. 56-94.

Campbell, Angus; Converse, Philip E.; Miller, Warren E.; and Stokes, Donald E. *The American Voter.* New York: John Wiley & Sons, 1960, pp. 120-167.

Converse, Philip E. *The Dynamics of Party Support: Cohort-Analyzing Party Identification.* Beverly Hills, Calif.: Sage Publications, 1976.

——; Miller, Warren E.; Rusk, Jerrold G.; Wolfe, Arthur C. "Continuity and Change in American Politics: Parties and Issues in the 1968 Election." *American Political Science Review* 63 (December 1969): 1083-1105.

Fiorina, Morris P. "An Outline for a Model of Party Choice." *American Journal of Political Science* 21 (August 1977): 601-625.

Miller, Warren E.; Miller, Arthur H.; and Schneider, Edward J. *American National Election Studies Data Sourcebook, 1952-1978.* Cambridge, Mass.: Harvard University Press, 1980.

Shively, W. Phillips. "The Development of Party Identification Among Adults: Exploration of a Functional Model." *American Political Science Review* 73 (December 1979): 1039-1054.

——. "The Nature of Party Identification: A Review of Recent Developments." In *The Electorate Reconsidered,* edited by John C. Pierce and John L. Sullivan, pp. 219-236. Beverly Hills, Calif.: Sage Publications, 1980.

*Wattenberg, Martin P., and Miller, Arthur H. "Decay in Regional Party Coalitions: 1952-1980." In *Party Coalitions in the 1980s,* edited by Seymour Martin Lipset, pp. 341-367. San Francisco, Calif.: Institute for Contemporary Studies, 1981.

Chapter 9: Candidates and Outcomes

Fenno, Richard F., Jr. *Home Style: House Members in Their Districts.* Boston: Little, Brown & Co., 1978.

Fiorina, Morris P. *Congress: Keystone of the Washington Establishment.* New Haven, Conn.: Yale University Press, 1977.

Jacobson, Gary C. *Money in Congressional Elections.* New Haven: Conn.: Yale University Press, 1980.

*Jones, Charles O. "The New, New Senate." In *A Tide of Discontent: The 1980 Elections and Their Meaning,* edited by Ellis Sandoz and Cecil V. Crabb, Jr., pp. 89-111. Washington, D.C.: Congressional Quarterly Press, 1981.

*MacNeil, Neil. "The Struggle for the House of Representatives." In *A Tide of Discontent: The 1980 Elections and Their Meaning,* edited by Ellis Sandoz and Cecil V. Crabb, Jr., pp. 65-87. Washington, D.C.: Congressional Quarterly Press, 1981.

*Mann, Thomas E., and Ornstein, Norman J. "The 1982 Election: What Will it Mean?" *Public Opinion* 4 (June/July 1981): 48-50.

*——. "The Republican Surge in Congress." In *The American Elections of 1980,* edited by Austin Ranney, pp. 263-302. Washington, D.C.: American Enterprise Institute for Public Policy Research, 1981.

Mayhew, David R. *Congress: The Electoral Connection.* New Haven, Conn.: Yale University Press, 1974.

Rohde, David W. "Risk-Bearing and Progressive Ambition: The Case of Members of the United States House of Representatives." *American Journal of Political Science* 23 (February 1979): 1-26.

Schlesinger, Joseph A. *Ambition and Politics: Political Careers in the United States.* Chicago: Rand McNally & Co., 1966.

Chapter 10: The Congressional Electorate

Abramowitz, Alan I. "A Comparison of Voting for U.S. Senator and Representative in 1978." *American Political Science Review* 74 (September 1980): 633-640.

Cover, Albert D. "One Good Term Deserves Another: The Advantage of Incumbency in Congressional Elections." *American Journal of Political Science* 21 (August 1977): 523-541.

Fenno, Richard F., Jr. "If, as Ralph Nader Says, Congress is 'The Broken Branch,' How Come We Love Our Congressmen So Much?" In *Congress in Change: Evolution and Reform,* edited by Norman J. Ornstein, pp. 277-287. New York: Praeger Publishers, 1975.

Ferejohn, John A. "On the Decline of Competition in Congressional Elections." *American Political Science Review* 71 (March 1977): 166-176.

Hinckley, Barbara. "The American Voter in Congressional Elections." *American Political Science Review* 74 (September 1980): 641-650.

——. *Congressional Elections*. Washington, D.C.: Congressional Quarterly Press, 1981.

Kuklinski, James H., and West, Darrell M. "Economic Expectations and Voting Behavior in United States House and Senate Elections." *American Political Science Review* 75 (June 1981): 436-447.

Mann, Thomas E., and Wolfinger, Raymond E. "Candidates and Parties in Congressional Elections." *American Political Science Review* 74 (September 1980): 617-632.

Chapter 11: The 1980 Elections and the Future of American Politics

*Burnham, Walter Dean. "The 1980 Earthquake: Realignment, Reaction, or What?" In *The Hidden Election: Politics and Economics in the 1980 Presidential Campaign,* edited by Thomas Ferguson and Joel Rogers, pp. 98-140. New York: Pantheon Books, 1981.

*Clymer, Adam, and Frankovic, Kathleen. "The Realities of Realignment." *Public Opinion* 4 (June/July 1981): 42-47.

*Katznelson, Ira. "A Radical Departure: Social Welfare and the Election." In *The Hidden Election: Politics and Economics in the 1980 Presidential Campaign,* edited by Thomas Ferguson and Joel Rogers, pp. 313-340. New York: Pantheon Books, 1981.

*Lipset, Seymour Martin. "The American Party System: Concluding Observations." In *Party Coalitions in the 1980s,* edited by Seymour Martin Lipset, pp. 423-440. San Francisco, Calif.: Institute for Contemporary Studies, 1981.

*McWilliams, Wilson Carey. "The Meaning of the Election." In *The Election of 1980: Reports and Interpretations,* Gerald M. Pomper with colleagues, pp. 170-188. Chatham, N.J.: Chatham House, 1981.

*Sandoz, Ellis. "Introduction: Revolution or Flash in the Pan?" In *A Tide of Discontent: The 1980 Elections and Their Meaning,* edited by Ellis Sandoz and Cecil V. Crabb, Jr., pp. 1-18. Washington, D.C.: Congressional Quarterly Press, 1981.

*——, and Crabb, Cecil V., Jr. "Conclusion: Electoral and Policy Realignment or Aberration?" In *A Tide of Discontent: The 1980 Elections and Their Meaning,* edited by Ellis Sandoz and Cecil V. Crabb, Jr., pp. 191-209. Washington, D.C.: Congressional Quarterly Press, 1981.

*Schneider, William. "The November 4 Vote for President: What Did It Mean?" In *The American Elections of 1980,* edited by Austin Ranney, pp. 212-262. Washington, D.C.: American Enterprise Institute for Public Policy Research, 1981.

*Sundquist, James L., and Scammon, Richard M. "The 1980 Election: Profile and Historical Perspective." In *A Tide of Discontent: The 1980 Elections and Their Meaning,* edited by Ellis Sandoz and Cecil V. Crabb, Jr., pp. 19-44. Washington, D.C.: Congressional Quarterly Press, 1981.

*Wildavsky, Aaron. "The Three Party System—1980 and After." *The Public Interest* 64 (Summer 1981): 47-57.

Additional Readings

The following readings on the 1980 and 1982 elections have appeared since the first edition of our book was published.

Abramson, Paul R. *Political Attitudes in America: Formation and Change.* San Francisco: W. H. Freeman & Co., 1983.

——, and Aldrich, John H. "The Decline of Electoral Participation in America." *American Political Science Review* 76 (September 1982): 502-521.

Axelrod, Robert. "Communication." *American Political Science Review* 76 (June 1982): 393-396.

Beck, Paul Allen. "Realignment Begins? The Republican Surge in Florida." *American Politics Quarterly* 10 (October 1982): 421-438.

Burnham, Walter Dean. *The Current Crisis in American Politics.* New York: Oxford University Press, 1982.

Eldersveld, Samuel J. *Political Parties in American Society.* New York: Basic Books, 1982.

Greenfield, Jeff. *The Real Campaign: How the Media Missed the Story of the 1980 Campaign.* New York: Summit Books, 1982.

Hibbs, Douglas A., Jr. "President Reagan's Mandate from the 1980 Elections: A Shift to the Right?" *American Politics Quarterly* 10 (October 1982): 387-420.

Jacobson, Gary C. *The Politics of Congressional Elections.* Boston: Little Brown & Co., 1983.

Mann, Thomas E., and Ornstein, Norman J. "Elections '82: The Voters Send a Message." *Public Opinion* 5 (December/January 1983): 6-11, 59.

Markus, Gregory B. "Political Attitudes During an Election Year: A Report on the 1980 NES Panel Study." *American Political Science Review* 76 (September 1982): 538-560.

Miller, Warren E., and Shanks, J. Merrill. "Policy Directions and Presidential Leadership: Alternative Interpretations of the 1980 Presidential Election." *British Journal of Political Science* 12 (July 1982): 299-356.

Shaffer, Stephen D. "Policy Differences Between Voters and Non-Voters in American Elections." *Western Political Quarterly* 35 (December 1982): 496-510.

White, Theodore H. *America in Search of Itself: The Making of the President, 1956-1980.* New York: Harper & Row, 1982.

Witt, Evans. "A Model Election?" *Public Opinion* 5 (December/January 1983): 46-49.

Index